Earl Warren and the Struggle for Justice

Earl Warren and the Struggle for Justice

Paul Moke

LEXINGTON BOOKS
Lanham • Boulder • New York • London

Published by Lexington Books
An imprint of The Rowman & Littlefield Publishing Group, Inc.
4501 Forbes Boulevard, Suite 200, Lanham, Maryland 20706
www.rowman.com

Unit A, Whitacre Mews, 26-34 Stannary Street, London SE11 4AB

British Library Cataloguing in Publication Information Available

Library of Congress Control Number: 2015949347
ISBN: 978-1-4985-2013-3 (cloth : alk. paper)
eISBN: 978-1-4985-2014-0

♾™ The paper used in this publication meets the minimum requirements of American National Standard for Information Sciences—Permanence of Paper for Printed Library Materials, ANSI/NISO Z39.48-1992.

Printed in the United States of America

To my parents, Clarence and Claudine,
who taught me the value of reading.

Contents

Preface

The origins of this book lie in the experiences of youth. For three years during the late 1960s and early 1970s, I attended one of the first fully integrated public secondary schools in central Ohio. The student body consisted of inner city and middle-class African Americans, white Protestants, and Jews. Although many teachers at the school taught stimulating classes, the real education took place informally, as students experienced in their own idiosyncratic ways the richness of their differences. One such experience stands out in my mind. It occurred in a public speaking class as Patti B., a shy African American cheerleader I had known for several years, addressed the class with a speech entitled "You Enslaved Me!" During her remarks, the usual diffidence I associated with her voice morphed into rage and indignation. When she finished, the students launched into a difficult discussion about individual and collective responsibility for the legacy of slavery in the United States. It marked the first time I remember having a serious conversation about social justice. Afterward, I wondered how many students ever had such a conversation, face-to-face, across the racial divide.

Unfortunately, during my high school years the exuberance and heartbreak of life as a teenager always seemed to displace deeper thoughts about social justice. The full meaning of the social experiment with desegregation in my high school escaped me at the time. Only later did I realize that the rich interracial experiences I had in the classroom, on the football field, and in social settings lay at the heart of Earl Warren's vision for public education.

As an undergraduate in the 1970s, I attended Wilmington College, an institution affiliated with the Society of Friends (Quakers) in southwestern Ohio. Small and relatively unknown, the College attracted the attention of Earl Warren in the early years of his tenure as Chief Justice of the United States. In a curious way, the story of Warren's involvement with Wilmington intersects with my own experience there, and it marks another inspiration for writing this book.

During my undergraduate years, I worked part-time at the College's dairy farm, milking cows. On Saturdays after a hard day's work, I often would treat myself to a sandwich and a beer at "Hammie's," a local bar. Located on an alley beside the railroad tracks on the "wrong side of town," Hammie's attracted an interracial group of working-class adults and college students. Charles "Hammie" Graham, the bar tender and owner, had a thoughtful manner about him as he filled his customers' orders, and later I learned that in the 1940s he had taken a controversial stand for the integration of local schools.

The legal background of the controversy dated back to the 1850s when the Ohio General Assembly passed legislation establishing racially separate common schools. Following the Civil War, it abolished the legal requirement of segregation but refused to dismantle the policies of segregation that local school boards had pursued over the previous twenty years. In portions of Ohio near areas where slavery had been legal, local school boards continued to assign elementary students on the basis of race. Such was the case in Wilmington and nearby Hillsboro, Ohio throughout the first half of the twentieth century.

In Wilmington, Midland School served as the segregated elementary school. Located in an industrial part of town beside two railroad crossings and not far from Hammie's Bar, the school had no indoor plumbing, and its students used older, handed-down textbooks. In 1939, Ted Lewis, a local black resident, challenged the assignment of his son, Charles, to Midland School. He filed a writ of mandamus action in the local Common Pleas court seeking the admission of his son to an elementary school closer to his home. The trial court rejected Lewis' challenge, and school officials sought compromise by offering to provide bus transportation for African American students who lived more than a mile away from Midland School. Lewis rejected the offer and with the help of Thurgood Marshall of the NAACP appealed the trial court's decision to the Ohio Supreme Court. In June 1940, the court rejected the appeal, holding that the Wilmington School Board had no legal duty to admit black students to the white schools nearest their homes.

Following the loss, attorneys for the NAACP lamented the relatively weak support Wilmington's black community gave to Lewis' challenge against the school board. Several attorneys thought the principal weakness involved the unwillingness of the plaintiffs, in a case alleging racial discrimination, to complain about anything other than the inconvenience of the distance their children had to travel to get to Midland School. Others perceived that the black community was reluctant to get involved in the case for fear that whites would retaliate by closing Midland School or by firing the black teachers who worked there. Precisely what factors would persuade the community to participate more enthusiastically in similar litigation, not only in Wilmington but nationwide, remained unclear.

At the conclusion of World War II, a group of Quaker pacifists came to Wilmington College and renewed the attack on segregated schools. When Hammie Graham and other African Americans sought to admit their children to the white schools, the school board again rejected their applications, and protests arose at local board meetings. Seymour Eichel, a Wilmington College undergraduate from New York City, led a small group of college students who spoke out in favor of the African American parents at a school board meeting. The school board retaliated by pressuring Wilmington College President Samuel Marble to stop the student protests. In an attempt to assuage them, Marble came to their next meeting. There, he asserted that the issue of school desegregation was national, not local in scope and that the college students had been respectful and were not the dangerous radicals that some members of the community had alleged. The board leadership obstinately disagreed. They launched a movement to curtail donations to the College and then cut back on the number of student teachers the College could place in the local schools. Then they persuaded the Wilmington College Board of Trustees to order President Marble to issue an ultimatum to the students: either stop the protests or face possible expulsion from the College. Caught in the web of power, Marble reluctantly complied. Although most of the student body obeyed Marble's request and ceased their protests, Seymour Eichel stood by his principles and withdrew from the school.

Just a few months later, in the fall of 1950, a newly constituted Wilmington School Board voted to phase out Midland as a segregated elementary school. They reasoned that running small segregated schools was inefficient and unnecessarily expensive. In the fall of 1953, less than a year before the Warren Court announced its decision in *Brown v. Board of Education*, Midland became a kindergarten for all students in the Wilmington Public Schools.

In neighboring Hillsboro, however, the commitment to segregated elementary schools remained firm. Historically, the local school board had maintained Lincoln School as an all-black institution. In the early 1950s, local protests and funding limitations persuaded the board to issue a vague promise that it would continue assigning students to Lincoln on the basis of race only until the 1956–1957 academic year, when the elementary schools attended by whites could be expanded and integrated.

In June 1954, just weeks after the first *Brown* decision, local resident Philip Partridge set fire to Lincoln School. A former city engineer in Wilmington, Partridge had been dismissed from his position after he wrote an editorial in the local paper in which he called the policy of segregation at Midland School "a disgrace." Following his dismissal, Partridge moved to Hillsboro and continued to oppose segregated schools. Later that year, he was convicted and received a one-to-fifteen year sentence for his crime; after serving approximately one year in prison, he left on parole.

After the fire, the Hillsboro School Board remodeled Lincoln School and once again assigned only black students to it. In the fall of 1954, a group of parents boycotted the public schools and filed suit in federal district court to block the continued assignment of elementary students on the basis of race. As part of their protest, they home schooled their children, and for a period of two years, Quaker volunteer teachers from Wilmington undertook weekly trips to Hillsboro to assist them. When a federal district judge rejected their claim for injunctive relief, the parents appealed to the U.S. Court of Appeals for the Sixth Circuit. The appellate panel reversed the trial court's decision and ordered the immediate admission of school children on a nonsegregated basis by the beginning of the 1956 academic year.[1]

Even though these events took place in the hinterland of rural Ohio, they did not escape the attention of Chief Justice Earl Warren. In May of 1954, immediately following the release of the Supreme Court's decision in the school desegregation case, Warren asked a group of law clerks to stay in Washington, D.C. over the summer to gather background information on local efforts to desegregate public schools. In making this assignment, Warren sought to provide background information for his fellow justices concerning the range of possible remedies that might be needed to alleviate the problems of segregated schools, an issue the Court would face in 1955 during the next phase of the *Brown* litigation. One section of the final report referenced the problems in Wilmington and Hillsboro.

The next year Chief Justice Earl Warren accepted President Sam Marble's invitation to speak at Wilmington College to commemorate the opening of Friends Hall, a new dormitory. Both leaders apparently saw the celebration as an opportunity for public reflection concerning the wisdom of integrated schools. Although the Chief Justice had rejected scores of speaking invitations in the wake of the *Brown* decision, he attentively selected Wilmington as a suitable place to address the public. His remarks, entitled "The Leaven in the Loaf," extolled the value of small colleges in improving civic education in the United States. In his speech, Warren made no direct reference to the *Brown* decision or to the controversies that had engulfed the local community. Yet indirectly, he praised the values of the Wilmington student body, saying: "I came here today to see if I might possibly imbibe some of the spirit that prevails on the campus of this little college—because I have some knowledge of that spirit . . . how it is developing and how it is helping people in other parts of this country." He found "leaven in the loaf" in Wilmington "because it leads young people not only to knowledge, but it leads them also to be good," an implied endorsement of the College's social justice mission.

Warren's speech at Wilmington College offers insight into his approach to the chief judgeship. Throughout his tenure in judicial office, Warren educated the American public about the work of the Court. In many of his major opinions, he wrote for members of the lay public, not for legal professionals. He consciously refrained from using legalese and communicated so that ordinary Americans could understand the constitutional values that the Court sought to uphold. For this same reason, Warren presented his "Leaven in the Loaf" speech to an audience in a troubled part of the country, where local residents had struggled to uphold the value of racial equality.

After an initial foray into graduate school, I returned to Wilmington College to teach social science courses to inmates at Lebanon Correctional Institution, then a reformatory for first-time offenders. Among the courses I taught was Constitutional Law. The twenty students in my class were young and from inner-city backgrounds, and many took the opportunity to earn college credit in prison quite seriously. The best student in the class, David K., was one of the most gifted students I have ever had the privilege of teaching. As a newly minted member of the Nation of Islam, David followed in the footsteps of Malcolm X: he used his time in prison to become literate, accepted the wrongfulness of his crime, and pondered the meaning of being black in America. Together, we studied the milestones of constitutional history. For David—and then for me—the course became a search for identity.

Through my inmate students' interpretations of leading constitutional decisions—*Dred Scott, the Civil Rights Cases, Plessy, Brown, Mapp*, and *Miranda*—I developed new perspectives on legal rights, perspectives grounded in the views of inner-city people of color, the poor, the criminally accused, and the institutionalized. The students' essays articulated the point of view of the socially dispossessed, an outlook often lacking in most academic discourse on constitutional law. Throughout many years of study in the fields of law and American politics, I have never forgotten that perspective. Perhaps that explains why the legacy of Earl Warren speaks so deeply to me.

The central theme of Warren's complex life involves the social imperative of inclusion. In my formative years in Ohio, I experienced firsthand the value and insight of educational diversity and inclusion. Unfortunately, relatively few students in today's classrooms experience these benefits. Literally and symbolically, my own high school illustrates the problem. The school now calls itself an "academy" and currently 97% of the student body is comprised of minority groups (mostly African American), 55% of the students qualify for the federal free lunch program, and only 55% of those in the district graduate.[2] In significant ways, Americans have turned their backs on Earl Warren's vision of integration, and public schools have resegregated along racial and class lines.

In this book, I address the question of how Earl Warren's life and major decisions have affected the struggle for social justice in the United States. In telling this story, I not only examine the personal and legal dimensions of Warren's work but also emphasize the broader social history and political context of his reforms in such fields as school desegregation, criminal justice, and voting rights. My perspective is at once biographical, legal, and historical. I seek to present the life, times, and thought of Earl Warren in a manner that avoids legal jargon and helps a new generation of readers better understand Earl Warren the person, politician, and jurist.

Many people have brought this book into being. Reference librarians at the Library of Congress Manuscript Division, the National Archives, the University of California Bancroft Library and Law Library, the University of Dayton, and Wilmington College assisted in framing research questions and obtaining archival materials. The staff of the Office of the Curator at the Supreme Court of the United States provided invaluable assistance with photographs and memorabilia, and Linda Duran-O'Malley of the Wilmington College publications staff assisted with mock-ups of photographic editing and layout. Professor Howard Tolley of the University of Cincinnati and Professor Richard Saphire of the University of Dayton School of Law provided countless hours of analysis and constructive criticism of my work. Professors G. Edward White, Stan Cain, Robert Frey, Ed Agran, Ursula McTaggart, Susan Wowrose, Freda Levenson, and Larry Gara gave thoughtful suggestions for improvement, as did Lenna Mae Gara, Laura Kloimwieder, Muriel Hiatt, and Jean Mulhern. Kathryn Tafelski and the staff of Lexington Books assisted with editing and final production.

Friends and family supported me through the many years of travel, research, and writing that it took to produce this work. Especially important were David and Teresa Evans, friends from my high school years, who assisted with lodging and transportation during my frequent trips to Washington, D.C. Above all, my wife Patti, our children Dan and Anna, and our beloved miniature Dachshund, Gretchen, offered encouragement during the long hours of research and writing. To each of you, a heartfelt thanks.

NOTES

1. For further information about the effort to desegregate the Wilmington and Hillsboro City Schools, see Lenna Mae Gara, "Separate and Unequal: The Closing of Midland School," *Timeline Magazine,* June/July 1991, 41.
2. Source: www.publicschoolreview.com/school_ov/school-id/62066.

Chapter 1

Earl Warren and the People's Court

Earl Warren (1891–1974) was a leading American politician and jurist in the middle four decades of the twentieth century. A Progressive Republican, he began his career as District Attorney in Alameda County California (the Oakland metropolitan area) in 1925 and later served as Attorney General and Governor of California. After several unsuccessful bids to secure the Republican nomination for president and a failed campaign in 1948 as the running mate of Thomas E. Dewey, Warren accepted a position as Chief Justice of the U.S. Supreme Court in October 1953. His sixteen years on the Court (1953–1969) brought significant legal reforms, especially in the areas of school desegregation, civil rights, and criminal justice.

Warren approached questions of public policy through a moral lens. In a variety of contexts that spanned many decades, he analyzed issues by posing a deceptively simple question: Is the government's conduct fair?[1] Typically, he answered from the point of view of the underdog: the corporation that lost a public contract due to corrupt bidding procedures; the black student forced to attend a school inferior to that attended by whites; or the innocent criminal defendant compelled to defend himself in the stationhouse or in court against a professional prosecutor.

The awareness of the disadvantaged "outsider" that formed the core of Warren's view of the world began in his adolescent years in the railroad yards of southern California. There, he saw the arbitrary and callous way managers dealt with injured workers. As a college student at the University of California before World War I, Warren embraced the ideals of the Progressive reformers, which stressed making state and local government nonpartisan and free from undue corporate influence and organized crime. As District Attorney in the 1920s and 30s, he fought against vice and public corruption. Later, as Governor of California in the 1940s and early 50s, he waged a bitter and ultimately unsuccessful campaign to provide health insurance for all Californians.

Throughout his career in public service, Warren's name and reputation were not always associated with the cause of liberal reform. During his years as an elected politician in the 1930s and 1940s, his positions at times seemed to contradict the ideals he espoused later in life. He often attacked labor unions and radicals. He overlooked the abuse of police power and enforced anti-vice laws unfairly, applying them more stringently in Asian neighborhoods than in other areas of Alameda County. Tragically, in a move that reflected the xenophobic underside of the Progressive movement, he advocated the removal of Japanese Americans from the Pacific Coast during World War II.

On the Supreme Court, Warren gradually embraced the ideals of social justice and extended legal rights to the "common people" of America. His vision of the Supreme Court as the conscience of the nation and his concern for the rights of political outcasts—racial minorities, indigent criminal defendants, and persons denied equal voting rights—provoked both support and resistance. Allies saw in Warren a crusader who breathed new life into the concepts of equal protection and due process that the Supreme Court long had used to legitimize racial segregation and police misconduct.[2] Many leading legal scholars of his day, including Archibald Cox,[3] Yale Kamisar,[4] and Charles Black[5] praised at least most of his major decisions. In contrast, Warren's detractors objected to the moralistic and results-oriented nature of his legal method.[6] Despite their differences, both sets of scholars acknowledged the groundbreaking nature of Earl Warren and the Warren Court.

Throughout its history, the Supreme Court has functioned both as a legal and a political institution. Based on its power of judicial review, the Court interprets federal law to manage the contours of government power, federalism, and individual rights, all inherently political issues. In the period before Warren took office, the Supreme Court pursued policies that blocked government interference with the functioning of free market capitalism, using doctrines such as freedom of contract, restrictions on congressional power to regulate the manufacturing process, and the "rule of reason" in anti-trust cases to do so.[7] During the Warren years, the Court moved in a decidedly different direction. In the field of voting rights reform—an area that Warren considered his most important contribution to American constitutional law—it used the Fourteenth and Fifteenth Amendments to curtail state restrictions on suffrage and in effect gave the federal government responsibility for protecting the ability of all citizens to participate on an equal basis in the democratic process. In the school desegregation cases, it required public school districts that had practiced intentional racial discrimination to dismantle their segregated systems.

Earl Warren's legal philosophy reflected a social justice vision. He challenged the distribution of opportunities and privileges throughout society and assigned rights and duties in order to achieve ethical outcomes. Warren refused to be constrained by strict adherence to the doctrine of *stare decisis* or precedent. Many of his key decisions overturned precedents, often because they left the enforcement of constitutional rights to the political branches, which consistently had failed to act. He interpreted constitutional provisions broadly and adapted the law to changing socioeconomic conditions in a manner not unlike judges throughout the history of England who built upon or overturned precedents in order to shape the common law. In other ways, the Warren Court was unique: whereas in earlier periods the Supreme Court made policy by simply striking down federal and state legislation, in the Warren era the Court used its equitable powers to require public officials to take affirmative steps to remedy legal violations on a systemic basis. On a level that was not true before its existence and would not be true afterward, the Warren Court nudged America into a new age.

In June 1969, as Warren prepared to retire from his position as Chief Justice of the United States, a reporter asked him how he would like the Warren Court to be remembered. Warren responded with a simple assertion: "The people's court." His answer revealed the disparity between the Warren Court and earlier Supreme Courts throughout American history. Initially characterized as the "least dangerous branch,"[8] the Supreme Court typically had protected the rights of property owners and corporations over the interests of slaves, workers, racial and ethnic minorities, and the poor.[9] Under Warren's leadership, the Court overturned the legal foundation of the Jim Crow caste system and applied large portions of the Bill of Rights to the states, thus initiating sweeping reforms of the criminal justice system. In so doing, the Warren Court transformed the American legal landscape.

Alexis de Tocqueville, author of the noted treatise *Democracy in America*, once wrote, "Scarcely any political question arises in the United States that is not resolved, sooner or later, into a judicial question." De Tocqueville's observation applies with particular force to Chief Justice Warren. During Warren's tenure on the Court, public-interest legal organizations such as the National Association for the Advancement of Colored People and the American Civil Liberties Union brought test cases involving racial equality, civil rights, voting rights, and due process, which elicited significant advances in human rights. Warren's first major decision, *Brown v. Board of Education*, immediately thrust him and his Court into the center of national and international attention. Warren's emergence as the author of the *Brown* decision, together with the difficulties he faced in helping America realize the promise of an integrated society, meant that for the remainder of his life his identity and reputation would be closely tied to the cause of racial equality.

By rigorously defending constitutional values, Warren led the Supreme Court into a position of growing prominence in American national government and in the everyday lives of American citizens.

To be clear, Warren did not take these steps alone. *Brown* was a unanimous decision, and many, if not all, of Warren's major opinions involved supermajorities. As Chief Justice, he has come to symbolize the achievements and controversies of what by convenience and convention has come to be known as the Warren Court. In some ways this designation is unfortunate. Warren had the good fortune of serving with some of the most intellectually rigorous and enlightened jurists in the country's history, including Justices Hugo Black, Felix Frankfurter, Robert Jackson, William O. Douglas, Arthur Goldberg, Thurgood Marshall, and William Brennan. Viewed in its totality, the work of the "Warren Court" involved the synergy of many great minds, as illustrated by the Black and Warren collaboration on criminal justice reforms or by Warren's work with Justice Brennan and William O. Douglas in the field of voting rights. To ascribe these achievements to Earl Warren alone would do a great disservice to the legal giants who served beside him on the bench.

That said, many of the best-known decisions of the Warren Court—including *Miranda v. Arizona* (1966), *Reynolds v. Sims* (1964), and *Loving v. Virginia* (1967)—did come from the pen of Earl Warren. Warren grounded his political philosophy in the concept of responsible citizenship. As he once phrased it, "Responsible citizenship is . . . the sheet anchor of our Republic. With it, we can withstand the storm; without it we are helplessly at sea."[10] For Warren, effective citizenship embraced love of country, belief in the Constitution and the purposes of government, and devotion to the rule of law. In the Constitution Warren found not only the foundation for the democratic process but also a "commitment to an open society with individual liberty, political freedom and equal opportunity for every citizen."[11] In his eyes, responsible citizens also maintained an allegiance to the rule of law, since the law represented "a means of declaring what is right and prohibiting what is wrong to provide protection for every individual."[12] To Warren, the ideal of responsible citizenship could not be maintained under circumstances of isolation or exclusivity. Rather, it must be shared with all others on an equal basis. "There are neither rights nor freedoms in any meaningful sense unless they can be enjoyed by all," he wrote.[13] Echoing the sentiments of Justice Brandeis, who once noted that "the great menace to freedom is an inert people," Warren cautioned against the evils of political indifference and apathy. "Who loves freedom must guard it with tenacity," he observed.[14]

As a judicial biography, the current work examines the complex web of experiences, ideas, and endeavors that comprise the life of Earl Warren. Understanding the life of another is a difficult and uncertain business, especially when viewed retroactively through the lens of memory, or recorded or printed materials. The challenge that confronts the biographer involves sifting through fragmented pieces of evidence to reconstruct, through careful analysis and historical imagination, the life, times, and accomplishments of another. As a field of study biography has its critics, who assail hagiography and fault the absence of hypothesis testing and objectivity in historical method. Yet those who insist upon formal claims, warrants, and evidence in biographical writing face their own challenges. Human lives, often chaotic and unpredictable, are anything but orderly. Instead, individuals might best be seen as independent actors, disconnected from the simplifying assumptions and hypotheses that academic researchers may seek to impose upon them.

The story of Earl Warren gives rise to many research questions, which concern matters of identity, ideology, and public persuasion. At a basic level, who was Earl Warren, and what persons, ideas, and values shaped his view of the world? What policies and approaches did he pursue as an elected official and as a member of the Supreme Court? Did his presence as Chief Justice make any difference in the substantive decisions of the Court? What impact did his decisions have on the reform of American political and social institutions? What role in American politics did Warren play off the bench, and did his decisions in matters of national security (such as the internment of Japanese Americans in World War II or in his capacity as Chair of the Warren Commission) reflect the values that he championed elsewhere? Finally, how did Warren's vision of American citizenship differ from that of other leaders of his day, and to what extent were his views accurate?

In framing initial answers to at least some of these questions, it may be helpful to consider an anecdote about Warren that sheds light on both his identity and his approach to the Office of Chief Justice. It concerns the way Warren managed the Court's weekly conferences, in which the Chief Justice leads the other justices in a discussion of the cases pending on the Court's docket. By all accounts, Warren was a master at employing this process to give a moral context to the issues. Warren researcher Bernard Schwartz[15] interviewed several of the justices of the Warren Court, and based upon their experiences, he stressed the way Warren influenced the brethren's perception of cases through the framing of legal issues in conference. Two examples illustrate Schwartz's point. In *Brown*, Warren began the December 12, 1953 conference (the first he chaired on the case) with the statement, "(T)he more I've read and heard and thought, the more I've come to conclude that the basis of segregation and 'separate but equal' rests upon a concept of the inherent inferiority of the colored race. I don't see how *Plessy* and the cases following it can be sustained on any other theory. If we are to sustain segregation, we also must do it upon that basis."[16] Likewise, in *Griffin v. Illinois*

(1956), a case involving whether poor criminal defendants had a constitutional right to a free transcript of their trial record for use on appeal, Warren began the conference by noting that a defendant who had the means to pay for a transcript should not have an advantage over one who did not. "We cannot have one rule for the rich and one rule for the poor," he asserted.[17] In both cases, Warren's initial framing of the issue on moral grounds proved pivotal to the outcome: *Brown* was a unanimous decision, and *Griffin* a 5–4 judgment in favor of the defendant, with the mercurial Justice Frankfurter joining the majority. In his interview with Schwartz, one of the members of the Warren Court, Justice Abe Fortas, noted, "It was Warren's great gift that in presenting the case and discussing the case, he proceeded immediately and very calmly and graciously, to the ultimate issues involved—the ultimate constitutional values, the ultimate human values. . . . (O)pposition based on hemstitching and embroidery of the law appeared petty in terms of Warren's basic value approach."[18]

Warren's Progressive vision and his pursuit of racial justice proved politically controversial. Richard Nixon, a fellow California Republican, often clashed with Warren, both during Nixon's rise to power in the 1940s and 50s, and in the 1968 Presidential campaign, when he attacked the Warren Court for being soft on crime and for making law under the guise of constitutional interpretation. In a speech during his 1972 campaign, Nixon elaborated on the reasons why he rejected the moral leadership of political elites, like the Supreme Court. To such elites, Nixon said, "the will of the people is 'the prejudice of the masses' and respect for majority rule is automatically denounced as 'political expedience.'" He continued, "It is time that good, decent people stop letting themselves be bulldozed by anybody who presumes to be the self-righteous moral judge of our society. There is no reason to feel guilty about wanting to enjoy what you get and get what you earn, about wanting your children in good schools close to home or about wanting to be judged fairly on your ability."[19]

Nixon's condemnation of the Warren Court's criminal justice and school desegregation reforms set the stage for a national debate about the role of the Supreme Court in American politics. The debate concerned not only practical questions involving busing, civil rights, and criminal procedure but also theoretical issues about the meaning of citizenship and constitutional democracy. Unlike Warren, Nixon deferred to the interests of the "great silent majority" in matters of civil rights and liberties, and he advocated the appointment of federal judges who favored the "strict construction" of the U.S. Constitution. As President, Nixon sought the expansion of executive authority. He maintained secrecy both in the conduct of war and in the pursuit of national security at home. Although he launched several transformative foreign policy initiatives including nuclear arms control and recognition of the People's Republic of China, Nixon's ethical lapses, unfair treatment of political adversaries and dissidents, and lack of transparency in the exercise of power proved divisive.

Throughout their careers as leaders of the Republican Party both in California and nationally, Warren and Nixon vied for control over Republican ideology and, ultimately, the hearts and minds of the American public. Warren's vision of American democracy stressed constitutional limits on political majorities and the role of the Supreme Court in a dialectical process with the political branches to ensure that the "nuts and bolts" of the political process remained democratic and that the rights of insular minorities received protection. In contrast, Nixon's vision emphasized the physical and material security of American citizens, the undemocratic nature of judicial elitism, and the protection of the interests of middle- and upper-class Americans in the face of civil and cultural disorder.

As Chief Justice of the Supreme Court, Warren approached the debate "with one hand tied behind his back." Constrained by his institutional role, Warren spoke largely through his judicial opinions, whereas Nixon, as a skillful campaigner and debater, had the advantage of extensive media coverage. Nixon's strident relations with the national press led to "infomercials" and televised forums before hand-picked, friendly audiences in his 1968 and 1972 presidential campaigns, providing him with frequent opportunities to shape issues and withhold damaging information from the public. Repeatedly, Nixon attacked the Warren Court for legislating from the bench on matters of racial integration and criminal justice reform. His mastery of media relations and widespread appeal to the concerns of the white working-class Americans gave him a decided political advantage over Warren.

The conflict between Warren and Nixon raised fundamental questions about political legitimacy. Arguably, Warren's tendency to interpret the Constitution in a manner that resolved long-festering social problems threatened the democratic order since he grounded his legal opinions in his own subjective views of the social good. Conversely, Nixon threatened the democratic order by concealing his own unethical and illegal conduct from the American public and transgressing Constitutional boundaries in the pursuit of heightened levels of presidential power. Nixon successfully appointed four justices to the Supreme Court, and they moved the Court in a much more conservative direction in school desegregation and criminal justice cases. Politically, his blueprint for undermining the foundation of the Democratic New Deal Coalition through cultural and patriotic appeals to the white working-class, suburban, and Southern voters proved successful, not only for his time, but also for later Republican presidential candidates. Yet Nixon's vituperative struggle with his perceived political enemies led to a criminal cover-up, scandal, and eventual resignation from the White House. The counterpoint between Warren and Nixon, as personal rivals and as ideological leaders of postwar America, forms a subtheme of the current work.[20]

Although the disgrace of Watergate and Nixon's subsequent resignation mean that Warren may have won his personal battle with Nixon, at least as a matter of historical reputation, in the period since 1970, the Republican Party and the "great silent majority" of Americans have retreated from Warren's social justice vision. Several factors have contributed to this outcome, including the economic strain of deindustrialization and globalization; government indifference to the interests of working-class Americans; and the political and cultural popularity of conservatism among white ethnic voters. In the process, the "Old" Jim Crow system that the Warren Court painstakingly sought to overturn has morphed into a new form of racial subordination under the auspices of the War on Drugs, mass incarceration, and the abandonment of inner-city America.

The gap between the social justice consciousness of the late 1960s (favored by Warren) and the regressive political climate of today (favored by Nixon) is not hard to trace. One measure of the change involves the recommendations of the Kerner Commission, a blue-ribbon panel charged with examining the causes and prevention of racial disorders in the wake of severe levels of civil unrest in the summer of 1967. After many months of study, the Commission concluded that the United States was "moving toward two societies, one black, one white, separate and unequal." Little to nothing came of the Kerner Commission's recommendations.

Within a few short years, the rhetoric of competitive individualism, personal responsibility, and color-blind justice dominated both the media and public policy in state and national governments throughout the country. Keeanga-Yamahtta Taylor and Michelle Alexander have extensively analyzed this transformation,[21] and they make several points. First, in the 1970s and 80s, a mass exodus of middle- and upper-class whites placed inner-city America in a condition of poverty. Serious problems with failing schools, deteriorating infrastructure, and heightened levels of unemployment ensued. Second, the FBI infiltrated and disrupted community organizations that sought to improve living conditions and redistribute resources in inner-city America; in the process, many radical activists received long prison sentences, or, in other cases, lost their lives to assassination. Third, affirmative action programs presented the illusion that hard work and individual merit could lift significant numbers of inner-city youth out of poverty. Black urban leaders symbolized this illusion of meritocracy, autonomy, and self-rule, but in fundamental respects they merely presided over the decay. In the meantime, key portions of the social welfare and employment training systems have been dismantled, and the sharing of resources among public schools that occurred under the auspices of racial integration has been abolished.

As a result, hyper levels of unemployment, gang activity, and crime now plague inner-city America.

Michelle Alexander persuasively argues that notwithstanding the progress of *Brown* and the civil rights movement, the racial caste system in the United States has not been terminated; instead, it has simply been restructured.[22] Alexander defines racial caste as a social system in which a stigmatized racial group is locked into an inferior position by law and custom. She contends that the drug war and the pursuit of mass incarceration have maintained structural racism in the United States, under a new system of policies and rhetoric. Her analysis of the history of racism includes a special focus on constitutional rules. She writes, "The Constitution was designed so the federal government would be weak, not only in its relationship to private property, but also in relationship to the rights of states to conduct their own affairs."[23] By announcing the end of "home rule" in the *Brown* decision and resuscitating the role of Reconstruction civil rights statutes such as 42 U.S. C. Section 1983 in the *Monroe v. Pape* (1961) case, the Warren Court curtailed federalism and states' rights, reasserted the primacy of national citizenship, and enabled individual plaintiffs to hold state and local officials accountable for the violation of their federal rights.

Although Taylor and Alexander correctly claim that conservatives such as Richard Nixon and Ronald Reagan reintroduced race as a wedge issue in American politics and erected a "New" Jim Crow system based on mass incarceration, their interpretation of the process by which structural racism emerged as a public policy issue in the "Second Reconstruction" of the 1950s and 1960s needs refinement. Like many other scholars, Taylor and Alexander assert that direct action was the key to the success of the civil rights movement and that the mass movement efforts of the SNCC and SCLC overshadowed the accomplishments of "elites" within the NAACP in this process. Important as the work of civil rights activists was, interpretations of the civil rights movement should not lose sight of the part that the Supreme Court played in protecting civil rights activists from their many antagonists. At various points in American history, social movements have faced strong legal headwinds that have prevented or delayed reform, as in the case of the abolitionist and women's rights movements. In contrast, the civil rights movement benefited from a sympathetic federal judiciary. But for key decisions involving the rights of protestors in sit-ins, the freedom to criticize public officials in the media, and rulings upholding the constitutionality of major civil rights statutes such as the Civil Rights Act of 1964 and the Voting Rights Act of 1965, the civil rights era might have had a very different outcome. It is here that study of the life and thought of Earl Warren becomes pivotal, for if a new movement for racial and economic justice is to encounter success in twenty-first-century America, legal institutions must not be hostile to it.

At this point, readers well may conclude that the questions I have raised about Earl Warren and the tentative answers I have framed may be of little relevance to their own lives. Why should they care about the life and politics of Earl Warren? In part, my answer comes from the insight of my grandmother, who grew up on the South Dakota prairie in the 1890s and had a fourth grade education. As I came of age, she often would say to me: "From every person you meet, you either learn how to be or how not to be." On several different levels, one can learn "how to be" by getting to know Earl Warren.

The first lesson involves the importance of listening. Never in law school, as an advocate in the courtroom, or as a judge on the bench, did Earl Warren rise to the level of an academic star. But what he lacked in analytical ability he made up in his skill at human interaction. Warren listened attentively to nearly everyone he encountered in five decades of public service. He remembered names and faces and regularly sought out new friends. In fundamental ways, Warren's view of the world broadened as result. In Sacramento, for example, Warren's close friendship with his African American chauffeur, Edgar "Pat" Patterson, deepened his understanding of the role that childhood socialization played in framing racial identity, a question that lay at the heart of the *Brown* litigation.

A second lesson involves how to approach the world of work. Warren was a skilled administrator who ran a tight ship in every position he ever had. Several secrets of his managerial success involve paying attention to organizational environment, preparing carefully for key meetings, and treating fellow employees with respect. Warren forged his skills as an administrator in the context of California's exponential growth following World War II, when he expanded public services to meet the needs of the new environment. As Chief Justice, in the face of heavy increases in the caseloads of federal judges, he extended the duties of the Administrative Office of the U.S. Courts, which provides managerial and support services for federal courts across the country. He developed a fierce work ethic and paid close attention to personal relationships. Shortly after his appointment to the Court in 1953, Warren introduced himself to every official, secretary, elevator operator, and janitor in the building, making a point to learn all of their names and family backgrounds. A staff member recollected that "He shook more hands in one day than some Justices (sic) had in twenty years."[24]

The final lesson involves race and the future of American politics. Whether the conversation concerns resegregated schools and American cities, racial discrimination in voting practices, or the treatment of ex-offenders as second-class citizens, legal policy on matters of race touches the lives of every person in the United States. Foreseeably, as the level of ethnic diversity increases in coming decades, issues involving race and justice will continue to loom large in matters of public policy. Students of the Court who want to know more about the history of such issues would be wise to study Earl Warren.

LITERATURE REVIEW

Previous Biographies of Warren

Earl Warren lived a rich life, and the literature about him approaches its subject from several different perspectives. Journalists, including Ed Cray[25] and Jim Newton,[26] offer detailed coverage of the many specific events of Warren's life but do not address the academic literature concerning the meaning and impact of his policies. Political scientists and law professors provide focused examinations of the Warren Court's opinions, philosophy, and social impact. In this vein, Lucas A. Powe Jr.[27] and Bernard J. Horwitz[28] have written accounts for lay audiences, while Bernard Schwartz,[29] Harry N. Scheiber and Melissa Cully Anderson,[30] and Philip B. Kurland[31] provide analysis and critiques appropriate for specialists and advanced students. While informative, these works give little to no discussion of Warren's background or key events involving him that took place off the bench, such as his prosecution of the *Point Lobos* cases in the 1930s, his involvement with the internment of Japanese Americans during World War II, or his chairmanship of the Warren Commission. Like the famous story of Goldilocks and the Three Bears, each either makes the porridge too hot or too cold.

Among the best books about Warren are two relatively early works, one by Warren's friend Jack Harrison Pollack[32] and the other by one of his law clerks, G. Edward White.[33] Both authors provide important personal and intellectual insights, but their work antedates the release of several crucial materials about Warren, including previously restricted files on the Warren Commission (released pursuant to the Kennedy Assassination Collection Act of 1992) and academic works that sharply criticize the Warren Court's school desegregation and criminal justice decisions. The FBI Headquarters files on the Warren Commission now available in the National Archives shed light on Warren's troubled interactions with J. Edgar Hoover and the strain Warren endured during his dual role as Chief Justice and Chair of the Warren Commission in 1964. Likewise, scholars Gerald N. Rosenberg[34] and William J. Stuntz[35] have written influential books highly critical of Warren and the Warren Court. For his part, Rosenberg argues that the Warren Court failed to achieve school desegregation because courts lack the administrative infrastructure, fiscal controls, and public relations posture to transform large institutions. Stuntz contends that the Warren Court's due process revolution in criminal justice undermined the informal and sympathetic neighborhood controls of the Gilded Age by imposing a rigid set of procedural mandates that bureaucratized the justice system and precipitated a backlash from law and order conservatives. Stuntz characterizes Warren's social justice reforms as ill-considered, quixotic, and socially damaging to the politically excluded groups that Warren sought to protect.

The current work responds to recent conservative scholarly criticism using newly available material. It examines the role that several of Warren's professors at the University of California played in the development of his view of the world. Professors William Carey Jones and Charles H. Lindley served as pillars of the Progressive movement in California, and their emphasis on informed citizenship, administrative expertise, and nonpartisanship in electoral politics helped shape Warren's own value system. Additional research into Warren's years as District Attorney of Alameda County has uncovered transcripts from the *Point Lobos* murder trial, arguably the most important criminal trial of Warren's career. The transcripts and a related unpublished dissertation by the late Miriam Feingold reveal the extent of Warren's involvement in psychologically coercive interrogations, a source of embarrassment when defense attorneys called him to the stand to testify about the matter.

Analysis of the *Brown* decision features Justice Robert Jackson's extensive working papers on the case, prepared most likely as a draft concurrence or possible dissent. The documents reveal the extent of Jackson's doubts about the merits of the NAACP's case and the difficulty of Warren's task in persuading Jackson to join a unanimous opinion in the favor of the plaintiffs. Supplementing these new sources of information on Warren are materials from specialized collections at the Library of Congress and Bancroft Library at the University of California. They include files from many of the justices on the Warren Court, NAACP files in leading cases of the civil rights movement, and, at Berkeley, files on Warren's years in state government, Jack Harrison Pollack's notes on Warren, and oral histories of principals in Warren's life. These materials add important details to the picture of Warren's life in American politics and law.

Judicial Biography

In recent decades, scholarship in the field of judicial biography has become surprisingly controversial. In a thoughtful essay that addresses the philosophical assumptions of judicial biography, Richard A. Posner highlights two epistemological difficulties.[36] The first concerns the so-called "hindsight problem." As Posner describes it:

> We know how things turned out, how a life turned out. We have no direct knowledge of how they would have turned out if something had been different, say in the subject's upbringing. The tendency to see the climactic events or crowning achievements of a life as latent in a person's character or early life is well-nigh irresistible, though we have no way of knowing whether things would have turned out differently had the person had a different character or different life experiences.[37]

The "hindsight problem" may be a factor in why the judicial biography has fallen into disfavor among contemporary political scientists and legal scholars. Political scientists have tended to promote empiricism in the study of political behavior and have shunned the modes of inquiry of the softer humanities, of which biography is broadly representative. For their part, legal scholars have avoided what may be an uncomfortable tension between the personal experiences of an individual judge and the process by which he or she makes judicial decisions. For them, the thorny problem may be that if there is a person behind the mask that interprets and administers the law, the very idea of the rule of law becomes suspect.

The second problem that Posner addresses involves the illusive search for the inner character or "essential self" of the judge. Posner voices skepticism about whether any person has an "essential self," much less a character that can be framed through analysis of social background, parental influences, or personality traits. He contends that there may be a disconnection between achievement and self, since many successful persons rise above the constraints of their backgrounds and personal characteristics. Posner describes most judges as dull and "boorish" people, a characterization that some commentators have applied to Earl Warren;[38] Posner concedes, however, that the most interesting judicial biographies may involve judges, like Earl Warren or Abe Fortas, who have had extensive political careers.

Other scholars share Posner's concerns about the poverty of judicial biography, albeit for different reasons. Professor Linda Przybyszewski, author of an insightful biography of the first Justice Harlan,[39] argues that many judicial biographers seek to escape the tension between "life" and "law" by relying upon a set of common but illusory devices. In her view, judicial biographers have an unfortunate tendency to establish the "greatness" of their judge by emphasizing the individual's "wisdom, economic progressivism, vindication by history, (or) integrity."[40] Others, she writes, measure "greatness" based on a judge's ability to further the "Holmesian values" of "philosophical skepticism, deference to the legislature in constitutional cases, and a direct, 'literary' style of opinion writing."[41] In contrast, Przybyszewski emphasizes religious values as a means of gaining insight into the world view of Justice Harlan.

If Justice Holmes is to be regarded as an archetype for judicial distinction because of willingness to defer to value judgments of elected officials, Earl Warren would fail to qualify for greatness. In fact, Warren represented the very antithesis of Holmesian skepticism of judicial authority. Yet many scholars (I among them) would contend that Warren qualifies for greatness because he used the power of judicial review to attack and partially defeat entrenched system of racial stratification. The dichotomy between Holmes and Warren reflects the tension between judicial restraint and judicial activism. Warren's activism and his willingness to strike down federal and state legislation arose from the need to protect minorities from the majoritarian political process. The jurisprudential roots of this position lay in the famous footnote four of the *Carolene Products* (1938) case.[42] There Justice Stone wrote that while the Supreme Court should defer to Congress in matters of social and economic legislation, it should use heightened levels of scrutiny to protect racial and political minorities, and fundamental rights.

Although the critics of judicial biography make many worthy points, overall the strengths of the discipline seem to outweigh the weaknesses. Studying the lives and accomplishments of individual justices fosters an understanding of the interplay between the Supreme Court and the society of which it is a part. It also helps to dispel the misconception that the interpretation of the law can be performed in a value-neutral manner. The literature of the discipline includes award-winning studies of John Marshall, Louis Brandeis, Hugo Black, Felix Frankfurter, and Abe Fortas, among many others. In their own idiosyncratic ways, each of these studies portrays the evolution of American law as a synthesis between human actors, the judicial process, and broad socioeconomic trends. As historians, judicial biographers necessarily must make qualitative judgments about the values, ideas, and substantive contributions of their justices, just as the justices themselves make value judgments in their own interpretations of the law. In highlighting these matters, judicial biographers enhance the reader's awareness of history and the dynamics and work product of the Supreme Court.

Legal scholars have written extensively on the jurisprudence of Earl Warren and the Warren Court. Much less is known about Earl Warren the person. An intensely private individual who shielded himself and his family members from public scrutiny, Warren shied away from social functions. He adjusted well to the monastic and scholarly life that the work of a successful Supreme Court justice demands. He presented himself to the public as an outgoing, big-hearted, and sensitive person, and those who worked closely with him often observed that the values he exhibited in public mirrored those he followed in his personal and working relationships. Former clerk and Warren biographer G. Edward White describes Warren's core characteristics as those of "integrity, nonpartisanship, honesty, humanity."[43] White continues, "He (Warren) was a genial companion but did not reveal his private thoughts; he held out his hand to the world, but retained his reserve."[44]

The shell that Warren used to shield his private life from the public often became impenetrable. Much of what is known about his private life comes from scripted images of his appealing family, created by campaign consultants Clem Whitaker and Leone Baxter, a political biography written by Irving Stone for Warren's 1948 vice-presidential campaign,[45] and a later biography written by Warren's close friend, Jack Harrison Pollack.[46] At least some of what emerges from these sources and from Warren's own *Memoirs* may have been scripted and should be taken with a grain of salt. Compounding the problem, Warren burned his correspondence with the brethren about their cases, in keeping with the traditions of the Court. Warren openly criticized former Chief Justice Harlan Stone for sharing his private Court papers with author Alpheus Mason, and in his *Memoirs* Warren revealed no secrets about the Court's internal deliberations. He made available to the Library of Congress only his correspondence, speeches, and formal drafts of opinions. These materials, together with extensive files at the University of California covering his years in local and state government, provide a more detailed and independent basis of knowledge about his persona.

Earl Warren and Progressivism

This work argues that Earl Warren embraced the values of Progressivism that he initially encountered as a college student and then applied throughout his career to advance the cause of social justice. Born in 1891, Warren grew up during the heyday of the Progressive movement. During his years at the University of California between 1908 and 1914, Warren assimilated the ethics and ideals of the Progressive reformers as he encountered them in the classroom and in extracurricular activities.

The Progressive era can be loosely defined as a period of discontent with economic and social changes in the American landscape during the late nineteenth and early twentieth centuries. Historian Richard Hofstadter has described the thrust of the Progressive movement as an effort to "restore a type of economic individualism and political democracy that was widely believed to have existed earlier in America and to have been destroyed by the great corporation and the corrupt political machine; and with that restoration to bring back a kind of morality and civic purity that was also believed to have been lost."[47] Warren shared the Progressives' criticism of urban corruption, the vice and squalor of immigrant ghettos, and the failure of elected officials to uphold the public interest in the face of corporate greed. Like many others of his generation, he entered public service in order to articulate and defend the public interest against attacks from without, whether in the form of corrupt corporate interests, dishonest politicians, dangerous political extremists, or alleged enemy aliens.

Historian Robert H. Wiebe[48] extends Hofstadter's analysis of the Progressive era by emphasizing the economic transformation of America between 1880 and 1920. Wiebe stresses the gradual shift in national values between the traditional mindset of the small town of the 1880s and the bureaucratic, managerial frame of mind of the 1920s. As industrial conglomerates and financial interests amassed great power during this period, community and political structures lagged behind, resulting in a crisis of confidence in local government. A new middle-class movement arose that exerted regulatory controls on monopolies, promoted public schools as a means of socializing immigrants, and extended the values of individualism and democracy. Wiebe argues that middle-class professionals (like Warren) failed to appreciate that the only realistic way to accomplish their objectives involved the development of centralized governmental structures. Although the reformers originally opposed centralized government bureaucracy, by the end of their careers, the professionals of the Progressive era erected a regulatory state that depended on legal institutions, trained experts, and the administrative apparatus of the New Deal to achieve their goals.

Other historians have struggled to identify the ideological meaning of Progressivism. Peter G. Filene[49] and John D. Buenker et al.[50] expressed concern about the many contradictions in, and broad appeal of, "progressive thought" to vast sectors of the American population. They challenged the very idea of a Progressive movement as "incoherent" and "conceptually muddled" and declared it ready for burial. Contemporary scholars, including Daniel T. Rodgers, acknowledge the inconsistencies of the Progressives but defend the underlying linguistic "tools" of the movement. In a leading essay on the subject, Rodgers writes, "Progressives could be found who admired the efficiency of the big corporation and who detested the trusts, who lauded the 'people' and who yearned for an electorate confined to white and educated voters, who spoke the language of social engineering and the language of moral uplift or (to make matters worse) did all these things at once."[51]

Rodgers argues that the Progressives lacked a clear political ideology and substituted instead a rhetorical discourse of "discontent" based on antimonopolism and the importance of social bonds and efficiency. Progressives vehemently opposed the various monopolies of their day in the fields of transportation, heavy industry, banking, and utilities. They decried the moral decay of the cities and proposed new measures of social control to fight vice. Above all, they sought to improve society through rational social engineering.[52] Toward this end, occupational groups in fields such as medicine, law, engineering, and social work used higher education and licensure requirements to define and control their status as professionals. They convinced legislators to create new regulatory agencies in federal, state, and local government in order to take power away from political parties and big corporations, leaving more authority in the hands of public administrators and experts.

Rodgers' critique of the underlying ideological ambiguities of the Progressives makes sense when used to evaluate the merits of the movement in its totality. As a professor of intellectual and social history, he tests whether the many divergent subthemes of the Progressives' broad political agenda can be reconciled and concludes that, in fundamental ways, its contradictions abound. To some extent, however, the inquiry differs when it is applied to the life and thought of one single actor, albeit one who played as important a role in twentieth-century political and legal reform as did Earl Warren. Perhaps this is because Warren never was, nor aspired to be, a deep political thinker. Instead, as an elected official and appointed jurist, he repeatedly guided the American ship of state in the direction of particular Progressive values, strengthening social solidarity, administrative efficiency, and the interests of a fair and secure community.

In this more narrow sense, Warren adhered to what Rodgers calls the discourse of discontent. He decried the moral decay of cities and opposed gambling, prostitution, and alcohol in the Prohibition era through the expansion of social controls. He attempted to improve society through rationalization, social engineering, and professional ethics. The thread of consistency that explains Warren's movement from the anticorruption and national security focus of his early years in California state and local government to his later advocacy of legal equality and civil rights on the Supreme Court lies in understanding Warren's Progressive vision of community.

Perhaps the central point of controversy in interpretations of Earl Warren's life involves the question of alleged inconsistencies between the law and order policies he pursued as an elected official and the individual rights agenda he endorsed as Chief Justice. How could a person whose reputation is so closely tied to the expansion of human rights in the form of famous decisions such as *Brown v. Board of Education* and *Miranda v. Arizona* have advocated so forcefully the internment of Japanese Americans during World War II? In a law review article that reflects what may be conventional wisdom about Warren among members of the legal community, Sandhya Ramadas[53] compares speeches and congressional testimony Warren gave in 1942 with his votes in cases involving national security in the 1950s and 1960s, including *Communist Party v. Subversive Activities Control Board*,[54] *Pennsylvania v. Nelson*, [55] and *Yates v. United States*.[56] Ramadas finds that Warren's support for the internment as a matter of national security cannot be squared with his later defense of individual sovereignty over the power of the state. She concludes that between 1942 and 1957 Warren's views concerning the function of law in society underwent an evolutionary transformation.

Ramadas grounds her argument in a comparison of Warren the politician of the 1940s with Warren the jurist of the 1950s. Yet how do these two points of comparison stack up against his behavior off the bench in the 1960s as he chaired the Warren Commission's investigation into the assassination of President Kennedy? In his approach to the Japanese internment *and* the work of the Warren Commission, Warren deferred to the centralized power of the national security state, which functioned autonomously as a "state within a state" outside the control of other branches of government within the separation of power system. If Warren's experiences as Chief Justice had fundamentally altered his world view on questions of national security, it is difficult to see why the state sovereignty perspective he supposedly discarded during the 1950s would suddenly resurrect itself in 1964.

The liberalizing trend that some scholars see in Warren's due process jurisprudence does not explain why Warren in times of crisis repeatedly agreed to surrender power to national security officials in the armed forces, the FBI, and other national intelligence organizations. Like many of his liberal counterparts in executive and congressional positions in the 1950s and 1960s, Warren trusted and empowered the national security state, even as it deceptively pursued a secretive and authoritarian agenda involving espionage, illegal surveillance, and counterintelligence that flew in the face of cherished constitutional values.[57] After Warren's passing, in the period following the death of J. Edgar Hoover and public disclosure of the excesses of the FBI and the Nixon White House during the late 1960s and early 1970s, Congress at least partially reasserted its authority over the national security state under the auspices of the Church Committee. But for Warren himself, the rule of law and the values of due process included a simple but important caveat: in circumstances where he perceived the interest of community safety to be under external threat, the law must defer to the interest of national security.

The philosophical underpinnings of Warren's view of community and citizenship lay in the precepts of American Progressivism. His commitment to clean and efficient government appears repeatedly during his college years, his service as Alameda County District Attorney, and as Attorney General and Governor of California. As District Attorney and state Attorney General, Warren prosecuted defendants for their involvement in corrupt street paving, bail bonding, and parole award schemes. He attacked vice in the gambling industry, closed prostitution rings, and stamped out illegal liquor distributors. As Governor, he rationalized public services in the fields of transportation, corrections, and mental health, and thereby expanded the positive state. In every elected and appointed position he ever held, Warren reorganized his administrative department and expanded its responsibilities, one of the hallmarks of Progressive administration. His vision of community embraced several elements, including fairness, equality, efficiency, and security.

As Chief Justice, Warren's school desegregation, legislative apportionment, and criminal justice decisions took social engineering and professionalism to a new constitutional plane. During the civil rights era, activists who participated in direct actions in the South often faced criminal convictions and other adverse legal actions in the lower courts. In reviewing appeals from these decisions, the Warren Court played a decisive role in the fight for civil rights and racial equality. Throughout his sixteen-year tenure on the Court, Warren never voted against the interests of civil rights activists, and in his leadership role as Chief Justice, he helped to build judicial majorities to defend their interests. In this sense, the Warren Court became a de facto arm of public administration in America: it undertook institutional reforms to fight racism and inequality through the enforcement of constitutional rights. In so doing, it called upon school administrators, law enforcement officials, and state election personnel to implement new legal standards under the supervision of the federal courts. These standards incorporated the constitutional values of racial equality, due process, voting rights, freedom of expression, and protection of the rights of suspects into the domain of public administration. The Court's decisions resurrecting 42 U.S.C. Section 1983 as a basis for holding state officials liable for the violation of federal rights reinforced this trend. In these ways, Warren's work on the Supreme Court extended the Progressive values he consistently embraced as an elected official in California. His deference to military and national security officials during the internment and the Warren Commission showed the primacy of safety in his views of community and the limitations and shortcomings of unbridled trust in the national security state.

Warren and Judicial Activism

Another central element of Warren's jurisprudence and the literature about him involves the concept of judicial activism. Judicial activism refers to the willingness of a court to use the power of judicial review to issue broadly based public policies from the bench. Judicial activism poses a dilemma for democratic theorists: in a democratic government, the formation of public policy is based upon the views of the people, yet in the absence of limitations on governmental power, the rights of minorities (be they religious, racial, political, or criminal) may be put in jeopardy. When unelected officials such as those in the federal judiciary rely upon vague constitutional language to announce new laws, critics voice concern about a lack of legitimacy. But, without a core set of values and a neutral judicial system to protect fundamental rights, political majorities run roughshod over minorities, and constitutional rights become meaningless.

In the period after the Warren Court, federal jurists and legal scholars have written extensively on the problems of legitimacy, legal method, and the power of judicial review. Although full discussion of these matters is beyond the scope of the current work, generally the debate concerns the proper role of courts in the process of defining and developing the law in a democratic society. At one extreme, too much creativity in the interpretation of the Constitution may make constitutional law tantamount to a justice's own subjective perception of the social good. At the other, rigid adherence to value preferences and institutional arrangements of the founding fathers may result in the perpetuation of undemocratic and immoral outcomes. The resulting tension pits those who gauge morality in terms of legitimacy against those who evaluate legitimacy in terms of morality.[58] Those taking the former position find legitimacy in judicial method and fear the intractability of making moral judgments under the guise of constitutional interpretation. Those adopting the latter position argue that focusing exclusively on legal method prevents the Constitution and the Supreme Court from serving their moral function in society.

Earl Warren favored the latter position. In his view, the legitimacy of the Court turned on the morality of its output. In arriving at a morally sound outcome in a given case, Warren thought the justices should search for governing principles based on history, precedent, and moral philosophy. At any particular time, their viewpoint might not be congruent with the opinions of a majority of elected representatives or the attitudes of the American public as a whole. Instead, viewed through a longitudinal lens, the Court's decision should be logically defensible, both in terms of its contribution to the historical evolution of substantive constitutional values and the underlying integrity of its moral precepts.

Whether one agrees or disagrees with Warren's position, the record shows that American courts have always been activist,[59] and as a co-equal branch of government, the judiciary consistently has shaped national policy involving federalism, the regulation of commerce, human equality, due process, and administrative law.

In his text on the Supreme Court, Professor Lawrence Baum defines judicial activism as the use of judicial power to make "significant changes in public policy, especially in policies that the other branches (of government) have established . . . . The Court intervenes in government policy most directly and most clearly," he writes, "when it strikes down the policies of the other branches on constitutional grounds."[60] Advocates of judicial restraint seek to constrain the Court's power through the use of narrow decisions that "minimize the Court's role in policy making."[61] As a result, decisions based on the principle of judicial restraint tend to support the political, cultural, and economic status quo. Conversely, advocates of judicial activism tend to issue decisions that reject dominant orthodoxy. The tension between broad and narrow approaches to the use of judicial power also affects many other aspects of the judicial craft, from differences in the interpretations of precedent to the application of rules that prohibit the use of the Constitution as the basis for decision if the issues in a case can be resolved through statutory interpretation. In these and many other ways, a given justice may either exercise or refrain from exercising judicial power.

Both liberals and conservatives have made policy from the bench. Just as the Taft and Hughes Courts practiced activism in striking down government regulations of business in the first four decades of the twentieth century, the

Warren Court pursued an activist agenda in the fight for racial equality and human rights during the 1950s and 1960s. Conservative justices have practiced judicial activism in the pursuit of *laissez-faire* policies that limit government regulation of business. On individual rights and social policy questions, they tend to defer to legislative majorities. Liberal leaning justices have actively defended individual rights and initiated reforms in public schools, mental institutions, and prisons. On matters of economic policy liberals defer to legislative bodies. Thus, much of the political rhetoric about judicial activism boils down to a question of whose ox is being gored.

During and immediately following the tenure of the Warren Court, conservative legal scholars attacked liberal judges as an "imperial judiciary" that made inappropriate decisions on matters of social policy in ways that went beyond the proper scope and capacity of what unelected judges should decide in a democratic political order.[62] This thesis contains several problems. Like their liberal counterparts, conservative judges often have been quite willing to use the power of judicial review to pursue their own values. Decisions by the Rehnquist and Roberts Courts involving the interstate commerce clause and federalism, the First Amendment rights of corporations in political campaigns, and the right to own guns illustrate this trend.

A recent case, *Kelo v. City of New London* (2005), exemplifies conservative judicial activism. There, the legal issue involved an economic development plan in New London, Connecticut that called for use of the city's power of eminent domain to transfer land from private homeowners to a private corporation. The city's ultimate goal involved the construction of a comprehensive business park to shore up the declining tax base of the area. Although the city offered private homeowners just compensation for the taking of their property, many had sentimental attachments to their homes, a factor that induced them to challenge the constitutionality of the city's plans.

Several legal precedents indicated that the New London development plan would have no constitutional problem if the city transferred the land in question to a utility, a common carrier, or an enterprise involving a public use. Alternatively, the land could be designated as a "blighted area" and then redeveloped without presenting constitutional problems. Based on these precedents, a majority of the Court voted 5–4 to sustain the constitutionality of the involuntary transfer, thus exhibiting a policy of judicial restraint. Writing in dissent, Justice Sandra Day O'Connor argued the city lacked the constitutional power to use eminent domain to transfer land from private party A to private party B. Her opinion, grounded in different interpretations of the relevant precedents, reflected a conservative activist approach. Pundits and state politicians across the nation supported Justice O'Connor's position. They argued that local governments should not be permitted to transfer land from A to B solely on the basis that B would enhance the value of the land more than A. Eventually, forty-three states passed laws prohibiting the use of the power of eminent domain in such situations. The *Kelo* case demonstrates that conservatives also pursue judicial activism, and when their policies receive widespread public support, their decisions can be perceived as constitutionally legitimate.

Perhaps the most distinctive doctrinal feature of the Warren Court involved its acceptance of an activist role for the Court in the protection of fundamental rights and human equality. In the New Deal period, judicial liberals criticized the activism of the Court in striking down regulatory legislation under the rubric of substantive due process. Consistently, until his retirement from the Court in 1962, Justice Frankfurter retained this point of view. Frankfurter saw federal courts as undemocratic institutions, and he believed federal judges should readily defer to the judgments of the political branches. The liberals on the Warren Court, including Justices Warren, Black, Douglas, Brennan, and later, Justices Goldberg, Fortas, and Marshall, assumed a more activist role for the Court in defending political and ethnic minorities and ensuring fundamental rights. They transformed the Equal Protection Clause from its status in the late 1920s as the "usual last resort of constitutional arguments" into the source of fundamental protections for voting rights and freedom from state-sponsored racial stratification systems.

Many scholars of the Warren Court have stressed the social backgrounds of several of the justices in explaining their willingness to protect and expand the constitutional rights of everyday Americans. Three of the leading figures on the Court grew up in low-income households—Justices Warren, Black, and Douglas—and their decisions in criminal justice, labor, and racial justice cases reflect a desire to stand up for the rights of the downtrodden. In contrast, most Supreme Court justices throughout American history have been from upper-class backgrounds, and it may be no accident that many of their decisions reflect an elitist point of view. On the Warren Court itself, the justices least likely to favor expansive doctrinal reforms on behalf of excluded groups, Justices Frankfurter and Harlan, came from relatively privileged backgrounds. Both of these justices relied upon the Case or Controversy requirement of Article III of the U.S. Constitution to restrict the types of cases that federal courts could hear. Their willingness to use the doctrines of standing, ripeness, mootness, and political questions to block access to the courthouse stood in stark contrast with the more lenient positions that many of their colleagues took on these questions.[63]

METHODOLOGY AND SCOPE

The methodology employed in this book involves archival research based on primary sources, oral histories, and secondary materials. Unlike comprehensive biographies, this book does not include a detailed narrative of the many events of Warren's life. Instead, it examines only the more prominent of Warren's experiences and then often in summary fashion. It focuses more carefully on the question of how Warren responded to four important social justice challenges of his day: his murder prosecution of the *Point Lobos* defendants in Alameda County during the Great Depression; his advocacy of exclusion zones and internment camps for Japanese Americans during World War II; his work on school desegregation, civil rights, and criminal justice cases on the Supreme Court; and his leadership of the Warren Commission's investigation into the assassination of President Kennedy.

In examining each of these challenges, the book explores the social meaning of Warren's life and ideas. It stresses the relationship between social context, Warren's decision making, and policy outcomes. Historical research of this nature is at once objective and subjective. It involves the parties who are concerned with controversies or litigation, the facts and history of their situations, the legal and political arguments they presented, and the steps Warren took in resolving their disputes. At least to some extent, these constitute matters of the objective historical record. Conversely, drawing inferences about the fairness of the outcomes necessarily involves the subjective process of weighing competing values and formulating conclusions about the reasonableness, motivation, and overall social utility of Warren's decisions.

The subjective research questions and methodology of this book make it important to be clear about the values that underlie my point of view. In my view, constitutional democracies must safeguard the rights of political and economic outsiders, such as the interests of racial and ethnic minorities. In the absence of such safeguards, capitalist societies have a tendency to develop rigid systems of stratification and privilege that block creativity, innovation, and opportunity. Ultimately, stratification systems pose destabilizing threats to political order. The establishment of constitutional safeguards to protect against injustice and stratification carries with it certain implications concerning the role of courts in society and the issue of judicial activism. On each of these matters, Earl Warren has been assailed for issuing broadly based policy judgments from the bench. Weighing the accuracy of these allegations necessarily involves value judgments, interpretation, and ideology.

The great philosopher of history R.G. Collingwood once noted that human events have an "outside dimension" and an "inside dimension." According to Collingwood, the "outside of an event" involves "everything belonging to it which can be described in terms of bodies and their movements," while the "inside of an event" refers to that "which can only be described in terms of thought." "The history of thought, and therefore all history," Collingwood wrote, "is the re-enactment of past thought in the historian's own mind."[64] Like all works of history, reenactments are interpretive and cannot be regarded as definitively true. Instead, like the current work, they might best be seen as a humble working hypothesis arising from one individual's recreation of another person's experience.

In interpreting the life and legacy of Earl Warren, this book proceeds in stages. The first, which embraces Parts One and Two of the book, follows a chronological format and examines the foundation of Warren's career in Bakersfield, Oakland, and Sacramento. Part One addresses Warren's childhood and his years as District Attorney. Part Two explores Warren's years in California state government, including his involvement in the Japanese internment of World War II, his years as governor, and his candidacies for national office in the late 1940s and early 1950s. Part Three, which follows a thematic format, examines Warren's years on the Supreme Court, with particular focus on the school desegregation, sit-in, voting rights, and criminal justice decisions. Part Four focuses on Warren's leadership role in the Warren Commission's investigation of the assassination of President Kennedy. The conclusion of the book evaluates the achievements of Warren's life and offers an assessment of the legacy of Earl Warren.

NOTES

1. Professor Jesse H. Choper, one of Earl Warren's former law clerks, often emphasized the moral dimension of Warren's approach to constitutional litigation. Jesse H. Choper, "Earl Warren—A Law Clerk's Memory of the Man and the Court," in *Earl Warren and the Warren Court: The Legacy in American and Foreign Law*, ed. Harry N. Scheiber (New York: Lexington Books, 2007), 357–61. Professor Chopper describes Warren as a "principled activist" whose central focus during oral arguments was to inquire of counsel whether the government's conduct was fundamentally fair.

2. For example, the Warren Court's school desegregation decision (*Brown v. Board of Education of Topeka*, 347 U.S. 483 [1954]) overruled *Plessy v. Ferguson*, 163 U.S. 537 (1896), and its exclusionary rule decision in *Mapp v. Ohio*, 367 U.S. 643 (1961) overruled *Wolf v. Colorado*, 338 U.S. 25 (1949). For further analysis of the Warren court's school desegregation and criminal justice decisions, see Chapters 6, 7, and 10, infra.

3. Archibald Cox, *The Warren Court: Constitutional Decision as an Instrument of Reform* (Cambridge, MA: Harvard University Press, 1968).

4. Yale Kamisar, "How Earl Warren's Twenty-Two Years in Law Enforcement Affected His Work as Chief Justice," *Ohio St. J. Crim. L.* 3, no. 1 (2005): 11–32; Yale Kamisar, "Earl Warren: Law Enforcement Leads to Defendants' Rights," *Law Quad Notes* 47, no. 3 (2005): 87–8; Yale Kamisar, "On the Fortieth Anniversary of the Miranda Case: Why We Needed It, How We Got It—And What Happened To It," 5 *Ohio St. J. Crim. L.* 163 (2007).

5. Charles Black, "The Lawfulness of the Segregation Decisions," 69 *Yale L. J.* 421 (1960).

6. See e.g., Philip B. Kurland, *Politics, the Constitution, and the Warren Court* (Chicago: University of Chicago Press, 1970); see also, Dennis J. Hutchinson, "Hail to the Chief: Earl Warren and the Supreme Court," 81 *Michigan Law Review* 922 (1983), available at http://chicagounbound.uchicago.edu/cgi/viewcontent.cgi?article=2526&context=journal_articles.

7. Famous examples of such decisions include *Lochner v. New York*, 198 U.S. 45 (1905) (freedom of contract), *Hammer v. Dagenhart*, 247 U.S. 251 (1918) (no congressional authority to ban child labor in the manufacturing process), and *Standard Oil Co. of New Jersey v. U.S.*, 221 U.S. 1 (1911) (establishing a judicially managed rule of reason in anti-trust actions).

8. In "Federalist No. 78," Alexander Hamilton described the federal judiciary as "the least dangerous branch" because it relies upon the power of reason to accomplish its objectives. In contrast, the executive branch relies upon the power of the sword, and the legislative branch relies upon the power of the purse. Alexander Hamilton, "Federalist No. 78," in *The Federalist Papers,* ed. Clinton Rossiter (New York: Signet Classics, 2003).

9. At various times in its history, the Supreme Court has defended the institution of slavery, *Dred Scott v. Sandford*, 60 U.S. (19 How.) 393 (1857), freed corporations from state economic regulations, *Lochner v. New York*, 198 U.S. 45 (1905), and upheld the constitutionality of Jim Crow laws that ensured white supremacy over blacks, *Plessy v. Ferguson*, 163 U.S. 537 (1896).

10. Earl Warren, *A Republic If You Can Keep It* (New York: Quadrangle Books, 1972), 170.

11. Ibid., 166–67.

12. Ibid.

13. Ibid., 169.

14. Ibid., 158.

15. Bernard Schwartz, *Super Chief: Earl Warren and His Supreme Court, A Judicial Biography* (New York: New York University Press, 1983); Bernard Schwartz, *A History of the Supreme Court* (New York: Oxford University Press, 1993).

16. Ibid., 292.

17. Ibid., 279.

18. Ibid., 292–93.

19. Richard Nixon radio address, October 21, 1972, courtesy Gerhard Peters and John T. Woolley, The American Presidency Project, Santa Barbara, CA, available at http://www.presidency.ucsb.edu/ws/?pid=3637.

20. For further discussion of the conflict between Warren and Nixon, see Chapters 5, 10, 13, and 14, infra.

21. Keeanga-Yamahtta Taylor is Assistant Professor at Princeton University's Center for African American Studies. Michelle Alexander is Associate Professor of Law at the Ohio State University College of Law.

22. Michelle Alexander, *The New Jim Crow: Mass Incarceration in the Age of Colorblindness* (New York: The New Press, 2012).

23. Ibid., 25.

24. Jack Harrison Pollack, *Earl Warren: The Judge Who Changed America* (Englewood Cliffs, NJ: Prentice-Hall, 1979), 165.

25. Ed Cray, *Chief Justice: A Biography of Earl Warren* (New York: Simon & Schuster, 1997).

26. Jim Newton, *Justice for All: Earl Warren and the Nation He Made* (New York: Riverhead Books, 2006).

27. Lucas A. Powe Jr., *The Warren Court and American Politics* (Cambridge, MA: Belknap Press of Harvard University Press, 2000).

28. Bernard J. Horwitz, *The Warren Court and the Pursuit of Justice* (New York: Hill and Wang, 1998).

29. Bernard Schwartz, *Super Chief: Earl Warren and His Supreme Court, A Judicial Biography* (New York: New York University Press, 1983).

30. Scheiber and Anderson, *Earl Warren and the Warren Court.*

31. Philip B. Kurland, *Politics, the Constitution, and the Warren Court* (Chicago: University of Chicago Press, 1970).

32. Pollack, *Earl Warren: The Judge Who Changed America.*

33. G. Edward White, *Earl Warren: A Public Life* (New York: Oxford University Press, 1982).

34. Gerald N. Rosenberg, *The Hollow Hope: Can Courts Bring About Social Change?* (Chicago, University of Chicago Press, 1991).

35. William J. Stuntz, *The Collapse of American Criminal Justice* (Cambridge, MA: Belknap Press of Harvard University Press, 2011).

36. Richard A. Posner, "Objectivity and Hagiography in Judicial Biography," 70 *N.Y.U.L. Rev.* 502 (1995).

37. Ibid., 506.

38. See ibid., 27n, where Posner notes that Dennis J. Hutchinson, in reviewing biographies of Earl Warren, wrote of Warren, "He was a dull man and a dull judge." Dennis J. Hutchinson, "Hail to the Chief: Earl Warren and the Supreme Court," 81 *Mich. L. Rev.* 922, 930 (1983).

39. Linda Przybyszewski, *The Republic According to John Marshall Harlan* (Chapel Hill, N.C.: University of North Carolina Press, 1999).

40. Ibid., 5.

41. Ibid., 8.

42. *U.S. v. Carolene Products Co.*, 304 U.S. 144, 152–53, no. 4 (1938).

43. G. Edward White, *The American Judicial Tradition: Profiles of Leading American Judges*, 3rd ed., (New York: Oxford University Press, 2007), 286.

44. Ibid.

45. Irving Stone, Earl Warren*: A Great American Story* (New York: Prentice Hall, 1948).

46. Pollack, Earl Warren*: The Judge Who Changed America*. Pollack spent many decades writing accounts of Warren and his family for the popular press.

47. Richard Hofstadter, *The Age of Reform from Bryan to F.D.R.* (New York: Knopf, 1955), 5.

48. Robert H. Wiebe, *The Search for Order,* 1877–1920 (New York: Hill and Wang, 1967).

49. Peter G. Filene, "An Obituary for 'The Progressive Movement,'" in *American Quarterly* 22, no. 1 (Spring, 1970): 20–34.

50. John D. Buenker, John C. Burnham, and Robert M. Crunden, "What Was Progressivism?" in *America* 51 (1969): 175–93.

51. Daniel T. Rodgers, "In Search of Progressivism" in *Reviews in American History* 10, no. 4 (Dec., 1982): 113–32.

52. Ibid., 125.

53. Sandhya Ramadas, "How Earl Warren Previewed Today's Civil Liberties Debate—And Got It Right In the End," 16 *Asian American L.J.* 73 (2009).

54. 351 U.S. 115 (1956).

55. 350 U.S. 497 (1956).

56. 354 U.S. 298 (1957).

57. For a thorough analysis of this interpretation, see William W. Keller, *The Liberals and J. Edgar Hoover: The Rise and Fall of a Domestic Intelligence State* (Princeton, NJ: Princeton University Press, 2014).

58. For further discussion of this issue, see Richard B. Saphire, "The Search for Legitimacy in Constitutional Theory: What Price Purity?" 42 *Ohio State L.J.* 335, 338 (1981).

59. See for example, Lawrence Baum, *American Courts: Process and Policy* (Boston: Houghton Mifflin,1990), 327.

60. Lawrence Baum, *The Supreme Court*, 10th ed. (Washington, D.C.: CQ Press, 2010), 162–63.

61. Ibid.

62. See for example, Raoul Berger, *Government by Judiciary: The Transformation of the Fourteenth Amendment* (Indianapolis: Liberty Fund, 1997); Donald Horowitz, *The Courts and Social Policy* (Washington, D.C.: Brookings Institution, 1977); and Nathan Glazer, "Toward an Imperial Judiciary," *The Public Interest* 40 (Fall 1975): 104–23. Since the late 1960s, several of these points of view have been reflected in Republican Party presidential platforms. For example, Republicans have denounced "judicial activism" and "legislating from the bench," favoring instead the jurisprudence of "strict construction." For their part, Democrats have endorsed the principle of a "living and breathing Constitution" in their approach to constitutional interpretation. The tension between these two positions recently has prompted one commentator to remark that "The jurisprudential divide on the Supreme Court regarding high-profile legal issues now appears to map almost perfectly onto the political divide that exists in the larger nation." See "In a Reversal, Rulings Could Goad Democratic Voters," *New York Times*, April 5, 2012 (remarks of Professor Justin Driver).

63. The doctrines of standing, ripeness, and mootness arise out of the requirements of Article III, Section 2 of the U.S. Constitution, which limit the power of federal courts to the resolution of cases and controversies. Hypothetical disputes between parties do not rise to the level of cases and controversies. Thus, federal courts lack the power to issue decisions if the parties do not have standing or if the issues in dispute lack ripeness or are moot. Generally speaking, parties have standing if they suffer a direct injury or harm that courts can remedy. Conversely, persons who merely dislike a given law lack standing to challenge it. Ripeness refers to the requirement that a plaintiff must suffer harm in order to litigate a case. Disputes involving hypothetical facts, or facts that either have not yet occurred or that are not fully developed, lack

ripeness. Moot cases involve disputes that have been fully resolved, such that there is no further remedial action that the federal court can take.

Issues of standing, ripeness, and mootness prevent federal courts from having subject matter jurisdiction. They are closely related to two other doctrines, which prevent federal courts from issuing advisory opinions and from hearing cases that involve political questions. Advisory opinions occur when parties invite federal courts to issue non-binding interpretations of law, whereas political questions involve matters that the Constitution commits to other branches of government for resolution. The rules governing standing, ripeness, mootness, advisory opinions, and political questions—collectively referred to as matters of justiciability—are notoriously vague and have been the basis for much disagreement among the justices over the years.

64. R.G. Collingwood, *The Idea of History* (Oxford: Clarendon Press, 1993), 204–15.

Part I

CHILDHOOD, EDUCATION, AND EARLY CAREER

Chapter 2

Coming of Age

Earl Warren's childhood and early adult experiences instilled in him the core values of independence, diligence, and humanitarian concern for others. His parents encouraged their children to pursue their own individual interests, both in school and in extracurricular activities. As a child, Warren became attracted to animals and the great outdoors. He spent many summers riding his burro in the Tehachapi Mountains outside of Bakersfield, California. In his adolescent years, Warren worked a variety of part-time jobs, including unskilled positions for the Southern Pacific Railroad. He grew up in a loving and supportive home and had a favorable self-image. As Warren matured, he adopted a humanitarian worldview that stressed the need for corporate and public responsibility in addressing the needs of injured persons, the ill, and the destitute. In his college years, Warren supported the Progressive movement, which reinforced his concerns about corruption, corporate greed, and vice. The quest for clean government, firm social safety nets, and the rights of social outcasts eventually became his central, lifelong concerns.

CHILDHOOD

Warren's parents, Methias and Chrystal Varran, led harsh and difficult lives. Born in Haugesund, Norway in 1864, Methias emigrated to the United States as an infant, together with his parents and older brother, Ole. The Varrans settled in rural Leland, Illinois, where Methias' father worked as a farmer and occasional carpenter. As they adjusted to American life, the family changed its name to Warren, and Methias became known as "Matt." In four short years, Matt's mother gave birth to two other boys, one of whom died in infancy. Shortly thereafter, she herself died.

Matt's father later moved the family to Eagle Grove, Iowa, where he remarried. The new family had eight more children by his second wife, and in desperation due to their father's declining health, Ole, Matt, and his younger brother moved to a neighbor's farm, where they helped doing chores. Matt stayed in school through the seventh grade but then left with Ole in search of work. Eventually, they arrived in Chicago, where Ole contracted a severe form of tuberculosis. Lacking the funds for medical help, Ole died in Matt's arms on Christmas Eve 1884. Ole's death left a deep impression. "Having lost the one most near and dear to him and being broke in a strange city," Earl Warren later recollected, "(My father) then swore that as long as he lived he would never be broke again."[1] In 1885, Matt moved to Minneapolis, where he obtained work in the railroad yards as a carpenter.

Earl Warren's mother, Christine ("Chrystal") Hernlund, also was an immigrant from Scandinavia. Born in the Swedish town of Halsingland, she came to America as an infant and settled with her family on the north side of Chicago. Her parents emphasized traditional Christian values, hard work, and abstention from tobacco and alcohol. In October 1871, the Great Chicago Fire left the family's home in ruins, and they resettled in Minneapolis. Chrystal eventually finished public school, and on Valentine's Day in 1886, at the age of eighteen, she married Matt Warren.

In 1887, Chrystal gave birth to their first child, Ethel. Two years later, they moved to California in search of a better life. Initially, Matt worked as a mechanic at the Hotel del Coronado in San Diego. In 1890, he again uprooted the family, this time for Los Angeles, where he worked as a carpenter for the Southern Pacific Railroad. The family resided in a small five-room house on Turner Street, near the original plaza of the city. There on March 19, 1891, Earl Warren was born.

Two events from Warren's early childhood figure prominently in the image that he later projected of himself. Both occurred when he was approximately three years old, too young to have remembered them clearly on his own. Warren's recollections of the incidents probably reflect the views of his parents, his older sister, his campaign consultants, or his own sense of what type of image may have made him attractive to potential voters as he ran for public office in the 1940s. Like John Marshall Harlan, who frequently told the story of his father chastising a slave driver in public for whipping a group of chained slaves,[2] Warren's stories have become mythical and, in that sense, provide valuable insights into his identity.

The first incident involved a neighbor's teenaged daughter, who died of either polio or spinal meningitis in anguish and great pain.[3] Warren purportedly overheard her screams, and at a later point, the experience may have reinforced in his mind the account of his Uncle Ole's death from tuberculosis in Chicago. In both cases, the poor victims died because they lacked the resources for appropriate health care.

The second incident occurred in 1894, when Matt Warren joined over 100,000 members of the American Railway Union in a strike against the Pullman Palace Car Company. The strike began as a wage dispute in Pullman, Illinois, a company town near Chicago, but eventually rail workers in other cities refused to service trains that used Pullman cars. Due to the purported "disruption" of mail service, federal officials obtained an injunction against the strike, and when union workers ignored the court order at the urging of labor leader Eugene V. Debs, President Cleveland called in federal troops to restore order. In Los Angeles, a young Earl Warren watched in horror as mobs roamed the streets burning railroad executives in effigy. The strike ended in failure, and Matt Warren, along with hundreds of fellow workers, found himself blacklisted and without a job.

Matt eventually found work with the rival Santa Fe Railroad in the desert east of Los Angeles. He then learned that the Southern Pacific Railroad had established a maintenance facility in Kern, California, one mile east of Bakersfield in the San Joaquin Valley and needed skilled craftsmen.[4] He acquired a position there, and in 1895 the Warren family moved into a home on Niles Avenue just across from the railroad yards. The east side of Bakersfield served as Ethel and Earl's home for the duration of their childhood.

In Earl Warren's youth, Bakersfield was a rough, frontier town. Its principal economic interests included ranching, farming, sheepherding, and railroading. By the turn of the century, engineers discovered major oil fields in the area, bringing a boom to the local economy. In those years, Bakersfield consisted of many working-class neighborhoods where itinerant workers lived. It also functioned as a center for alcohol, gambling, and vice. One researcher estimates that in 1900, during Warren's childhood, Bakersfield had approximately 7,000 residents, more than 100 saloons, and about 500 prostitutes.[5] An ethnically diverse community, it featured single Chinese men who worked as unskilled railroad workers, Basque and French sheepherders, Jewish merchants, and white former Midwesterners, like the Warrens.

Official census figures for 1900 confirm this picture. Of the 16,480 residents of Kern County in 1900, 8,623 were foreign born, and 10,504—nearly 63%—were male. Between 1890 and 1900, the female population of the County declined precipitously, from 8,889 in 1890 to 5,976 in 1900.[6] Despite its ethnic diversity, Bakersfield remained highly segregated. Asians lived on the outskirts of town, railroad workers lived to the north side of the Southern Pacific mainline, sheepherders to the south, and the vice district lined K Street.

Matt Warren worked at night as a car inspector for the Southern Pacific, and eventually he became a supervisor and master craftsman in the car repair shops. He stayed with the railroad until his retirement in the 1930s. By all accounts, the family led a Spartan existence, and Matt and Chrystal taught the value of frugality and self-improvement. Both worked hard to save funds for their children's education. Earl started grammar school at the unusual age of five, and by the end of his first year, his teachers promoted him to the third grade. As a result, he became the youngest and smallest child in his class, and this adversely affected both his self-confidence and his participation in athletics. An average student whose academic interests gravitated toward history and English, his most meaningful youthful experiences lay outside the classroom in his encounters with pets and after-school employment.

Warren's closest friend while growing up was his burro, "Jack," obtained from sheepherders who spent their summers in the nearby Tehachapi Mountains. The youthful Warren rode Jack bareback and without bridle cross-country, and he spent much of his youth alone, exploring, hunting, fishing, and finding swimming holes. This sparked a lifelong love for these activities. Every day after school, Warren would feed Jack treats, and the two became inseparable. When Warren prepared to leave for college, his family sold Jack to the owner of a local shoe store, who used the burro to haul a wagon to advertise the store. Frequently, however, Jack would escape his stall and head to the Warren household, where he would bray loudly for treats. One day after school, Warren learned that Jack had been poisoned, most likely by a neighbor who disliked all the noise. Years later in his *Memoirs*, a heartbroken Warren remarked, "My sorrow at (Jack's) passing remains to this day."[7]

Warren's after-school jobs included hauling ice on a wagon and working for the railroad. As a "call boy," he located train crews to inform them that they needed to report to work to man trains. This meant wandering the seedy hotels, brothels, and gambling joints of town in search of wayward crewmembers. Although Warren's parents strictly forbade his participation in vice, he nevertheless saw the underside of Bakersfield, at least from a distance. Occasionally, Warren's coworkers seriously injured themselves on the moving train cars. Warren helped carry them to a special room for the amputation of limbs. Tragically, the Southern Pacific Railroad often dismissed its injured workers and retaliated against them if they sought damages for the injuries they sustained. They became cripples, with no access to financial compensation at all.[8]

COLLEGE AND EARLY CAREER

In 1908, Warren graduated from Kern County Union High School in a class of sixteen, and he was one of only four in the class who went on to college.[9] In the fall of 1908, he enrolled at the University of California majoring in political science.

Warren became a rather carefree student and placed his priorities on developing friendships at fraternal organizations such as the La Junta Club and the Skull and Keys Society. In these groups, Warren balanced the consumption of kegs of beer with discussions of literary works by Upton Sinclair, Jack London, and Frank Norris. He often found this extracurricular reading more engaging than his formal studies at the university, and the muckraking and Progressive themes in the books he read influenced him. He especially enjoyed Frank Norris' novel, *The Octopus*, which stressed the corruption and monopolistic power of the Southern Pacific Railroad in the San Joaquin Valley and in California state politics. Undoubtedly, the conflicts between ranchers, wheat farmers, and the all-powerful railroad featured in *The Octopus* brought to mind the familiar world of Bakersfield that Warren himself had experienced.

In his public statements, Warren often discounted the effect that his professors had upon him. "No book or professor had a profound influence on me," he once said, "not even in law school. Companionship was the greatest thing I found at the university and it still stands out in my mind today as more important than anything I learned in classes."[10] Based on this statement, most Warren biographers discount the role that formal education may have played in the formation of his political values.

Although Warren certainly did not excel in academics at this stage in his career, the ideas he encountered in his courses at Berkeley and later in law school at Boalt Hall reinforced his humanitarian instincts. Many of his professors had strong ties to the Progressive Party in California, and they often expressed their political views and real-world experiences in class. Given the relatively largely number of courses Warren took from Progressive professors such as William Carey Jones and Charles H. Lindley, the ideas he encountered in the classroom nudged him in the direction of Progressivism.

During his six years as an undergraduate in political science and as a law student in the Department of Jurisprudence at Berkeley, Warren studied under Professor William Carey Jones, a specialist in Roman law who played a central role in the founding of the law school at the University. Like several of his colleagues on the jurisprudence faculty, Professor (and later, Dean) Jones closely identified with Progressive values and became active in community affairs. Jones wrote the charter for City of Berkeley and incorporated reforms such as the city manager system into it. His academic articles emphasize efficient administration and the importance of citizenship, nonpartisanship, and the public welfare in democratic life, themes that Warren would rigorously pursue throughout his adult life. Histories of Boalt Hall (as the law school at the University of California is known) note that Professor Jones and his colleagues often referred to their Progressive political activities and viewpoints in the classroom during the period when Warren studied there.[11]

Another of Warren's professors, Charles H. Lindley, joined the Progressive Party and became actively involved in municipal reform in San Francisco.

Professor Lindley worked closely with Hiram Johnson, an alumnus of Boalt Hall, who served as an assistant prosecutor in the graft prosecution of San Francisco mayor Eugene Schmitz. As a student, Warren followed the Schmitz trial and volunteered to serve as a poll watcher in San Francisco municipal elections. In 1911, Warren supported Hiram Johnson's successful campaign for Governor of California.

At the time of his matriculation, the University of California had no formal law school other than the Hastings College of Law across the bay in San Francisco. The study of jurisprudence at Berkeley consisted of a combination of undergraduate courses in political science, history, and political economy with a series of upper-level classes in Roman law and Anglo-American common law. The two principal professors in the program, William Carey Jones and Bernard Moses, taught courses in history, political science, and jurisprudence. The grandson of Missouri Senator Thomas Hart Benton, Professor Jones graduated from the University of California in 1871 intending to work as an attorney, but instead he accepted an administrative position as recorder of the faculties. In 1877, he moved to the faculty, where he taught Latin and, beginning in the early 1880s, a senior course in Roman law. Professor Moses, who at one time headed the Department of Political Science, earned his doctorate at the University of Heidelberg, where he became deeply committed to rigorous academic scholarship in the German tradition. Textbooks for Professor Moses' required "Political Science" class included Cambell's *Austin's Jursiprudence*, Cooley's *Constitutional Law*, and Smith's *English Institutions*.[12]

In Warren's freshman and sophomore years, the vast majority of students who intended to pursue careers in the law combined three years of lower division coursework in elementary and commercial law with one year of upper-level classes in international law, constitutional law, and Roman law. After they earned bachelor's degrees, graduates would work as clerks for several months in law offices and then apply for admission to the bar. Professor Jones proposed that the University charter its own law school, and in 1910, it secured funds for the construction of a new law building.

The law school at Boalt Hall, originally known as the Department of Jurisprudence, opened in January 1911, during Warren's junior year. In the 1911–1912 academic year, 89 students enrolled. In order to gain admission, students had to complete three years of undergraduate course work in elementary law, jurisprudence, Roman law, and international law. The School of Jurisprudence adopted an academic approach to the study of law that differed significantly from the utilitarian approach favored at Hastings. In addition to the required two years of upper division coursework, students had to complete a dissertation project.

The faculty of the Department of Political Science and the faculty of Jurisprudence at Boalt Hall consciously incorporated Progressive ideas into their curricula. Progressivism became a pervasive part of California politics in the first two decades of the twentieth century, in part because of reaction against the excesses of the Southern Pacific Railroad and in part because of a perceived need to counter the problem of graft in municipal government and expand public schools in order to socialize immigrant children.

The University naturally embraced the movement to expand the power of experts in solving society's problems, and on an informal basis, its mission encouraged faculty members to serve as consultants for municipal and state government. In Warren's years at Berkeley, David Barrows of the Political Science Department and Professor William Carey Jones of the Department of Jurisprudence worked as advisors to the City of Berkeley addressing a myriad of municipal problems. Jurisprudence lecturer Max Thelen specialized in the regulation of railroads, and he later served on the California State Railroad Commission during the administration of Governor Hiram Johnson. Professor Charles H. Lindley studied the law of lands, mines, and water, and he developed close ties with Hiram Johnson during the 1911 gubernatorial campaign. These faculty members helped to shape the nature of the student academic experience—both in the classroom and outside the classroom—during Warren's years as a student in the Departments of Political Science and Jurisprudence.[13]

Professor William Carey Jones' essay, "Present Day Problems of Democracy," provides an example of his Progressive philosophy. There, he wrote:

> Never was a people more responsible for its difficulties than is the American nation today. But, again, never did a people have more fully in its own hands the power and opportunity to surmount peaceably its difficulties . . . . (A) sense of civic obligation has been developed which demands good local government. . . . We are becoming alive to the necessity of good and efficient administration of our State governments. And by this token we are becoming better citizens of the Republic. Citizenship above partisanship. Public welfare above private interest . . . they are emblems that point the way to a sure and steady progress toward the resumption of political power by the people, to a new realization of the ideals of democracy.[14]

The central themes of this passage—efficient public administration, citizenship, nonpartisanship, public welfare over private interest—appear repeatedly in Warren's public policies, legal decisions, and books at later periods in his life.

Jones' other published materials confirm his ideological ties to the Progressive movement. In *Elements of Civil Government* (1891), he underscores the "evils" of political parties, caucuses, and conventions, which "call for the most earnest thought from every intelligent citizen." He continues, "Such evils are the influence and corruption practiced by political 'bosses,' the buying of votes, and 'treating' to liquor. They are especially prevalent in larger cities."[15] Jones stressed the moral obligation of individual citizens to "take a keen interest in the honor, integrity, and wellbeing of the government," themes that Warren also emphasized.[16]

Although Warren's academic transcripts at the University of California are private and unavailable, it is highly likely that he enrolled in William Carey Jones's classes. Jones, functioning as Dean of the Jurisprudence Department, threatened Warren with dismissal from law school because Warren failed to participate in class discussions. Warren stood his ground in the conversation and successfully argued that the departmental rules contained no formal requirement that he participate in class as long as he passed his exams.[17] It is unlikely that Jones would have confronted Warren in the absence of personal knowledge about Warren's reticence in class. In addition, several Warren biographers make a point of saying that following his conversation with Warren, Professor Jones refrained from calling on Warren in his subsequent Constitutional Law class.[18] Available records do establish that the third-year curriculum in Warren's last year of law school (1913–1914) featured Professor Jones' Constitutional Law class, and it is therefore highly probable that Warren enrolled in it.

Throughout his years at Berkeley and at Boalt Hall, Warren remained, at best, an average student. One of the reasons he disliked academics in law school concerned his professors' extensive reliance on the casebook method in teaching their classes.[19] Warren's distaste for the casebook method led him to supplement his legal education with volunteer and employment opportunities outside the classroom. Over time, the focus of his volunteer experiences involved poll watching in San Francisco and court watching in major graft prosecution cases in the Bay Area. These experiences reflect his growing interest in Progressivism. Likewise, the topic for his senior paper, "The Personal Liability of Corporate Liability in the State of California," shows his concern for corporate responsibility and the need for expanded state regulation of corporate malfeasance.

One of the trials Warren watched as a student involved the bribery trial of San Francisco Mayor Eugene Schmitz, the County Board of Supervisors, and their attorney, "boss" Abe Ruef. Warren enjoyed watching the trial because it featured the themes of corruption and corporate greed. As the complex trial dragged on, a would-be juror became angry when prosecutors dismissed him from the venire. The juror took revenge in the courtroom by shooting the lead prosecutor, Francis J. Heney, in the head. Although Heney survived the shooting, responsibility for prosecuting the case fell to one of Heney's assistants, Hiram Johnson. Johnson eventually won a conviction against Ruef, and the remaining cases either were dismissed or reversed on appeal.[20] Building on his reputation as a fighter against corruption, Johnson successfully ran for Governor of California in 1910. His campaign had a profound impact on Earl Warren.

Johnson's platform included a proposal to make several changes in state law designed to end the dominance of corporations like the Southern Pacific Railroad in state politics. These proposals—which voters eventually passed as amendments to the California Constitution—included the rights of recall, referendum, initiative, and cross-filing. The first three reforms enabled voters to remove sitting politicians, initiate legal changes through the ballot, and eliminate unpopular legislation. The fourth reform, cross-filing, permitted candidates to run as "nonpartisans" in the primary elections of both major parties, and it eventually became an integral part of Warren's political strategy. Every time he ran for statewide public office in California, Warren positioned himself as a political moderate by cross-filing as a Democrat.[21]

After several years as governor, Hiram Johnson nominated himself to the United States Senate, where he became an ardent isolationist. Although Johnson fell short of his ultimate goal of restricting the power of corporations in the legislature, his structural reforms, and especially his support for the ballot initiative, fundamentally altered the shape of California politics over the next century. Johnson's commitment to nonpartisan government, his opposition to corporate corruption and organized crime, and his intolerance of vice heavily influenced Warren's own political views.

When he graduated from Boalt Hall in 1914, Warren had acquired the identity of what historian Robert H. Wiebe (1966) has described as "the new middle class." Warren joined the ranks of urban professionals who endorsed rational public administration and scientific management as a means of eliminating corruption and improving the delivery of community services in municipal and state government.

Initially, Warren apprenticed at a variety of law offices in Oakland, and when the U.S. entered World War I, he enlisted in the Army and entered the officers' corps at the rank of second lieutenant. After training at Camp Lewis, Washington, he provided bayonet instruction for the duration of the war at Camp Lee, Virginia. He then returned to Oakland and, in May of 1920, accepted a position as Deputy District Attorney at the Alameda County District Attorney's Office.

Warren's first case involved the prosecution of John Taylor, a former "socialist" candidate for mayor of San Francisco. Taylor faced criminal charges under a newly adopted syndicalism law that prohibited individuals and organizations from advocating the violent overthrow of private industries or the government. Warren charged Taylor with knowingly belonging to the Communist Labor Party—whose platform advocated industrial sabotage—and with committing acts that aided and abetted industrial sabotage. At trial, Warren introduced evidence that the Communist Labor Party sought to capture and control state government in the name of the masses and transfer of all private property to "the people." Warren won a conviction on both counts in the trial court, but the California Supreme Court overturned Taylor's conviction on the aiding and abetting charge because of a lack of evidence that Taylor acted on his beliefs.[22] As a result, the trial court sentenced Taylor to fourteen years in prison. Taylor stood convicted solely because of his political beliefs and his membership in the Communist Labor Party.

Syndicalism laws such as the one Taylor violated originally targeted the activities of the Industrial Workers of the World, a radical union that organized workers in the American West. In the aftermath of World War I, as communists gained power in Russia and, briefly, in Germany, prosecutors in America applied these laws to many different radical groups, including anarchists, communists, and socialists. In 1919, anarchists bombed the home of U.S. Attorney General Mitchell Palmer, and later that same year, they planted a bomb on Wall Street in New York City that killed 38 people. These and similar attacks triggered a wave of antiradical repression known as the Palmer Raids.

Prosecutors in Alameda County brought many cases as a part of this nationwide effort, and their actions proved both legally and politically controversial. Their most famous case involved Anita Whitney, a radical social worker and feminist who had family ties to former Supreme Court Associate Justice Stephen Johnson Field and prominent industrialist Cyrus W. Field. They charged Whitney with violating the same California syndicalism law that Warren later used against John Taylor. In 1927, the U.S. Supreme Court upheld Whitney's conviction, thereby sustaining the constitutionality of the California Syndicalism Act. In his famous concurrence in *Whitney*, Justice Louis Brandeis advocated a "free market of ideas" approach to First Amendment rights. He contended that government censorship should be discouraged in the absence of a clear and present danger.[23] Decisions such as *Taylor* and *Whitney* sparked opposition to the repression of political radicals, and eventually, organizations such as the American Civil Liberties Union arose to challenge these acts of political censorship.

Earl Warren worked diligently and competently, and his supervisors noticed the quality of his efforts. In 1923, he accepted a promotion to Chief Deputy District Attorney, assuming responsibility for civil cases at the prosecutor's office. In this capacity, he established close relationships with several members of the Alameda County Board of Supervisors and with Joe Knowland, conservative publisher of *The Oakland Tribune*. In 1925, when District Attorney Ezra Decoto accepted a position on the State Railroad Commission, the Board of Supervisors narrowly approved Warren as Alameda County District Attorney.

One of Warren's first steps as District Attorney was to reorganize his staff into various areas of specialization, including a civil division, a homicide division, a fraud division, and a criminal investigation division. Using daily staff meetings to maintain control, he demanded long hours from his staff and recruited highly competent persons for positions of major responsibility. These included Helen MacGregor, a law school graduate who became executive secretary, J. Frank Coakley, head of the criminal division, and Warren Olney III, who became Warren's closest aide. All three would serve him faithfully not only in Alameda County but in the Attorney General's and Governor's offices as well.

During the late 1920s and early 1930s, Warren and his staff fought corruption in the Alameda County Sheriff's Office, raided Chinese lotteries and houses of prostitution in Emeryville, and exposed a corrupt system of bidding for street paving contracts in Oakland. His attorneys and investigators thoroughly prepared their cases for trial, and together they achieved one of the highest successful prosecution rates in California.

With the assistance of his staff, Warren gradually expanded his statewide reputation for independence, integrity, and professionalism. Known as a hard-nosed prosecutor, Warren strictly enforced laws against organized crime, graft, and political radicalism. In 1931, when Columbia University Professor Raymond Moley conducted a comprehensive study of district attorneys nationwide, he called Earl Warren the best district attorney in the United States.[24] By 1934, Warren expanded the scope of his activities outside Oakland by chairing the California Board of Criminal Identification and Investigation, creating a criminal laboratory for rural counties, and sponsoring a postsecondary program in law enforcement studies at San Jose State University. His pioneering work in these fields led to a friendship with FBI Director J. Edgar Hoover, who shared Warren's goal of making the field of law enforcement more professional.

Berkeley police chief August Vollmer also played an important role in Warren's developing views about law enforcement. Famous for his advocacy of police training programs and administrative structures that kept chiefs of police independent from urban politics, Vollmer opposed police brutality and coercive methods during custodial interrogations. As early as the 1920s, Vollmer criticized the intimidation and manipulation of suspects in the Berkeley Police Department and advocated training in scientific investigation as an alternative to interrogation. Vollmer's officers assisted Warren in raids against vice operations in Emeryville and Oakland, and the Berkeley Police Department also performed laboratory work for the Alameda County District Attorney. During the early 1930s, Vollmer headed the Wickersham

Commission's subsection on police, and he wrote the chapter on police administration. The seeds of Warren's faith in police professionalism and his later opposition to involuntary confessions began in his associations with August Vollmer in the 1920s.[25]

FAMILY LIFE

Despite the significant commitment of time and energy that Warren devoted to his career, he maintained a modest social life. In 1924, while attending a Sunday brunch at the Piedmont Baths in Oakland, he met Nina Elisabeth Myers. It was close to love at first sight. Nina (pronounced "Ny-na") was 5' 2", attractive, and, like Warren, of Scandinavian background. She came from difficult family circumstances. Originally christened Nina Elisabeth Palmquist, she was born in Sweden in 1893 and emigrated to the United States as an infant. Her father was a Baptist minister who initially settled in San Diego. Her mother died of uremic poisoning when Nina was just five, leaving her father to raise five children alone. He later moved the family to Oakland, where he remarried. In rapid succession, three members of the family succumbed to tuberculosis: her father in 1907, one of Nina's brothers in 1919, and another brother in 1920. "We were so poor, and everybody was dying. We didn't have pleasant memories," she later said.[26] Nina married an aspiring jazz pianist, Grover Cleveland Myers, and in 1919, the couple had a son, Jim Myers. Three months later, Grover Myers himself died of tuberculosis. To save money, Nina moved in with her stepmother and found work in a women's specialty shop nearby. She devoted herself to her work and soon became manager of the shop.

Over the next year, Earl's romance with Nina blossomed, and on October 14, 1925, they married. Shortly after the marriage, Warren adopted Jim, and when the boy turned five, the newlyweds decided to send him to Del Monte Military Academy. School regulations permitted only one home visit a month, and Jim faced a rather Dickensian childhood. He was philosophical about his experience: "Mother came to send me to a military academy—it gave me a chance to get a good start in schooling, and it gave them a chance to get to know each other."[27] Jim remained at Del Monte until the age of ten, when he returned to Oakland. He then became an integral part of the Warren family.

After their wedding, the Warrens moved into an apartment in Oakland, and in the next six and a half years, they had five more children. Their first child, Virginia, was born in 1928. By 1934, the family also included Earl Jr., Dorothy, Nina, and Bobby. At that point, the family moved to more spacious accommodations on Vernon Avenue in the Merritt Lake district, close to downtown Oakland. They lived in this home until Warren became Governor of California in 1942.

As a rising leader in the California Republican Party, Warren jealously guarded the privacy of his family. Nina dedicated her principal attention to raising the children, and, apart from occasional parties, she remained free of political and social obligations. Raising a large family in the depression years on the limited salary of a public official presented challenges, and money remained tight even as Warren assumed positions of greater leadership in California politics. With careful budgeting, they managed.

Ever devoted to his family, Warren cared for the children every Sunday so that Nina could enjoy some time to herself. Together, he and the children would visit the Oakland Zoo, go swimming at local pools, chase the geese at Merritt Lake, lunch in San Francisco's Chinatown, or visit his sister, Ethel. Warren avoided bringing work home as much as possible, and he faithfully kept the dinner hour as a time of refuge to enjoy with his family. They attended Baptist services in Oakland, but the children's active involvement in varsity and recreational sports gradually led to a decline in family religious activities.

The family stayed in Oakland until 1942, when Warren won his bid to become Governor of California. They then moved to Sacramento, where the five younger Warren children spent their adolescence and graduated from high school. Popular magazines often ran stories about the photogenic Warren family during these years. The stories featured Nina's management of home life in the Victorian governor's mansion, the athletic accomplishments of the Warren children, and the healthy balance between work and family life that Warren himself struck. In the 1940s and 1950s, the children completed their formal education and pursued a variety of careers. Jim served in the Pacific theater in World War II and later pursued a successful career in real estate and in the wine industry. Earl became a judge in Sacramento, and Robert ("Bobby") worked as an administrator for the California Department of Corrections. Virginia married television celebrity John Charles Daly, host of the famous quiz show "What's My Line." She later served as volunteer secretary for the Supreme Court Historical Society. Dorothy married a professor at UCLA, but the marriage failed in the 1960s. At that point, she moved to Washington, D.C. and lived for a time with her parents. She then remarried and lived in the Washington area until her death in 1986. In the early 1950s, Nina Elizabeth ("Honey Bear") rose to national prominence because of her fight with polio. She eventually recovered, attended UCLA, and then married Dr. Stewart Brien, an obstetrician in Los Angeles.

Over the years, the Warren family remained close even as Warren himself rose to political prominence on the state and national stage. Warren's approach to parenting reflected the values of independence and freedom of personal development that his own parents used in his upbringing. Just as he pursued his interests in animals and exploration, he encouraged his children to follow their diverse athletic and extracurricular interests. Warren's strong sense of independence, reflected in his desire to supplement his legal classes with a part-time job in a law firm, indicates his favorable self-esteem and his willingness to act forcefully to affect change.

Warren's developing worldview as a student at the University of California shows the importance of humanism, Progressive ideology, and professional public administration in his approach to government. Several faculty members in the Departments of Political Science and Jurisprudence at Berkeley appear to have influenced Warren's Progressive views concerning the importance of citizenship and the need for nonpartisanship and professionalism in public affairs. As District Attorney, Warren exhibited Progressive values in reorganizing the office, challenging corruption in urban politics, and combating vice.

NOTES

1. Earl Warren, *The Memoirs of Chief Justice Earl Warren* (New York: Madison Books, 1977), 14.
2. See Przybyszewski, *The Republic According to John Marshall Harlan*, 25 (see chap. 1, n. 39).
3. Ibid., 12.
4. Some scholars speculate that Matt Warren secretly sided with management during the strike, making his "blacklisting" a ruse. See Cray, *Chief Justice: A Biography of Earl Warren*, 19, note. However, others have not found support for this assertion.
5. Newton, *Justice for All*, 20.
6. Data on population and housing from the Twelfth Census of the United States in 1900 is available online at www.census.gov/prod/www/abs/decennial/1900.htm).
7. Warren, *Memoirs*, 31.
8. Ibid., 30.
9. Ibid., 26–7.
10. Quoted in James F. Simon, *In His Own Image: The Supreme Court in Richard Nixon's America* (New York: David McKay Co., 1973), 57.
11. Sandra P. Epstein, *Law at Berkeley: The History of Boalt Hall* (Berkeley: Institute of Government Studies Press, University of California at Berkeley, 1997), 51–3.
12. Ibid., 6.
13. For further information on the faculty of the Department of Jurisprudence at the University of California during the first two decades of the twentieth century, see Ibid., 50–6.

14. William Carey Jones, "Present Day Problems of Democracy," paper included in collected writings of William Carey Jones, bound and shelved in Faculty Library, Boalt Hall, University of California, 1–23, quoted in Epstein, *Law at Berkeley*, 51.

15. Edward Carey Jones, *Elements of Civil Government* (Sacramento: State of California Printing Office, 1891), 97–8.

16. Ibid., 118.

17. For further details about the conversation, see Pollack, *Earl Warren: The Judge Who Changed America*, 31–2.

18. Ibid., 32.

19. Warren, *Memoirs*, 42.

20. Charles Fickert, the newly elected District Attorney, dismissed the remaining bribery cases. Newton, *Justice for All*, 32.

21. Although recall, referendum, and initiative all remain crucial aspects of California elections law today, in 1958 voters adopted a constitutional amendment that eliminated the cross-filing option. In 2010, they also approved a "single primary" system. The latter enables eligible voters to vote in the primary election for any candidate for congressional or state political office without regard to the political party of either the candidate or the voter.

22. *People v. Taylor*, 203 p. 85 (1921).

23. In 1969, in one of its final decisions, the Warren Court overruled *Whitney v. California*, thus accepting Brandeis' argument that advocacy of violent revolution in the abstract did not rise to the level of an imminent danger. *Brandenburg v. Ohio*, 395 U.S. 444 (1969).

24. See Yale Kamisar, "How Earl Warren's Twenty-Two Years in Law Enforcement Affected His Work as Chief Justice," 3 *Ohio St. J. Crim. L.* 11 (2005–2006), available at http://moritzlaw.osu.edu/osjcl/Articles/Volume3_1/Symposium/Kamisar_3–1.pdf, pp. 12–13.

25. For further analysis of Warren's relationship with Vollmer, see Gene E. Carte and Elaine H. Carte, *Police Reform in the United States: The Era of August Vollmer, 1905–1932* (Berkeley: University of California Press, 1975), 47–9, 71.

26. Cray, *Chief Justice: A Biography of Earl Warren*, 40.

27. James Warren, et al., *"Earl Warren: The Governor's Family,"* Earl Warren Oral History Project, typeset of an oral history conducted 1970–1975 by Amelia R. Fry and Miriam Feingold Stein, Regional Oral History Office, The Bancroft Library, University of California, Berkeley, 1980, p. 69.

Chapter 3

The D.A. on the Waterfront

Earl Warren's success in prosecuting vice and political corruption cases in Alameda County brought him into the political limelight. As prosecutor, he had the reputation of being tough, nonpartisan, and fair. On the campaign trail, he was a formidable opponent. Outgoing and friendly, he remembered names and faces well, put people at ease, and spoke articulately on behalf of centrist values. He developed strong ties with conservative organizations such as the Masons, the Elks, and the xenophobic Native Sons of California, and he won the endorsement of influential *Oakland Tribune* publisher and Republican insider, Joe Knowland. After the 1930 campaign, he never faced meaningful opposition for reelection as district attorney.

Warren's rise to statewide political prominence in California during the 1930s occurred against the background of union strife in the San Francisco Bay Area. In the prohibition era, Warren oversaw prosecutions against rum-runners, mobsters, and corrupt politicians, and this earned him the respect of law enforcement officials nationwide. In the 1930s, he gained additional public attention by enforcing laws against militant labor unions that attempted to organize workers in the difficult days of the Great Depression. In San Francisco, widespread public opposition led to lax enforcement of criminal syndicalism and antiunion laws. However, in conservative Alameda County, Warren played a leading role in the counterattack against labor militancy. As a law and order Republican, he opposed union violence.

The stock market crash of 1929 and the ensuing Great Depression brought enormous hardship to the people of the United States and the State of California. More than 300,000 new agricultural workers migrated to California during the 1930s, driven largely by drought and Dust Bowls in the prairie states, where farm wages plummeted by more than 50% between 1929 and 1933. Many of the new migrants settled in the Central Valley and the

Imperial Valley regions of California, and squalid shanty towns and camps without sufficient sanitary facilities led to shocking levels of poverty, malnutrition, and disease. Novelist John Steinbeck and photojournalist Dorothea Lang provided stirring images of the profound hardship of this time.[1] As confidence in the capitalist system waned, the unemployed embraced unions and militant politics in a desperate attempt to transform their shattered lives.

Labor unions long had been an important factor in the California workplace, especially in the northern part of the state. In 1906, dockworkers in San Francisco gained union recognition, and in the three decades leading up to the 1930s, they along with ship workers and lumbermen fought for union hiring halls, an eight-hour day, and improved working conditions. Following World War I, as the wartime economy cooled and conservatives gained political power, unions faced troubled times. Between 1921 and 1934, wages for seamen declined by almost 50%, and employer-sponsored unions, known as "Blue Books," replaced autonomous worker unions throughout the Bay Area.

Franklin Roosevelt's landslide election in 1932 led to a new period of labor reform. Adoption of the National Industrial Recovery Act of 1933 (N.I.R.A.) permitted workers to form unions and engage in collective bargaining. In the struggle to organize workers in the fields, canneries, and shipyards of California, radicals in the Communist Party fought with conservatives for control of the unions. Communist activists organized the disenfranchised, particularly Mexican and Filipino farm workers, whom no one else would help. Employers resolved to resist these efforts. In rural counties, they recruited vigilantes to beat union organizers, often driving them out into the desert and leaving them without clothes, money, food, or water.[2] In urban areas, they relied upon police and the courts to protect non-union (scab) workers and keep the docks open.

In Northern California, the struggle between unions and owners intensified. During the 1930s, the docks in San Francisco, Alameda, Oakland, and Richmond formed the second busiest harbor in the United States, and Bay Area dockworkers resented the "shape-up" system that employers used to select workers for day work. Under this system, straw bosses, acting as hiring agents, selected workers each day for jobs. Straw bosses demanded kickbacks in order to pick workers for job assignments, and those with ties to unions or those who refused to pay simply did not work. Under the N.I.R.A., federal leaders eliminated corrupt "Blue Book" unions, replacing them with a hiring system jointly run by the workers' union—the International Longshoreman's Association (I.L.A.)—and management. Despite this victory, the I.L.A. failed to win concessions on the issues of higher wages and improvements in working conditions. Other workers, including those on the ships, continued to chafe under the injustices of the shape-up system. In May 1934, 34,700 dock and ship workers all along the Pacific Coast—from San Diego, Los Angeles, and San Francisco, to Portland, and Seattle—went out on strike.

The Waterfront Employers Union, a coalition of ship owners, vowed to fight the strike, waging a battle in the media and the courts for public support. In San Francisco, their strategy called for recruiting non-union workers, using a municipal railroad to transport goods from the docks to remote warehouses, and drafting union and non-union teamsters to deliver the goods to market. For the first six weeks of the strike, union workers conducted mass rallies along the Embarcadero to keep the docks closed, even as their leaders negotiated with the owners and federal labor officials. Their efforts led to a proposed settlement on wage and working conditions for the dockworkers, but the I.L.A. refused to support the proposal as long as other ship workers remained uncovered.

By early July, after owners suffered millions of dollars in lost profits, the situation deteriorated. Workers set up barricades along the Embarcadero, and over a period of three days San Francisco police attacked them. On "Bloody Thursday," July 5, 1934, thousands of striking workers gathered on the waterfront and protestors threw rocks at police. Officers fired into the crowd, killing two workers and wounding another. In protest, union leaders organized a peaceful funeral march for the slain workers, and the participants, including many World War I veterans dressed in uniform, conducted a funeral march that extended for over a mile and a half. In an impressive show of solidarity, unions then sponsored a four-day general strike in San Francisco, which brought the city to a standstill. They astutely maintained the support of local residents by permitting the teamsters to deliver food, dairy products, and beer into the city.

Across the Bay in Oakland, District Attorney Earl Warren did not escape the turmoil of labor-management relations in the local community. His initial encounter with the radicalism of the depression years began in 1934 when he assumed a formal position of leadership in the California Republican Party. The controversial gubernatorial election of that year, which featured the famous novelist and erstwhile socialist Upton Sinclair and his opponent, stalwart Republican Frank F. Merriam, tested Warren's commitment to traditional patriotic values. Two years later when labor violence again erupted on the waterfront, Warren served as lead prosecutor in a criminal conspiracy and murder case involving leaders of a shipping union. Popularly known as the *Point Lobos* or *King* murder trial, it became the most significant case of Warren's prosecutorial career.

RESISTING EPIC

Warren's first move into statewide politics in 1934 began when he expressed tentative interest in running for state attorney general. The incumbent, 71-year-old Ulysses Sigel Webb, was a Republican, and Warren ultimately decided that it would be best to bide his time and avoid a bruising intraparty squabble. Warren retained his position in Alameda County and, in a move that showed unusual ambition for a county prosecutor, drafted proposals for two state constitutional amendments. The first broadened civil service protection for state workers, and the second expanded the responsibilities of the state attorney general. Under Warren's proposals, the attorney general would become the full-time, chief law enforcement officer of the state, and prosecutors and judges would receive the right to comment on a defendant's failure to testify or denial of guilt at trial.[3] In 1934, voters overwhelmingly approved both amendments.

Warren's second step came in September 1934 when he accepted a position as Chair of the California Republican Party. That fall, Republican Lieutenant Governor Frank F. Merriam faced a tight race for governor against Democrat Upton Sinclair and third-party Progressive Raymond Haight. Sinclair campaigned on an "End Poverty in California" plan that assured full employment through a series of state-run industrial and agricultural cooperatives.[4] Voters in California had given Franklin Roosevelt overwhelming support in the 1932 presidential election, and the severity of the depression made the economy and social welfare policy central issues in the gubernatorial campaign. Unemployment in California hovered at 28%, and the recent general strike in San Francisco caused great concern among conservatives. As a centrist who attempted to strike an independent position attracting support from moderates on both the left and the right, Warren stepped cautiously into this fray.

Sinclair's rhetorical flourishes ultimately led to his undoing. At times, his critique of capitalism deteriorated into a diatribe against business leaders, and his anti-Semitic remarks about those who financed the Hollywood film industry galvanized opposition to his plan for public ownership of movie studios. Louis B. Mayer, cofounder of the Metro-Goldman-Mayer studio, made propagandistic newsreels that portrayed Sinclair supporters as indolent tramps and left-wing radicals who leached off hardworking Californians. MGM's *California Election News* shorts featured staged interviews with ordinary Californians about the upcoming election. Supporters of Sinclair, dressed as greasy mechanics or African Americans sitting in luxury automobiles, stressed their candidate's ties to the Soviet Union, where radical ideas like his were "working well." Inarticulate and unpolished, they appeared and sounded wholly unconvincing. In contrast, well-dressed supporters of Merriam clearly emphasized their appreciation for the jobs they currently had as well as their confidence that Merriam would enhance prosperity in California. Another segment showed a freight train entering California with scores of hobos on the top of freight cars, while a narrator read a statement criticizing Sinclair's EPIC plan because it would attract unemployed bums to the state.[5]

The Merriam campaign hired Clem Whitaker and Clem's associate and future wife, Leone Baxter, as consultants. Whitaker and Baxter designed an innovative media campaign featuring negative attacks on Sinclair in newspaper articles, billboards, and radio spots. Their methods became a blueprint for future political contests both in California and across the nation, and they made fear of Sinclair the principal issue. Unwittingly, Sinclair handed them potent ammunition by making an off-hand joke in a conversation with FDR's Emergency Relief Administrator, Harry Hopkins. Sinclair said that if his End Poverty program were adopted, "Half the unemployed of the U.S. will come to California." A reporter overheard the comment, publicized it, and within days Whitaker and Baxter produced a relentless series of negative news articles and billboards that said, "Take California out of the Red; the Red out of California."

As the new Chairman of the California Republican Party, Warren sided with Merriam. In a series of speeches in late October, he attacked Sinclair by appealing to bipartisan values. He characterized the contest as "a crusade of Americans and Californians against Radicalism and Socialism" and "a battle . . . between two conflicting philosophies of government—one that is proud of our flag, our governmental institutions and our honored history, the other that glorifies the Red Flag of Russia and hopes to establish on American soil a despotism based upon class hatred and tyranny."[6] Warren wisely appealed to bipartisan values and the popularity of Roosevelt's New Deal. Although the contest remained close, Sinclair never recovered from his gaffe, and Merriam eventually won the three-way race with 49% of the vote.

A bitter Sinclair never forgave Warren for his role in the campaign. On election night, as Merriam declared victory, Sinclair refused to concede, citing irregularities in the polling places that may have cost him 125,000 votes. Following Merriam's address from the NBC studios in Los Angeles, Sinclair took the microphone and struck back: "My face burns when I think of the lies and forgeries circulated by men with millions to spend to defeat me. However, it won't go on. We're not going to stop. This is only one skirmish, and we're enlisted for the war."[7]

Shortly thereafter, Sinclair wrote a book about his experience entitled, *I, Candidate for Governor: And How I Got Licked* (1935). In it, he portrayed the election as "a revelation of what money can do in American politics; what it will do when its privileges are threatened."[8]

Warren's involvement in Merriam's campaign reflected his desire to please the leadership of the California Republican Party. Although he genuinely abhorred leftist political groups and above all sought an orderly society, in 1934 he was a relative newcomer to state politics. Lacking an independent powerbase and aspiring to higher office, he followed the right-wing leaders of his party and readily did their bidding.

Merriam's 1934 gubernatorial campaign represents a milestone in American politics because it marked the first time that professional consultants organized a multipronged media campaign to lift a politician to public office. On another level, Merriam's failure to win a majority of the vote taught another lesson, one not lost on the District Attorney from Alameda County: if one could stake out a position in the center and attract enough support from both Democrats and Republicans, s/he stood a good chance of winning in California politics.

THE *POINT LOBOS* CASE

On March 22, 1936, police found the body of Chief Engineer George W. Alberts aboard the freighter S.S. *Point Lobos* in the dockyards of Alameda. Alberts, an ardent anticommunist who opposed the Marine Firemen, Oilers, and Wipers Union (MFOWU), apparently had been stabbed to death. Warren's strategy in the murder investigation focused on finding conservative members of the MFOWU who opposed the militant leader of the Union, Earl King, and who would be willing to provide tips about the crime.

With the help of an informer, Warren's investigators used an undercover plant and a hidden microphone to engage a witness in a series of incriminating conversations about the crime. Albert Murphy, a disgruntled officer in the union, eventually cooperated by implicating five other men in the crime. Murphy accused Earl King—the local head of the MFOWU—and several other persons with ties to the Union, including Ernest Ramsay, Frank Connor, George Wallace, and Ben Sakovitz, of killing Alberts. Because Murphy came forward with vital criminal evidence, Warren declined to bring charges against him.[9]

Police arrested George Wallace, an illiterate laborer with limited command of spoken English, in Brownsville, Texas as he attempted to flee into Mexico. They brought him back to Alameda County, where prosecutors held him in a Berkeley hotel and interrogated him without the benefit of counsel. Wallace admitted that he served as lookout on the night of the crime and agreed to testify on behalf of the state. Behind the scenes, Warren struck a deal with Wallace's attorney, Public Defender Willard Shea, to spare Wallace a first-degree murder charge in return for his testimony. By making this arrangement, Warren cleverly divided the defense attorneys and kept Wallace from recanting his confession. When the case later went to trial, the other criminal defendants deeply resented Wallace and saw him a snitch. Defense attorneys unsuccessfully argued that the defendants should not have been tried in a single case because one of the alleged coconspirators would be testifying against the others.

The most controversial aspect of the investigation involved the arrest and interrogation of Frank Conner, a so-called "black gang" delegate of the MFOWU on the *S.S. Point Lobos*. As "black gang" delegate, Conner assumed responsibility for reporting antiunion activity on the ship to union officials. Following Albert's murder, Conner fled to Seattle, where police found him in a hotel, drunk and stricken with a bad cold, in early September 1936. Conner recently had been hit by a car and had spent nine weeks in the hospital recovering from a knee injury. Despite his weakened physical state, investigators flew Conner to Oakland and immediately took him to a Berkeley hotel for questioning. Beginning at 9 p.m., they interrogated a sick, hungover, and fatigued Conner until 2:30 a.m., when they handcuffed him to a chair and allowed him to "sleep" for four hours until the interrogation resumed at 7 a.m.

Later that day, Conner appeared at trial for arraignment. He wanted to be represented by union attorney, Henry C. Levinski, but when Levinski failed to attend the interrogation as it resumed later that afternoon, Conner became angry. One of Warren's investigators, Oscar Jahnsen, then read Conner an article from a local newspaper, which stated that "Henry C. Levinski, Seattle attorney, . . . declared that he could not be certain whether or not he would represent Conner."

An emotionally distraught and physically drained Conner then spilled his guts to the D.A.'s men:

> You see, it is this way. They have me. I'm not a Communist, and I saw the ship's delegate, King, send those men over. I did not ask for them. All I asked for was a patrolman, but because I was the delegate it looks like I ordered the job done, but they can't blame it on me, the dirty bastards. If they do not come when I get over to the jail and see King, I will tell him plenty. The dirty sons of bitches. When I was in court they would not look at me. If they do not come over tomorrow, I will tell you all.[10]

Warren's interrogators urged Conner to make a formal statement on the record immediately, which Conner agreed to do. Apparently motivated by fear that his union bosses planned to pin the murder on him, he confessed. Shortly afterward, Connor entered the hospital with acute bronchitis and a fever of 101. Several days later, under the advice of his attorney (Levinski), he repudiated his confession, contending it had been coerced.

On the strength of Conner's disclosures, police arrested King and Ramsay and sent them to the Piedmont City Jail, where their defense attorneys would be unlikely to find them. Prosecutors bugged the cell and equipped it with a decoy "inmate" but obtained no incriminating evidence from either King or Ramsay. Warren assumed personal responsibility for prosecuting the cases and obtained grand jury indictments for conspiracy and murder against all five suspects. In a statement to the press, Warren said, "It was a paid assassin's job, and the basis of the plot was communistic." In response, union officials called a strike to protest the trial and to win concessions on wage and overtime issues. For ninety-nine days, 40,000 maritime workers on the West Coast walked off their jobs. The union also organized demonstrations outside the court house throughout the two month long trial, and picket lines formed in front of Earl Warren's home.

During the bitterly contested trial, the attorneys sparred over several technical issues, including the alleged involuntariness of the confessions and whether prosecutors could use the confession of one defendant as evidence against the others. Beneath the surface, another controversy arose over the process for selecting jurors in Alameda County. At the time of the *Point Lobos* cases, the jury commissioner gathered names of potential jurors from church directories, fraternal organizations such as the Elks and the Knights of Columbus, and even individuals suggested by the judges themselves. The jury rosters reflected a bias in favor of middle-class whites who did not represent a fair cross-section of the broader community. Prosecutors also benefited from a secret supplemental system of information about jurors who had served in previous cases. They knew how jurors had voted in previous trials, as well as their political affiliations, criminal records, and potential degree of support for the prosecution.

Attorneys for both sides thought Edward Tyrrell, the judge originally assigned to the case, would not be up to presiding over such a complex murder trial. Judge Frank Ogden replaced Tyrrell. Ogden previously had worked for Warren in the D.A.'s Office, and this raised suspicions about his impartiality. The most hotly debated issue during the trial concerned the voluntariness of Conner's confession. On direct examination, Conner testified that at the time of his questioning he had been without sleep for nearly 48 hours. He alleged that prosecutors had interrogated him for nearly 21 hours without his attorney being present, even though he repeatedly had asked to consult with counsel. Conner asserted that he had been feverish and in great pain from his knee injury and bronchitis. Interrogators had given him the third degree, sharply questioning him and rapidly changing the subjects of the interrogation to keep him off balance. When he disagreed with their contentions, they accused him of lying. At 2:30 in the morning, the questioning temporarily subsided, and prosecutors handcuffed him in an uncomfortable position thus depriving him of sleep.

Following this testimony, defense attorney Resner took the unusual step of calling Earl Warren himself to the stand, using a procedure known as *voir dire* during the middle of the trial to question the witness as if he were on cross-examination. Resner began by challenging the basis for "kidnapping and mistreating" a prisoner instead of taking him immediately to the county jail:

Resner: Couldn't you talk to anyone in the jail?

Warren: When they get over there and talk to all the . . . lawyers in the jail, there is not much use in talking to them.

Resner: Don't you know there are private rooms in the jail where you can talk to Mr. Conner?

Warren: Very true.

Resner: You know defense attorneys are confined to talking to their clients in these rooms. I suppose the reason you kept him in that hotel room was so that he was out of the reach of his counsel?

Warren: As far as I knew, Conner did not have an attorney at that time.[11]

At the conclusion of this questioning, Resner presented a fifteen-minute argument to support his motion to exclude Conner's confession from the evidence. Afterward, Judge Ogden summarily overruled the motion, ruling simply, "The recorded conversation will be admitted into the evidence." At that, Resner lost control and angrily accused the court of committing prejudicial error. "I want to state that the admission of the statement shows your Honor's bias and prejudice in this case, and they are not going to have a fair trial, and they are not getting a fair trial," he shouted. Judge Ogden countered that the defense had made "no legal showing as to the involuntary nature of the conversation" and found Resner in contempt of court. He sentenced Resner to a $50 fine or ten days in jail. Before the end of the trial, Resner apologized to the court, and Judge Ogden suspended the sentence.

In his closing argument before the jury, Warren stated, "I am going to say at the outset that (this trial) has been one of the most unpleasant experiences that I have ever had in my legal career, not with all the counsel here in this case, but with some of them." He continued, "All I want is the law enforced, all I want to see is life and property safe in this community. . . . Ladies and gentlemen, I just want to say this to you. That you never have and never will sit in a more important case than this case right here and what you do in this case will mean much to the future of this country."[12]

A central point in Warren's closing argument involved the failure of the defendants to take the stand to deny their guilt. In his closing remarks to the jury, Judge Ogden noted that the defense witnesses lacked credibility and that much of the defense's proffered evidence appeared weak. Ogden observed that, in his opinion, Conner gave his confession voluntarily and that it squared with other evidence in the case.[13]

The jury returned second-degree murder convictions against all four defendants, and all defendants except Wallace appealed their convictions. In their appeals, the defendants argued that the evidence against them included involuntary confessions and prosecutors had recorded their conversations behind the backs of defense counsel. The appellate courts eventually rejected these arguments and upheld the defendants' convictions.

Following the conclusion of the original proceedings, jury tampering allegations arose. They concerned undisclosed ties between a juror, Julia Vickerson, and one of the lead prosecutors in the case, Assistant District Attorney Charles Wehr. After Wehr's death in 1939, Vickerson alleged that during the two years before the trial she had loaned Wehr over $15,000, which he never repaid. This raised the inference that the two had been romantically involved at the time of the trial. In subsequent legal proceedings, state courts ruled that Vickerson's allegations lacked credibility and did not warrant a retrial of the *Point Lobos* defendants.

The defendants served nearly five years at San Quentin until December 1941 when Governor Cuthbert L. Olson granted three of them pardons.[14] The pardons outraged then State Attorney General Earl Warren and served as a major factor in Warren's decision to run against Olson in the gubernatorial election of 1942.

Much has been made of the conduct of Earl Warren's office during the *Point Lobos* criminal investigation and subsequent trial. Warren's critics complained that his staff conducted incommunicado interrogations, bugged hotel rooms and jail cells to obtain evidence, and intervened to influence the appointment of a trial judge who would be favorable to their side.

This criticism has force. Warren's staff did use patently unfair methods, and to the extent that Warren knew about and authorized their activities, he deserves criticism. Warren's defenders argue that the methods in question were commonplace in American law enforcement in the 1930s and that it is unfair to judge the Warren of the 1930s by constitutional and ethical standards of the 1960s. This argument understates the extent of criticism that custodial interrogations received during the 1930s. In 1931, the federal Wickersham Commission devoted a significant portion of its report to the problem of lawlessness in law enforcement and, specifically, to the issue of "third degree" techniques in custodial interrogations. As early as 1897, the Supreme Court had condemned the use of compelled self-incrimination in federal cases,[15] and in 1936, one year before the *Point Lobos* convictions, the Court issued its first decision striking down a state criminal conviction based on an involuntary confession that police beat out of a suspect.[16] Just a few years later, the Supreme Court condemned psychological manipulations during custodial interrogations, including the use of sleep deprivation, which prosecutors had relied upon in the *Point Lobos* investigations.[17]

As a reformer who pushed for greater professionalism in American law enforcement, and one whose own relationships with J. Edgar Hoover and August Vollmer made him familiar with the reforms that federal and state law enforcement officials had pursued in this area, Warren knew or should have known that the conduct of his agents was legally suspect. If not, by the end of the *Point Lobos* prosecutions and the subsequent appeals, the point clearly had been made. While none of the *Point Lobos* defendants won the reversal of a criminal conviction, Warren refrained from using these controversial tactics again.

THE ATTORNEY GENERAL

Following the conclusion of the *Point Lobos* trial in the winter of 1937, California Attorney General Ulysses S. Webb notified Warren that he would not stand for reelection, and Warren decided to run for the office. In the spring of 1938, Warren positioned himself as a moderate by cross-filing in both the Republican and Democratic primaries. Campaigning on a platform of expanded state responsibility for coordinating law enforcement activities and more rehabilitation programs for offenders, he narrowly won the Democratic primary in August against a field of six other candidates. His decisive victory in the Republican Primary meant that his election in the fall was a foregone conclusion.

During the primary campaign, a crisis in Warren's personal life intervened. In May 1938, Warren received the shocking news that his father, Matt Warren, had been found dead in his East Bakersfield home, the victim of a criminal attack.

Matt Warren had retired from the Southern Pacific Railroad in the early 1930s. Over the years, he had started a home rental business in his neighborhood, using scrap materials from the railroad as construction supplies. This brought in supplemental income after his retirement. The frugality that he had exhibited since his youth grew to excessive proportions later in life, and many described him as irascible. Chrystal had left Matt in the late 1920s, moving to Oakland to be closer to the children and to the medical care she needed for deafness and cataract problems. As the Great Depression deepened, Matt's role as property owner made him a controversial figure in the neighborhood, especially when his tenants encountered problems with late payment and eviction. Rumor had it that Matt stored cash in his home. His living circumstances remained parsimonious, and his cluttered household included furniture, construction materials, and tools needed in his rental business that he kept in disarray across the backyard.

Early on a hot Saturday evening, Matt apparently fell asleep while reading the newspaper. An unknown intruder entered the property from the rear and picked up a pipe in the backyard. Proceeding through the back door of the house, the intruder struck Matt on the back of the head with the pipe, crushing

Matt's skull. The intruder then dragged Matt's body into the bedroom, stole his wallet, and fled on foot.

On Sunday morning May 15, 1938, Warren was giving a campaign speech at a hotel in Berkeley when he received a telegram informing him of his father's death. He immediately left for Bakersfield with Nina and several trusted aides. The press caught up with him there, and he gave a brief, tearful interview. It would be one of only two times in Warren's career when he broke down in public.

Bakersfield police assumed primary responsibility for the investigation, with supplemental assistance from Warren and his staff. Eventually, local police identified a suspect, the son of one of Matt Warren's tenants. The suspect recently had been convicted of several robberies in East Bakersfield and had just begun serving a sentence in San Quentin. The police used coercive tactics in interrogating the suspect and also proposed planting a decoy and a hidden microphone in his jail cell. Warren vetoed the microphone proposal, saying, "I don't believe in Dictaphones."

Warren's chief investigator, Oscar Jahnsen, responded angrily when he learned that the Bakersfield police used coercive interrogation tactics against the suspect. In a later interview, Jahnsen stated:

> We just kept on working (on the investigation), and then we picked up a man who seemed to fit. . . . I was sure we had our man. I questioned him and grew even more certain. I made notes on his story and then left him to check out facts which he had given me. Before I left, I told the others to let him alone.
>
> . . . I went back to where I'd left the suspect. When I got there, I found that they'd decided to question him themselves.
>
> They had been working on him for hours. No food. A light working on him. They hadn't touched him, of course. They knew better than that. But they'd been breaking him down, one after the other. By the time I got there, he was on the verge of collapse. I blew my top. I said to them that they'd blown the case. I told them that Earl Warren would never stand for a confession that was extorted from a suspect.
>
> (Later),(t)he boss (Earl Warren) said I'd done the right thing.[18]

Warren's comments about the Dictaphone and his aversion to coercive measures during custodial interrogation provide insight into the evolving nature of his values as a criminal justice professional. Just one year earlier, his own staff had used a similar strategy in the *Point Lobos* investigations, and at the trial, Warren had been challenged on the witness stand about them. Now, in the tragic context of his father's own death, he refused to adopt unseemly and arguably illegal investigatory methods. Critics of Warren's later Supreme Court decisions—which held that at least some of these practices violated the federal constitution—might well have remembered this important episode in

Warren's own life. The principles Warren stood for applied universally, even to his own profoundly troubling circumstances. In the end, the murder of his father remained unsolved, and Warren and his family grieved in private.

In the fall of 1938, Warren handily won his bid to become Attorney General of California, but he was the only Republican to win executive office in Sacramento that year. The Democratic candidate for Governor, Culbert L. Olson, defeated the incumbent Frank Merriam and thereby became the only Democratic Governor of California up to that point in the twentieth century. Almost from the start, Warren feuded with Olson. Initially, they battled over the pardon of Tom Mooney, a labor activist who had been convicted for involvement in the San Francisco Preparedness Day bombing of 1916.[19] Over the next two decades, labor leaders in California insisted that Mooney had been framed, and Olson made this an issue in his campaign for governor. Early in his administration, when Olson informed Warren about a tentative plan to issue Mooney a full pardon, Warren responded that while California law gave the governor the discretion to issue pardons, he did not think it advisable to blame law enforcement officials for wrongdoing in the Mooney trial. Olson ignored Warren's counsel. In a speech before the California Assembly, Olson pardoned Mooney and pointedly blamed state prosecutors for presenting false testimony at the trial. An infuriated Warren vowed that he would never meet face-to-face with Olson again. Over the next four years, they became vehement enemies.

Warren's first major case as Attorney General involved a political corruption scandal arising out of pardons issued by the previous governor, Republican Frank Merriam. Newspaper reporters informed Warren about rumors that a Merriam staff member and relative by the name of Mark Lee Megladdery had been selling gubernatorial pardons. In one of his last acts of office, Merriam had appointed Megladdery to a Superior Court judgeship. Warren's investigation into Megladdery's bank accounts showed deposits far above Megladdery's salary, and in late January, Megladdery resigned his judgeship. Warren prosecuted him for bribery, won a conviction, and sent Megladdery to prison at San Quentin.

Warren then concentrated on vice cases involving gambling at dog tracks and on ships operating off the coast of Los Angeles. The most famous of these cases concerned three gambling ships operated by purported mobster Tony Cornero three miles off Santa Monica Bay. Warren and his lead prosecutors Olney and Jahnsen developed a legal theory that the State of California's territorial jurisdiction extended from one headland of the Bay to the other, which in effect meant that it reached ten miles from the shore. Using a flotilla of police boats, they conducted a daring raid and surrounded and later seized the gambling ships and their crews. The California Supreme Court sustained Warren's headlands theory of jurisdiction and with it, Cornero's conviction.

The Court ordered Cornero to pay a fine, destroy his gambling equipment, and take his ship out of California waters.

Throughout the late 1930s and early 1940s, Warren's conflicts with Governor Olson also included battles over pardons for the *Point Lobos* defendants and civil defense issues. Olson's political strategy featured appeals to union leaders, and he used his pardon power to win their support. In the fall of 1940, Olson announced that he was considering giving pardons to three of the *Point Lobos* defendants; the fourth defendant, Wallace, who had turned state's evidence against his codefendants, remained ineligible for a pardon because of a previous criminal conviction. Warren publicly opposed Olson's proposed pardons, calling them "shocking." When the state parole board, which Olson had appointed, announced its decision to release the three defendants from prison, Warren denounced the move in the strongest possible terms:

> The murderers are free today, not because they are rehabilitated criminals but because they are politically powerful Communistic radicals. Their parole is the culmination of a sinister program of subversive politics, attempted bribery, terrorism and intimidation which has evidenced itself in so many ways during the past three years.[20]

A second conflict between Olson and Warren arose over civil defense. Early in 1941, as concern about the wars in Europe and Asia deepened, Warren arranged for a meeting of law enforcement officials from across the state to discuss the need for central planning in the event of an emergency. They agreed upon a plan to create nine different regions in the state with assigned responsibility for coordinating evacuation and police services. Olson viewed Warren's efforts with suspicion and countered with the creation of a State Council of Defense, which included the formation of a state guard that would be responsible for defending California if federal officials called the California National Guard into active duty. The legislature resisted this approach and approved only a fraction of the funds that Olson sought for it. He retaliated by cutting funding for civil defense efforts at the Attorney General's office. The ensuing conflict over control of civil defense planning galvanized Warren's tentative interest in running for governor, and by late 1941 he became the leading Republican candidate in the 1942 gubernatorial election.

Warren's formal ties to the executive leadership of the state Republican Party ended when he became Attorney General. He insisted on maintaining a position of neutrality as the state's chief law enforcement officer. This meant resigning from his positions as Chair of the California Republican Party and as a member of its executive committee. But behind the scenes, he maintained close ties with Joe and William Knowland, and he also expanded his inner circle by reaching out to two influential Democrats, Jess Steinhart and Bill Sweigert, who worked as attorneys in San Francisco. The Knowlands encouraged Warren to run for governor, and they helped persuade downstate Republicans that he was the only viable candidate who had a chance of beating Olson. Steinhart and Swigert strengthened Warren's ties to moderate Democrats. Sweigert, who had been educated in Jesuit schools, steered Warren in a direction of greater sensitivity to the problems of the poor.

The protracted struggle between labor and management in California during the 1930s pitted the forces of reform and workers' rights against the forces of conformity and law and order. The conflict raged on many fronts, and in fundamental respects, it ended in a draw. Workers won union recognition and improvements in wages and working conditions, yet management defeated Sinclair's incipient socialist campaign and repressed militancy and violence on the waterfront. The battle took place not so much in the streets as in the media, the polls, and the courthouse, as both sides sought to win public support.

Earl Warren had a starring role in this fight, both in his capacity as chair of the state Republican Party and as lead prosecutor in the *Point Lobos* case. He emerged from the victorious Merriam gubernatorial campaign and the *Point Lobos* trial with a reputation as a law and order conservative, which he later emphasized in his attacks against Governor Olson. Nevertheless, the controversial criminal investigation techniques that Warren used placed him in the embarrassing and uncomfortable situation of having to defend his methods on the witness stand in a high-profile murder trial. The experience reshaped Warren's policies concerning the rights of suspects during custodial interrogations and reinforced his evolving high expectations of criminal justice professionals.

NOTES

1. John Steinbeck's *The Grapes of Wrath* provides a classic portrayal of the harsh reception the Okies received in California in the 1930s, while Dorothea Lang's sensitive portraits of the migrants offer stark images of the great physical and emotional price that poverty imposed upon workers, parents, and children in these years.

2. For a detailed account of vigilante violence against union organizers in California during the depression, see Kevin Starr, *Endangered Dreams: The Great Depression in California* (New York: Oxford University Press, 1996).

3. The U.S. Supreme Court upheld a similar New Jersey law in *Twining v. New Jersey*, 211 U.S. 78 (1908). However, in 1964, it overruled *Twining*, with Earl Warren voting with the majority. *Malloy v. Hogan*, 378 U.S. 1 (1964).

4. Under Sinclair's "production for use" plan, inactive businesses and farms would be reorganized into cooperatives. Goods and services produced in the

cooperatives would be available for workers' consumption and would not be sold on the open market for the owners' profit.

5. Segments of *MGM California Election News* shorts from the 1934 gubernatorial campaign are available online at https://www.youtube.com/watch?v=tPQfLqnsLEg. For further analysis of the role of the MGM shorts in the 1934 campaign, see Greg Mitchell, *The Campaign of the Century: Upton Sinclair's Race for Governor of California and the Birth of Media Politics* (New York: Random House, 1992), 415–16.

6. Earl Warren radio address, October 21, 1934, Earl Warren Papers, pre-gubernatorial papers, 1934 Campaign file, California State Archives, Office of the Secretary of State, Sacramento, California, quoted in Newton, *Justice for All*, 84, 50n.

7. Mitchell, *The Campaign of the Century*, 533–34.

8. Upton Sinclair, *I, Candidate for Governor: And How I Got Licked* (Pasadena, Calif.: the Author, 1935), 1.

9. Prosecutors never located Ben Sakovitz. Investigators believe that he escaped to New York, where he went into hiding and that he later enlisted in the Abraham Lincoln brigade and fought on the side of the loyalists in the Spanish Civil War. During World War II, police arrested Sakovitz in North Africa, but he escaped from custody while returning by ship to the United States.

10. *People v. King et al.*, Tr., II, pp. 843, 847a-849, 855, 862–863, 872–894, 898, 900–901, 927, 931–950, 953–956, 960, 970, 1009, 1012–1014, 1023, 1125, 1129, 1220–1225, 1247, 1250, 1256–1258, 1316. For further details about the *Point Lobos* trials, see Miriam Feingold, "The King-Ramsey-Conner Case: Labor, Radicalism, and the Law in California, 1936–1941," unpublished dissertation, University of Wisconsin, 1976.

11. *People v. King, et al.*, Tr., II, 767–865.

12. *People v. King et al.*, Tr., VI, 3852–932.

13. Ironically, both Warren's argument about the defendants' failure to take the stand and Ogden's comments about the paucity of the defense evidence were permissible under California law because of a state constitutional amendment that Warren himself had drafted. Today, neither of these statements would be permissible based on several Warren Court decisions, including *Malloy v. Hogan*, 378 U.S. 1 (1964) (Fifth Amendment privilege against self-incrimination applies to state criminal proceedings as well as federal ones); *Miranda v. Arizona*, 384 U.S. 436 (1966) (prior to custodial interrogation suspects must be warned about their constitutional rights to silence and the assistance of counsel); and *Messiah v. United States*, 377 U.S. 201 (1964) (police may not interview a defendant behind the back of counsel after indictment).

14. Because George Wallace had a previous criminal background, authorities did not release him from San Quentin until several years later.

15. *Bram v. U.S.*, 168 U.S. 532 (1897).

16. *Brown v. Mississippi*, 297 U.S. 278 (1936).

17. See e.g., *Ashcroft v. Tennessee*, 322 U.S. 123 (1944).

18. Robert B. Powers, *"Law Enforcement, Race Relations:* 1930–1960," Earl Warren Oral History Project, typescript of an oral history conducted June 10, 1969 by Amelia Fry, Regional Oral History Office, The Bancroft Library, University of California, Berkeley, 1971, I-6a.

19. On July 22, 1916, San Francisco officials sponsored Preparedness Day, a massive parade to build support for American involvement in World War I. In the midst of the parade, a bomb exploded, killing ten and wounding forty innocent bystanders. Prosecutors accused two local radicals, Tom Mooney and Warren Billings, of the crime, and the pair was convicted and sentenced to death. Before the sentence could be carried out, President Woodrow Wilson created a Mediation Commission and charged it with resolving labor disputes that threatened the war effort. The Commission investigated the Preparedness Day Parade in San Francisco and the violence that gave rise to the convictions. An attorney for the War Department, Felix Frankfurter, assisted the Mediation Commission and in that capacity worked on the Mooney/Billings case. Writing on behalf of the Commission, Frankfurter urged President Wilson to use his influence to obtain a retrial of Mooney's case. California Governor William D. Stephens responded by commuting Mooney's death sentence to life imprisonment; eventually, both Mooney and Billings received pardons. Frankfurter later served as an Associate Justice on the U.S. Supreme Court from 1939–1962.

20. Earl Warren statement, November 27, 1941, attorney general office papers, King-Ramsay-Conner file, California State Archives, Office of the Secretary of State, Sacramento, California.

Part II

FINDING A NATIONAL VOICE

Chapter 4

The War at Home

Japan's devastating attack on Pearl Harbor on December 7, 1941 profoundly influenced all Americans, including Attorney General of California, Earl Warren. Not only did the coming of war present Warren with the formidable question of what steps California should take to bolster its defenses and enhance the national war effort, but it also raised the disconcerting issue of how Californians should respond to the Japanese Americans in their midst. With characteristic vigor, Warren confronted these challenges head-on. His efforts established his national reputation as a competent and effectual administrator, yet they also precipitated significant controversy and dissent.

During the two-year period leading up to Pearl Harbor, Earl Warren and his staff studied how the Nazis used subversion and sabotage as a part of an integrated strategy during the invasions of France, the Netherlands, and Norway. Warren and his assistant, Warren Olney III, realized that the West Coast contained several airplane and ship-building operations of vital strategic importance. The Japanese assault on Pearl Harbor destroyed much of America's Pacific fleet, and in the first twelve months of the war, naval resources for the protection of the West Coast became desperately thin. In a meeting with Warren shortly after the attack, Admiral John Greenslade, Naval Commander on the Pacific Coast, admitted that the Navy had only two destroyers to patrol the entire 1,000-mile coastline. This convinced Warren that a grave danger of invasion existed. Public officials, including Warren, did not want to alert the Japanese about America's vulnerability to attack, so instead of referring to a risk of "invasion," they used the term "sabotage." This focused public attention on the possibility of attacks by enemy agents from within.

For years, the question of how Californians treated local residents of Asian descent had been a significant issue. Large numbers of Chinese immigrants arrived in California in the 1860s and 1870s, and smaller numbers of

Japanese came in the 1880s. Hardworking and assiduous, they labored in the railroad and agriculture industries. Within one generation, they began to own truck farms, small businesses, and homes. Nativists resented their presence in the State, and organizations such as the Native Sons of the Golden West pressed politicians to adopt discriminatory laws, such as the federal Oriental Exclusion Act and the state Alien Land Law.

The first of these laws, originally passed in 1882, barred Chinese nationals from emigrating to the United States and prohibited Chinese Americans from becoming U.S. citizens; the Immigration Act of 1924 extended these prohibitions to other Asian groups, including the Japanese.[1] Under the Alien Land Law of 1913, aliens ineligible to become citizens could no longer own land in the State of California. This created a distinction between first- and second-generation immigrants, who then became known in the Japanese American community as "Issei" and "Nisei." Derived from the words "first" and "second" in Japanese, the terms described, respectively, those who emigrated from Japan to the new world and those in the second generation who were the children of the immigrants.

Within days of Pearl Harbor and the American declaration of war, the Roosevelt Administration issued an order excluding enemy aliens from zones near vital military installations. For the most part, the order did not apply to persons of Japanese, German, or Italian ancestry who had been born in the United States. In the crucial period between the beginning of the war and the announcement of the exclusion of Japanese Americans from the West Coast on February 19, 1942, no known acts of sabotage in California or other Pacific states took place. Reported acts of reprisal against Japanese Americans also were few. To the extent that anti-Japanese hostility did arise in the early months of the war, it came from public officials, not from the media or the citizens at large.

As Attorney General and would-be candidate for governor in the fall of 1942, Earl Warren engaged the issue. On December 8, 1941, only hours after the Pearl Harbor attack, he met with county law enforcement officials to discuss ways to enhance state security. Following the meeting, Warren announced, "We are at war and are immediately confronted with the most serious law enforcement problem of all time. Sabotage is just as much a part of Axis Warfare as are military and naval operations." In another speech he said, "I have come to the conclusion that the Japanese situation as it exists in this state today, may well be the Achilles heel of the entire civilian defense effort. Unless something is done it may bring about a repetition of Pearl Harbor."[2]

By the middle of January, conservative groups such as the Native Sons of the American West and the American Legion passed resolutions approving the removal of California's Japanese residents. In Los Angeles, all city and county employees of Japanese ancestry temporarily lost their jobs. On January 24, Supreme Court Justice Owen Roberts issued a panel report on the role of sabotage in the Pearl Harbor attacks, which concluded, without empirical evidence, that spies had passed information about American military installations in Hawaii to the Japanese military and thereby assisted in the assault.[3] The Report enflamed citizen hostility against the Japanese.

By late January, Warren started to build a rationale for the removal of all Japanese American residents from sensitive areas of the state, where they might pose a risk to national security. He argued that if Japanese Americans did not receive special protection, they might fall victim to attacks by angry Americans. He also expressed concern that the "alien" and "insular" nature of the Japanese would lead them to commit treasonous acts. On January 31, Warren issued a statement asserting that it was impossible to distinguish between "Japanese enemy aliens, of whom we are sure there are many here, and Japanese American citizens generally loyal to the United States."[4] He noted that the Japanese, unlike their German and Italian counterparts, had remained culturally and geographically segregated from other Americans and that law enforcement officials knew relatively little about their activities. It would be difficult, he argued, for public officials to conduct hearings to determine who was loyal to America and who posed a threat of sabotage. He also articulated a concern about Nisei—dual citizens of Japan and America. Many had attended elementary school in Japan and, while there, they may have developed cultural and political ties to the Empire before returning to their families in the United States.

Warren organized a study of maps to determine where Japanese Americans lived in California and the proximity of their residences and land holdings to assets of strategic value. In early February, he sent urgent letters to county district attorneys and other law enforcement officers throughout the state, seeking their assistance in identifying potential security risks posed by Japanese Americans. The result, many argue, was a case study in manipulation. Warren's correspondence with Lowell L. Sparks, District Attorney of Placer County, is illustrative. After receiving Warren's request for information, Sparks sent a tongue-in-cheek reply dated February 19, 1942: "There are only two Japanese residing in Auburn (California), one running a fish market and the other a general merchandise store. In addition to this, there is a building viewed as a Japanese Church."[5] Yet by the time Warren and Assistant Attorneys General Warren Olney III and Herbert Wenig analyzed the data, a very different picture emerged. In testimony before House of Representatives Select Committee Investigating National Defense Migration (the so-called Tolan Committee) on March 11, 1942, Warren stated, in specific reference to Japanese Americans in Placer County, California:

> Sheet Three shows a large number of Japanese congregated in the vicinity of Auburn, with easy access to the railroad and highway through Donner Pass. These lines have a large number of vulnerable tunnels, trestles and slides, and are not only main lines to the East but are supply lines between the Naval Ammunition Dump at Hawthorne, Nevada and the Pacific Naval Bases.[6]

The circumstantial nature of this evidence, in conjunction with the use of a broad test for what constituted an asset of strategic value, made it a simple matter to document the relationship Warren sought to prove. Census data provided information on the ethnic composition of residents in California counties, and everything from manufacturing plants, power lines, irrigation and water reservoirs to oil fields, rail lines, and radio stations could be considered a military asset in a time of war. The Japanese Americans owned small truck farms on the outskirts of major metropolitan areas in relatively close proximity to utilities, industrial plants, or other vital infrastructure. Under Warren's approach, virtually any ethnic group could be shown to be a threat to national security. In the case of Placer County, the District Attorney's report remained the most credible information available, yet Warren and Olney transformed an innocuous report about a fish market into a threat to the vital supplies of ammunition for U.S. Navy bases on the entire Pacific Coast.

Warren and his staff rebutted these criticisms by arguing that when considered from a statewide perspective, the proximity of Japanese properties to military assets went beyond mere coincidence. In a later interview, Warren Olney III made the case succinctly:

> (A)ll or practically all of these Japanese were ostensibly engaged in agricultural pursuits, (yet) there were a number of large agricultural areas having only a few strategic points in them, and the maps disclosed that in such areas the Japanese were congregated at the strategic points and at those points alone . . . .
>
> We came to the conclusion that the explanation of these patterns was really quite simple and that it lay in the manner in which Japanese society in California was organized. At that time the Japanese population in California was very thoroughly organized. There were Japanese agricultural, commercial, educational, social, religious, and patriotic associations in every Japanese community. . . . They were all quite closely integrated by means of interlocking directors and officers, honorary advisers, and interlocking membership among the ordinary members.
>
> . . . At the top of this organizational pyramid were the Japanese Association of America in Northern California and the Japanese Central Association in Southern California. Their connection with the Japanese Government had always been very close.[7]

The FBI conducted another phase of the investigation. It sent detailed questionnaires to Japanese Americans in selected California locations, principally those near Sacramento, and sought consent to search houses, farms, and businesses for contraband. The questionnaire asked how long family members had lived in the United States, to what organizations they belonged, whether they sent any money to Japan, and what their viewpoints were about the war. In each reported instance, Japanese families cooperated eagerly and consented to the searches. Most searches revealed no contraband, but occasionally agents confiscated cartons of fireworks, searchlights, ordinary radios, and small arms and ammunition used in connection with ranching activities. Authorities detained T. Yanagisaki of Mills, California for questioning when his answers to the questionnaire revealed that he was 41 years of age and over the previous 15 years had sent 93,000 yen to Japan. He explained that he planned to retire in Japan, distrusted American banks, and was sending funds to a relative for safekeeping. After several hours of questioning, the FBI released him.[8]

From these and other sources of information, Warren concluded that all alien Japanese should be removed from all territories in California within 200 miles of the Pacific Coast until the end of the war.[9] Warren met frequently in San Francisco with General Dewitt, the U.S. Army's commanding officer at the Presidio, to convince him to adopt this policy. Initially, Dewitt voiced skepticism about the plan, but by January 30, he recommended that Secretary of War Henry Stimson order Japanese immigrants and Japanese American citizens away from sensitive areas on the West Coast. Although Stimson agreed with Dewitt's recommendation, he encountered resistance from the U.S. Department of Justice and Attorney General Francis Biddle. The Department of Justice opposed the idea both because FBI Director J. Edgar Hoover thought evacuation unnecessary and because respected attorneys such as Edward J. Ennis, Director of the Alien Enemy Control Unit, had concluded that the plan was unconstitutional.

On February 19, President Roosevelt sided with Stimson and issued Executive Order 9066, which authorized the Secretary of War to designate selected military areas within the United States "from which any or all persons may be excluded."[10] The vague and open-ended order gave military officials the discretion to apply the new regulation primarily against Japanese American residents. Later in the spring, President Roosevelt issued Executive Order No. 9102, creating the War Relocation Authority and assigning it responsibility for evacuating persons from restricted areas of the country.

The Warren, Dewitt, and Stimson recommendations that gave rise to Executive Order 9066 stressed the exclusion of Japanese Americans on the Pacific Coast from areas where they might pose a security threat. In the initial months of the program, federal officials allowed persons of Japanese ancestry to resettle in inland communities on their own. When protests from these communities arose, violence directed against Japanese Americans appeared imminent. By late March, the Western Defense Command sharply curtailed the voluntary evacuation program and sent approximately 110,000 Japanese in Washington, Oregon, and California to assembly centers. Then, beginning in September, the Japanese Americans went to internment camps in remote and desolate locations in California, Utah, Arizona, Montana, Idaho, Colorado, and Arkansas.

The internment program in the continental United States represented one of the most egregious government violations of civil liberties in American history. It imposed a series of unjustifiable hardships on innocent people, over half of whom were under the age of 18. In most instances, the government gave Japanese families only several days' notice before they had to report to assembly centers. This meant that hasty arrangements had to be made for the disposition of property. Land, houses, cars, agricultural implements—all went at fire sale prices. Government regulations permitted each detainee to take only one suitcase. Thus, family heirlooms, furniture, and other property either had to be sold or stored in neighbors' basements or attics, in the care of persons who, in many cases, would never be seen or heard from again. By mid-spring, as Allied soldiers at Bataan and Corregidor in the Philippines surrendered to Japanese troops only to face starvation, mutilation, and lingering death on the Bataan Death March, the climate turned increasingly hostile against the Japanese in America.

In the face of community opposition, YMCAs and Baptist, Quaker, and Congregationalist churches provided temporary shelter, food, and support for Japanese families in the difficult days before the families reported to assembly centers. In the San Francisco Bay area, officials located the assembly center at the Tanforan Race Track in San Bruno, near the present-day San Francisco Airport. Famous horses like Seabiscuit once had bedded there, but as entire Japanese families lived in unclean horses' stalls for nearly five months, life became unreasonably difficult.

Ruth Kingman, whose husband served as Executive Officer of the Berkeley YMCA, did advocacy work for the internees on behalf of the Pacific Coast Committee on American Principles and Fair Play. Kingman recalled the story of Harvey Itano, a Nissei who was valedictorian in the graduating class at the University of California that spring. At the ceremony in the Cal football stadium, President Robert Gordon Sproul announced Itano's name as valedictorian. Many in the audience recognized Itano's Japanese surname and correctly inferred that Itano was an internee. Sproul continued, "I'm sorry but he cannot be with us today. He is serving his country elsewhere." At that, nearly all of the graduates and members of the audience gave the absent Itano a standing ovation. Itano eventually left the camps early under the auspices of a special relocation program, and he entered graduate school in St. Louis, where he graduated with honors. He later worked as a medical researcher at Johns Hopkins University.[11]

In the fall, the internees moved to camps in remote locations, where they faced harsh and overcrowded conditions. At Gila, Arizona, the camp opened without heat, and by late fall, the nighttime temperature plunged to 16 degrees Fahrenheit.[12] Surrounded by barbed wire and armed patrols, the internees enjoyed little privacy or living space. Initially, they worked in the fields, producing vegetables and meat for their own consumption. Soon local farmers opposed this arrangement since it deprived them of markets for their products. In response, the government discontinued the internees' gardens. Work projects then shifted to the production of camouflage nets for use in the European theater and the construction of detailed models of the entire Japanese fleet for allied bomber crews to study. In many of the centers, federal officers organized work corps programs patterned after the Civilian Conservation Corps, but the residents resisted them. Instead, they created enterprise partnerships with the War Relocation Authority to provide consumer goods for their fellow internees. Eventually, cabinetry shops, mattress factories, sawmills, and bakeries became common at the camps.

Before the conclusion of the war, some older Japanese Americans grew disillusioned because they had lost their livelihood as farmers and had little prospect of regaining a foothold in the American economy after the conclusion of war. They asked to be returned to Japan, a request that the American government eventually granted.[13] Those remaining in the camps tried to make the best of a bad situation. Parents entertained their children with artwork, music, and storytelling, and they established schools. But growing up in the internment camps often left severe and lifelong psychological scars as the children coped with feelings of shame, humiliation, isolation, and anger.

Dillon S. Myer served as director of the War Relocation Authority, the agency that assumed responsibility for running the camps. A trained agriculturalist from Ohio State University whose previous government experience consisted of administrative work for the U.S. Soil Conservation Service, Myer did his best to improve conditions at the camps. He later recalled, "It took me one trip (to the camps) to find out this (relocation) was something that shouldn't be done. It was a very inhuman thing to do." Myer's background working on his family farm in Ohio gave him insight and a moral compass that he brought to his new assignment. As he expressed it, "I came in, fortunately, with an open mind. I didn't have any original opinions about it excepting that I believed in the Bill of Rights, and that guided us all the way through our program. We used that as our anchor, what I used to call our endpost to hook our fence to. . . . We believed in every citizen having his day in court, and all the kind of opportunities that the Bill of Rights stood for."[14]

Myer helped create a Nisei college relocation program that permitted bright young people in the camps who had not been educated in Japan to relocate in the eastern United States in colleges and universities. He lobbied extensively to persuade federal officials to create a Japanese American unit in the U.S. Army, and when American forces stopped the Japanese advance at the Battles of Coral Sea and Midway, he pressed for closure of the camps. In December 1944, the directive finally came to begin to close the camps, and Myer placed Japanese families throughout the country rather than isolating them in "ghettos" on the Pacific Coast. In this way, they integrated more fully into American society and encountered less risk of political reprisal.

Myer's proposal for a Japanese American unit within the U.S. Army came to fruition in the summer of 1943. Initially, the Pentagon activated a unit from Hawaii known as the 100th Infantry Battalion, which served in Oran, North Africa, the invasion of Salerno, Italy, and the arduous battle for Monte Cassino. The 100th fought valiantly and suffered heavy losses. Eventually, about 1,250 Japanese Americans from the internment camps also volunteered for military service, and they joined the surviving members of the 100th to form the 442nd Infantry Regimental Combat Team. The 442nd faced challenging assignments at Anzio and in northern Italy, and, in what may have been its crowning achievement, it liberated a surrounded unit of G.I.s outside Biffontaine, France. The 442nd suffered one of the highest casualty rates of the war in proportion to its size, and the unit received seven Presidential Unit Citations and 21 Medals of Honor.

In late 1944 and early 1945, as WRA officials encouraged internees to apply for relocation away from the West Coast and Japanese American veterans began coming home, they faced the daunting prospect of reintegrating into American society. Under Myers' plan, they relocated to nearly every state in the union and absorbed back into the general population, in most instances, without recrimination. However, on the West Coast, where many sought to return to their previous careers, they continued to face discrimination. The State of California brought legal actions to confiscate land that "alien" Japanese families held in violation of the state's Alien Land Law. In 1948, the Supreme Court struck down these laws as unconstitutional, but not before many farms owned by Japanese American had been sold.

In Hood River, Oregon, the local commander of the American Legion removed the names of Japanese American servicemen from a plaque that had been erected to honor veterans of the war. Myer and other officials of the War Relocation Authority organized a boycott of Hood River apples, and local bankers convinced the legionnaires to replace the names. Japanese American schoolchildren faced hostility from teachers and fellow students alike, and in California, the State Assembly debated a bill to bar all Japanese Americans from the state. T.E. "Pat" Frayne of the War Relocation Authority recalled the steps the agency took to resist this legislation:

> With all the public opinion against them, as evidenced in the attacks on Japanese-Americans when they came home and attempts to keep them out, even in the legislature, why Vic Firth and I had to go up to Sacramento. We went up to Sacramento to visit Jack Tenney and Hugh Burns who had a resolution in there to declare it the sense of the legislature that no Japanese-American would be permitted to return to the state.
>
> John F. Shelley, a state senator, later Congressman in Washington and later mayor of San Francisco . . . was conscious of the discrimination against the Japanese-Americans. So he went up to DeWitt General Hospital where a number of veteran Japanese, some with legs off, had been cared for and brought a group of them down to the Senate chambers at a time when George Hatfield from Modesto had a resolution in there also barring Japanese-Americans from ever returning to California. . . . So Shelley said, when this resolution was about to be brought up, "Gentlemen, I would like to have you hear a few words from some American war veterans, wounded American war veterans. So in troops this group, some on crutches. One of them hesitantly got up there and the Senate suddenly discovered they were all Japanese-Americans. And this one who made the talk, hesitantly, told about how he, as a returning war veteran, had been received with hostility as had his companions, and they couldn't understand it. They had done their best for their country. . . . When they were through, why, the senatorial chambers applauded them.

George Hatfield walked over to Shelley and said, "You win, Jack." He withdrew his resolution.[15]

During their confinement, a handful of internees challenged the constitutionality of their detentions. The U.S. Supreme Court issued decisions in four of these cases, *Hirabayashi v. U.S.* (1943),[16] *Yasui v. U.S.* (1943),[17] *Korematsu v. U.S.* (1944),[18] and *ex parte Endo* (1944).[19] In *Korematsu*, the most important of the cases, the Court sustained the constitutionality of the exclusion order (Executive Order 9066) using a national security rationale. Writing for the majority, Justice Black admitted, "Compulsory exclusion of large groups of citizens from their homes, except under circumstances of direct emergency and peril, is inconsistent with our basic governmental institutions."[20] Nevertheless, Justice Black concluded that the government must have power to protect its citizens in wartime: "[W]hen, under conditions of modern warfare, our shores are threatened by hostile forces, the power to protect must be commensurate with the threatened danger."[21] Black denied that the government's exclusion order represented an act of racial discrimination. "Korematsu was not excluded from the Military Area because of hostility to him or his race," Black wrote. "He was excluded because we are at war with the Japanese Empire . . . and because (military authorities) decided that the military urgency of the situation demanded that all citizens of Japanese ancestry be excluded from the West Coast temporarily."[22]

Korematsu marked one of the first times in American history that the Supreme Court used strict scrutiny to analyze government action that discriminated against persons based on immutable characteristics such as ethnicity and national origin. Sadly, even under this highest level of judicial protection, the Court did not require individualized hearings to determine if particular citizens actually represented a security threat before they were expelled from the West Coast and held in detention. A majority of the justices found that the imperative of national security in wartime represented a compelling state interest, and the justices refused to second-guess military officials on questions of national security. The *Korematsu* decision carried the potential for future harm, a point not lost on Justice Robert Jackson, who wrote a blistering dissent in the case. Jackson expressed alarm that his colleagues had sanctioned an unconstitutional military order, a precedent that he analogized to "a loaded weapon, ready for the hand of any authority that can bring forward a plausible claim of an urgent need."[23]

On December 18, 1944, the same day that it issued a decision in *Korematsu*, the Court announced the outcome of *Ex parte Endo*. Mitsuye Endo, a resident of Sacramento, California detained under Executive Order 9066 at the internment camp in Tule Lake, California, applied for permission to leave the camp and move to nonrestricted area of the country under a special War Relocation Authority program. Authorities conditionally granted her application because they could find no evidence that she had been disloyal. The special program required applicants to make arrangements for living and employment in a community outside the camps, and Endo, like many other internees, found it impossible to meet this requirement. In many communities, the public opposed the relocation of the Japanese Americans.

Endo filed a petition for a writ of habeas corpus in federal district court, arguing that as a loyal citizen she should be entitled to immediate release. The district judge denied her petition, and the Court of Appeals certified the legal question to the Supreme Court. Writing for a unanimous Court, Justice William O. Douglas ruled that the War Relocation Authority had no power to detain loyal citizens and that Endo should be released. In the meantime, just a few hours before the Court issued its decisions in the *Endo* and *Korematsu* cases, the Army revoked the West Coast exclusion orders, officially ending the internment program.

In effect, the Supreme Court upheld the constitutionality of the curfew orders and evacuations on the grounds of military necessity, but it stopped short of an outright endorsement of the unlimited detention program. Executive Order 9102 did not expressly authorize detention of citizens as part of the relocation program, and this provided the Court a convenient means of avoiding the ultimate issue. The various opinions in *Korematsu* implied that the justices would be unlikely to approve of a drastic curtailment of liberty in the absence of individual hearings under the normal criminal process. Thus, Mitsuye Endo received her freedom, and Fred Korematsu lost his challenge against the constitutionality of the evacuation orders.

In his written comments about these decisions, Myer reveals the frustration that WRA officials felt at the time:

> We had urged the Solicitor General [Charles Fahy] on several occasions to proceed with the case, but at each meeting he insisted that we make the case moot by allowing Miss Endo to go without conforming to any of the provisions of our leave policy. We continued to argue that we wanted the court to act for the reason that we were quite certain of the outcome and that we wanted the backing of a Supreme Court decision in order that we might abolish any further need for leave regulations for anyone like Miss Endo who was free to relocate. There is no doubt in my mind that the prospect of a ruling against the validity of detention in the Endo case was one of the major factors which finally persuaded the War Department to revoke the exclusion orders.[24]

THE NEW GOVERNOR

As a candidate for governor in the 1942 campaign, Earl Warren repeatedly used the internment issue against his opponent, Culbert Olson. In contrast to Warren, who consistently noted the threat that Japanese Americans posed to state security, Olson appeared inconsistent, vacillating between public pronouncements opposing the internment and others endorsing it. Olson also appeared vulnerable on the issue of civil defense. Although the state Republican leadership applauded Warren's position on these issues, the GOP's big donors distrusted his moderate stances on other matters. In order to preserve a GOP majority in both houses of the California Assembly, they directed their campaign contributions to Republican legislative candidates. This pushed Warren into a posture of financial and political independence from downstate Republican business interests, a position that he welcomed. Warren ran a frugal campaign, cross-filed in the Republican, Democratic and Progressive primaries, and struck an ideological position as a moderate who would not necessarily be bound by the dictates of insiders within his own party. For the first time, he featured his family in the campaign, and they provided a softer, more human side to the image of hard-nosed prosecutor that Warren himself presented.

As a matter of electoral strategy, Warren's approach succeeded. He won the GOP primary with 635,230 votes and narrowly lost the Democratic primary to Olson by only 110,000 votes. The combined total of over one million votes for Warren in the Democratic and Republican primaries made the fall gubernatorial election almost moot. Warren won a significant victory in November, and his bipartisan strategy served as a blueprint for his subsequent victories in the 1946 and 1950 gubernatorial elections. Yet Warren's strategy did not guarantee that he would be a successful governor. Although moderates like Warren tended to do well in statewide contests in California in the 1940s, right-wing Republicans predominated in the gerrymandered legislative districts. When Warren's reform measures wandered too far from the Republican right, they encountered resistance in the legislature.

Warren gave his first inaugural address in early January 1943. He set a tone of fiscal restraint and advocated expansion of social welfare programs. He requested tax cuts and proposed improvements in schools, mental institutions, and state prisons. His plans for new government projects met with resistance from conservative legislators, who did not applaud once during his speech.

Warren's priority in his first administration involved winning the war. Because the command and procurement aspects of war effort remained principally in federal hands, he focused on the threat posed by Japanese Americans. Two speeches he gave to national audiences illustrate this theme. The first, which he gave at the 35th Annual Governors' Conference in Columbus, Ohio on June 21, 1943, was the most bellicose speech he ever gave on the topic. With a broad brush, he painted the Japanese as a security threat, saying:

> (T)here are in this country over 150,000 potential aiders and abetters of . . . warfare. They are, or at least were until recently, in relocation centers in various parts of this country. Large numbers of them are reservists in the Jap military forces. Others have been taught the art of sabotage preparatory to this struggle. All have been indoctrinated with the imperial designs and have had them coupled with Shintoism—the religion of the race.[25]

Warren then attacked the efforts of the War Relocation Authority (WRA) to place selected Japanese in university settings in the eastern United States: "Recently, we have read of the social experiments in these relocation centers and the movement within our government to release the most of them as harmless to the security of our home front. But please don't be deceived. No more dangerous step could be taken."[26]

In January 1944, Warren amplified on these themes in a speech before the Newspapers Publishers Association in Portland, Oregon. There, he asserted that the Shinto religion "makes the Emperor a deity" and that "the WRA . . . has not performed in full accordance with its responsibilities . . . (assuming) an attitude of resentment toward relocation and one of defiance toward all public opinion."[27] Warren eventually ended his public rebuke of War Relocation Authority officials. Following high-level meetings with WRA officials, he issued statements welcoming Japanese Americans back to California after the camps closed. Yet he did not step forward with meaningful programs to ensure fair compensation for the homes and property they had lost. Instead, he benefited from his harsh treatment of the Japanese, both by using the issue successfully in the 1942 gubernatorial campaign and by incorporating it as a theme in national speeches he gave in 1943 and 1944 to raise his profile among the Republicans across the country.

Undoubtedly, Warren's advocacy of the Japanese internment represents one of the most controversial stages of his career. In his defense, the possibility of Japanese attacks against vital American military interests on the West Coast represented a legitimate concern, particularly in the early stages of the war. In addition, the United States desperately needed all available naval strength to maintain supply lines to Australia, and the defense of Britain required planes and other military hardware. Diverting scarce military resources to provide additional security for local factories would strain the Pentagon, and if a Japanese attack did occur, the outcome would be unpredictable. As Warren Olney put it, "(I)f the Japanese attacked the Pacific coast, it would be a desperate affair, and in the middle would be 122,000 Japanese civilians whose sentiments and loyalties were impossible to gauge and whose conduct as individuals was impossible to predict."[28] Californians feared Japanese Americans during the war, and Warren simply reflected and acted upon their apprehension.

On the other hand, there are strong reasons to doubt the wisdom of Earl Warren's actions against Japanese Americans during the war. As noted, nearly half of the persons sent to the internment camps were children, and at no point did officials make any serious effort to ascertain on an individual basis who posed a risk of being disloyal and who did not. The experience of Japanese Americans in Hawaii offers compelling evidence of the fallacies of Warren's approach.

In Hawaii, national security officials sought to include Japanese Americans as much as possible in the service of their country during a time of war. In 1939, FBI Special Agent Robert L. Shivers, who headed the Honolulu Office of the FBI, undertook a careful examination of the nearly 160,000 Japanese Americans who lived in the Hawaii Territory. With the help of Japanese American civic leaders, Shivers identified 736 Issei who posed a potential threat to American national interests. On December 7, 1941, after the Pearl Harbor attack, law enforcement officials arrested these persons and held them in confinement for the duration of the war. Shivers then persuaded FBI Director J. Edgar Hoover and Lt. General Delos C. Emmons, the military governor of the Hawaii Territory, that the remainder of the population remained loyal to America.

During the early stages of the war, Emmons organized groups such as the Varsity Victory Volunteers to recruit men into noncombat service as laborers. He also resisted orders to create internment camps on outlying islands for the remainder of the population, arguing that America needed their labor for the war effort. Eleanor Roosevelt later took up Emmons' cause and worked successfully behind the scenes to persuade her husband that the FBI had identified and incapacitated those who threatened national security in Hawaii. As a result, nearly 159,000 Japanese Americans on the islands avoided internment camps during World War II.

Unlike California, Hawaii lay in close proximity to the war zone, and it had a population of Japanese Americans that exceeded that of California by nearly 70%.[29] Yet the FBI's actions in Hawaii showed the feasibility of identifying and incapacitating the relative few who posed a legitimate threat to national security without the need for incarcerating the broader population. For the duration of the war, no reported acts of sabotage involving Japanese Americans in Hawaii took place. For these reasons, Warren's policy smacked more of administrative convenience and ugly stereotyping than the enhancement of national security.

Warren's approach to the Japanese internment also reflected his conservative associations, the undeveloped and unclear nature of his political philosophy during the 1940s, and his genuine concern for the security of California. Coming of age in East Bakersfield, where residents shunned Asians as second-class citizens, he was the product of his time and place. Warren's later associations with xenophobic groups such as Native Sons of the Golden West reinforced these racist viewpoints and tacit assumptions. Warren's philosophical commitment to Progressivism included ambivalence about race. His concern for public security, while realistic in view of the weakened level of American naval protection along the Pacific Coast during the early stages of the war, became much less plausible by February 1943, when the successful allied invasion of Guadalcanal moved the nerve center of the war eastward toward the Solomon Islands and the Philippines. From this point onward, the national security premise of Warren's argument became weak.

During his many years of public service following the conclusion of World War II, Warren never apologized for his role in the Japanese internment. Public apologies for actions taken long in the past were simply not his style. At one point later in his career, while giving an address at his alma mater, Warren noticed a group of twenty-five angry Japanese American students sitting at the front of the hall. Following his speech, he uncharacteristically refused to take questions from the audience. On his way out of the auditorium, the students confronted him, seeking an apology for the Japanese internment. One student asked, "Is it true that you of all the principal figures involved, are the only one who has refused to admit error?" Warren gave a muted response:

"Yes. It is true that I never apologize for a past act. Besides, that is just a matter of history now." Only in his *Memoirs,* published posthumously, did an equivocal apology appear:

> I have since deeply regretted the removal order and my own testimony advocating it, because it was not in keeping with our American concept of freedom and the rights of citizens. Whenever I thought of the innocent little children who were torn from home, school friends, and congenial surroundings, I was conscience-stricken. It was wrong to react so impulsively, without positive evidence of disloyalty, even though we felt we had good motive in the security of our state. It demonstrates the cruelty of war when fear, get-tough military psychology, propaganda, and racial antagonism combine with one's responsibility for public security to produce such acts. I have always believed that I had no prejudice against the Japanese as such except that directly spawned by Pearl Harbor and its aftermath.[30]

On its face, Warren's apology appears heartfelt and genuine. Yet his remarks also seem backhanded, replete with an implicit denial that he himself was prejudiced against Japanese Americans and, as well, a plausible rationale for why he acted as he did. A careful reading of the apology reveals that the primary reason Warren was "conscience-stricken" arises out of the "innocent little children who were torn from home, school friends, and congenial surroundings." The pangs of conscience do not necessarily extend to adults. Warren ends his statement by noting, "I have always believed that I had no prejudice against the Japanese as such *except that directly spawned by Pearl Harbor and its aftermath* (emphasis supplied)." He seems to conclude that he was justified in his belief that adult Japanese Americans were not wholly innocent bystanders during the war years. To him, they represented a public danger, and as an elected public official, he saw it as his responsibility to act in defense of the country.

Available public records provide two additional details about Warren's thoughts concerning the interment. In June 1942, Warren gave a speech to the Stanford Law Society entitled "Martial Law in Time of War."[31] In his remarks, Warren argued that the enemy alien problem should be handled by military officials under the auspices of martial law until the war emergency came to an end. He reviewed the history of legal precedents for military tribunals in time of war, including the Supreme Court's decision in *Ex parte Milligan* (1866).[32] There, the Court decided 5-4 that Congress lacked the constitutional power to authorize military tribunals to issue criminal punishments without jury trials, unless, due to invasion, the tribunals functioned in territory where the federal courts could not operate. Warren supported the position articulated by the dissenting justices, who argued that if the country was exposed to military danger, Congress should be given the flexibility to determine on its own where and when military tribunals should replace ordinary federal courts. In this way, Warren concluded, the country would benefit from the expedience of the military and the rule of normal law would return at the end of the war. Although Warren repeated these arguments in his testimony before the Tolan Committee, the federal government never formally declared martial law as a basis for its internment policy.

The second piece of evidence comes from an interview that researchers at the University of California conducted with Robert Cozzens, the Assistant National Director of the War Relocation Authority. In the interview, Cozzens recalled that in late 1944 he met personally with Governor Warren for several hours to discuss the postwar relocation of the Japanese in California. According to Cozzens, in this meeting Warren stated that he knew the Japanese internment "was unconstitutional all the time."[33] This admission can be interpreted in several different ways. Warren may have meant that the position he articulated in his Stanford Law Society speech reflected a minority position of the Supreme Court and therefore did not represent the law of the land. Alternatively, he may have wanted to confess that he advocated a policy he knew was wrong for his own political gain or, more charitably, that, in his mind, the imperative of domestic security trumped the human rights and constitutional concerns.

The many public statements Warren gave articulating a national security rationale for the internment counsel toward the latter interpretation. Like Lincoln, who once famously asserted in reference to the Constitution in wartime, that "often a limb must be amputated to save a life; but a life is never wisely given to save a limb,"[34] Warren may have felt that the war justified his unconstitutional actions. This tragic judgment questioned the loyalty of innocent immigrants whose only wrongdoing arose from the accident of birth. In the end, the sacrifice and quiet dignity of the internees stands as a lasting testament to the ideals of American citizenship.

NOTES

1. From the outset, the naturalization laws of the United States discriminated against individuals who were not "white." The first naturalization law, passed by the U.S. Congress in 1790, stated that any alien "being a free white person . . . may be admitted to become a citizen." Naturalization Act of 1790, 1 Stat. 103. Following the Civil War, blacks became eligible for naturalization, and in the 1940s American Indians, Filipinos, East Indians, and Chinese also became eligible. However, it was not until 1952 that persons of Japanese or other Asian descent became eligible to apply for American citizenship.

2. Quoted in Mortin Grodzins, *Americans Betrayed: Politics and the Japanese Evacuation* (Chicago, University of Chicago Press, 1949), 94.

3. The Roberts Commission's allegation that Japanese spies played a role in the Pearl Harbor attack was only a minor theme in the overall Report. Nevertheless, newspapers throughout the United States, including the *Los Angeles Times*, emphasized the finding in bold headlines. The Commission Report also charged the U.S. military commanders of Pearl Harbor, Admiral Husband Kimmel and Lieutenant General Walter Short, with dereliction of duty, and they were later forced into retirement. Before the end of the war, both the Navy and the Army conducted formal courts of inquiry and secretly found that neither Kimmel nor Short were guilty of negligence. While the Roberts Commission Report played an important role in changing public opinion toward Japanese Americans, Roberts himself was one of three justices on the U.S. Supreme Court who dissented in *Korematsu v. U.S.*, 323 U.S. 214, 225 (1944).

4. *New York Times*, January 31, 1942, 8.

5. Collection on the Pre-Evacuation Location of Japanese Americans, 1944, Placer County File, State of California, Office of the Attorney General, The Bancroft Library, University of California, Berkeley.

6. Collection on the Pre-Evacuation Location of Japanese Americans, 1942, Warren testimony to Tolan Committee, March 11, 1942, p. 24, State of California, Office of the Attorney General, The Bancroft Library, University of California, Berkeley.

7. Warren Olney III, *"Law Enforcement and Judicial Administration in the Earl Warren Era,"* Earl Warren Oral History Project, typescript of an oral history conducted 1970–1981 by Meriam F. Stein and Amelia R. Fry, Regional Oral History Office, The Bancroft Library, University of California, Berkeley, 1981, pp. 230–31.

8. Collection on the Pre-Evacuation Location of Japanese Americans, 1942, file 1:2, Letter from G.W. Griffin, Special Agent, to file, dated 2/19/1942, San Francisco, re: F.B.I. Searches of Alien Japanese Property, The Bancroft Library, University of California, Berkeley.

9. *Los Angeles Times*, February 3, 1942.

10. Executive Order 9066, February 19, 1942.

11. Ruth W. Kingman et al., *"The Japanese-American Relocation Reviewed, Volume II: The Internment,"* Earl Warren Oral History Project, typescript of an oral history conducted 1974 by Rosemary Levenson, Amelia Fry, and Miriam Feingold Stein, Regional Oral History Office, The Bancroft Library, University of California, Berkeley, pp. 4-b–15-b.

12. Robert Cozzens et al., Ibid., p. 15.

13. In July, 1944, a new federal law made it possible for American citizens to renounce their citizenship, and approximately 5,500 internees at the Tule Lake Segregation Center in California decided to do so. More than 1,300 of them were repatriated to Japan. For further information about this unhappy chapter in the history of the internment, see www.tulelake.org/history.html.

14. Dillon S. Myer et al., *"Japanese-American Relocation Reviewed, Volume II: The Internment,"* p. 4a.

15. Robert Cozzens et al., Ibid., pp. 62–3.

16. 320 U.S. 81 (1943).

17. 320 U.S. 115 (1943).

18. 323 U.S. 214 (1944).

19. 323 U.S. 283 (1944).

20. *Korematsu*, 323 U.S. 214, 220 (1944).

21. Ibid.

22. Ibid., 223.

23. Ibid., 426.

24. Dillon S. Myer, *Uprooted Americans: The Japanese Americans and the War Relocation Authority during World War II* (Tucson: University of Arizona Press, 1971), 267. The plaintiffs who challenged the Japanese internment showed great courage. Not only were they vilified by "Jap-hating" Americans but many within their own community also disapproved of their actions. Japanese cultural traditions call for acceptance of authority and a stoical "keep it inside" ethic known as "*gaman*." According to this custom, when one rises to challenge authority, one must be successful or else suffer humiliation and community ostracism. Because they lost their cases, Fred Korematsu and Gordon Hirabayashi lived with this humiliation for many decades after the war, and it was only in the 1980s and 1990s that they regained at least some of their social standing. With the help of legal activist Peter Irons, an emeritus professor of political science at the University of California, San Diego, they reopened their cases in federal court. Irons introduced evidence that federal officials, including the then U.S. Solicitor General, had withheld documents from the U.S. Supreme Court in the internment cases that would have shown that Army officials no longer thought that internment was a necessary national security measure.

The federal court used a rare procedure known as *coram nobis* to expunge the detention records of the petitioners in these cases, on the grounds of newly discovered evidence of manifest injustice, even as the original Supreme Court decisions that justified the constitutionality of the internment remained on the books. In 1988, Congress passed legislation formally apologizing for the treatment of Japanese Americans during World War II and granting at least partial reparations for the economic harm that the internees suffered. One decade later, President Clinton granted Fred Korematsu the Presidential Medal of Freedom, the highest honor that the U.S. government bestows upon a citizen.

25. Speech given at the 35th Annual Meeting, Governors' Conference, Columbus, Ohio, June 21, 1943, Container 787, Speeches and Writings File, Earl Warren Papers, Manuscript Division, Library of Congress, Washington, D.C.

26. Ibid.

27. Speech given at the Newspapers Publishers Association, Portland, Oregon, January, 1944, Container 787, Speeches and Writings File, Earl Warren Papers, Manuscript Division, Library of Congress, Washington, D.C.

28. Warren Olney III, *"Law Enforcement and Judicial Administration in the Earl Warren Era,"* p. 235.

29. Census data show that 159, 534 Japanese Americans lived in Hawaii in 1940, whereas 93,717 Japanese Americans lived in California that year. See http://www.census.gov/prod/www/abs/decennial/1940.html.

30. Warren, *Memoirs*, 149.

31. Warren, Address to Stanford Law Society: Martial Law in Time of War (June 4, 1942) (transcript available in the California State Archives, Earl Warren Papers). For a review of Warren's speech and his subsequent positions on national security and due

process issues, see Sankhya Ramadas, "How Earl Warren Previewed Today's Civil Liberties Debate—And Got It Right in the End," 16 *Asian American L. J.* 73 (2009).

32. 71 U.S. 2 (1866).

33. Robert Cozzens et al., *"The Japanese-American Relocation Reviewed: Volume II: The Internment,"* p. 60.

34. Abraham Lincoln to Albert G. Hodges, April 4, 1864, in *The Collected Works of Abraham Lincoln,* vol. 7, ed. Ray P. Basler (Washington, D.C.: Abraham Lincoln Association, 1959), 281.

Chapter 5

California's Favorite Son

As his first term as governor approached its end, Warren shifted his focus from winning the war to preparing California for growth. During the 1940s, California experienced a massive in-migration. The mild climate and unpopulated rural areas offered suitable locations for military bases and training grounds, and San Diego, Long Beach, and Oakland attracted naval installations and industrial sites for the construction of planes, ships, and war material. In a speech to the Commonwealth Club of San Francisco in December 1945, Warren noted that employment in the airplane manufacturing industry in California had increased from 37,000 workers in 1940 to 328,000 workers at the peak of the war, and in the shipbuilding industries, it increased from 6,000 workers to over 300,000 workers. Civilian employment in the state peaked at 3.5 million in 1944.[1] Many service members and women who came to California for military training before shipping abroad planned to return to the state after the war to settle down.

Nor was growth merely a function of the war. In the decade between 1940 and 1950, California's population grew from 6,900,000 people to 10,650,000, and by 1952, its population approached 11.5 million, making it the second most populous state in the nation. Warren foresaw the demands on state government that these trends foreshadowed. He obtained legislative approval for special funds for the transition to a peacetime economy, including monies for unemployment relief and postwar construction.

Warren envisioned a California of 20 million people. Accordingly, he engineered improvements in the state's justice, mental health, transportation, and irrigation systems. In an arid region unsuited for a large population, this meant significant changes in natural water systems. Throughout the Central Valley, which extends from Sacramento in the north, through the San Joaquin Valley into the Imperial Valley in the south, California remained barren and dry throughout much of the year. In the winter and spring, mountain snows would melt, leading to destructive flooding in areas like the Sacramento Valley. Cities like Los Angeles needed water, as did farmers and ranchers in rural areas. With the cooperation of the legislature, Warren created a State Water Resources Board that oversaw water development throughout the state. The Board worked in tandem with federal agencies such as the Bureau of Reclamation and the Army Corps of Engineers to design water delivery and storage systems.

Balancing water rights between urban and rural interests in California often sparked controversy, and at several points Warren intervened to protect ranchers in the Owens Valley from Los Angeles water developers.[2] Warren secured $55 million in state funds to supplement federal resources for the construction of the Shasta Dam in the Central Valley. Astutely, he often supported agricultural interests in this region since its voters often determined the outcome of close California elections.

In the fall of 1944, as the presidential election approached, Republican officials sought Warren as a lead speaker for their national convention and as a possible running mate for New York Governor Thomas E. Dewey. Warren's keynote speech at the convention denounced the centralization of government under Franklin Roosevelt's New Deal and pointed to innovations and effective leadership at the state level. But Warren distanced himself from the Dewey campaign, reasoning that in the middle of a war, the American people would not endorse a change in the White House. Warren's involvement in the fall presidential campaign ended in October when he entered the hospital with a serious kidney infection. He spent three weeks in recovery, and during his recuperation, he reflected on how working-class Americans coped with the financial burden of paying for health care.

When he returned to work, Warren announced a new proposal for compulsory health insurance that would help moderate income citizens obtain health care. He argued that affluent Californians had the means to afford private health insurance and the poor already received state health-care benefits, but the working class had nothing save its own relatively small resources to rely upon in a medical emergency. Under Warren's plan, employees would pay 1.5% of their own salaries up to $4,000 a year into a prepaid health insurance plan, and employers would match these funds. An eleven-member Health Service Authority would establish a fee schedule for the delivery of medical services.

Above all, Warren wanted to engage the legislature in a dialogue about how to improve health care for the residents of California. He signaled his openness to changes in the details of his plan. However, the powerful California Medical Association resisted the reforms. Doctors did not want to lose control over the pricing and delivery of medical services, and they accused Warren of saddling California businesses with heavy taxes and threatening freedom of choice among patients, doctors, and hospitals. They hired Warren's former consultants, Whitaker and Baxter, to attack the health care plan. Soon charges of "socialized medicine" dominated the media.

The California Medical Association's sizable campaign contributions and their close relationships with Republicans in the State Assembly doomed Warren's plan. His principal ally in the legislature, Assemblyman Albert Wollenberg, failed to get the bill to floor by a narrow vote of 38–39, and the measure died in committee. Warren's prescient efforts on behalf of health care reform continued into his next two terms as governor, but in the end, he met with only partial success. Funding for medical education programs and mental health treatment centers increased, and disability coverage for off-the-job illnesses and accidents expanded modestly.

On the civil rights front, Warren quietly pursued a reform agenda. In 1945, Mexican-Americans in Orange County filed a lawsuit challenging the mandatory segregation of their children in public schools. Federal District Judge Paul J. McCormick ruled that the segregated school system denied the plaintiffs the equal protection of the law. The defendant school officials appealed to the federal Court of Appeals for the Ninth Circuit, and the State of California filed a friend of the court brief on behalf of the plaintiffs. The appellate court upheld the judgment for the plaintiffs on narrower grounds and avoided the constitutional question.[3] As governor, Warren issued public statements in support of the plaintiffs, and he attacked the concept of segregated schools.

In a second case, *Shelley v. Kraemer* (1948), Warren filed a friend of the court brief on behalf of the African American plaintiffs who challenged the constitutionality of racially restrictive covenants in real estate. The covenants restricted the right of property owners to sell land to racial minorities, which kept urban blacks segregated in overcrowded ghetto neighborhoods. In 1946, as the appeals were pending before the Supreme Court, Warren issued statements in support of the African American plaintiffs. The Supreme Court later held that racially restrictive covenants could not be enforced in state or federal courts without violating the Equal Protection Clause.[4]

Warren's health care and civil rights reforms cemented his relations with moderate Democrats even as they alienated right-wing conservatives. As the 1946 gubernatorial election approached, extremists on both sides had difficulty fielding viable candidates. Warren pursued his customary strategy of running a modest campaign, refusing big corporate campaign donations, and cross-filing in the Democratic primary. His opponent, Attorney General Robert Kenny, served as the only Democratic statewide official at the time. Warren won the Democratic primary by over 60,000 votes and once again achieved a decided victory in the fall.

In his second term as governor, Warren continued to focus on the problem of growth. He stressed the inadequacies of California's highways and proposed a gas tax to pay for the construction of new roads. Oil executives opposed Warren's plan and raised gas prices in order to induce voters and legislators to reject it. Angered by the rejection of his health care initiatives, Warren fought back. He sought and obtained the assistance of the U.S. Department of Justice in investigating price-fixing and anti-trust violations in the California oil industry and worked behind the scenes to strike special deals with key legislators. The Assembly endorsed Warren's gas tax proposal, and a massive highway construction program began.

Warren's popularity in voter-rich California made him a natural candidate for higher office. New York Governor Thomas E. Dewey, badly defeated in the 1944 presidential race, again sought the Republican nomination in 1948, and he wanted Warren as his running mate. Uneasy about his relations with Dewey, concerned about the financial strain of moving to Washington, D.C., and still uncomfortable in the partisan environment of national politics, Warren balked. But when Dewey countered in a late night meeting at the Republican National Convention that the upcoming election would perhaps be Warren's last opportunity to enter the national stage as a Republican candidate, Warren relented. He agreed to serve as Dewey's running mate in the fall campaign. Upon hearing the news, the Warren family voiced lukewarm support for the idea. Intuitively, Nina seemed to know that her husband would be uneasy in a back-up role, and the children disliked the prospect of moving yet again, this time to far away Washington.

The 1948 Republican presidential campaign became a case study in overconfidence. The old New Deal Coalition within the Democratic Party could not unite behind Harry S. Truman. The left-wing of the party gravitated toward Progressive Henry A. Wallace of Iowa, while Southern conservatives endorsed South Carolina Dixiecrat, Governor (and later U.S. Senator) Strom Thurman. Pundits in the Dewey campaign believed the election was Truman's to lose. They counseled Dewey to avoid controversy and serious discussion of the issues in the hope that Truman's unpopularity and the division within the Democratic Party would assure victory in the fall.

Warren conducted a 21 state, whistle-stop campaign, joined by Nina, daughter Virginia, and his principal speechwriter, Bill Sweigert. The leadership of the Dewey campaign urged restraint in Warren's public speeches. This frustrated Sweigert, who often had to rewrite the speeches at the last minute. "My life was a life of misery on that train," he later wrote.[5] Warren's remarks on the campaign trail often featured innocuous comments about the weather, local geography, patriotism, and wholesome children. Although foreign policy issues such as the Cold War and the Marshall Plan posed important issues for voters in the fall of 1948, foreign policy had never been Warren's strong suit, and Dewey's staff desired a low-key campaign.

The Republican strategy backfired. Truman campaigned effectively against the "do-nothing" Republican Congress, and voters in the heartland feared that a return to Republican rule would mean a return to the Great Depression. Although Truman won 49.6% of the popular vote, and Dewey trailed with 45.1%, in several large states (including New York, California, Illinois, and Ohio), Truman won by less than 1% of the vote. The loss in California disappointed Warren, but he seemed to see defeat coming. No Republican candidate for president had won California in many years, and Dewey had alienated potential supporters in the Central Valley by refusing to clarify his stance on federal support for irrigation projects. Warren scholars speculate that the outcome of the election, one of the closest in American history, might have been different if he had led the Republican ticket.

Following the 1948 campaign, Warren returned to his duties as governor and prepared for a reelection bid in 1950. In 1949, anti-Communism emerged as a major issue, as Mao Zedong's victory in China, the nuclear arms race between the United States and the Soviet Union, and conflict in Korea dominated the headlines. In California, State Senator Jack B. Teeney introduced a so-called loyalty oath bill designed to protect students from indoctrination by perceived radical faculty members, especially those at the University of California.

Article XX of the California Constitution already required state employees to take an oath to "support the Constitution of the United States and of California," and it expressly provided that no other loyalty oath could be required as a qualification for public office. Teeney's bill would have added the requirement that state employees must swear that they did not believe in or belong to any organization that advocated the violent overthrow of the U.S. government. When the University of California Regents implemented a campus requirement that all officers and employees of the University disclaim subversive beliefs and associations or else face expulsion, the faculty resisted, seeing a threat to academic freedom.

Prudently, Warren stayed out of the fray until Lieutenant Governor Goodwin Knight dropped his plans to run for governor in the 1950 Republican primary. He then joined University of California President Robert Gordon Sproul in seeking a compromise that upheld the free speech rights of the faculty. Warren issued public statements challenging the Regents' oath as ineffectual and probably unconstitutional. "Any Communist would sign it and laugh," he asserted. A protracted fight in the Board of Regents ensued, and, at one point, 62 university faculty members refused to sign a compromise oath, which would make it illegal for Communists to retain their positions on the faculty.

Warren sought to defuse the controversy by introducing legislation in the State Assembly requiring *all* state employees to take a loyalty oath. On its face, his proposal suggested that he was more interested in protecting the reputation of his alma mater than in protecting the civil liberties of dissenters. In response, the legislature passed the Levering Act. The Act amended Article XX of the California Constitution by inserting a requirement that the employee swear s/he had never belonged to an organization within the past five years that advocated the violent overthrow of the government. Notwithstanding his concern about its constitutionality under the First Amendment, Warren signed the bill into law. The final version included both a pledge not to advocate the overthrow of the government and a statement that within the past five years the employee had not been a member of any organization that advocated this position.

In the meantime, by April 1951, 110 scholars had left the University of California over the campus loyalty oath issue, and the faculty leadership challenged the Regents' Oath in court. In a famous decision that endorsed academic freedom and freedom of expression, California District Court of Appeals Judge Paul Peek struck down the Regents' Oath.[6] The California Supreme Court later affirmed Peek's decision, determining that the legislature had preempted the Regents' authority to issue rules on the issue of loyalty when it amended Article XX of the State Constitution. The Court then set aside Peek's broader assertions about academic freedom.[7] In a later decision, the California Supreme Court upheld the constitutionality of the Levering Act because advocacy of revolution did not fall within the scope of the "orderly conduct of government" and therefore did receive protection under the First Amendment.[8]

The final text of California's loyalty oath, as set forth in the amended Article XX of the State Constitution, applies to all state, county, and local employees. However, subsection 3 of the Article defines "public officer and employee" to mean "every officer and employee of the State, *including the University of California* . . . ." Because this language expressly singled out the employees of the University of California, Warren and the university faculty lost an important public relations and civil liberties battle in this matter.

In the gubernatorial election of 1950, Warren faced Democrat James Roosevelt, son of former President Franklin D. Roosevelt. Roosevelt waged a competitive campaign, but the public supported Warren's massive school and road construction projects. In addition, the adoption of the Levering Act defused opposition over the loyalty oath issue. On Election Day, Warren took every county in the state, winning by over 1.1 million votes.

Despite the overwhelming victory and his election to an unprecedented third term, Warren's celebration was short lived. Nina ("Honey Bear"), the Warrens' youngest daughter, had been fighting muscle pain for several days, and on Election Day she lost feeling in her legs. The family doctor summoned the Warrens to return home, and there he diagnosed Nina with poliomyelitis. In tears as he appeared before reporters, Warren struggled to accept the news. That afternoon, Nina's paralysis spread to her diaphragm, and doctors took her to an isolation ward at Sutter Hospital in Oakland, where doctors placed her in an iron lung. When the news became public, support poured in from all over the nation. Thousands of well-wishers sent recovery cards and telegrams, including President Truman and actress Dinah Shore. After seven weeks in the hospital, Nina returned home to her mother's care, and for the next eight months, she worked diligently at physical therapy. By April, she swam every day, and in June, she walked across the stage to accept her diploma from McClatchy High School. Instead of attending college that fall, Nina took a year off to further her recovery, and by the time she entered college at U.C.L.A. the following year, the polio was in full remission.

Warren's overwhelming victory in the gubernatorial election again raised his profile in the upcoming presidential campaign. Throughout 1951, Warren sought and obtained the endorsement of GOP leaders, including U.S. Senators William Knowland and (for a time) Richard Nixon of California. Ohio Senator Robert Taft and former allied Supreme Commander Dwight D. Eisenhower also emerged as leading candidates for the Republican nomination. As a dark horse, Warren reasoned that if the convention became deadlocked between Taft and Eisenhower, he might emerge as a viable compromise candidate. In the meantime, he assembled a state delegation to the GOP convention that would pledge loyalty to him and made plans to run in the Wisconsin and Oregon primaries.

In November 1951, another medical crisis ensued. Warren experienced pain in his right side, and doctors discovered a malignant growth in his colon that required immediate surgery. Warren sought to keep his status as a cancer patient out of the public limelight, but eventually word of his condition leaked out. Doctors removed two feet of his colon, and they judged the operation successful. However, the 60-year-old Warren emerged in a physically weakened condition and needed lengthy recovery time.

As Warren regained his strength in the early spring of 1952, he concentrated on assembling delegates for the upcoming GOP nominating convention. He invited Senator Richard Nixon to serve as one of the at-large delegates, but Nixon remained aloof. Miffed at Warren's failure to endorse him in his Congressional and Senate campaigns, Nixon disapproved of Warren's bipartisan and moderate positions on many domestic and international issues. Although his background in some respects resembled that of the California Governor, differences in values, personality, and vision eventually led to a serious and prolonged conflict between the two California politicians.

Like Warren, Richard Nixon came of age in very modest circumstances. Born in 1913 in Yorba Linda, California, then a small town in desolate region of northeastern Orange County, Nixon faced a life of adversity. His father, Frank, a strict and emotionally detached taskmaster, worked a series of odd jobs as a manual laborer and farmer. After going bust in an unsuccessful effort at growing lemon trees, Frank Nixon moved his family to nearby Whittier, California, where he opened a small grocery store and gas station. Richard's mother, Hannah, a devout and conservative Quaker, raised her five sons with high expectations for their future success. But tragedy struck the family. When Richard was twelve, a classmate threw a rock that hit his 7-year-old brother, Arthur, in the head, causing a concussion. Arthur came down with a fatal case of tubercular meningitis, and Richard blamed himself for failing to protect his younger brother on the playground. In Richard's high school years, his older brother, Harold, contracted tuberculosis. After a long battle with the disease that drained the family of financial resources, Harold died at the age of 23. In an article in *Ladies Home Journal*, Hannah later observed that when Harold died Richard "sank into a deep, impenetrable silence. . . . From that time on it seemed that he was trying to be three sons in one, striving even harder than before to make up to his father and me for our loss."

By the time he graduated from high school, Nixon had a reputation as a shy loner who loved to read. He did well academically and gained admission into Harvard and Yale, but his family's tight financial circumstances meant that instead he attended Whittier College, a Quaker institution of higher learning in his home town. Although he excelled on the debate team and earned a spot as a back-up on the football team, he unsuccessfully applied to an exclusive campus fraternity known as the Franklins. The rejection reinforced feelings of resentment against "elites" that began in his poverty-stricken childhood. Graduating near the top of his class, Nixon attended Duke University School of Law. Due to limited funds, he worked his way through school and lived in a small cottage that lacked adequate plumbing. In 1937, he graduated third in a class of 25. After unsuccessfully seeking employment at prestigious Wall Street law firms, he returned to Whittier to work at a law office. Following Pearl Harbor, he accepted a position with the Office of Price Administration in Baltimore. In August 1942, he enlisted in the Navy and served in a non-combat position in the South Pacific Combat Air Transport until his discharge in August 1946.

Later that fall, Nixon decided to run for Congress as the representative of the 12th District of California. His opponent, Democratic incumbent Jerry Voorhis, had served five terms in the House of Representatives, adopting a position as a New Deal Democrat. In the campaign, Nixon accused Voorhis of having ties to communist organizations such as the prolabor CIO-PAC. To many voters, the allegations of disloyalty appeared as inappropriate hits below the belt. Nevertheless, Nixon won that November. As a new member of Congress, he accepted a position on the House Un-American Activities Committee, where he organized the investigation of Alger Hiss. A State

Department official in World War II and President of the Carnegie Endowment for International Peace, Hiss faced charges that he was a communist spy who had infiltrated the Roosevelt administration during the 1930s. Nixon's dogged investigation, based upon information he received from FBI contacts, eventually led to Hiss' perjury conviction. Political fallout from the investigation split America into two camps: one, loosely affiliated with liberalism, saw Nixon as a sinister figure who destroyed an honorable man in order to gain political power. The second, loosely associated with conservatism, saw Nixon as a courageous fighter who tenaciously exposed a communist agent and removed him from key positions of power.

Nixon's work on the Hiss case precipitated a rise in his national prominence, and in 1950 he ran for U.S. Senate against Democrat Helen Douglas of California. Adopting a campaign strategy similar to the one he used against Jerry Voorhis in 1946, Nixon avoided the real issues and appealed instead to voters' fears by stridently attacking Douglas's alleged "pro-communist" voting record. In the process, his campaign became a vituperative effort to destroy Douglas both personally and politically. Adlai Stevenson, unsuccessful Democratic candidate for president in 1952 and 1956, once described Nixon's campaign style as "Nixonland—a land of slander and scare, of sly innuendo, of a poison pen, the anonymous phone calls, and hustling, pushing, shoving—the land of smash and grab and anything to win."[9]

Nixon defeated Douglas in the 1950 Senate election but in the process earned himself the nickname "Tricky Dick" for the unscrupulous and misleading way he conducted the campaign. As a stalwart opponent of communism, he had strong support from Republican conservatives, which enhanced his appeal to would-be candidates like Dwight Eisenhower, whose policy positions as a moderate internationalist drew opposition from Old Guard Republicans such as Robert A. Taft. As the Governor of California and the GOP's popular vice-presidential candidate in the close 1948 campaign, Earl Warren also saw himself as a player in the upcoming campaign.

In an effort to persuade Nixon to serve as an at-large delegate for California's GOP nominating convention, a structure that would operate under Warren's leadership and control, Warren engaged Nixon in negotiations. Eventually the two sides agreed that in exchange for serving as a delegate, Nixon would receive the right to select 23 of California's 70 delegates to the Convention. Nixon also entered into a legally binding "Statement of Preference" indicating his support for Warren. By April, however, Nixon struck a secret deal with the Eisenhower campaign, in effect agreeing to secure part of the California delegation for Eisenhower in exchange for front-runner status as Vice President on the Republican ticket.

Following the California primary that spring, Nixon fired the opening salvo in his protracted fight to win the nomination for Eisenhower. He sent a questionnaire to 23,000 California Republicans asking them to respond to a hypothetical question: if Warren failed to win the nomination and decided to release his delegation, which of the remaining Republican candidates would be the strongest nominee for President? The letter infuriated Warren and his supporters, who regarded it as "a stab in the back."[10] Nixon defended himself by arguing that Warren had no chance of becoming the Republican nominee and that he merely wanted to determine whether Taft or Eisenhower had more support among California Republicans. Of course, Nixon's own political ambitions lay with Eisenhower.

From Warren's point of view, Nixon's Machiavellian maneuvers set the tone for a frustrating and ugly convention. During the train trip from California to the convention in Chicago, Nixon lobbied the California delegation, urging them to support Eisenhower for President. He urged the delegates to vote for Warren on the first ballot but announce ahead of time that they would commit to vote for Eisenhower in the second round. Pursuing this strategy would enable California to extend its influence in the new administration since Eisenhower then would select Nixon as his running mate. Much to Warren's dismay, when the train arrived in Chicago the buses that carried the California delegation to their hotel featured "Eisenhower for President" signs.

At the convention, the delegates were badly split: the successful candidate needed 604 votes to secure the nomination, and on the first day 530 delegates supported Taft and 427 supported Eisenhower. A dispute arose before the Credentials Committee concerning the seating of delegates from six southern states. Each of the six states sent two separate delegations, one supporting Taft and the other supporting Eisenhower. As a practical matter, the 85 seats at stake in the controversy would be enough to determine the outcome of the nomination. Taft controlled the Credentials Committee, and convention rules allowed the Committee to determine the seating of the disputed delegates. The Committee voted to seat 68 of the disputed delegates, 50 of whom supported Taft. In response, Eisenhower supporters introduced a Fair Play Amendment on the floor that, if adopted, would have blocked the pro-Taft delegations from the disputed states from voting to seat themselves. The uncommitted state delegations and the "favorite son" delegations would determine the outcome of the credentials fight.

As one of the largest of the "favorite son" delegations, California with its 70 votes would be decisive. The "unit rule" of the California delegation gave Warren control over its vote, and he could have kept his nomination hopes alive by splitting the 70 votes evenly between Taft and Eisenhower. However, Warren saw the issue from a moral point of view: voters in the southern states had cast votes for Eisenhower delegates, and the Taft political insiders wanted to ignore the voice of the people. Warren decided to let the California delegates cast their own individual ballots, rather than voting them as a bloc. At his urging, the California delegates overwhelmingly supported the Fair Play Amendment, by a vote of 62-8. Once the Fair Play Amendment passed, Eisenhower secured the nomination. Later that night, Eisenhower chose Dick Nixon as his running mate.

Although Warren dutifully campaigned for Eisenhower that fall, he resented Nixon for the rest of his life. In September a bitter Warren supporter leaked a story to the press concerning an $18,000 "secret fund" that Nixon supporters had raised for him. The issue mushroomed before the nation, and pressure mounted on Eisenhower to select a new running mate. In the face of widespread press criticism of Nixon, Eisenhower maintained a public posture of silence. This prompted Nixon to give a speech on national television to defend himself and his place on the GOP ticket. In his famous "Checkers Speech," Nixon argued that the fund existed solely for legitimate campaign expenses and that donors did not receive special privileges. Following a detailed accounting of his family's finances, he revealed that one of the gifts he had received was a puppy, "Checkers," which his family decided to keep because his young daughters had fallen in love with it. With the help of Checkers, Nixon regained public support and, of equal importance, persuaded Eisenhower to stick with him.

The political fund controversy of September 1952 reinforced Nixon's smoldering resentments against the establishment "elitists" and kindled an emerging bitterness toward the national media. In his *Memoirs*, Nixon later wrote that in the wake of the 1952 fund crisis, he became "bitterly disillusioned by the performance of the press. I regarded what had been done to me as character assassination, and the experience permanently and powerfully affected my attitude toward the press in particular and the news media in general."[11]

Nixon's deft handling of the campaign fund crisis arose not merely because of his appeals to everyday Americans on such matters as Checkers the dog and Pat Nixon's inability to afford anything but a "good old Republican cloth coat" but also because of the subtle way he manipulated political opponents. Calling on his Democratic adversaries, Adlai Stevenson and John Sparkman, to disclose their own personal finances, Nixon stated, "I would suggest that under the circumstances both Mr. Sparkman and Mr. Stevenson should come before the American people as I have, and make a complete statement as to their financial history. If they don't it will be an admission that they have something to hide. . . . *Because, remember, a man who's to be President and a man who's to be vice president must have the confidence of all the People* (emphasis supplied)."[12] In this way, Nixon implicitly challenged a reluctant Eisenhower to make public his own tax statements for the previous ten years. In another part of the speech, Nixon said that he was tendering the decision about his political future "to the public and the Republican National Committee" and not to Dwight Eisenhower himself. By referring the decision to the Committee, Nixon snubbed Eisenhower. Aides to Eisenhower who were present as Ike watched Nixon's speech reported that when Nixon made these remarks, Ike jammed a pencil into his legal pad so hard that the pencil broke.

Earl Warren's resentment against Nixon for the events that transpired at the 1952 Republican National Convention arose in part from simple human jealousy. The two California politicians got off on the wrong foot from the very start of Nixon's 1946 congressional campaign, but the real conflict arose because both of them competed for increasing levels of responsibility within the Republican Party. For his part, Warren had done extensive campaign work for the Party in 1944, run for vice president in 1948, and now had unsuccessfully sought the presidency. In contrast, Nixon was a 39-year-old neophyte who had served only six years in Congress. On the other hand, at a time of heightened Cold War tensions, Nixon had more extensive knowledge of international affairs than the more domestic-minded Warren. As a conservative who could appeal to the right-wing of the Party, Nixon could help Eisenhower build party unity, whereas Warren, as another liberal Republican, added relatively little. That Warren had failed to deliver California to the GOP in the 1948 campaign only deepened the concerns about him.

The controversies of the 1952 GOP convention meant that Eisenhower owed a major political debt to Warren. However, following the fall election, Eisenhower informed Warren that there would be no place for him in the Cabinet. At age 62 and in his tenth year as Governor, Warren faced an uncertain future. Running for a fourth term would be difficult: his relations with Lieutenant Governor Knight had become strained, and Knight appeared to be the heir apparent among the California GOP leadership. Having spent his entire career in public service, a move into the corporate sector appeared unrealistic. Nor did the private practice of law seem viable. It had been many years since Warren had been in the courtroom, and his skills as an advocate were rusty. Having recently survived cancer, he also considered early retirement, but with several of his children about to enter college, family expenses remained high. Warren anxiously awaited Eisenhower's next move.

On November 28, Eisenhower offered Warren the "first vacancy" that came up on the Supreme Court. Warren quietly accepted the arrangement and waited for an opening to occur. During the next four months, Warren appointed several close friends and staff members to other public offices. They included State Controller Thomas Ruche to fill Richard Nixon's vacant Senate seat and Helen MacGregor to the California Youth Authority. Speculation in Sacramento grew that there would be no fourth term for Warren as Governor.

In the spring, Attorney General Herbert Brownell notified Warren that Eisenhower had difficulty filling the office of Solicitor General, the attorney responsible for representing the federal government before the U.S. Supreme Court. Brownell reported that Eisenhower thought additional legal experience would be good for Warren before he assumed a post on the Supreme Court. Warren asked for time to think about the offer and in early June left with his family to visit Europe. Brownell later made a formal offer, and in early August, Warren secretly accepted it with the understanding that he would remain first in line for a Supreme Court appointment. Eisenhower delayed making a public announcement, but on September 3, Warren issued a statement indicating that he would not run for reelection for a fourth term. Five days later, Supreme Court Chief Justice Fred Vinson unexpectedly suffered a massive heart attack and died.

Vinson's death left Eisenhower in a quandary. When he had promised Warren "the next vacancy" on the Court, Eisenhower apparently meant the next vacancy as Associate Justice, not Chief Justice. Eisenhower appeared to prefer others with more legal experience for the chief justice position. His short list included former New York Governor Thomas E. Dewey and Democrat John W. Davis, who had just presented the initial oral argument in the Supreme Court on behalf of the State of South Carolina in the *Brown v. Board of Education* case. Each of these possible candidates declined for reasons of age, ill health, or disinterest. Nevertheless, Eisenhower wanted Warren to become Solicitor General, gain more legal experience, and then join the Court.

On September 25, 1953, Attorney General Brownell contacted Warren in California to confirm the plan to move Warren into the Solicitor General's position. Warren insisted that Eisenhower's promise of "the first vacancy" meant precisely that. Brownell reported back to Eisenhower, and on September 30, Eisenhower nominated Warren as Chief Justice.

On Friday October 2, Warren resigned as governor and said farewell to the people of California. During his tenure in office, the state had nearly doubled in population, and as its chief executive, Warren had effectively managed that growth, building new schools, highways, and waterways, and reengineering the state's mental health and correctional systems. As a progressive, he sought nonpartisan government and an end to political corruption. In a narrow sense, he accomplished that goal, by ruling from the center, remaining independent of both major political parties, and running a clean administration. In a broader sense, however, Warren's vision of a democratic society remained unfulfilled. Warren sought political equality and a governmental system that followed the public interest, free from the corrupting influence of political bosses, unrestrained corporations, and smoke-filled backrooms. In the face of progressive reforms, political insiders simply found new ways to exercise their power, principally through the creation of interest groups, lavish campaign contributions, and negative media campaigns. As the fight over Warren's health care initiative showed, these methods worked quite well, especially in the context of legislative politics. It remained to be seen whether Warren's vision of a society free from the domination of privileged insiders might best be realized by means of the judiciary.

NOTES

1. Speech given at the Commonwealth Club of San Francisco, December 21, 1945, Container 787, Speeches and Writings File, Earl Warren Papers, Manuscript Division, Library of Congress, Washington, D.C.

2. For further reading on the environmental and political consequences of water development in California, see Marc Reisner, *Cadillac Desert: The American West and Its Disappearing Water* (New York: Viking Press, 1986). A documentary film "Cadillac Desert: The Transformation of Nature" (1996) also is available.

3. *Westminster School District v. Mendez,* 161 F.2d 774 (9th Cir. 1947).

4. *Shelley v. Kraemer*, 334 U.S. 1 (1948).

5. William Sweigert, *"Administration and Ethics in the Governor's Office and the Courts, California, 1937–1975,"* Earl Warren Oral History Project, typescript of an oral history conducted 1972–1975 by Amelia R. Fry, Regional Oral History Office, The Bancroft Library, University of California, Berkeley, 1987, p. 106.

6. *Tolman v. Underhill*, 229 P. 2d 447 (1951), *rev'd in part*, 39 Cal. 2d 708 (1952).

7. *Tolman v. Underhill*, 39 Cal. 2d 708 (1952).

8. *Pockman v. Leonard*, 39 Cal. 2d. 676 (1952).

9. Adlai Stephenson, Speech in Los Angeles, California, October 27, 1956, as quoted in *The New America*, ed. Seymour E. Harris, John Bartlow Martin, and Arthur Schlesinger, Jr. (Port Washington, NY: Kennikat Press, 1971), 249.

10. *New York Times*, October 3, 1952, 1.

11. Richard M. Nixon, *RN: The Memoirs of Richard Nixon* (Norwalk, CT: Easton Press, 1988), 108.

12. Richard M. Nixon, *Richard Nixon: Speeches, Writings, Documents*, ed. Rick Perlstein (Princeton, NJ: Princeton University Press, 2008), 78.

Warren family in the 1890s. From left, Chtystal Warren, Earl Warren, Methias Warren, and Ethel Warren. Chtystal instilled in her children the values of mutual respect, frugality, and self-development. Matt worked long hours in the railroad yards and saved for the children's education. Ethel struggled with illness as a child and did not attend college. She became a widow relatively early in life and received periodic support from her brother. *Source*: Courtesy of the Collection of the Supreme Court of the United States.

Warren at age 11 in Bakersfield. As a child, Warren and his many pets spent countless hours exploring the nearby Tehachapi Mountains. Warren's father used the construction materials in the background to build rental properties in East Bakersfield. At the time of his death in 1938, Matt Warren owned approximately one hundred small homes, but the Warren family realized only a small profit from their development. *Source*: Courtesy of the Collection of the Supreme Court of the United States.

Cadet Earl Warren at Camp Lewis, Washington where he received officers' training in the spring of 1918. *Source*: Courtesy of the Collection of the Supreme Court of the United States.

Warren during his years as Deputy District Attorney of Alameda County, circa 1925.
Source: Courtesy of the Collection of the Supreme Court of the United States.

District Attorney Warren and his deputies conduct a raid on an illegal still in Emeryville during the Prohibition Era. *Source*: Courtesy of the Collection of the Supreme Court of the United States.

The extended Warren family, Christmas 1937, on the front steps of the Warren home, 88 Vernon Street, in Oakland. Top row from left: Earl Warren, Bud Plank (nephew), James C. Warren (adopted son), Nina Warren. Middle row from left: Chtystal Warren , Dorothy Plank (niece), Matt Warren, Ethel Plank (sister). Bottom row from left: Bobby Warren, Nina "Honey Bear" Warren, Dorothy Warren, Earl Warren Jr., Virginia Warren. The photograph is the one of the last pictures of Matt Warren, who died at the hands of a murderer only a few months later. *Source*: Courtesy of the Collection of the Supreme Court of the United States.

Methias Warren, father of Earl Warren. Date unknown. *Source*: Courtesy of the Collection of the Supreme Court of the United States.

Warren prepares to leave Oakland for Bakersfield upon learning of the murder of his father, May 1938. No one was ever convicted of the crime. From left to right, Inspector George Helms, Nina Elizabeth Warren, and Earl Warren. *Source*: Courtesy of the Collection of the Supreme Court of the United States.

Attorney General Earl Warren in July 1942. *Source*: Photograph by Gabriel Moulin Studies, San Francisco, California. Courtesy of the Collection of the Supreme Court of the United States.

Warren Campaign Poster 1942. As a Progressive, Warren appealed to bipartisanship, leadership skills, and the public interest in his many campaigns for statewide office between 1938 and 1952. *Source*: Courtesy of the Collection of the Supreme Court of the United States.

Campaign Photographs, 1942. During his bid for governor in 1942, Warren hired public relations consultants Leone Baxter and Clem Whitaker, who took a series of family photographs for the campaign. Baxter and Whitaker presented a soft, family image of Warren that opponents found difficult to attack. *Source*: Courtesy of the Collection of the Supreme Court of the United States.

Campaign Photographs, 1942. Warren hired public relations consultants Leone Baxter and Clem Whitaker, who took a series of photographs during his bid for governor in 1942. *Source*: Courtesy of the Supreme Court of the United States.

Governor Warren and family are on the steps of the governor's mansion. The family is carrying luggage as they move into the executive mansion. In a clockwise motion (LR): Virginia, Dorothy, Nina Elizabeth ("Honey Bear"), Earl Jr. Robert, Nina Elizabeth and Earl Warren. *Source*: Courtesy of the Collection of the Supreme Court of the United States.

Nina Warren during the Sacramento years. Family-oriented, warmhearted, and thoughtful, Nina shied away from the public and devoted herself to the home front during her husband's political career. *Source*: Courtesy of the Collection of the Supreme Court of the United States.

The Warren family in the 1940s. Seated in the front row (L-R) Dorothy and Nina Elizabeth "Honey Bear" Warren. Second row seated in chairs (L-R) Nina Elizabeth, Robert, and Earl Warren. Standing at rear (L-R) Earl Jr. and Virginia Warren. *Source*: Courtesy of the Collection of the Supreme Court of the United States.

The Warren family in the 1940s. From left, Bobby Warren, Nina "Honey Bear" Warren, Dorothy Warren, Earl Warren, Jr., Virginia Warren, James Warren, Nina Warren, and Earl Warren. *Source*: Courtesy of the Collection of the Supreme Court of the United States.

Warren with his family on the back platform of his campaign train, the "Warren Special," circa fall 1948. *Source*: Courtesy of the Collection of the Supreme Court of the United States.

Earl Warren for President campaign pamphlet, 1952. *Source*: Courtesy of the Collection of the Supreme Court of the United States.

Governor Earl Warren at the California State Fair in Sacramento, July 1948. *Source*: Courtesy of the Supreme Court of the United States.

Warren on the front steps of the Supreme Court Building on October 5, 1953, the day before he took the oath of office. Photograph by Harris & Ewing. *Source*: Courtesy of the Collection of the Supreme Court of the United States.

The Supreme Court, October 1954. Front Row, from left: Felix Frankfurter, Hugo Black, Earl Warren, Stanley Reed, William Douglas. Back Row, from left: Tom Clark, Robert Jackson, Harold Burton, Sherman Minton. This Court issued the unanimous decision in Brown I. Justices Frankfurter and Black, seated next to each other in the front row, engaged in protracted debate during the 1940s, 1950s, and early 1960s. *Source*: Courtesy of the Collection of the Supreme Court of the United States.

Chief Justice Warren in the winter of 1960, as the due process revolution and the struggle for civil rights in the South began to intensify. Photograph by Harris & Ewing. *Source*: Courtesy of the Collection of the Supreme Court of the United States.

The Warren Court at the beginning of the 1962 term. In nominating Arthur Goldberg to replace the retiring Felix Frankfurter, President Kennedy ushered in a new liberal majority on the Supreme Court. Chief Justice Warren worked closely with Associate Justices William Brennan, Arthur Goldberg, Hugo Black, and William Douglas in this era. *Source*: Courtesy of the Collection of the Supreme Court of the United States.

Chief Justice Earl Warren walks the U.S. Capitol Grounds with newly appointed Associate Justice Arthur Goldberg, early October 1962. Warren wanted Goldberg to succeed him as Chief Justice, but Goldberg resigned from the Court in July of 1965 to become U.S. Ambassador to the United Nations. *Source*: Photograph by Getty Images, all rights reserved.

The Warren Commission in 1964. From left to right are Representative Gerald Ford, Representative Hale Boggs, Senator Richard Russell, Chief Justice Earl Warren, Senator John Sherman Cooper, John J. McCloy, Allen Welsh Dulles, and General Counsel J. Lee Rankin. Behind them is a photograph of the slain President. *Source*: Courtesy of the Collection of the Supreme Court of the United States.

Outgoing Chief Justice Earl Warren with President Richard Nixon and newly appointed Chief Justice Warren Burger on the steps of the Supreme Court, June 23, 1969). *Source*: Courtesy of the Collection of the Supreme Court of the United States and the Washington Post.

Two pillars of the Second Reconstruction, Chief Justice Earl Warren and Associate Justice Thurgood Marshall, share a drink on the yacht "Sequoia" at one of Chief Justice Warren's retirement parties in the spring of 1969. *Source*: Photograph by Elizabeth Black, courtesy of the Supreme Court of the United States.

Retired Chief Justice Earl Warren at the Offices of the Sacramento Bee, circa January 1974. On the back frame of this photograph, Nina Warren noted that it was her favorite photo of her husband. The occasion marked Warren's last trip to Sacramento before his death in July of 1974. *Source*: Courtesy of the Supreme Court of the United States.

Commemorative Stamp of Warren. One of the best-known images of Warren, this drawing brings to mind Warren's many crucial decisions, including Brown I and II, Reynolds v. Sims, Miranda v. Arizona, and Loving v. Virginia. Warren appeared on the front cover of Time Magazine four times during the 1940s and 50s. *Source*: Courtesy of the Collection of the Supreme Court of the United States.

Part III

EARL WARREN ON THE BENCH

Chapter 6

"A Day That Will Live in Glory"

In October 1953, Earl Warren moved to Washington, D.C. to assume his new responsibilities as Chief Justice of the United States. On several levels, he faced insecurity. Professionally, he was about to enter a judicial institution whose internal procedures, traditions, and personnel were largely unfamiliar. At least Warren was not a complete stranger to the Court. On twenty-five occasions during his years in active practice, he had presented oral arguments there.[1] However, mastering the work of a justice on the high court involved a steep learning curve. As governor of the second largest state in the union, Warren often had been in the limelight, and he had a large staff to carry out the business of state. Now he found himself cloistered in the quiet of his Supreme Court chambers, largely cut off from public interaction and attention.[2] His staff consisted of a few secretaries and three law clerks. As Chief Justice, his relations with the public would be more formal, and he would speak largely in the context of judicial opinions. No longer could he initiate public policy as he did from the Governor's office in Sacramento. Instead, he could only address the issues that the parties to lawsuits brought before him.

An additional source of insecurity arose from Warren's political position. He began his tenure on the Court as a recess appointee, which meant that he served in a temporary capacity until formal confirmation hearings took place in the Senate the following spring. Personally, he lived on his own, at least for the next several months, while Nina stayed in Sacramento to wrap up family business. He found suitable accommodations at the Sheraton Park Hotel in Woodley Park, in a seven-room suite that would serve as the family home during the coming decades in Washington.[3]

Almost from the start, Warren's recess appointment triggered controversy. Harvard Law Professor Henry M. Hart, Jr. raised constitutional objections to the idea of a recess appointment for Chief Justice of the United States.

Writing on behalf of five colleagues, Hart urged President Eisenhower to call the Senate into special session to act on Warren's nomination before Justice Black swore Warren into office. Hart argued, probably correctly, that as a recess appointee Warren lacked the necessary independence that the framers of the Constitution demanded of the Chief Justice. "His every vote, indeed, his every question from the bench, is subject to the possibility of inquiry in later committee hearings and floor debates to determine his judicial fitness to continue in judicial office," Hart wrote.[4] Although Eisenhower ignored Hart's protests, the Court issued only minor decisions during the first several months of Warren's tenure. It postponed making decisions on major cases until after his confirmation hearings.

Warren approached his new assignment with a friendly, easygoing manner and a fierce work ethic that featured careful preparation and diligent homework. All of his colleagues on the Court had been appointed by either President Roosevelt or President Truman. Three justices had backgrounds in the U.S. Senate (Hugo L. Black, Harold H. Burton, and Sherman Minton); two had been law professors (Felix Frankfurter and William O. Douglas); four had administrative experience with the federal government (William O. Douglas, Stanley F. Reed, Robert H. Jackson, and Tom C. Clark); and one had served as a judge on the federal court of appeals (Sherman Minton). On his first day at work, Warren visited each of them in their chambers. He also made it a point to meet every member of the Supreme Court staff, including secretaries, guards, janitors, and elevator operators. African American staff members remarked that it was the first time they had ever become acquainted with a Chief Justice.

Using the traits of hard work and diligence that long had been his trademark, Warren gradually adapted to the demands of his new position. By his own account, the most challenging aspect of his job involved its massive reading load. Warren had always been a slow reader, but he often defended his careful approach to the workload with a quip from Abraham Lincoln: "I am a slow walker, but I never walk backward."

The heavy administrative responsibilities at the Court,[5] together with the time-consuming oral arguments and conferences, meant that Warren had to read briefs and study cases every night. Eventually, he adopted a routine that involved a twelve-hour workday. Typically, he would awaken at 7 a.m. and read in bed until 8:30 a.m. Then he would eat breakfast and drive to the Court, arriving at 9:30 a.m. He would do administrative work in the morning, hold oral arguments in the early afternoon, and stay at the office until just after 6 p.m. After dinner, he would read until midnight. This schedule enabled Warren to avoid the notorious Washington rush hour traffic. On Saturday mornings, he would return to the office for "reflection" and then take his law clerks out to lunch in the afternoon.

In selecting Warren as his nominee for Chief Justice, President Eisenhower paid a political debt from the 1952 campaign. Eisenhower also had other goals in mind. First and foremost, he sought to alter troubled personal dynamics within the Court, which for several years had deteriorated into infighting and public outbursts of incivility. The tension became most apparent in 1946 when Justices Robert Jackson and Hugo Black clashed publicly over who should serve as Chief Justice following the sudden death of Chief Justice Harlan Stone.[6]

In addition to this disagreement, the justices split bitterly over the First Amendment rights of political radicals (*Dennis v. United States*, 1951) and the death penalty appeals of alleged atomic spies Julius and Ethel Rosenberg. Eisenhower hoped that Warren would quiet the controversy on the Court and use his diplomatic skills to build morale.

Although Warren's warm personal manner helped to assuage the tensions among the justices, in other ways he did not meet all of Eisenhower's expectations. Eisenhower sought a Supreme Court that would not provoke public controversy or force the executive branch into uncomfortable policy dilemmas that might compromise its public support. Like all presidents, Eisenhower could shape the broad direction of the Court through the nomination process. Yet he could not direct the issues that litigants brought before the Court nor shape the justices' rulings on the merits. As the question of school desegregation wound its way before the federal courts and the American people, no one, least of all Dwight Eisenhower, could control the outcome.

"NINE SCORPIONS IN A BOTTLE"

When Warren joined the Court, he had the good fortune of serving with some of the most creative and intellectually gifted jurists in the country's history, including Felix Frankfurter, Hugo L. Black, and Robert H. Jackson. Widely respected for their command of precedent, analytical ability, and persuasive writing skills, each of these justices made major contributions to American law, whether in terms of legal method or in the drafting of groundbreaking decisions involving separation of church and state, freedom of expression, separation of powers, and criminal procedure. Yet behind the scenes and occasionally even in their formal opinions, their big egos led to acrimonious infighting. During the seven years of the Vinson Court, the justices repeatedly lived up to Oliver Wendell Holmes' famous description of his colleagues as "nine scorpions in a bottle."

The divisiveness arose in part out of personality conflicts between Justices Frankfurter, Jackson, and Black and in part because of Vinson's shortcomings as Chief Justice. As a former U.S. Representative from Kentucky who served for one year as Secretary of the Treasury in the Truman Administration, Vinson lacked the legal and intellectual skills for a position on the high court. His close personal and political ties with President Truman, which dated back to their years in Congress, led to charges that Vinson lacked judicial independence, which made it difficult for him to build consensus on the Court.

In the 1952 term, the Supreme Court failed to reach a unanimous decision in 81% of its cases, whereas nearly one decade earlier 40% of its decisions were unanimous.[7] Major disagreements arose among the justices concerning the interpretation of the Constitution and the proper role of the Court in a democratic society.

Between 1900 and 1935, the Supreme Court struck down state and federal laws that regulated business. A majority of the justices at that time endorsed the conservative political philosophy of *laissez-faire*, which favored free trade and the "invisible hand" of the marketplace over government regulation of business. The justices used three legal tools to incorporate this philosophy into their interpretation of the Constitution. In cases such as *Schechter Poultry Co. v. U.S.* (1935), they interpreted Congress' power to regulate interstate commerce narrowly. In *U.S. v. Butler* (1937), they used the doctrine of dual federalism under the Tenth Amendment to protect state autonomy from federal intrusion. They also devised a substantive due process approach to the Fourteenth Amendment Due Process Clause, protecting freedom of contract as a matter of "liberty" and placing absolute limits on the power of government to regulate business. The most famous example of the Court's *laissez-faire* decisions arose in *Lochner v. New York* (1903), where the justices struck down a New York law that restricted bakers to a ten-hour day. The Court held that the New York law violated the right of employees to contract with their employers to work more than ten hours each day. Similar decisions struck down child labor and minimum wage laws.

By the mid-1930s, a majority of the Court used these tools to strike down major aspects of Franklin Roosevelt's New Deal, even as the nation faced economic collapse and large majorities demanded federal action. The casualties included the National Industrial Recovery Act, the Agricultural Adjustment Act, and the Bituminous Coal Conservation Act. As congressional leaders introduced new bills involving labor law and social security, it appeared unlikely that the Court would sustain the constitutionality of these initiatives. Newspaper editors described the four justices who formed the core of these rulings as the "Four Horsemen," a biblical reference to the Four Horsemen of the Apocalypse (pestilence, war, famine, and death) from the Book of Revelation.

In 1937, President Roosevelt responded with an ill-fated judicial reorganization proposal, popularly known as his "Court-Packing Plan." The plan would have given the right to appoint one justice for every sitting justice who was over 70½ years of age, up to a maximum of six justices. His plan met with fierce public and congressional opposition. Ironically, shortly before Roosevelt unveiled his plan, the Supreme Court voted privately in conference in *West Coast Hotel Co. v. Parrish* (1937) to sustain the constitutionality of a Washington State minimum wage law. In effect, this decision endorsed the power of state legislatures to regulate business, one goal of Roosevelt's reforms.

Shortly after the Court released its opinion in *Parrish*, one of the Four Horsemen, Justice Willis Van Devanter, announced his retirement. Roosevelt nominated Senator Hugo L. Black to replace Van Devanter, and the Senate approved Black's nomination. In the coming years, Roosevelt made seven other appointments to the Supreme Court, taking care to select nominees who supported his view that the Court should defer to the political branches when it came to the framing of social and economic policy.

Roosevelt's overriding concern about eliminating what he termed the Supreme Court's "horse and buggy approach" to interstate commerce illustrates the limitations of focusing on one issue as a president makes nominations to the Supreme Court. While Roosevelt's nominees uniformly opposed the economic due process decisions of the previous era, they did so for different reasons. For his part, Justice Frankfurter saw excessive judicial activism as the principal evil of the *Lochner* period, and he urged greater deference to state and federal legislatures in the formation of public policy. Often, this led him to oppose the imposition of sweeping reforms from the bench, whether they arose in the context of criminal justice, civil liberties, or voting rights cases.

On the other hand, Justice Black viewed the *Lochner* era as problematic because of the Court's tendency to interpret the Constitution too loosely. As a textualist, he read the Constitution literally and sought to follow the intent of the framers rather than inventing his own construction of vague constitutional language. Unlike Frankfurter, Black insisted that the Court should have broad power to enforce the Constitution to protect the rights of political and racial minorities. In the coming era, as issues of individual and civil rights replaced economic regulation as the central questions before the Court, the two justices would spar mightily from their perches on the bench.

Warren's role as Chief Justice—together with his own vision of what the duties of this office entailed—thrust him into the middle of the raging debate between Frankfurter and Black. On issues such as federalism, the role of federal courts, the judicial method of strict construction, and the search for the appropriate meaning of the Fourteenth Amendment Due Process Clause, the tension between Justices Frankfurter and Black would be central to the constitutional jurisprudence of the Warren Court until Frankfurter's retirement in 1962. During his first two years on the Court, Warren often sided with Frankfurter, especially in cases involving criminal justice and federalism. Warren's background as a state prosecutor and his relatively undeveloped judicial philosophy initially attracted him to Frankfurter's philosophy of judicial restraint. By 1956, however, Warren shifted his allegiance to Justice Black. For the duration of his years on the bench, Warren would favor Black's view that the protections of the Bill of Rights should apply to the states under the Fourteenth Amendment Due Process Clause and that federal courts should actively protect individual rights.

In the fall of 1953, the immediate question before the Court involved the explosive issue of school segregation. From the outset, Earl Warren faced the daunting task of building consensus among the justices on the issue of human equality. A troubled nation would watch his movements closely.

FIGHTING THE COLOR LINE IN EDUCATION

The first major case on the Court's docket was *Brown v. Board of Education of Topeka*, scheduled for re-argument in mid-December, 1953. *Brown* involved a consolidated set of cases challenging racially segregated schools in South Carolina, Kansas, Delaware, Virginia, and (in a separate case) the District of Columbia. Originally, the parties had argued the case in December 1952, but the justices were divided on the merits and remained unclear about how to proceed.[8] In May, following months of indecision, Justice Frankfurter urged that the case be postponed into the following term, suggesting that the new Eisenhower Administration deserved the right to offer its views in a case of such national import. He prepared a list of questions for the parties to address prior to oral argument in the fall. In late May, the Court formally agreed with Frankfurter's approach. Over the summer, the parties researched and rebriefed the case, and they prepared to address the Court again, this time with Chief Justice Earl Warren presiding.

The issue before the Court in *Brown* arose out of America's experience with slavery. States that practiced slavery adopted slave codes that strictly forbade any formal or informal education of blacks. To the extent that slaves became literate at all, they did so principally by two means: learning from white children and conducting segregated religious services. Black house servants learned from white children as the children studied reading and writing, and the servants then passed this knowledge to others, often in the form of religious services conducted in the woods far from the inquisitive eyes of the master.

During Reconstruction, the Freedmen's Bureau opened hundreds of schools in the South, and by 1870, approximately nine thousand teachers served

200,000 students of color. Although hostile white supremacists destroyed schools in Georgia, Texas, South Carolina, and Kentucky, many teachers courageously continued their work. Despite their efforts, most blacks in the Reconstruction years had no access to education whatsoever: estimates indicate that nearly 80% of black children in the South received no education at all.[9]

In the North, education of blacks took place in segregated schools. As early as 1850, state courts in Massachusetts, Ohio, New York, and Indiana upheld the right of local school districts to educate black children in segregated facilities. Even after the adoption of the Fourteenth Amendment in 1868, with its guarantee of equal protection of the law for all persons, the Indiana Supreme Court sanctioned segregated public schools, ruling that the 1851 Indiana State Constitution, "was made and adopted by and for the exclusive use and enjoyment of the white race."[10] Courts in other northern states rejected the notion that black and white children should attend integrated schools. In 1871, for example, the Ohio Supreme Court ruled, "Equality of rights does not involve the necessity of educating white and colored persons in the same school."[11]

Federal efforts to reconstruct the South ended after the disputed presidential election of 1876. In that election, Democrat Samuel J. Tilden received 164 Electoral College votes, Republican Rutherford B. Hayes received 165 votes, and 20 votes from three Southern states were in dispute. After backroom political bargaining, Hayes gained the presidency in exchange for federal promises to end Reconstruction and provide financial support for a transcontinental railroad in the South.[12] Over the next three decades, white supremacists erected a Jim Crow political culture in the South, mandating racial segregation in public facilities, widespread disenfranchisement of African Americans, and retaliation against blacks who attempted to challenge the *status quo*.

In 1890, as a part of the Jim Crow movement, Louisiana passed a law requiring racial segregation on passenger trains operating in the state. Popularly known as the Separate Car Act, the law required railroads to provide "separate but equal" accommodations for black passengers. Ironically, rail corporations in Louisiana had unsuccessfully lobbied against the law, arguing that segregation made it more expensive to operate trains. As an "octoroon" of Creole descent (meaning that seven of his eight great-grandparents were "white" and one was "black") Homer Plessy was considered black under Louisiana law. Plessy regarded the Louisiana law as a violation of his right to equal protection of the law under the Fourteenth Amendment. With the help of a white friend and a local civil rights association, he made plans to challenge it. Plessy sat beside his white friend in the car for white passengers, and at the appropriate moment, his friend complained to the conductor. Plessy refused to move into the black car, and the conductor kicked him off the train.

Plessy filed suit in Louisiana state courts, and when both the trial court and the state supreme court ruled against him, he appealed to the U.S. Supreme Court. In a 7–1 ruling, the Supreme Court also rejected his claim. Writing for the majority, Justice David Josiah Brewer held that laws segregating persons by race did not stamp black citizens with a badge of inferiority and that if separate accommodations were equal, they did not violate the Equal Protection Clause. Brewer reasoned that laws "distinguishing" between the races were not "discriminatory" since they involved social rather than political rights. "We consider the underlying fallacy of the plaintiff's argument to consist in the assumption that the enforced separation of the two races stamps the colored race with a badge of inferiority," he wrote. "If this be so, it is not by reason of anything found in the act, but solely because the colored race chooses to put that construction upon it. . . . If one race be inferior to the other socially, the Constitution of the United States cannot put them on the same plane."[13]

Justice John Marshall Harlan dissented. In his now famous opinion, Harlan exposed the central flaw in Brewer's reasoning by rejecting the distinction between "political" and "social" rights. In simple but eloquent terms, Harlan summarized what the principle of equal protection of the law should mean: "Our Constitution is color-blind and neither knows nor tolerates classes among citizens," he wrote.[14]

By giving legal sanction to racial discrimination, the *Plessy* decision relegated blacks to a subordinate role in the political, social, and economic arenas of American life. The Court's assertion that conditions for blacks were "equal" to those of whites created a legal fiction of the highest order. Jim Crow schools in the South received little or no public funding. Classroom instruction for blacks took place in tar papered shacks that lacked suitable heat or indoor plumbing. Even as late as the 1930s, teachers in Jim Crow schools often lacked basic literacy, especially in the fields of mathematics and science. Textbooks were out-of-date cast offs from white schools, and black students walked to school even as whites passed them on the road in publicly owned school buses. Although black parents realized the importance of education, their own illiteracy meant they could provide little supplemental instruction or support at home.

Educational funding statistics from 1930 show the severe racial disparities that occurred in American schools in that era. Alabama spent $37 on each white child and $7 on each black child. Georgia spent $32 for whites and $7 for blacks. Mississippi spent $31 for whites and $6 for blacks, while South Carolina spent $53 for whites and $5 for blacks. Across the South in the 1930s, only 14% of all black students attended high school, and the range extended from a low of 5% in Mississippi to a high of 20% in North Carolina.[15] Even as late as 1945, severe racial disparities existed in the professional schools of the Jim Crow South: fifteen medical schools served whites and none served blacks; four dental schools served whites and none served blacks; sixteen law schools served whites and one served blacks, and seventeen engineering schools served whites and none served blacks.[16]

In the face of this desperate situation, the National Association for the Advancement of Colored People (NAACP) developed a comprehensive political and legal strategy to open up the doors of educational opportunity for black students. In 1933, NAACP activists Charles Hamilton Houston and Nathan Margold studied the *Plessy* decision and identified two alternative avenues for attacking Jim Crow schools. The first and easier route focused on the element of "equal" in the Supreme Court's "separate but equal" formula. Using objective measures such as disparities in school funding, teacher pay, and classroom facilities, plaintiffs could challenge the Jim Crow system on a case-by-case basis. The second route would strike at the root of the problem by developing evidence that even in a hypothetical world where black and white schools were fundamentally equal, legal segregation itself represented a badge of slavery.

After months of careful debate, the NAACP leadership reached a decision concerning how to proceed. Given the prospect of white resistance if elementary schools became the initial focus for the integration movement, they determined that their first attacks on segregation would occur at the level of professional and graduate schools. Whites would be unlikely to perceive such challenges as fundamental threats to the established social order, in part because graduate students already had been brought up in segregated institutions. Furthermore, starting the legal challenge at the graduate level would place great fiscal pressure on states that adopted Jim Crow policies. In most cases, it would be cost prohibitive to create two separate law schools, medical schools, or engineering schools, one for blacks and one for whites.

For the time being, the attack against Jim Crow in elementary and secondary schools would be limited to inequalities in teacher pay or physical facilities under the existing "separate but equal" rule. However, proceeding on a case-by-case basis against all the segregated school districts in the United States would eventually bankrupt the NAACP and slow the prospect of reform to a snail's pace. Therefore, once courts resolved this first round of cases and established favorable precedents, the NAACP would launch a frontal attack on *Plessy*.

Throughout the late 1930s and 1940s, NAACP staff attorneys challenged segregated professional and graduate schools. In precedent-setting cases such as *Missouri ex rel. Gaines v. Canada* (1938), *Sweatt v. Painter* (1950), and *McLaurin v. Oklahoma State Regents* (1950), the NAACP forced the states to integrate their professional and graduate schools. Likewise, in numerous lower court cases, the NAACP attempted to equalize the salaries of black teachers and administrators to those of whites.

The effort to recruit plaintiffs for these cases was not easy. Threats of retaliation were commonplace, and school boards used a seemingly endless series of administrative rules to block reform. Other problems arose within the black community itself. In many school districts, black teachers and administrators resisted the NAACP's initiatives, arguing that they would face layoffs if courts closed all-black schools in the name of integration.

Black intellectuals like W.E.B. Du Bois endorsed this criticism. In a series of essays published in *The Crisis*, Du Bois argued that there was no "magic" in integrated schools and that black students who attempted to enroll in white schools might face violence and psychological harm. School districts simply needed to increase funding for black institutions, and then the path for improvement would be open.[17] Even in the face of these controversies, the NAACP worked diligently to identify suitable plaintiffs, build local community support, and oversee the work of local attorneys.[18]

The NAACP's effort to recruit plaintiffs for the school desegregation cases benefited from the massive social changes that took place in black America as a result of the World War II. The United States needed black workers in the armed forces and in war-related industries, thus offering avenues of opportunity for isolated blacks in the rural South. Long oppressed by Jim Crow conditions, they now experienced life in other parts of the world where others treated them with respect. After the war, black veterans returned home seeking expanded opportunities for their children. As an advocacy organization, the NAACP membership swelled. In the six-year period between 1940 and 1946, NAACP national membership increased from 50,000 to 450,000, and the number of its local branches increased from 88 in 1938 to 14,000 in 1948.[19] Parents saw the NAACP's desegregation reforms as a means of upward mobility for their children, and at a local level, many fought for their constitutional rights, even at great personal cost.

Briggs v. Elliott—Clarendon County, South Carolina

The plaintiffs whom the NAACP recruited for the school desegregation test cases illustrate these themes. The Clarendon County case, *Briggs v. Elliott*, involved one of the poorest rural counties in South Carolina. Nearly 80% of its black residents were farm workers, and over two-thirds of its black families earned under $1,000 per year. In 1947, local NAACP organizer, teacher, and minister Reverend Joseph DeLaine and his wife, Mattie, recruited local parents to sign a petition requesting bus transportation for black students in the county. Levi Pearson, a local farmer, signed the petition because his children had to walk nine miles every day to attend Scott's Branch High School. Public school officials refused their request, and the matter went to court. Several weeks later, the judge dismissed the case due to jurisdictional problems.

The NAACP's Thurgood Marshall then came to Clarendon County to convince concerned citizens to broaden their complaint so that it demanded equal treatment in curriculum, school facilities, and textbooks, as well as transportation. At that point, Harry and Eliza Briggs served as the lead plaintiffs. Harry Briggs, a Navy veteran from World War II, worked as a farmer and local service station attendant. Eliza, his wife, worked as a maid in a local motel. When the case went to federal court under NAACP sponsorship, local residents retaliated against the plaintiffs. The DeLaines lost their positions in the local school, suffered arson attacks against their church and home, and narrowly survived a drive-by shooting. Levi Pearson lost his ability to harvest and pay for his crops, and Harry and Eliza Briggs both lost their jobs.

During pretrial hearings, Judge J. Waites Waring persuaded Thurgood Marshall to amend the plaintiffs' complaint to present a facial constitutional challenge against South Carolina school segregation laws.[20] In effect, this meant that under then-current federal practice, a three-judge panel would hear the case, and the NAACP would present its argument that the South Carolina segregation laws, regardless of their particular application, would always be unconstitutional. The new posture of the case raised both political and legal problems. Politically, although Judge Waring appeared to be favorably inclined toward the plaintiffs, the other two judges who now joined him on the bench, John J. Parker and George B. Timmerman, seemed less certain.[21] Legally, Marshall's case became more complex when the state defendants admitted that the segregated schools in Clarendon County were unequal to the facilities that whites attended. The defendants presented evidence that the Governor of South Carolina already had approved a comprehensive plan for improving black schools in the state.[22] In response, Marshall pursued the strategy that Charles Hamilton Houston and Nathan Margold had devised two decades before. He attempted to show that even if black and white schools were mirror images of one another, state segregation laws made black students unequal to whites.

Ultimately, Marshall turned to the developing field of social psychology for evidence of the adverse consequences of racial segregation. "I told the staff that we had to try this case just like any other one in which you would try to prove damages to your client," he said. "If your car ran over my client, you'd have to pay up, and my function as an attorney would be to put experts on the stand to testify how much damage was done. We need exactly that kind of evidence in the school cases."[23]

Relying upon expert witnesses such as Professor Kenneth Clark of the City College of New York and Helen G. Trager of Vassar College,[24] Marshall sought to prove the psychological damage that legal segregation imposed upon black students. In their research, Clark and Trager had used a method known as "projective play" to gain insight into the self-concepts of young children. Working independently, they observed black and white children in extended role-play situations involving doll characters of different racial backgrounds. Under the theory of "projective play," the world of play would provide a "safe" environment that would encourage children to reveal genuine feelings that they otherwise might not discuss openly with interviewers. At trial in Clarendon County, Marshall put Trager, Clark, and other social scientists on the stand as expert witnesses.

Trager had spent three years studying 250 children in the Philadelphia Public Schools in a research project that sought to design a new curriculum for the improvement of democratic social relations in elementary classrooms. She testified at length about her findings:

> First, even at 5 years old, we found that all of the children were aware of group differences, that is racial differences. . . . [O]ne difference . . . between the reactions of Negro and white children . . . was that the white children talked freely about race and race differences; whereas the Negro children showed obvious discomfort and avoidance. . . . Both Negro and white children perceived the Negro group . . . as meaning that you are not liked by people, that you won't be asked to play, that you won't be allowed to do things that other children can do. . . . The Negro children, unlike the white children, showed a tendency to expect rejection.[25]

When asked how the children internalized the social message of segregation, Trager responded:

> In our testing situations, where both Negro and white children were asked to play with dolls, . . . the white children who tended to give the worst clothes to the Negro doll and the good clothes to the white doll, who gave the worst houses to the Negro doll because that is where that person [or doll] would live, who gave the lowest type of work to the Negro doll, were also the children who had the highest amount of hostility toward Negro people. . . . I think that increase of hostility, which was apparent in our children, when they associated low status with Negroes, is precisely what we want to avoid if we are going to have any kind of peace and good human relations, and democratic human relations in our society.[26]

When Robert L. Carter asked if she thought segregated schools ever could correct the psychological harm of racism, Trager laid out the moral principle that lay at the heart of the plaintiffs' case: "Segregation is a symbol of, a perpetuator of, prejudice."[27]

Kenneth Clark supplemented Trager's testimony by presenting a detailed overview of his doll experiments in northern cities such as Philadelphia and Boston and in Southern areas such as Arkansas. In preparation for the trial,

Clark also had conducted his experiment with sixteen black children between the ages of six and nine at Scott's Branch school in Clarendon County South Carolina. He found that ten of the children preferred the white doll to the black one, that eleven of the students said the black doll looked "bad," and nine said the white doll was the "nice" one. When asked about the conclusions he had drawn from his various studies about racial segregation and the development of black children, Clark replied:

> [D]iscrimination, prejudice and segregation have definitely [sic] detrimental effects on the personality development of the Negro child. The essence of this detrimental effect is a confusion in the child's concept of his own self-esteem—basic feelings of inferiority, conflict, confusion in his self-image, resentment, hostility towards himself, hostility towards whites, intensification of . . . a desire to resolve his basic conflict by sometimes escaping or withdrawing.[28]

Defense attorney Robert Figg had not prepared carefully for Clark's cross-examination, and, being unfamiliar with Clark's work, he made a tactical decision to avoid rigorous questioning. In retrospect, this was a crucial mistake, for the Supreme Court would later attach significance to the social science evidence. To be sure, Clark's work contained serious flaws. The language that formed the substance of his doll experiment was vague, and students might have had different conceptions of what the crucial terms "bad doll" and "good doll" meant. His Clarendon County sample was too small to form the basis of meaningful conclusions, and Clark's previous work involving larger numbers of students showed that students in segregated schools in the South actually had a better self-concept than those in integrated schools in the North.[29] In the other school desegregation cases that became part of the *Brown* case on appeal, the defendants presented expert witnesses to challenge Clark's work. They claimed that Clark's doll experiments lacked standardization and scientific validity. However, the record in the Clarendon County case revealed none of these problems.

The three-judge panel in Briggs ruled 2–1 in favor of the defendants, relying on the *Plessy* "separate but equal" framework and crediting the state's promise to build a new school for black students in Clarendon County. Judge Waring issued a twenty-page dissent, in which he relied heavily on Trager and Clark's testimony concerning the adverse psychological effects of segregation on young children. Waring wrote:

> The mere fact of segregation, itself, had a deleterious and warping effect upon the minds of children. . . . (T)he humiliation and disgrace of being set aside and segregated as unfit to associate with others of different color had an evil and ineradicable effect upon the mental processes of our young which would remain with them and deform their view of life until and throughout their maturity. . . . Segregation is per se inequality.[30]

Brown v. Board of Education of Topeka—Kansas

In Topeka, the legal issues initially concerned unsafe conditions faced by elementary students as they traveled to segregated schools. Linda Brown, a first grader at Monroe School, had to cross a busy railroad-switching yard to catch a school bus to get to her school. As a black student, Linda could not attend all-white Sumner School, located just a few short blocks from her house. Linda's father, Oliver Brown, a quiet and unpretentious man who worked as a welder for the Santa Fe Railroad, served as an assistant pastor at St. John African Methodist Episcopal Church. Widely respected in the local black community, he was not an outspoken political activist. Unlike the plaintiffs in Clarendon County, he held a union position at the railroad, and this protected him from retaliation. Like Harry Briggs and Levi Pearson in South Carolina, he simply wanted a better opportunity for his children to pursue the American Dream.

The NAACP-sponsored lawsuit in Topeka raised many of the same issues as the *Briggs* case. Dr. Louisa Holt from the University of Kansas testified as an expert witness for the plaintiffs. Holt presented social science evidence about the damage segregation caused to the self-esteem of black children. She emphasized the importance of social sanctions in the process by which segregation laws harm blacks. "The fact that (separation) is enforced, that it is legal, I think, has more importance than the mere fact of segregation by itself does because it gives legal and official sanction to a policy which inevitably is interpreted by white people and by Negroes as denoting the inferiority of the Negro group," she testified.

The three-judge panel issued a unanimous decision in favor of the defendants. Judge Walter A. Huxman ruled that two Supreme Court precedents, *Plessy v. Ferguson* (1896) and *Gong Lum v. Rice* (1927), gave the State of Kansas the authority to segregate its schools. Huxman reasoned that although the Supreme Court had adopted the *Plessy's* separate but equal rule in the context of public transportation, its ruling relied upon earlier state court decisions such as *Roberts v. City of Boston* (1849), which had sustained racially segregated schools. In *Gong Lum*, the Supreme Court had denied the petition of a Chinese American high school student who sought to be assigned to a white high school in Mississippi. In effect, *Gong Lum* sustained the power of the state to classify students by race.

The one bright spot in Judge Huxman's decision lay in his discussion of the facts of the case. Adopting the undisputed testimony of Dr. Louisa Holt, he found:

> Segregation of white and colored children in public schools has a detrimental effect upon the colored children. The impact is greater when it has the sanction of the law; for the policy of separating the races is usually interpreted as denoting the inferiority of the Negro group. A sense of inferiority affects the

> motivation of a child to learn. Segregation with the sanction of law, therefore, has a tendency to retard the educational and mental development of Negro children and to deprive them of some of the benefits they would receive in a racially integrated school system.[31]

This factual finding became highly useful for the NAACP attorneys as they prepared their appeal before the Supreme Court.

Other Cases

The *Briggs* and *Brown* trials represented two of four similar cases that the NAACP brought against segregated schools nationwide in 1951. In the other cases, *Davis v. Prince Edward County* (Virginia) and *Belton v. Gebhart* (Delaware),[32] the NAACP also recruited plaintiffs who were respected spokespersons in the local black community. Attorneys argued that segregation was in and of itself unequal, and expert witnesses presented social science evidence about the damage segregation caused to the self-esteem of black children.[33] In all but one of these cases, the trial courts sustained the constitutionality of the segregated schools under *Plessy*. The lone exception occurred in Delaware case, where the court ordered the black plaintiffs to be admitted into white schools in the interest of equal justice without overturning *Plessy* itself. The plaintiffs directly appealed the decisions to the U.S. Supreme Court, and the Court consolidated the four state cases into the *Brown v. Board of Education of Topeka* case.[34]

A separate challenge against segregation in the District of Columbia Public Schools occurred in *Bolling v. Sharpe* (1954). Plaintiffs' counsel in *Bolling*, James Madison Nabrit, Jr., acted independently from the NAACP in framing the constitutional arguments he presented at trial. Avoiding the issue of inequality in the condition of black and white schools, Nabrit focused solely on the constitutionality of segregation itself. When the trial judge ruled against him on the merits, Nabrit appealed, over the objections of the NAACP, which disagreed with his approach to the case. On appeal, the Supreme Court separated *Bolling* from the other school segregation cases since the issues in the case involved the conduct of federal rather than state public officials. The Court later ruled that the principle of racial equality grounded in the Fourteenth Amendment Equal Protection Clause applied to the federal government through the Fifth Amendment Due Process Clause.

THE SUPREME COURT ARGUMENT—ROUND I, 1952

The South Carolina defendants hired John W. Davis to present their argument before the high court. A former congressman from West Virginia, Davis had served as Solicitor General of the United States during the Wilson administration and run unsuccessfully for President as a Democrat in 1924. One of the most respected attorneys of his era, he had extensive experience representing clients before the Supreme Court. In his brief before the Court, Davis argued that the best interest of black students would be served if they remained in segregated schools, where they would be free from harassment and intimidation from hostile whites. States like South Carolina that planned to equalize black and white schools would assure blacks a brighter academic future than the uncertain prospect of integration, he contended.

Davis listed examples of successful black Americans who had been educated in segregated elementary schools. They included Richard Wright and W.E.B. Du Bois. With the precedents of *Plessy* and *Gum Long* on his side, Davis was confident of victory. He noted that even the Supreme Court's most recent unanimous decisions in *Sweatt* and *McLaurin* had used the separate but equal framework. If an injustice existed in the *Brown* cases, he concluded, it involved the lack of equal facilities for blacks, not the issue of segregation itself.

The legal team Thurgood Marshall assembled to pursue the NAACP appeal made three central points in their brief. First, they argued that under the Japanese internment cases (*Hirabayashi* and *Korematsu*), racial classifications were suspect, and in peacetime, could only be justified on the basis of a compelling governmental interest, which the state defendants had not presented on the facts in *Brown*. Second, they sought to distinguish *Plessy* and *Gum Long* on the grounds that *Plessy* was a transportation case and *Gum Long* had not addressed directly the question of the constitutionality of government racial classifications. Third, they asserted that the recent graduate school desegregation cases such as *Sweatt* and *McLaurin* showed that the Supreme Court had relied upon intangible factors in determining whether blacks and whites enjoyed equal educational opportunities. The "intangible factors" the Court relied upon in those cases included the ability of students to engage in discussions with other students outside the classroom. If these factors mattered in those cases, then they mattered here, where expert witnesses repeatedly emphasized the psychological harm that enforced segregation caused to young black children.

The NAACP supplemented its brief with an Appendix summarizing the findings of social science researchers who had investigated the psychological effects of segregation on black youth. Scandinavian social psychologist Gunnar Myrdal, author of the best selling book *An American Dilemma*, was the only scholar whose name appeared in the Appendix. The brief did not discuss Kenneth Clark's doll experiments. In addition, the NAACP sought to influence the justices by promoting law journal commentary and seeking to place sympathetic law clerks on the Court. Although the organization had no direct involvement in the personnel or decision making of the Court, its ties to influential law professors at Ivy League schools offered an opportunity to urge professors to recommend suitable law students for positions as clerks for the Justices.

In both their brief and their argument before the Court, the NAACP attorneys pitched their case to Justice Felix Frankfurter, whom they viewed as critical to their success. At the oral argument, Frankfurter expressed doubt about Robert Carter's effort to distinguish *Brown* from the precedents *Plessy* and *Gum Long*. Frankfurter thought (correctly it turned out) that if the plaintiffs were going to win, these precedents would have to be overturned. Frankfurter also seemed to focus on the difficult question of what the framers of the Fourteenth Amendment intended about segregated schools, an issue the plaintiffs did not address in detail.

Arguing for the Defendants, John W. Davis stressed several points. First, he contended that the plaintiffs' social science evidence raised policy issues for the legislature, not legal questions for the Court. Second, he asserted that segregated schools had existed in the District of Columbia before the Civil War, and following the ratification of the Fourteenth Amendment, Congress never had eliminated them. In effect, this meant that the framers of the Fourteenth Amendment did not intend to abolish segregated schools. He closed his argument with an appeal to federalism and the interest of the people in running their own schools. "Do not," he concluded, "force the children into what may be an unwelcome contact." As he left the Court, Davis predicted that the justices would decide in his favor, perhaps by a vote of 6–3.

On December 13, 1952, the justices met in conference to share their initial views. Although the Court's conferences are strictly confidential, several justices kept notes on the meeting.[35] Based on source materials in the Library of Congress, which consist primarily of the justices' fragmentary notes, National Public Radio reporter Nina Totenberg prepared a docudrama of the conference.[36] From her analysis, as well as the work of other scholars who have addressed the question, it appears that the justices were deeply troubled by the implications of the case and were uncertain about how to proceed.[37]

Chief Justice Vinson began the discussion by noting that Congress could not have intended for the Fourteenth Amendment to abolish segregated schools since the same legislators who passed the Fourteenth Amendment also had enacted laws segregating the District of Columbia public schools. "The abolition of the separate school system in the South raises serious practical problems," he said. . . . [W]e face the complete abolition of the public school system. Boldness is essential, but wisdom is indispensable."

As the member of the Court with greatest seniority, Justice Black spoke next. His personal roots as an elected politician from the Deep South gave added meaning to his words. According to Burton, Black found the issues in

Brown to be "painful," but he agreed with the plaintiffs that the purpose of segregation was to make blacks unequal to whites. Even though the decision might mean the end of Democratic Party control in the South, he would vote to reverse the trial courts.

Justice Reed voiced a position in favor of retaining *Plessy* as precedent and equalizing schools under the separate but equal framework. "Negroes have not thoroughly assimilated," he asserted, and states are "authorized to make up their own minds."[38] Justice Clark, who in his early years on the Court sided with Chief Justice Vinson the vast majority of the time, also seemed to favor this point of view. Justice Frankfurter was undecided but appeared to be leaning toward affirming the lower courts. Although he had a long record of opposing racial inequality during his tenure on the Court and seemed to be in favor of striking down segregated schools in the District of Columbia, the prospect of outlawing segregation in the states troubled him.

Justice Jackson shared the view that the Court's institutional limitations counseled against its assuming a primary role in making fundamental changes in American society. As he saw it, the issues in *Brown* were primarily political and not legal. But he was conflicted. "I find nothing in the text that says it's unconstitutional, nothing in the opinions of the courts, nothing in the history of the Fourteenth Amendment," he said. "It will be bad for Negroes to be put into white schools. But segregation is nearing an end. If there are two or three deaths on this Court, this will come. There is no way out."

Justices Burton and Douglas, who tended to be more outspoken than the other justices in their defense of personal freedom, voiced their support for the plaintiffs. Thus, at the end of the first conference, it appeared that four justices would have voted to reverse (Justices Black, Douglas, Burton, and Minton) and five justices would have sustained the judgments below.

In a Memorandum for the File that he wrote on May 17, 1954 (the day the Court released its opinion in the school desegregation cases), Justice William O. Douglas confirmed this interpretation of the December 12, 1952 conference. Noting that the justices decided not to take a formal vote during this conference due to the likelihood that there might be some leaks, he wrote:

> In the original conference, there were only four who voted that segregation in the public schools was unconstitutional. Those four were Black, Burton, Minton, and myself. Vinson was of the opinion that the *Plessy* case was right and that segregation was constitutional. Reed followed the view of Vinson and Clark was inclined that way. In the 1952 conference Frankfurter and Jackson viewed the problem with great alarm and thought that the Court should not decide the question if it was possible to avoid it. Both of them registered the view that segregation in the public schools was probably constitutional. Frankfurter drew a distinction between segregation in the public schools of the District of Columbia and segregation in the public schools in the States. He thought that segregation

> in the public schools of the District of Columbia violated due process but he thought that history was against the claim of unconstitutionality as applied to the public schools of the States.[39]

During the winter and spring of 1953, the Court seemed uncertain about how to proceed. The issues in the *Brown* case appeared to overwhelm Chief Justice Vinson, the one person best situated to strike a compromise between the various factions of the Court. During his years on the Court, Vinson had done much to support the NAACP, using the equalization element of the separate but equal doctrine to force recalcitrant states to provide meaningful educational opportunities for black professional and graduate students. Now that *Plessy* itself lay under attack, he became uneasy. His lack of leadership, in conjunction with some of colleagues' uncertainty about and tepid interest in the sociological basis for the Plaintiffs' complaint, made the future of the case unpredictable.

Behind the scenes, Justice Frankfurter sought to delay a decision. He argued that in a case of this magnitude, the Eisenhower Administration deserved the right to present its views before the Court. Anxious about Justice Jackson's unwillingness to thrust the Court into the center of the school desegregation controversy, Frankfurter realized that the Court would need to speak with a unanimous voice. He asked one of his clerks, Alexander Bickel, to undertake a painstaking review of historical records to determine what the framers of the Fourteenth Amendment intended concerning segregated schools.

At a conference in May, the justices agreed to postpone the *Brown* case into the subsequent term. They ordered the parties to address several questions, which would become the basis for a second oral argument in the fall. The questions concerned whether the framers of the Fourteenth Amendment intended to prohibit segregated schools and, if they did not, whether the Court nevertheless had the power to do so.[40]

The Supreme Court Argument—Round II, 1953–1954

At the NAACP offices in New York, the order came as unwelcome news. Finances were extremely tight, and developing answers to the Court's questions appeared difficult. The plaintiffs hired several historians to assist in the project, including eminent scholars such as John Hope Franklin and C. Vann Woodward, as well as a host of researchers and volunteers. Howard Jay Graham, a deaf researcher at the Los Angeles County Law Library, Jacobus ten Broek, a blind professor at the University of California, Berkeley, Alfred H. Kelly, a professor of history at Wayne University in Detroit, and William R. Ming, a black law professor at the University of Chicago, assisted in the effort. Together, they probed the complex history of the Reconstruction Era to formulate answers to Frankfurter's questions.

The principal obstacle to the research concerned the legislative debate over the Civil Rights Act of 1866, a bill that originally contained an assurance that the freedmen would face "no discrimination in civil rights or immunities." On the floor of both the House and the Senate, conservatives voiced opposition to the "no discrimination" clause. Their arguments included the point that Pennsylvania, Ohio, and Indiana had laws requiring the racial segregation of schools, and these laws conflicted with the proposed language. The sponsor of the bill, Ohio Representative John A. Bingham, then withdrew the "no discrimination" clause, and the amended bill passed into law when Congress overrode President Andrew Johnson's veto.

Representative Bingham went on to sponsor the Fourteenth Amendment itself. His proposed constitutional amendment contained the sweeping provision that "no state shall deny to any person the equal protection of the law." After thorough review of the legislative history in the *Congressional Globe*, the NAACP research team could find only one tangential reference to segregated schools in the legislative history.[41] This left open the question of whether the Fourteenth Amendment provided new rights that went beyond the limitations of the Civil Rights Act of 1866 or whether the more specific statements from the earlier debate, in which legislators voiced opposition to the idea of prohibiting segregated schools, actually reflected the will of the Congress. Compounding this problem, public schools were largely undeveloped in the South, both at the time of the Civil War and during the remainder of the Nineteenth Century. Traditionally, the planter class in the South had educated its youth by means of private tutors, and poor whites remained largely illiterate. Several states in the region did not even adopt compulsory school attendance laws until after 1900. Richard Kluger reports that in 1868, at the time of the adoption of the Fourteenth Amendment, 13 states had no school segregation laws or prohibited segregated schools, eight states authorized local school districts to operate segregated schools, five states explicitly or implicitly excluded black children from public schools, and five states prohibited school segregation (three of these later restored school segregation practices).[42]

For several months, the NAACP research team struggled over how to reconcile these contradictory facts. The more he thought about the problem, the more Marshall realized that he stood on the prongs of a dilemma. On the one hand, in order to take the Court's questions seriously, he had to address the specifics of the Congressional debate, yet doing so only revealed the uncomfortable fact that many elected representatives did not want to eliminate segregated schools. On the other hand, he could argue that the specifics of the congressional intent were not clear, and the general principle of nondiscrimination laid out in the Fourteenth Amendment should win out. However, this seemed to beg the questions that the Court had posed and appeared disrespectful.

Professor Alfred H. Kelly urged Marshall to resolve this dilemma by arguing that Representative Bingham had introduced the Fourteenth Amendment in order to provide Congress with the constitutional power to outlaw all forms of racial discrimination, a power that it lacked in 1866. In effect, the Amendment paved the way for the wholesale prohibition of racial classifications that Bingham originally had sought in the 1866 Civil Rights Act. Marshall ultimately decided to use this argument in his brief.

In the meantime, Justice Frankfurter had been assembling an extensive report on the school segregation cases, apparently in an effort to clarify his own thinking. He asked his law clerk, Alexander Bickel, to analyze the legislative history of the Fourteenth Amendment as it pertained to the problem of school segregation; in late August, Bickel finished the massive project. Relying on the removal of the "no discrimination" language from the 1866 Civil Rights Act, Bickel concluded that the Reconstruction Congress probably would not have passed legislation prohibiting the segregation of schools. On the other hand, he found it plausible that in adopting the broad nondiscriminatory terms of the Fourteenth Amendment, the Congress wanted to give future generations the authority to eliminate segregation. The unclear intent of the legislature left the path open for the Court to grant the plaintiffs the relief they sought. This meant that the Court would have to base its decision not on the intent of the framers but on the argument that conditions in American life and in state public education had changed since the adoption of the Fourteenth Amendment in 1868.[43]

The issues that Bickel examined in his report foreshadowed the conflict between preserving racial equality and confronting the limitations of the Court's institutional role in mandating sweeping changes in American life. Justice Frankfurter acknowledged these conflicts in a memorandum to the Conference that he prepared in the late summer of 1953. In it, he cautioned against deciding *Brown* on the basis of the justices' personal views about segregation. "However passionately any of us may feel, however fiercely any of us may believe that such a policy of segregation as undoubtedly expresses the tenacious conviction of Southern States is both unjust and shortsighted, he travels outside his judicial authority if on the basis of his private feelings he declares unconstitutional the policy of segregation," Frankfurter wrote.

Instead, Frankfurter thought the Court should focus on the legal issue of whether under the Equal Protection Clause "the necessary process of welding a nation out of . . . diverse elements can be imposed as a matter of law upon the States in disregard of the deeply rooted feeling and tradition, based upon local situations, to the contrary." In resolving this issue, Frankfurter asserted, the Court should not "rely upon a fixed formula defined with finality at a particular time." The guarantee of equality enshrined in the Constitution "does not reflect . . . the social arrangements and beliefs of a particular epoch. . . .

(The) law must respond to transformation of views as well as to that of outward circumstances," he concluded.[44]

Within days of the release of Bickel's memo, Chief Justice Fred Vinson died suddenly of a heart attack. At the memorial service, one of Frankfurter's former clerks, Philip Elman, recalls a remark that Frankfurter made. Taking Elman aside, Frankfurter looked him in the eye, and said, "Phil, this is the first solid piece of evidence I have ever had that there really is a God."[45]

The second oral argument in *Brown* took place over a three-day period in December 1953. At the conclusion of his argument, John W. Davis referred to a story from Aesop's fables about a dog with a bone that sees his own reflection in a pond. Mistakenly thinking that the dog in the pond had a bigger bone, he dropped the bone to grab the reflection, only to lose the only bone he had. So it was with the black plaintiffs, Davis argued. They rejected generous offers of state assistance for the construction of new schools in the uncertain quest for integration.

In his closing argument, Thurgood Marshall emphasized the absurdity of segregated schools. "I got the feeling on hearing the discussion yesterday that when you put a white child in a school with a whole lot of colored children, the child would fall apart or something. Everybody knows that is not true," he said. "Those same kids in Virginia and South Carolina—and I have seen them do it—they play in the streets together, they play on their farms together, they go down the road together, they separate to go to school, they come out of school and play ball together. They have to be separated in school."

The Eisenhower Justice Department, represented by Assistant Attorney General J. Lee Rankin, [46] presented an *amicus curiae* argument on behalf of the NAACP plaintiffs. Rankin argued that federal district courts should have the responsibility of overseeing the desegregation of schools in the South and that school boards should implement desegregation plans "with all deliberate speed." The phrase immediately caught the attention of Justice Frankfurter.

Three days after oral argument, the Court again met in conference to consider the case, this time with Earl Warren leading the discussion. According to available records,[47] Warren began the conference by requesting that no vote be taken that day and so that discussions could be informal and open ended.[48]

Warren highlighted the moral dimensions of the case. "The more I've read and thought," he said, "the more I've come to conclude that the basis of segregation and separate but equal rests upon a concept of inherent inferiority of the colored race." He refrained from blaming anyone and recognized that the Court would need to be sensitive to the fact that conditions in different regions of the country differed. Eliminating segregation in the Deep South without upheaval and strife, he purportedly said, "would require all the wisdom at the command of the Court."

It was a fresh approach to the thorny issues in the case. By subordinating issues of judicial power, framers' intent, and precedent to the more central question of what racial inequality meant to the ideals of American democracy, Warren subtly shifted the burden of proof to those who would uphold the trial courts' decisions. Implicitly, he accepted Frankfurter's position that the case could not be resolved on the basis of legislative history and that the Court should be free to consider the meaning of equal protection in light of contemporary social conditions. He stressed the importance of how the Court would frame a remedy for the problem of segregated schools.

After the conference, it appeared that Justice Reed continued to oppose a decision in favor of the plaintiffs, and Justices Frankfurter and Jackson were likely to issue separate concurrences. According to Justice Jackson's law clerk, E. Barrett Prettyman, Jackson remained skeptical of "a recasting of society by judicial fiat," since "any constructive policy for abolishing (segregation) must come from Congress."[49] Patiently, diplomatically, Warren met individually with each justice in an effort to build consensus.

Justice Douglas' Memorandum for the File confirms the fact that the Court remained divided after the second oral argument in *Brown*. He wrote:

> At the conference following that argument in December 1953 Black was absent but he sent in his vote indicating that he thought that segregation in the public schools was unconstitutional. His vote, together with Burton's, Minton's and my own made four. Chief Justice Warren was very clearly of the view that segregation in public schools was unconstitutional. That made a bare majority for the reversal of the judgments below. Reed voted the other way. He thought that segregation was constitutional. Clark was inclined that way although doubtful. So was Frankfurter and so was Jackson. The latter two expressed the hope that the Court would not have to decide these cases but somehow avoid these decisions.[50]

In January 1954, the Senate Judiciary Committee took up the matter of Warren's confirmation to the Court. Senator William Langer of North Dakota delayed the confirmation in subcommittee by voicing concern about Warren's alleged ties to unions and organized crime. During February, Langer convened secret meetings of the Committee, hearing testimony from Roderick J. Wilson, who alleged, without substantial evidence, that Warren had assisted the interests of organized crime in California. Warren Olney III, who headed the California Crime Commission, attended the session and then extemporaneously spoke out in Warren's defense. When Wilson's charges proved unsubstantiated, the Committee voted 12-3 in support of Warren's nomination. On March 1, 1954, the Senate voted 40-0 to confirm Warren's nomination,[51] and on March 20, 1954, Justice Robert Jackson administered the oath of office to Warren.

In the meantime, Justice Jackson had been working on a paper that he may have intended to serve as the basis for a concurring opinion in *Brown*. Various drafts of the document, which he revised between December 7, 1953 (immediately following the second oral argument) and March 1, 1954, show a gradual evolution away from an initial position in favor of the defendants.[52] One passage from an early version of the draft shows his support for the defendants' arguments:

> (W)e cannot oversimplify this decision to be a mere expression of our personal opinion that school segregation is unwise or evil. We have not been chosen as legislators but as judges. . . . (T)he thoughtful layman, as well as the trained lawyer, must wonder how it is that a supposedly stable organic law of our nation this morning forbids what for three quarters of a century it has allowed.
>
> . . . Thus, despite my personal satisfaction with the Court's judgment, I simply cannot find, in surveying all the usual sources of law, anything which warrants me in saying that it is required by the original purpose and intent of the Fourteenth or Fifth Amendment.[53]

Jackson also criticized the plaintiffs' effort to ground the decision in sociological and political considerations. "I have no doubt that segregation has psychological consequences," he asserted, "but I know too that the woes of the colored child are by no means solved merely by forcing him into white company. And if we should regard the feelings and reactions of those who are coerced into segregation I suppose we should also weigh the effect of those who are coerced out of it." He expressed a clear preference for congressional resolution of the issue. Asking the Court to outlaw segregation, he concluded, "is to say that the Court should intervene to promulgate as a law that which our Constitutional representative system will not enact."

The final draft of the working paper, approximately twenty-four pages in length, ends abruptly. Like many of Jackson's opinions, it is well written and cogent. It also bears a remarkable, almost uncanny resemblance to many of the arguments that arose in opposition to the *Brown* decision during the next several years. His concerns about the absence of evidence regarding any intent on the part of Congress to overturn segregation in the course of the debates over the Fourteenth Amendment, the alleged weaknesses of the sociological evidence in the case, and his concern about coercing whites to associate with blacks would sound repeatedly in the future public attacks against Warren's opinion.

Yet the most illuminating change in the various drafts of Jackson's working paper concerns the gradual recognition of the importance of education in postwar American society and the thorny problem of unequal educational opportunity in Jim Crow society. These themes may, and probably were, points that Warren emphasized in his frequent discussions with Jackson over the winter about the merits of the case. That said, the final draft of Jackson's working paper states that he "favor(s) at the moment going no further than to enter a decree that the state statutes requiring or authorizing segregation merely on account of race or color are unconstitutional." That the Court "embark upon a supervised revamping of the educational system of the South proposes what is manifestly beyond judicial power or functions."[54]

Jackson's law clerk, E. Barrett Prettyman Jr., may have played an important role in dissuading Jackson from concurring separately in the case. In a responsive memo, Prettyman contended that Jackson's analysis "should *begin*, not with doubts and fears—not with a negative attitude, but with a clear and affirmative statement of your legal opinion. You have stated this position in only two out of 23 pages," Prettyman continued, "and these two pages are almost at the end of the opinion. They are almost an afterthought."[55]

In a recent speech at the Chautauqua Institution, Prettyman shared additional details about Justice Jackson's unpublished opinion in *Brown*. Prettyman reported that he reviewed Jackson's opinion for the first time on March 15, 1954, and two weeks later, Jackson suffered a heart attack and was hospitalized. As of that time, Jackson had not shared his memo with any of the other justices, although it is likely that Jackson and Warren had met extensively over the winter to discuss Jackson's views. When Chief Justice Warren brought Jackson a first draft of the *Brown* opinion at the hospital, Prettyman waited down the hall, and the two justices conferred. After Warren left, Prettyman read the opinion. He recalled that although Justice Jackson expressed disappointment that Warren's opinion did not rely more on the law, Jackson was "overwhelmingly relieved that it contained none of the attributes he had feared, and delighted that it was an opinion he could join."[56]

Prettyman also shared his thoughts concerning why Jackson willingly joined the Warren opinion when it differed significantly from his own views. Prettyman stated:

> The Warren opinion, for example, treated the history of the Fourteenth Amendment as equivocal, whereas Jackson thought it quite clear that the Framers did not intend to wipe out segregation. The Warren opinion relied in part on sociological studies that Jackson apparently thought were not a proper element of equal protection. And, most importantly, Warren based his conclusion primarily on the harm that segregation did to Negro children, whereas Jackson based his on the disappearance over time of any claim that the two races were constitutionally unequal.
>
> I think the answer to why Jackson was willing to join Warren despite these differences is that Jackson liked the simplicity and directness of the Warren opinion; he thought even laymen could understand it; and, as I have said, he was grateful that it did not place the blame on anyone. Remember, unanimity of the Justices was not yet realistically expected.[57]

Whether Earl Warren ever saw Prettyman's original memo to Justice Jackson is unknown, but Warren's draft and final opinions in *Brown* follow almost exactly Prettyman's counsel. They begin with a frank discussion of the inconclusive nature of the framers' intent regarding segregated schools, and then state forthrightly that "In approaching this problem, we cannot turn the clock back to 1868 when the Amendment was adopted, or even to 1896 when *Plessy v. Ferguson* was written. We must consider public education in the light of its full development and its present place in American life throughout the Nation." Warren's draft opinion in *Brown* persuaded Jackson to retreat from his position that he would only join the majority if the Court openly acknowledged that a ruling striking down school segregation had no basis in law.

In the early spring, as the Court prepared to hold its first formal vote in the *Brown* cases, Warren circulated a memorandum as a starting point for the conference discussion. In it, he laid out eleven elements of his approach to the case. He proposed that the District of Columbia case should be considered separately from the state cases and that the decision on segregation should be resolved in the current term. The question of what remedy the plaintiffs would receive would be postponed into the upcoming term. Then, in several short paragraphs Warren outlined his thoughts on the merits. His words are worth quoting in full:

> On the question of segregation in education, this should be the end of the line. . . . We must answer the question—*Can* we have 'separate but equal' public schools?
>
> We must hold that the doctrine of separate but equal as stated in *Plessy v. Ferguson* cannot apply to public education, but we should not go beyond that. The applicability of the doctrine in other contexts must await future decision.
>
> The opinion should emphasize the change in public education since adoption of the Fourteenth Amendment and its present status in American life. . . .
>
> The opinion should be *short,* readable by the lay public, non-rhetorical, unemotional and, above all, non-accusatory. No section of the country and no segment of our population can justly place full responsibility for segregation on others. They must assume a measure of that responsibility themselves.[58]

Warren's clerk, Earl Pollock, worked closely with the Chief Justice in drafting the final opinion. Pollock noted, "If there were three things of great value and stimulation to him, they were (1) equality, (2) education, and (3) young people."[59] The original draft of the opinion, written in long hand on yellow legal paper, features cursive handwriting no different from that appearing in the papers students write every day. Warren was left handed, and at an early age, his teachers tied his left hand behind his back to force him to write with his right hand. The result was handwriting that mirrored exactly the letters from models on the walls of elementary classrooms. Yet the simplicity of the handwriting masked the depth of composition. To black America, Warren's plain and simple document was no less significant than the potent words of Abraham Lincoln's Emancipation Proclamation or the "terrible swift sword" of Grant's Army of the Potomac.

On May 7, Warren shared his draft opinion with the rest of the Court. He personally delivered it to Justice Black at the Justice's backyard tennis court in Alexandria, Virginia. Justice Frankfurter, who also had been considering a separate concurrence, responded favorably to the draft.

Standing alone, Justice Reed continued to have doubts about the decision. Warren repeatedly met with Reed, trying to be sensitive to Reed's concerns yet remaining steadfast that a unanimous opinion would be the most desirable outcome. George Mickum, Justice Reed's clerk who was present at one of their last meetings regarding the case, recalls Warren as saying, "Stan, you're all by yourself in this now. You've got to decide whether it's really the best thing for the country." The apparent price for Reed's assent was a pledge to allow a gradual phase-out of segregation in the South.

On Monday May 17, 1954, Chief Justice Warren read the Court's opinions in *Brown* and *Bolling v. Sharpe* (the District of Columbia case) from the bench. Just moments before Warren began, Justice Jackson, acting against his doctors' orders, appeared at the Court for the reading of the opinion.[60] The brevity of the *Brown* opinion encouraged newspapers to print it in full.

Warren began the opinion by noting that the views of the drafters of the Fourteenth Amendment on the question of segregated schools were "inconclusive" and that the public education in the United States was a much more extensive enterprise in 1954 than it had been in 1868. "Today, education is perhaps the most important function of state and local governments," he wrote. "In considering whether segregation deprived black children of equal educational opportunities (w)e cannot turn the clock back to 1868 when the Fourteenth Amendment was adopted, or even to 1896 when the [Fourteenth] Amendment *Plessy v. Ferguson* was written." The Court needed to "consider public education in light of its full development and its present place in American life throughout the nation." Given the critical importance of education in contemporary America, Warren reasoned, segregation deprived black students of equal educational opportunities. Separating them from others based on their race "generates a feeling of inferiority" that "may affect their hearts and minds in a way unlikely ever to be undone."

In a footnote, he grounded this assertion in the social science evidence that the plaintiffs introduced at trial and in the Appendix they had submitted to the Court. Addressing the issue of whether the cases would be treated as class actions, and thus binding on schools not specifically before the Court, Warren held that "the plaintiffs and others similarly situated" are deprived of the equal protection of the law. Because of the "wide applicability" of the decision, he ordered rehearing the following term on the issue of how to formulate decrees in the cases.

Shortly after Warren announced the Court's decision, the Voice of America broadcast news about the decision in 34 languages throughout the world.[61] Initially, the public responded enthusiastically, both stateside and abroad. Polls showed that a significant and growing number of Americans supported it.[62]

Felix Frankfurter credited Earl Warren for the unanimous *Brown* decision. On May 17, 1954, Frankfurter sent a note to the Chief. It read:

Dear Chief:
This is a day that will live in glory. It is also a great day in the history of the Court and not in the least for the course of deliberation which brought about the result. I congratulate you.

Very Sincerely,
/Felix Frankfurter/[63]

NOTES

1. See G. Edward White, *Earl Warren: A Public Life*, 147. Warren's first oral argument before the Court in 1932 coincided with Oliver Wendell Holmes' last day on the bench.

2. In a 1972 interview, Warren addressed the challenges he faced in making the transition between politician and jurist during his early days on the Supreme Court. He stated, "(T)he thing that was hard for me to get over was this—for all my life I had been dealing with people and their group problems, talking them over as you and I are talking now, learning from actual contact with people before I made a decision on anything. When I came to the Supreme Court it was altogether different. I never saw an individual who was involved in any litigation. We never see a litigant in the Court. All we know is that that (sic) printed record that we get of the testimony in the trial, the printed briefs of counsel, and maybe a half hour of argument, or an hour of argument on each side of the podium in our court. And the change from dealing with human beings to what you might call statistics only, was really a shock for me and it took a long time to overcome it. But I did it just by dropping everything else and paying no attention to politics or current events and just sticking to our legal work." "Brandeis Television Recollections: A Conversation with Earl Warren," broadcast on December 11, 1972, WBGH-TV, Boston, Container 846 pp. 2–4, Speeches and Writings File, Earl Warren Papers, Manuscript Division, Library of Congress, Washington, D.C.

3. Located at the intersection of Connecticut Avenue and Woodley Road, N.W. near the National Zoo, the Sheraton Park Hotel at various times served as home to many famous celebrities, including President Eisenhower, Richard Nixon, former Chief Justice Vinson, and actress Marlene Dietrich. Today, the facility bears the name

Mariott Wardman Park Hotel and Conference Center, and its grounds cover more than 16 acres.

4. Henry M. Hart, Jr., Letter to the Editor, "Hart Says Confirmation First," *Harvard Crimson*, October 5, 1953, available at http://www.thecrimson.co/article/1953/10/2/hart-says-confirmation-first-to-the/. Recently several federal courts of appeal have issued conflicting opinions about the constitutionality of the President's power to make recess appointments.

5. For further discussion of the administrative responsibilities of the Chief Justice, see Chapter 14.

6. Jackson and Black also sparred over the appropriateness of Jackson's leave of absence from the Court to serve as Chief Prosecutor at the Nuremburg War Trials and Black's failure to recuse himself when his former law partner functioned as lead counsel in two pending cases.

7. Richard Kluger, *Simple Justice: The History of Brown v. Board of Education and Black America's Struggle for Equality* (New York: Knopf, 1975), 582.

8. Following the first oral argument, Justices Black, Douglas, Burton, and Minton apparently leaned in favor of striking down the segregation laws. The remaining justices, with the exception of Frankfurter, were either undecided, unclear about the grounds of decision, or were opposed.

9. Peter Irons, *Jim Crow's Children: The Broken Promise of the Brown Decision* (New York: Penguin Group, 2002), 9.

10. *Cory v. Carter*, 48 Ind. 327, 357 (1874).

11. The Court continued, "It would seem, then, that under the constitution and laws of this State, the right to classify the youth of the state for school purposes, on the basis of color, and to assign them to separate schools for education, both upon well recognized legal principles and the repeated adjudications of this court, is too firmly established to be now judicially disturbed." *State, ex rel. Garnes v. McCann*, 21 Ohio St. 198, 208 (1871).

12. For further information, see C. Vann Woodward, *Reunion and Reaction: The Compromise of 1877 and the End of Reconstruction* (Boston: Little, Brown, 1966) and C. Vann Woodward, *The Strange Career of Jim Crow* (New York: Oxford University Press, 1974).

13. *Plessy v. Ferguson*, 163 U.S. 537, 551–52 (1896).

14. Ibid., 559 (Harlan, J., dissenting).

15. Peter Irons, *Jim Crow's Children*, 33.

16. David W. Levy, "Before Brown: The Racial Integration of American Higher Education," in *Black, White, and Brown: The Landmark School Desegregation Case in Retrospect*, ed. Clare Cushman and Melvin I. Urofsky (Washington, D.C.: Supreme Court Historical Society, 2004), 69–70 (quoting Fred McCuistion, *Graduate Instruction for Negroes in the United States* (Nashville: George Peabody College, 1939)).

17. W.E.B. Du Bois, "Does the Negro Need Separate Schools?" *J. Negro Education* 4, no. 3 (July, 1935): 328–335, reprinted in *W.E.B. Du Bois: A Reader*, ed. Meyer Weinberg (New York: Harper and Row, 1970), 286.

18. For further information about these efforts, see Mark V. Tushnet, *The NAACP's Legal Strategy against Segregated Education, 1925–1950* (Chapel Hill: University of North Carolina Press, 1987).

19. James T. Patterson, *Brown v. Board of Education: A Civil Rights Milestone and Its Troubled Legacy* (New York: Oxford University Press, 2001), 2.

20. Kluger, *Equal Justice*, 304.

21. In 1930, the NAACP had opposed Judge Parker's nomination to the U.S. Supreme Court on the grounds that he had made racist remarks in his 1920 campaign for governor of North Carolina, and the Senate rejected his nomination. At the time of the trial in *Briggs v. Elliot*, Parker served on the U.S. Court of Appeals for the Fourth Circuit in Richmond, Virginia.

22. Governor Byrnes' plan included construction of a new $261,000 high school for black students in Summerton, the county seat of Clarendon County.

23. Kluger, *Simple Justice*, 316.

24. Marian J. Radke and Helen G. Trager, "Children's Perceptions of the Roles of Negroes and Whites," *Journal of Psychology* 29, no. 1 (1950): 3–33. Their research project was known as the Philadelphia Early Childhood Project.

25. Container 139, pp. 4–5, Testimony of Experts of Clarendon County School Case, Direct Examination by Robert L. Carter, May 29, 1951, Transcript of Helen G. Trager, Legal File 1940–1952, Part II, Records of the NAACP, Manuscript Division, Library of Congress, Washington, D.C.

26. Ibid., 9.

27. Ibid., 10.

28. Container 139, pp. 588–92, Testimony of Experts in Clarendon County School Case, Direct Examination by Robert L. Carter, Transcript of Kenneth Clark, Legal File 1940–1952, Part II, Records of the NAACP, Manuscript Division, Library of Congress, Washington, D.C.

29. For additional details on this point, see Kluger, *Simple Justice*, 355–56.

30. *Briggs v. Elliott*, 98 F. Supp. 529, 547–8 (E.D. S.C. 1951) (Waring, J., dissenting).

31. *Brown v. Board of Education of Topeka*, 98 F. Supp. 797 (D. Kan. 1951) (Finding of Fact 8).

32. *Davis v. County School Board of Prince Edward County*, 103 F. Supp. 337 (E.D. Va.1952); *Belton v. Gebhart*, 87 A. 2d 862 (Del. Ch. 1952).

33. Analysis of the pretrial and trial aspects of all of these cases is beyond the scope of this chapter. For further information about these cases, including the student strike in Farmersville, Virginia that triggered the school desegregation litigation in Prince Edward County, Virginia, see Kluger, *Simple Justice*.

34. Under federal practice at this time, cases decided by three-judge panels could be appealed directly to the U.S. Supreme Court, by passing the U.S. Circuit Courts of Appeal.

35. Because the Supreme Court's conferences are private, students of the Court often rely upon the justices' private papers to reconstruct what transpired during closed-door deliberations. Yet relying upon the perceptions and recollections of any one justice may be misleading. One of the ways scholars can determine whether private notes are accurate is to compare them with other sources of information, for example, memoranda written by other justices or interviews conducted with reporters or biographers. In this case, Justice Douglas' extensive notes on the conferences

(Containers 1149 and 1150, Original Conference notes, transcriptions, and Docket Book Pages re Segregation Cases, Supreme Court File, William O. Douglas Papers, Manuscript Division, Library of Congress, Washington, D.C.) do appear to square with both formal memos that other justices wrote for their colleagues, with Chief Justice Warren's own recollections as set forth in his *Memoirs*, and with Justice Burton's diary, which contains references to the conference discussions on the school desegregation cases (see e.g., Container 3, Tuesday May 18, 1954, Diaries, Harold H. Burton Papers, Manuscript Division, Library of Congress, Washington, D.C.; see also, Container 184, Legal File, Robert Houghwout Jackson Papers, Manuscript Division, Library of Congress, Washington, D.C.). For further insight into the strengths and weaknesses of using private papers in judicial research, see S. Sidney Ulmer, "Bricolage and Assorted Thoughts on Working in the Papers of Supreme Court Justices," *Journal of Politics*, 35, no. 2 (May, 1973): 286–310.

36. Ms. Totenberg's report is available at http://www.npr.org/templates/story/story.php?storyId=1537409. The docudrama originally was broadcast on December 8, 2003.

37. See e.g., Michael J. Klarman, *From Jim Crow to Civil Rights: The Supreme Court and the Struggle for Racial Equality* (New York, Oxford University Press, 2004), 293–301 and the notes therein.

38. Ibid., 294.

39. Container 1150, "Original Conference notes, transcriptions, and Docket Book Pages re Segregation Cases," Supreme Court File, William O. Douglas Papers, Manuscript Division, Washington, D.C. Professor Klarman's own review of the available evidence leads him to the same conclusion as Justice Douglas. Klarman believes Justices Black, Douglas, Burton, and Minton thought school segregation violated the Fourteenth Amendment, Justices Vinson and Reed wanted to uphold *Plessy v. Ferguson*, and Justices Frankfurter, Jackson, and Clark were ambivalent. Klarman, *From Jim Crow to Civil Rights*, 298.

40. Among the questions the Court asked the parties to brief were the following: (1) "What evidence is there that the Congress which submitted and the state legislatures and conventions which ratified the Fourteenth Amendment contemplated or did not contemplate, understood or did not understand, that it would abolish segregation in public schools?" (2) "If neither the Congress in submitting nor the states in ratifying the Fourteenth Amendment understood that compliance with it would require the immediate abolition of segregation in public schools, was it nevertheless the understanding of the framers of the amendment (a) that future Congresses might in the exercise of their power under Sec. 5 of that amendment, abolish segregation, or (b) that it would be within the judicial power, in light of future conditions, to construe the amendment as abolishing such segregation of its own force?" Container 570, Supreme Court File, Earl Warren Papers, Manuscript Division, Library of Congress, Washington, D.C.

41. The reference concerned a statement on the record by Wisconsin Senator Timothy Howe in which Howe voiced an objection to a Florida school law that taxed both blacks and whites for white schools but required that blacks pay the full cost of black schools. For further information on this history, see Kluger, *Simple Justice*, 631.

42. Ibid., 633–34.

43. In a one-page Memorandum for the Conference dated December 3, 1953, Justice Frankfurter described Alexander Bickel's review of the legislative history of the adoption of the Fourteenth Amendment as a "fair, well-balanced summary of the story." Frankfurter then asserted that "the legislative history of the Amendment is, in a word, inconclusive, in the sense that the 39th Congress as an enacting body neither manifested that the Amendment outlawed segregation in the public schools or authorized legislation to that end, nor that it manifested the opposite." Container 571, Supreme Court File, Earl Warren Papers, Manuscript Division, Library of Congress, Washington, D.C.

44. Justice Frankfurter's memorandum consists of a two-page document he wrote during the summer of 1952. Following Chief Justice Vinson's death, Frankfurter circulated it among the brethren on September 26, 1952. Container 571, State Segregation Cases, Supreme Court File, 1930–1974, Earl Warren Papers, Manuscript Division, Library of Congress, Washington, D.C.

45. Phillip Ellman, interview with National Public Radio reporter Nina Totenberg, available at http://www.npr.org/templates/story/story.php?storyId=1537409. The interview is part of a report on the Supreme Court's deliberations on the *Brown* case, originally broadcast on December 8, 2003.

46. Later J. Lee Rankin served as General Counsel of the Warren Commission, which investigated the assassination of President Kennedy.

47. See note 35. Other sources that examine the Court's internal deliberations in this conference include Richard Brust, "The Court Comes Together," *ABA Journal*, April 1, 2004, and S. Sidney Ulmer, "Earl Warren and the Brown Decision," *Journal of Politics*, 33, no. 3 (Aug., 1971): 689–702.

48. Warren's strategy was to avoid asking his colleagues to form conclusions too quickly. ". . . (W)hen a person once announces he has reached a conclusion, it is more difficult for him to change his thinking," he later wrote. Warren, *Memoirs*, 285.

49. For a summary of Prettyman's recollections, see Brust, "The Court Comes Together." Chief Justice William H. Rehnquist, who clerked for Justice Robert Jackson in 1952–1953, wrote that both Justices Frankfurter and Jackson indicated an intention to write separate, concurring opinions in the case. William H. Rehnquist, "Chief Justice Warren's Role in Brown v. Board of Education," in *Brown at 50: The Unfinished Legacy*, ed. Deborah L. Rhode and Charles J. Ogletree, Jr. (Chicago: American Bar Association, 2004), 48.

50. Container 1150, Original Conference notes, transcriptions and Docket Book Pages re Segregation Cases, Supreme Court File, William O. Douglas Papers, Manuscript Division, Library of Congress, Washington, D.C.

51. For further information about Warren's confirmation hearings, see Newton, *Justice for All*, 281–91.

52. Container 184, Legal File, Robert Houghwout Jackson Papers, Manuscript Division, Library of Congress, Washington, D.C.

53. Ibid.

54. Ibid. Justice Jackson's uneasiness about thrusting the Court into the role of overseeing the transformation of public schools in the South contrasts sharply with

Chief Justice Warren's approach to the issues before the Court in *Brown*. In a memo to one of his clerks, Gerald Gunther, prepared on July 6, 1954, in which Warren chartered a study of the progress and challenges to school desegregation throughout the country, Warren wrote, "I believe we should know as many conditions (about the movement toward integrated schools) that must be faced as it is possible to ascertain. It would also seem desirable to me to know all of the proposals for defeating integration. Frequent evaluation of these proposals and of counter proposals should be helpful." Container 574, Supreme Court File, Earl Warren Papers, Manuscript Division, Library of Congress, Washington, D.C. Had Jackson lived, the framing of the Court's unanimous opinion in *Brown II* may have been yet more of a challenge for Chief Justice Warren than it otherwise was.

55. Quoted in Kluger, *Simple Justice*, 691.

56. Ibid., 697.

57. E. Barrett Prettyman, Jr., "Thoughts on Justice Jackson's Unpublished Opinion," October 8, 2003, available at: http://www.roberthjackson.org/the-man/speeches-articles/speeches/speeches-related-to-robert-h-jackson/thoughts-on-justice-jacksons-unpublished-opinion/.

58. Container 571, Segregation State Cases File, memo of May 5, 1954, Supreme Court File, 1930–1974, Earl Warren Papers, Manuscript Division, Library of Congress, Washington, D.C.

59. Quoted in Kluger, *Simple Justice*, 695.

60. Just a few months later, in October, 1954, Jackson suffered a fatal heart attack.

61. Kluger, *Simple Justice*, 708.

62. David G. Barnum, "The Supreme Court and Public Opinion: Judicial Decision Making in the Post-New Deal Period," *Journal of Politics*, 47, no. 2 (May, 1985): 652, 657, 12n.

63. Container 571, Supreme Court File, Earl Warren Papers, Manuscript Division, Library of Congress, Washington, D.C.

Chapter 7

All Deliberate Speed

In his opening remarks to the Conference after the second oral argument in *Brown*, Chief Justice Warren emphasized the delicate political task that the justices faced in confronting the issue of segregated schools. "It will take all the wisdom of this Court to do this with a minimum of commotion and strife," he asserted. "How we do it is important. We must abolish in a tolerant way the practice of segregation in the public schools."[1]

The *Brown* decision eventually struck down school segregation laws and policies in twenty-one jurisdictions, including four Western States (Arizona, Kansas, New Mexico, and Wyoming), eight Border States (Delaware, Kentucky, Maryland, Missouri, North Carolina, Oklahoma, Tennessee, and West Virginia), and nine Deep South states (Alabama, Arkansas, Florida, Georgia, Louisiana, Mississippi, South Carolina, Texas, and Virginia). In addition, at least two Midwestern States (Ohio and Indiana) gave some school districts the option of segregating schools, practices that later gave rise to litigation.

Polls taken in the summer of 1954 suggested that approximately 40% of the American public immediately supported the *Brown* decision. In the Deep South, only about 10% of the population supported it.[2] Embedded in these simple statistics lay the seeds of the acrimonious battles that lay ahead on issues of civil rights and racial justice.

Warren addressed the issue of racial inequality through the art of political compromise. He secured unanimous agreement among the justices for the principle that the Constitution prohibits racial segregation in the public sector by agreeing to implement the prohibitions slowly. As Justice Black expressed it, "People are going to fight this (*Brown* decision). . . . We should move gradually, like a glacier."[3] For the moment, the terms of the compromise remained hidden from public view. The justices asked the parties in *Brown* to brief the issue of what remedy the Court should order to rectify the constitutional violations it had found. Oral argument would take place in April 1955.

In the weeks following release of the first *Brown* decision, the Court extended the principle of racial equality into new territory by means of a series of *per curiam* decisions. These decisions, usually issued in summary fashion by the entire Court without a written opinion, ordered the admission of black students to the University of Florida and Louisiana State University. Subsequently, the Court abolished segregation in publicly owned amphitheaters, golf courses, and housing projects.[4] The summary decisions avoided any deeper discussion of whether federal law might guarantee access to places of public accommodation, such as private restaurants and hotels.

When the parties presented their arguments to the Court that spring, they recommended diametrically opposite remedies. The NAACP sought immediate implementation of the *Brown* ruling, while the school boards asserted that the Court should set no deadlines for their districts at all. The U.S. Department of Justice advocated a middle position: school districts that had intentionally segregated by race should be required to formulate desegregation plans "with all deliberate speed."

In conference, Chief Justice Warren and Justice Frankfurter voiced optimism that a gradual approach to desegregation, in conjunction with judicial sympathy for the position of white Southerners, would soon persuade moderate Southerners to embrace desegregation. Conversely, Justices Black and Douglas, who perhaps understood the South better, thought that the best course for the Court involved a clear articulation of the principle of racial equality under the Constitution. Because they thought the desegregation of Southern schools would take a decade or more, they opposed a gradualist decree. Eventually, the justices agreed to use gradualist language in the degree, and they also agreed that the complex and nuanced business of desegregating public schools would best be conducted at the district court level. Chief Justice Warren wanted to give the lower courts direction. "We should say something that will help the District Courts," he said. "We ought to give them guidance. It would be rather cruel to ship these (cases) back and let them flounder."

The Court's final decision in *Brown II*, a mere seven paragraphs long, gave local schools boards the primary responsibility for drafting school desegregation plans, subject to district court supervision. The Court ordered school districts that had intentionally segregated by race to formulate desegregation plans "with all deliberate speed," and in fashioning remedies, the lower federal courts would be "guided by traditional equitable principles."

In one of his briefs before the Court in the first round of the *Brown* case, Assistant Attorney General Lee Rankin used the phrase "deliberate speed."

He apparently borrowed it from Oliver Wendell Holmes' opinion in *Virginia v. West Virginia* (1918); Holmes, in turn, attributed the phrase to the language of English Chancery, but scholars (including Justice Felix Frankfurter) who attempted to find specific references to the phrase in British common law have encountered frustration. Richard Kluger argues that the phrase actually had its origins in Francis Thompson's 1893 poem, "The Hound of Heaven." In law, the phrase came to mean that one should move forward but without any expectation of a firm deadline for completion.

Under the framework of the *Brown II* decision, school districts that had practiced unlawful segregation faced the complex task of establishing nondiscriminatory schools. Broadly considered, this entailed making changes in district boundaries, transportation systems, personnel, curriculum, pupil assignments, and extracurricular activities.

By the spring of 1956, several states made significant progress. School districts in the West and Midwest planned to abandon their racial segregation policies, and a number of Border States, including Kentucky, Maryland, Missouri, North Carolina, and West Virginia, appeared to be phasing in the policy of desegregation in good faith. However, in the states of the Deep South a drumbeat of resistance against *Brown* began, including a rising tide of criticism against Earl Warren and his colleagues on the Supreme Court.

Opponents of *Brown* took several steps to obstruct it. In Virginia, several counties closed their public schools rather than desegregate, and in Tennessee and Delaware, violence broke out. Leading Southern politicians, including Senators Strom Thurmond, Sam Ervin, Harry Byrd, and Richard Russell, adopted a "Southern Manifesto," which declared the *Brown* decision "a clear abuse of judicial power." They promised to use "all lawful means to bring about a reversal of this decision which is contrary to the Constitution and to prevent the use of force in its implementation."

Eventually, over one hundred members of Congress endorsed the manifesto. Two states, Mississippi and South Carolina, amended their state constitutions to abolish public schools, and throughout the Deep South, White Citizens Councils and the Ku Klux Klan began campaigns of intimidation and violence to resist the movement toward racial equality. At their peak, the White Citizens Councils across the South attracted a membership approaching 250,000 persons.

Legally, the burden of implementing *Brown* fell on federal district courts, especially those in the South. Courageous judges such as John Minor Wisdom, Frank Johnson, and J. Skelly Wright faithfully enforced the *Brown* decision in the face of protracted opposition. Other federal judges in the South, who had been appointed through the political power of segregationist senators, did their utmost to resist integration. Among them was Judge John J. Parker, who wrote the original lower court opinion in the *Briggs v. Elliot* case (Clarendon County, South Carolina). During the remand of *Briggs*, Parker devised a narrow interpretation of *Brown* known as the "Briggs Dictum" that became the blueprint for how recalcitrant school districts could resist *Brown*.

Developing a distinction between integration and desegregation, Parker ruled that the Supreme Court only required school districts to refrain from denying any person admission to public schools on the basis of race. Under this narrow interpretation, school districts had no affirmative obligation to dismantle segregated schools. Instead, they could adopt "freedom of choice plans" and "transfer policies" that subtly perpetuated one-race schools. White parents whose children attended majority-minority schools could "petition out," and black parents who wanted their children to attend integrated schools had to "petition in." These individualized petitions expanded the discretion of administrators in overseeing the process of desegregation and made it easier to deny transfers based on allegedly nonracial factors such as behavior problems or lack of academic merit.

THE BACKLASH, 1956–1964

As the most important political leader in the United States during the 1950s, President Eisenhower did not welcome the *Brown* decision. Initially, when reporters asked about his views of the case, he replied that he was "duty-bound to accept it." However, he stopped far short of approval. "The Supreme Court has spoken, and I am sworn to uphold the constitutional processes in this country, and I am trying. I will obey," he said.

In later years, when reporters asked him about *Brown*, Eisenhower responded bluntly, saying, "You can't legislate morality." When he heard this comment, Dr. Martin Luther King Jr. issued a famous retort. Acknowledging that racial understanding was "ultimately an issue of conscience and morality," King said, "the purpose of law was to establish justice in the lesser realm of ordinary life."[5] Earl Warren became deeply frustrated with Eisenhower's unwillingness to endorse the cause of racial equality.

To Warren, the Republican Party stood for the emancipation of the slaves and the promise of the Reconstruction Amendments. On a personal level, Warren strongly admired Abraham Lincoln. Throughout most of his working life, he had hung a portrait of Abraham Lincoln on his office wall. His aides reported that during his time as Governor of California, whenever Warren faced difficult problems, they would find him alone in his office staring silently at Lincoln's portrait.

In the 1940s, under the influence of Edwin "Pat" Patterson and other black friends, Warren's support for civil rights grew. School desegregation and the later battles over civil rights pitted the principled and idealistic Earl Warren against pragmatic politicians such as Dwight Eisenhower and Richard Nixon. The future of the Republican Party lay in the balance.

In his *Memoirs*, Warren revealed his distaste for Eisenhower when it came to issues of racial justice. "I have always believed that President Eisenhower resented our decision in *Brown v. Board of Education* and its progeny," he wrote. Warren related an incident that occurred at a White House dinner shortly before the Court issued its decision in *Brown*. Warren sat to the immediate right of President Eisenhower, and John W. Davis, lead counsel for the state defendants in the *Brown* case, also sat at the table. During the meal, Eisenhower effusively praised Davis, and afterward, the President took Warren by the arm and spoke of the Southern states' efforts to preserve racial segregation. "These are not bad people," he said. "All they are concerned about is to see that their sweet little girls are not required to sit in school alongside some big overgrown Negroes."[6]

That incident, and the subsequent release of the Court's decision in *Brown*, strained relations between the two Republican leaders. At one point, Eisenhower publicly admitted that appointing Warren to the Supreme Court "was the worst damn fool mistake I ever made."[7]

In the political campaigns of 1956, candidates for public office in the Deep South vehemently opposed school desegregation. In Arkansas, Governor Orval Faubus faced Jim Johnson in the Democratic primary. Johnson had strong ties to the White Citizens Council, and both candidates adopted extremist views on desegregation issues. Faubus advocated interposition—a discredited legal doctrine that empowered states to oppose Supreme Court decisions on sovereignty grounds—and promised that no school district in the state would have to desegregate against its will. He won both the primary and the general election.

In the fall of 1957, the school board in Little Rock, Arkansas planned to desegregate Central High School by allowing nine black students, selected on the basis of academic achievement, to attend classes. On September 4, 1957, a hostile mob gathered outside the school to resist integration. Governor Faubus called out the National Guard to prevent the black students from entering the school. One of the students, Elizabeth Eckford, walked alone into a hostile mob, which beat and spat upon her.

Photos of Eckford's courageous stand made the national news and inspired calls for President Eisenhower to provide federal protection for the students. Eisenhower waffled and eventually met personally with Governor Faubus to urge him to remove the troops and allow the desegregation plan to move forward. Faubus returned to Little Rock and then callously ignored the President. He again ordered the National Guard to block the black students from attending Central High School.

On September 20, federal judge Ronald Davies ordered Governor Faubus to remove the troops. Little Rock Police Officers escorted the nine black students into the school through a side entrance. An ugly mob then attacked the school, and the nine students barely escaped. Three days later, President Eisenhower finally issued an order for the crowds to disperse and directed "an overwhelming force" of 1,000 troops from the 101st Airborne to protect the black students. At least some federal troops remained at Central High School for the remainder of the school year.

In May 1958, school officials filed a motion with the federal court seeking permission to delay the integration of Central High School for three years. Judge Harry Lemley granted the request, and the NAACP appealed his ruling, setting the stage for the legal battle known as *Cooper v. Aaron* (1958). The United States Court of Appeals for the Eighth Circuit overturned Judge Lemley's order, and the school board appealed to the Supreme Court. The Court expedited the appeal and heard the oral argument in special session on September 11, 1958.

During oral argument in *Cooper*, a heated exchange took place between Chief Justice Warren and Richard Butler, attorney for the Little Rock School Board. In the course of an argument based on Governor Faubus' policy of nullification, Butler contended that "if the governor of any state says that a United States Supreme Court decision is not the law of the land, the people of that state, until it is really resolved, have a doubt in their mind and a right to have a doubt." At that, Earl Warren countered, "I've never heard such an argument made in a court of justice before. And I've tried many a case, over many a year. I have never heard a lawyer say that the statement of a governor, as to what was legal or illegal, should control the action of any court."[8]

The very next day, the Court issued a *per curiam* opinion holding that the *Brown* decision represented the supreme law of the land and that the states must honor it. Faubus' nullification doctrine flew in the face of the Supremacy Clause of the federal constitution and lacked a foundation in the law. Warren badly wanted the Court's decision in *Cooper* to remain unanimous in order to reinforce the strength of its message to recalcitrant politicians like Governor Faubus. However, after signing the original decision, Justice Frankfurter issued a concurring opinion, in which he appealed to the humanitarian interests of attorneys and civic leaders of the South. "The Constitution does not require agreement," Frankfurter wrote. "But active obstruction or defiance is barred. The responsibility of those who exercise power in a democratic government is not to reflect inflamed public feeling but to help form its understanding."[9]

As a matter of law, the Supreme Court's *Cooper* decision cleared the way for the lower federal courts to review school desegregation plans without interference from state and local politicians. Yet as a matter of politics, the decision radicalized the South and virtually guaranteed that extremists who opposed desegregation would gain political power. In Little Rock, Governor Faubus ordered Central High School to shut down for the 1958–1959 school year, and the school remained closed until the fall of 1960.

In Alabama, incumbent Big Jim Folsom lost the 1958 gubernatorial election to former state Attorney General Jim Patterson. Folsom had adopted a moderate stance on racial issues in contrast to Patterson's segregationist position. Similar trends took place in Georgia, Louisiana, and South Carolina. In Arkansas, Mississippi, and Alabama, segregationists remained in control of the governors' offices for the next several years, as Faubus, Patterson, and (in Mississippi) H. Ross Barnett won their bids for reelection. They announced policies of "massive resistance" in the face of opposition from federal courts, and later, from civil rights activists.

One of the "massive resistance" strategies involved closing the public schools rather than desegregating them. In Virginia, the legislature cut off state funds for any school district that agreed to desegregate. This policy led to the closure of public schools in Norfolk and Charlottesville until parents voted to reopen the schools on a desegregated basis with the use of local funds. However, in Prince Edward County, site of one of the original challenges that became part of the *Brown* decision, public schools remained closed. In 1959, when Virginia Supreme Court of Appeals struck down the school-closure law under the Virginia Constitution,[10] the state legislature responded by passing a new statute that abolished compulsory attendance laws. The legislation made the operation of public schools a local option and provided tuition grants that students could use in attending (segregated) private schools.

By 1960, Prince Edward County was the only county in Virginia in which the public schools remained closed. For a five-year period between 1959 and 1964, white students in the county relied upon state and local tuition grants to attend segregated private academies, while black students remained largely uneducated. In a televised broadcast entitled "The Lost Class of 1959," CBS reporter Edward R. Murrow raised public awareness about these conditions.

In 1964, the Supreme Court accepted jurisdiction in the Prince Edward County case, *Griffin v. School Board*.[11] During oral argument, the school board's counsel, J. Segar Gravatt, asserted that responsibility for educating students belonged to state and local government, not the federal courts. This prompted Chief Justice Warren to respond that Prince Edward County had given black children the "freedom to go through life without an education."[12]

The Court held that Prince Edward County had violated the equal protection clause when it closed its public schools and appropriated public funds to send white children to segregated private academies. Writing for a 7–2 majority, Justice Black noted, "There has been entirely too much deliberation and not enough speed in enforcing the constitutional rights which we held in *Brown v. Board of Education* had been denied Prince Edward County children."[13]

Other state legislatures in the Deep South also adopted the massive resistance strategy of closing the public schools rather than submitting to desegregation. These included Georgia and Louisiana. However, parents in Atlanta and New Orleans desperately wanted the public schools to stay open, and school officials in these jurisdictions eventually decided to adopt watered-down "freedom of choice" plans that kept white students largely where they were and offered only a limited number of transfers to black students.

By 1964, ten years after the original *Brown* decision, 98% of black students in the South still attended all-black schools.[14] In part, the delay arose because the Supreme Court failed to confront the inadequacies of the Briggs Dictum. The Court refrained from taking this step because it wanted Congress and the President to enforce the *Brown* decision. Eventually, after civil rights activists conducted direct actions in the South and following President Kennedy's assassination, Congress passed the 1964 Civil Rights Act and the 1965 Elementary and Secondary Education Act. These statutes cut off federal funds for school districts that maintained dual systems of education in violation of the *Brown* decision, and they precipitated change in the South.

In the meantime, valuable time had been lost, and the opponents of school integration—including Dixiecrats and conservative Republicans—worked tirelessly to obstruct the *Brown* decision through a seemingly endless series of legal and political countermeasures. Finally, in 1966, Judge John Minor Wisdom of the Fifth Circuit U.S. Court of Appeals filled the vacuum in Supreme Court oversight by issuing a stinging attack on Judge Parker's Briggs Dictum. In his opinion in *U.S. v. Jefferson County Board of Education* (1966), Wisdom stressed that school boards in the South had an affirmative obligation to dismantle their segregated systems. He wrote:

> *Briggs,* decided only six weeks after *Brown II,* is one of the earliest cases in this field of law. The portion of the opinion most quoted is pure dictum. *Briggs* did not paraphrase the law as the Supreme Court stated it in *Brown* or as the law must be stated today in the light of *Aaron v. Cooper* . . . . These and other decisions compel states in this circuit to take affirmative action to reorganize their school systems by integrating the students, faculties, facilities, and activities.[15]

Judge Wisdom continued:

> We do not minimize the importance of the Fourteenth Amendment rights of an individual, but there was more at issue in *Brown* than the controversy between certain schools and certain children. *Briggs* overlooks the fact that Negroes collectively are harmed when the state, by law or custom, operates segregated schools or a school system with uncorrected effects of segregation.

> Denial of access to the dominant culture, lack of opportunity in any meaningful way to participate in political and other public activities, the stigma of apartheid condemned in the Thirteenth Amendment are concomitants of the dual educational system. The unmalleable fact transcending in importance the harm to individual Negro children is that the separate school system was an integral element in the Southern State's general program to restrict Negroes as a class from participation in the life of the community, the affairs of the State, and the mainstream of American life: Negroes must keep their place.[16]

In its last two major school desegregation decisions, the Warren Court accepted Judge Wisdom's rationale by rejecting the subterfuge of "freedom of choice" plans where school boards could not show that such plans had been effective in dismantling dual educational systems. Further, the Court abandoned its own "all deliberate speed" doctrine. In *Green v. County School Board* (1968), the Court emphasized that school boards had the burden of making a transition to a unitary, nondiscriminatory system. "The burden on a school board today is to come forward with a plan that promises realistically to work, and promises realistically to work *now*," Justice Brennan wrote. Where "freedom of choice" plans left schools with the vestiges of their dual systems, these plans were simply not effective. By focusing on segregated schools as systems, the Court emphasized the importance of six factors, including facilities, staff, faculty, extracurricular activities, transportation, and student assignments. All would have to be desegregated in order to eliminate racial discrimination "root and branch."

Then in *Alexander v. Holmes County Board of Education* (1969), the Court abandoned the "all deliberate speed" rule, holding that segregated schools must immediately terminate their dual systems and operate only on a unitary basis. This decision, in conjunction with the threat of the loss of federal funds under the 1964 Civil Rights Act, led to significant improvements in racial integration in Southern schools. In 1968, 25% of all black students in the South enrolled in schools with white majorities, and in 1972, this percentage exceeded 36%.[17] By the early 1970s, the South had the most integrated schools in the United States. As education policy researcher Gary Orfield and his colleagues have documented, with the increase in integrated schools came a decrease in the black-white academic achievement gap.[18]

Professor Michael J. Klarman[19] correctly argues that the *Brown* decision radicalized southern politics. During the latter half of the 1950s, segregationists used opposition to *Brown* as a means of gaining power across the Deep South, and they adopted policies of massive resistance. These policies delayed the implementation of *Brown* significantly, but they also had the effect of inciting greater levels of violence against civil rights protestors who conducted peaceful direct action initiatives on the streets of the South in the 1960s. The savage attacks that extremists used against civil rights protestors, in turn, increased public support for racial reform. These events, which will be examined at greater length in chapter 9, highlight the importance of Warren Court's *Brown* decision in the chain of events that transformed American racial relations in the short span of fifteen years.

THE SOCIAL MEANING OF *BROWN*

In the aftermath of the *Brown* decision, conservative legal scholars attacked what they saw as the failure of the Court to ground its decision in the tradition of constitutional law. Initially, the assault focused on alleged weaknesses in the NAACP's social science evidence. Ernst Van den Haag[20] and A. James Gregor[21] contended that the Kenneth Clark's doll experiments did not control for noneducational factors such as neighborhood peer groups or religious institutions that may have contributed to negative self-concepts among black children. Others assailed the Warren Court for failing to ground the school desegregation decisions in neutral principles of constitutional law that transcended the immediate result in any given case.[22]

Defenders of the Warren Court took issue with these positions. Barton J. Bernstein[23] argued that the *Plessy* decision itself rested on faulty social assumptions: Justice Henry Billings Brown, author of *Plessy*, failed to offer even a scintilla of social evidence for his opinion, which rejected the proposition that "the enforced separation of the two races stamps the colored race with a badge of inferiority." In an influential essay, Charles L. Black, Jr. [24] asserted that the true basis of *Brown* lay not in the social science evidence but in the imperative of placing blacks and whites on an equal footing. Jim Crow segregation systematically excluded blacks from the economic, political, and educational advantages of American life, Black asserted, and thus kept them in an inferior position.

Social theorists also studied the meaning and impact of the school desegregation decisions. In a thoughtful essay about how school children learn about *Brown*, Professor Diana E. Hess summarizes this literature well.[25] She identifies four competing schools of thought concerning the school desegregation decisions, the "rightful icon," "liberation referent," "well-intentioned error," and "unfulfilled promise" positions. [26] Each is associated with the work of one or more leading scholars, and taken together the various schools provide a useful framework for evaluating alternative perspectives on *Brown*.

The "rightful icon" school asserts that "the Court did the right thing, at the right time, and for the right reasons," [27] and it represents the dominant way instructors cover *Brown* in the classroom. This school includes NAACP attorneys such as Thurgood Marshall and Jack Greenberg who, thinking in legal terms, saw the *Brown* decision as ending the legitimacy of the Jim Crow system. To them, *Brown* deserved iconic status because it cut the racial caste system from its constitutional moorings, and they celebrated this important accomplishment. Author Louis Lomax expresses the exultation black Americans felt the day the Court announced its decision in *Brown*:

> It would be impossible for a white person to understand what happened within black breasts on that Monday. An ardent segregationist has called it 'Black Monday.' He was so right, but for reasons other than the ones he advances: That was the day we won; the day we took the white man's laws and won our case before an all-white Supreme Court with a Negro lawyer, Thurgood Marshall, as our chief counsel. And we were proud . . . .[28]

But there are other points of view. A second position, which Hess labels the "*Brown* as liberation referent" school, stresses the role of the school desegregation decisions in inspiring other oppressed groups to petition the courts to extend civil and constitutional rights. For example, over the past fifty years organizations such as the National Council of La Raza, the League of United Latin American Citizens, the National Organization of Women, and National Gay and Lesbian Task Force successfully have used the courts in the fight for legal equality. Advocates of the "liberation" position contend that Warren Court precedents involving discrimination against discrete and insular minorities (e.g., *Brown*) and the right to privacy in matters of intimate relations (e.g., *Griswold v. Connecticut*) provided a broad framework for the extension of human rights in later decades.

The "*Brown* as well-intentioned error" school consists of scholars who view the school desegregation decisions as creating more symbolic and tangible benefits for the white community than for blacks. Derrick A. Bell (1991; 2000) argues that *Brown* improved America's reputation for fairness and racial equality at a time when the struggle against international communism made it important for the United States to win the hearts and minds of persons in the developing world. Indeed, Warren himself played a key role as a good will ambassador in India and East Asia during the 1950s. Bell also argues that black students would have been better off if the Court had accepted South Carolina's plan for the construction of new black schools that would be mirror images of white schools. Bell's position assumes the good faith of southern states in fulfilling their promises about equal funding for schools, a historically dubious proposition. His argument also assumes that in the absence of state good faith, the Court would have been effective in mandating and overseeing the redistribution of educational resources.

The final school, designated as the "*Brown* as unfulfilled promise" position, corresponds most closely with the argument presented in the current book. Scholars in this school endorse the integrationist goals of the *Brown* decision, but they criticize the failure of courts, school boards, and American citizens generally to abide by the letter and spirit of the school desegregation decisions. Writers Jonathan Kozol and Gary Orfield express concern about the growing resegregation of American schools. They stress the role that the Burger and Rehnquist Courts have played in ending federal court supervision of unequal public schools in such decisions as *Rodriguez v. San Antonio Independent School District* (1974), *Milliken v. Bradley* (1974), and *Missouri v. Jenkins* (1995).

Orfield sharply criticizes what he sees as the ideologically driven nature of recent Supreme Court school desegregation decisions.[29] He argues that courts need to be more mindful of empirical studies showing the harm that racial and economic isolation does to minority students in "re-segregated" inner-city schools, as well as the benefits of attending school in integrated settings. Students educated in isolated inner-cities confront an array of problems including academically underprepared peer groups, under-qualified instructors, dysfunctional family and neighborhood environments, and an increased incidence of serious behavioral and health problems. In contrast, according to Orfield's research, students of color who attend racially and economically integrated schools often reach higher levels of learning and academic attainment.

Orfield also criticizes the conservative "white flight" hypothesis. According to this hypothesis, demographic factors such as white flight overshadow discriminatory state action as the proximate cause of racially isolated schools. Orfield contends that the pattern of white migration to the suburbs began long before the Supreme Court issued its *Brown* decision and has continued long afterward. His empirical studies make it difficult to argue that a causal relationship exists between court-ordered desegregation and white flight.

Given the intense concentration of minority students in urban areas and the large number of whites in the suburbs, Orfield concludes that the only feasible means of integrating racial minorities into white schools involves a broadly based, metropolitan, and "inter-district" school desegregation plan. This approach has proved successful in a number of cities throughout the nation. Unfortunately, however, the Supreme Court in the 1970s prohibited school districts from adopting metropolitan-wide school desegregation plans in the absence of proof that suburban school boards violated the law.

The tension between optimistic perceptions of *Brown* evident in the "iconic" and "liberation" positions and the pessimistic overtones of the "well-intentioned error" and "unfulfilled promise" schools mirrors similar trends in public opinion about school desegregation. To optimists, *Brown* symbolizes the ability of a downtrodden people to use the courts to achieve significant social change. The decision contains an intriguing cast of characters, a moral story of good versus evil, and a court that took the high road to uphold the claims of the underdog. To pessimists, *Brown* may be more symbol than substance.

A 2004 Gallup poll suggests that Americans view the social implications of Brown from profoundly different perspectives. Ninety percent of the respondents in the sample agreed that educational opportunities for black children have improved since 1954.[30] Yet when the Gallup researchers asked a follow-up question about educational parity and race, they discovered a significant gap between white and black respondents. When asked whether they agreed with the statement that black children have not achieved educational parity with whites, 68% of the black respondents agreed with the assertion, whereas only 34% of whites did. The majority of whites apparently perceived the problem of *de jure* segregation as a historical artifact, whereas most blacks contended that the problem of racial apartheid in American schools continues in new form. In fact, many poor students of color are educated in isolated settings, but their isolation is primarily the result of economics and class, not law. For these students, it may be a distinction without a difference.

The many conflicting perspectives regarding the meaning of the school desegregation cases reveal important truths about political ideology in the United States. They expose a basic contradiction between America's rhetorical commitment to a substantively fair society and the hard individual and collective effort needed to achieve a just social order. Competing social agendas make it difficult to strike a balance between the demands of a capitalist market economy and the constitutional principle of racial equality. Just as a capitalist society must reward individual initiative and achievement, so must a fair society remedy the contemporary effects of past discrimination and maintain stable and functioning communities that offer equal opportunities for upward mobility. To its credit, the Warren Court raised these issues in an open and groundbreaking dialogue with the American public, but the difficult path toward racial equality shows that its work in many respects remains incomplete.

The various perspectives on *Brown* also reveal differences in the body politic concerning judicial activism and the appropriate role of the Supreme Court in framing public policy. As scholars and jurists debate the appropriate level of deference courts should give to majoritarian political institutions that ignore long-standing injustices perpetrated against ethnic, religious, or political minorities, the role of value choices in the framing and administration of constitutional law becomes paramount. The science of law contains a healthy measure of the art of politics, and the process of constitutional adjudication necessarily involves value choices about the interpretation of precedents and the weighing of contrary interests.

In arriving at final decisions, especially in major cases like those involving school desegregation, the justices follow their sense of what the needs of the country are. In *Brown*, the Court unanimously rejected the constraints of a rigid caste system. In their own moderate way, the justices legitimized the struggle against colonialism, apartheid, and second-class citizenship that people of color waged across the world in the 1950s and 1960s. In this sense, the Court's decision followed the tide of history.

In the end, many social and political forces influenced the evolution of school desegregation policies in the United States, both during Warren's tenure on the Court and in the period following his passing. Presidential candidates, community activists, and—ultimately—the American people themselves all would have their say. As conservatives gained control of the Supreme Court during the last three decades of the twentieth century, the Court gradually abandoned its effort to achieve racial balance in school districts with a history of *de jure* segregation. The concluding chapter of this book offers an analysis and critique of these trends.

Today, nearly sixty years after the school desegregation decisions, the legacy of *Brown* is still unfolding. The Court's decisions in this area of the law mean different things to different people, and, as recent studies suggest, segregation in American schools by race and income remains an unmet challenge. According to a 2012 report from the Civil Rights Project at the University of California, Los Angeles, based on data from the U.S. Department of Education, 80% of Latino students and 74% of black students attend schools where the majority of students are not white. Conversely, white students generally attend schools in which approximately 75% of their peers are white.[31] Based on these statistics, racial isolation in American schools remains as much of a problem today as it was in 1954.

As morally justifiable as the *Brown* decision was, it inevitably raised important questions about the limits of judicial authority in a constitutional democracy. How far could unelected judges go in creating a new vision for American society before they undermined respect for the law and induced widespread noncompliance?

The intransigence of white supremacists and their elected allies in the aftermath of *Brown* presented one answer to this question. As long as the Supreme Court stood alone, without the support of the political branches of federal and state governments or even professional associations such as the American Bar Association, it remained on uncertain ground.

In his *Memoirs*, Earl Warren devoted many pages to this issue. He expressed disappointment in the American Bar Association and the Eisenhower Administration for failing to support the Court.[32] In many respects, during the first nine years of the *Brown* regime, the Court remained isolated, without the support of leading politicians or mainstream professional organizations. Nevertheless, as the interest group that had spawned the *Brown* decision, the NAACP did not rest on its laurels. From the very beginning, its struggle against segregated schools involved grassroots political organizing. As one of the leading civil rights advocates of his generation, Thurgood

Marshall realized that courts alone could not achieve the cultural and civic revolution that the NAACP had in mind. In an interview with the *New York Times* on January 3, 1960, Marshall stated, "I consider the lawsuits to be a holding action, a way of getting things open so that they can operate. But the final solution will only be when the Negro takes his part in the community, voting and otherwise."

The next phase of the movement for racial equality would address these issues in a broader context, involving an expansive, grassroots-driven agenda that included access to public accommodations, voting rights, and fair housing.

In retrospect, the school desegregation decisions posed a great dilemma for the justices as they determined whether to attempt a sweeping transformation of American society by means of legal pronouncements. The power of judicial review gives unelected federal judges the ability to decide, under the rubric of constitutional adjudication, major political, economic, and social questions of fundamental importance to the American people. Throughout its history, the Court often has pursued a policy of self-restraint, which has minimized its conflicts with the political branches. Only rarely—as in the *Dred Scott* decision in the 1850s or in the conflict between the Four Horsemen and President Roosevelt during the New Deal—have the Court's decisions sparked major political unrest. As the institution that comes closest to being a neutral, disinterested voice in American politics, the Supreme Court insisted on compliance with the moral principle of equality at a time when politicians of both parties, in the interest of gaining reelection, refused to act.

The late Archibald Cox, Professor of Law at Harvard and former Solicitor General of the United States, once observed, "Law, to command consent, must deserve it." If public opinion is any measure, Earl Warren's vision of the law as reflected in *Brown* passes the test. According to Gallup polls, in 1954, 40% of the American public approved of the *Brown* decision; in 1961, 63% did, and by 1994, 87% supported it.[33] Today, most legal scholars view *Brown* as a legitimate decision, which, in the words of Professor Michael Perry, "is generally thought to represent the Court at its best."[34]

NOTES

1. Container 1150, Original Conference Notes, December 12, 1953, William O. Douglas Papers, Manuscript Division, Library of Congress, Washington, D.C.

2. Barnum, "The Supreme Court and Public Opinion," 652, 657 12n.; see also A. Wade Smith, "Tolerance of School Desegregation," *Social Forces* 59, no. 4 (1981): 1256–74.

3. Justice Black's remarks during the Court's April 16, 1955 conference in *Brown II*, together with the descriptions of all of the Justices' comments from this conference

contained in the current Chapter, are necessarily impressionistic. They are based upon the conference notes of Chief Justice Warren and Justices Burton, Douglas, and Jackson available in the Library of Congress. See Container 574, Segregation Cases, Earl Warren Papers, Manuscript Division, Library of Congress, Washington, D.C.; Container 244, Segregation Cases, 16 Apr. 1955, Harold H. Burton Papers, Manuscript Division, Library of Congress, Washington, D.C.; Containers 1149 and 1150, Segregation Cases, William O. Douglas Papers, Manuscript Division, Library of Congress, Washington, D.C.; and Container 184, Legal File, Robert Houghwout Jackson Papers, Manuscript Division, Library of Congress, Washington, D.C. See also, Klarman, *From Jim Crow to Civil Rights*, 314, 49n. and 50n; *The Supreme Court in Conference (1940–1985): The Private Discussions Behind Nearly 300 Supreme Court Decisions*, ed. Del Dickson (New York: Oxford University Press, 2001; and Nina Totenberg's Series on *Brown v. Board of Education*, as broadcast on National Public Radio's *All Things Considered*, December 8, 9, and 10, 2003, available at http://www.npr.org/templates/story/story.php?storyId=1537409.

4. For further discussion of these cases, including citation, see Chapter 9, note 4.

5. Quoted in Taylor Branch, *Parting the Waters: America in the King Years, 1954–1963* (New York: Simon and Schuster, 1989), 213.

6. Warren, *Memoirs*, 291.

7. Quoted in Todd S. Purdum, "Presidents, Picking Justices, Can Have Backfires," *New York Times*, July 5, 2005.

8. A tape recording of the oral argument in *Cooper v. Aaron* is available at http://www.oyez.org/cases/1950–1959/1958/1958_1.

9. 358 U.S. 1, 24 (1958)(Frankfurter, J., concurring).

10. *Harrison v. Day*, 200 Va. 439, 106 S.E.2d 636 (1959).

11. 377 U.S. 218 (1964).

12. Quoted in Peter Irons, *Jim Crow's Children*, 193.

13. 377 U.S. 218, 229.

14. Gary Orfield and Erica Frankenberg, "Reviving Brown v. Board of Education: How Courts and Enforcement Agencies Can Produce More Integrated Schools," in Rhode and Ogletree, *Brown at 50*, 189.

15. 372 F.2d 836, 862 (1966).

16. Ibid., 866.

17. Quoted in Gary Orfield and Erica Frankenberg, "Reviving Brown v. Board of Education: How Courts and Enforcement Agencies Can Produce More Integrated Schools," in Rhode and Ogletree, *Brown at 50*, 191.

18. Ibid., 187.

19. Klarman, *From Jim Crow to Civil Rights.*

20. Ernest Van den Haag, "Social Science Testimony in the Desegregation Cases," 6 *Villanova L. Rev.* 69 (1960).

21. A. James Gregor, "The Law, Social Science, and School Segregation: An Assessment," 14 *Case W. Res. L. Rev.* 626 (1963).

22. Herbert Wechsler, "Toward Neutral Principles of Constitutional Law," 73 *Harvard L. Rev.* 1 (1959).

23. Barton J. Bernstein, "*Plessy v. Ferguson*: Conservative Sociological Jurisprudence," *Journal of Negro History* 48, no. 3 (July, 1963): 196–205.

24. Charles L. Black, Jr., "The Lawfulness of the Segregation Decisions," 69 *Yale L.J.* 421 (1960).

25. Diana E. Hess, "Brown as a Classroom Icon," in Cushman and Urofsky, *Black, White, and Brown,* 275–95.

26. Hess also identifies a fifth school known as the "*Brown* as irrelevant" school, which I address in Chapter 9.

27. Hess, "Brown as a Classroom Icon," 280.

28. Quoted in Simon, *In His Own Image*, 29 (see Chapter 2, note 10).

29. See e.g., Gary Orfield and Hohn T. Yun. "Resegregation in American Schools" (Cambridge, MA: The Civil Rights Project, Harvard University, 1999), available at http://www. civilrightsproject. harvard. edu/research/deseg/reseg_schools99. php.

30. Gallup Poll, April 27, 2004, see http://www.gallup.com/poll/11521/race-education. The survey was based on interviews with 3,017 adults; it was subject to a margin of error of ± 2% and a 95% confidence level.

31. "Civil Rights Project Reports Deepening Segregation & Challenges Educators & Political Leaders to Develop Positive Policies," available at http://civilrightsproject.ucla.edu/news/press-releases/crp-press-releases-2012/civil-rights-project-reports-deepening-segregation-and-challenges-educators-and-political-leaders-to-develop-positive-policies/. See also, "American Schools Still Heavily Segregated By Race, Income: Civil Rights Project Report," *Huffington Post*, September 20, 2012, available at http://www.huffingtonpost.com/2012/09/20/american-schools-still-he_n_1901583.html.

32. See Warren, *Memoirs*, 319, 330.

33. Julie Ray, "Reflections on the 'Trouble in Little Rock,'" Part II. March 4, 2003 at Gallup.com.

34. Michael J. Perry, *The Constitution, the Courts and Human Rights: An Inquiry into the Legitimacy of Constitutional Policymaking by the Judiciary* (New Haven: Yale University Press, 1982), 1.

Chapter 8

The Super Chief

In the 1956 term, Warren framed his identity as a jurist. In his first two years on the Supreme Court, Warren stood in the shadow of Felix Frankfurter. Especially in cases involving federalism and the rights of suspects, the two justices voted in favor of the states and pursued the philosophy of judicial restraint. Beginning in the 1956 term, Warren gravitated toward liberals Hugo Black and William O. Douglas in freedom of expression, criminal justice, and anti-trust cases. By the end of the 1961 term, the Warren Court issued major decisions protecting the rights of political dissidents and granting federal courts the power to review legislative apportionment cases. Statistics shed light on Warren's transformation from a protégé of Felix Frankfurter to a reliable member of the Court's liberal wing. In his first year on the Court, Warren opposed Justice Black in twenty-two cases. However, by his third year, Warren sided with Black in all but two decisions.

Warren's metamorphosis reflects the importance of interpersonal interaction in the development of his political and legal thought. Warren's leadership style as Chief Justice featured frequent informal meetings with colleagues, either in their chambers or over lunch. His colleagues recall receiving telephone calls from the Chief, in which Warren would say, "I've a point to check with you. May I come over?"[1] Warren's collaborative style affected both his tactical and social leadership of the Court. In his informal meetings, he discussed the development of legal doctrine and shared preliminary thoughts on case selection and case assignments. Given Warren's admitted weaknesses in legal scholarship, especially during his first few years on the Court, this approach had merit.

Warren's opinion in the *Brown* case showed that he had a gift for expressing dry legal concepts in engaging language that everyday people could understand. As a result, he became widely sought as a speaker. Beginning in the 1955–1956 term, he gradually spent more time in the public spotlight, speaking at law schools, writing essays for popular journals, and conducting official visits abroad. The speaking and writing engagements offered opportunities for reflection.

In November of 1955, Warren published a popular essay in *Fortune* magazine in which he speculated on the challenges that the American legal system might face in the coming generation. In his essay, he expressed his own developing philosophy of law as well as his thoughts on the growing resistance to the school desegregation decisions. In one passage, he wrote:

> In all times and places (man) has had a sense of justice and a desire for justice. Any child expresses this fact of nature with his first judgment that this or that "isn't fair." A legal system is simply a mature and sophisticated attempt, never perfected but always capable of improvement, to institutionalize this sense of justice and to free men from the terror and unpredictability of arbitrary force. Unfortunately, the same human nature that craves justice and freedom under law is too often willing to deny them to others. Thus the struggle for law is never-ending, and our generation is inevitably engaged in it.[2]

Warren's insight that fairness and freedom from arbitrary force form the core of progressive legal systems highlights the role that morality played in his approach to the law. He advanced the proposition that law must openly embrace equity and fairness, even as others criticized him for issuing legal decisions that they found too simplistic and result-oriented. Warren's remarks provide a veiled yet accurate characterization of American society in the 1950s. One side of human nature—the civil rights movement—sought to secure constitutional rights for black citizens; the other side—the forces of massive resistance—sought to deny these rights to others. The problem of inequality loomed large in Warren's worldview. As he matured intellectually, Warren stressed the importance of inclusion, freedom of political expression, and ending discrimination.

Warren's enhanced public profile included an international dimension. During the Court's summer recess of 1956, as Earl and Nina traveled to Europe, Secretary of State John Foster Dulles contacted them to ask if they would be willing to alter their travel plans because the government of India had invited them for an official visit. The Warrens accepted the invitation and immediately left on a 17-day speaking tour of India. Their journey took them to Bombay, Delhi, Calcutta, and Utter Pradesh, the most populous region of India.

The Indian people showed a keen interest in the *Brown* decision. On the day the Court released its decision, the Voice of America provided extensive radio coverage of the case in South Asia, and the U.S. Information Agency widely disseminated published reports about it in a campaign to improve the international image of the United States during the Cold War. The school desegregation cases struck a chord in a country that had its own legacy of discrimination.

Wherever they went, the Warrens encountered cheering crowds. In a ceremony at Delhi University, Warren received an honorary degree, and he spoke before a large audience. The Vice Chancellor of the University later remembered, Warren "rose to fame in 28 minutes of that Monday afternoon as he read out his momentous decision outlawing segregation in American public schools."[3]

Back at home, *Life* magazine featured a story on the Warrens' visit to India, which included photographs of Earl and Nina as they rode a beautifully adorned elephant. Other photos featured them greeting throngs of villagers in Utter Pradesh and preparing to address the Supreme Court of India.[4] The trip built political support for a series of legislative reforms designed to protect the fundamental rights of members of the former untouchable class in India.[5]

Warren later joined a human rights project known as "World Peace through the Rule of Law." In 1966, he gave an address to the organization's leaders in Athens, Greece. There, he called for the creation of an international court with jurisdiction to enforce judgments on issues of human rights and international law. In his address, he also praised the ancient Greek political leader, Solon. Using words that he often repeated in other venues, Warren remarked that approximately 2,500 years ago someone asked Solon how justice could be achieved in Athens. Solon's answer, in substance, was that it would occur when those who were not injured by injustice were as outraged as those who had been. It was a timely and appropriate reference.

THE PUBLIC FACE OF EARL WARREN, 1954–1962

Earl Warren was an intensely private person, and given the Court's heavy workload, he spent most evenings at home burning the midnight oil. His strained relations with President Eisenhower and Vice President Nixon meant that he and Nina spent relatively little time at official White House functions during the Eisenhower era.

Warren's family occupied the core of his social life. Following his appointment as Chief Justice, his daughters Virginia and Dorothy moved from California to the D.C. area, and in 1960, Virginia married John Charles Daly, host of the popular television game show, "What's My Line?" She later worked for the Supreme Court Historical Society, assembling biographical and archival materials.

Twice a year, at Christmas and over the summer, the Warrens returned to California, which they always considered their home. They held family

Christmas dinners at their friend Ben Swig's Fairmont Hotel in the fashionable Nob Hill neighborhood of San Francisco. In later years, they celebrated Christmas at Jim Warren's vineyards in the Napa Valley. Other members of the family lived nearby: Earl Junior in Sacramento, Honey Bear in Beverly Hills, and Robert in the Davis area. The family remained close even though they resided at opposite ends of the country.

In his *Memoirs*, Warren wrote that he deliberately avoided cocktail parties in Washington, D.C. because he believed that justices should refrain from voicing their opinions in informal settings, where surreptitious reporters might overhear them. "I cut off all connection with the members of the press who had been so friendly with me through the years, and refrained from all public discussions," he stated.[6]

Of equal importance, Nina disliked cocktail parties. "For years in Washington, I received at least one invitation a day to a cocktail party and sometimes two or three," Warren continued. "I went to none. My wife never drank and did not like cocktail parties, so that was not a grave deprivation for us."[7]

Journalist Drew Pearson's "Washington Merry-Go-Round" broadcasts provide occasional glimpses into the Warrens' limited appearances at official White House functions. Warren's quick-witted comebacks at parties often made good copy. In one incident, the White House hosted a dinner in his honor, and Mrs. Cora Clarkson entered into a conversation with the Chief Justice. Mrs. Clarkson, who had just returned from visiting the Charles Englehard gold mines in South Africa, asked Warren if he had ever known a girl prettier than Jane Englehard. Without batting an eye, Warren responded, "Yes, I married one."[8]

Perhaps the most famous controversy that arose from Warren's appearances at social functions occurred in the fall of 1959 when he got into an intense argument with *New York Herald Tribune* journalist Earl Mazo at a party. Mazo had just released a biography of Richard Nixon, and portions of it had appeared in *Look* magazine. In his book, Mazo examined an incident in the 1950 race for U.S. Senate in California when Republican candidate Richard Nixon had unsuccessfully sought an endorsement from Governor Warren. Warren disagreed with Mazo's interpretation of the episode.

Although Warren would later deny it, press reports indicated he called Mazo "a damned liar" at the party. "You are just trying to promote the presidential candidacy of Nixon. . . . I don't care what you write about Nixon as long as you don't try to build him up over my body," Warren shouted. "I don't like it when you use me, when you use this book to step on my head—to go over my body to promote Nixon." Raising his arms with his wrists together as if he were in handcuffs, Warren then exploded, "You people are persecuting me because you know I can't strike back."[9]

The host of the party, Barnet Nover, diplomatically ushered the two men into a side room, where they continued their discussion for several more minutes. They emerged on speaking terms.

As this incident shows, Warren still harbored bitter feelings toward Nixon. The conflict between them appeared to have reached a crescendo at the 1952 Republican Convention, but the wound still had not healed. In 1957, the American Bar Association invited Warren to speak at its summer meeting in London. After Warren accepted the offer, the ABA also wanted to extend an invitation to Vice President Nixon. Warren vetoed the idea, writing David Maxwell, then president of the ABA, "If you let that fellow in, count me out."[10] The ABA board decided not to invite Nixon.

Warren's antipathy toward Nixon lasted until his final days, and it illustrates Warren's dualistic, "light vs. dark" orientation toward political conflict. Whether his opponent took the form of Nixon, the defense attorneys in the *Point Lobos* case, or California Governor Culbert Olson, Warren responded to adversity on an intensely personal level. He rarely seemed to forgive or forget the affronts of the past. Instead, political adversity appeared to spark his personal ambition.

In contrast, in the period since the 1952 election, Nixon had assumed a subordinate role to President Eisenhower and gained important insights into both global politics and the nature of the presidency itself. Eisenhower assigned Nixon and Secretary of State John Foster Dulles as the administration's principal spokespersons on American foreign policy. Nixon traveled widely to Southeast Asia, Africa, South America, and the U.S.S.R. and became one of the most active vice presidents in the nation's history. In pursuit of the administration's policy of containing communism, he developed working relationships with foreign leaders as well as ties with American corporate and military leaders. In the 1954 midterm electoral campaigns, he appeared frequently on behalf of GOP candidates, but in the end the Republican Party stumbled badly in the face of Democratic victories in congressional and gubernatorial races throughout the country.

Following his massive heart attack in September 1955, President Eisenhower considered dropping Nixon from the 1956 ticket and replacing him with Deputy Secretary of Defense Robert Anderson, or with Chief Justice Warren. In the spring of 1956, Warren issued a public statement in which he denied any interest in resigning from the Court in order to run for political office. Eisenhower eventually decided to keep Nixon as his running mate. They won the 1956 presidential campaign, yet again the GOP failed to gain control of Congress. The recession of 1957 led to a further erosion in the performance of GOP candidates in the midterm 1958 elections. The GOP selected Nixon as its presidential candidate in the 1960 campaign, but Eisenhower worked behind the scenes in an unsuccessful effort to persuade Robert

Anderson to enter the race. Ike never seemed wholly convinced that Nixon would make a suitable president.

During the campaign, Nixon ran as a moderate on the issue of civil rights. In an address on school desegregation in August 1960, he asserted, "Law alone, while necessary, is not the answer to the problems of human rights."[11] Nixon benefited from his success in breaking the filibuster of the 1957 Civil Rights Act in the U.S. Senate, but he lost vital support among black voters by failing to speak out against the conviction of Dr. Martin Luther King Jr. for conducting a sit-in at an Atlanta lunch counter. For his act of civil disobedience and an outstanding driver's license violation, the trial court sentenced King to four months at hard labor at a Georgia State Prison camp. Several days later, John Kennedy phoned Coretta Scott King offering support, and Robert Kennedy contacted the trial judge to inquire about King's right to bail. That afternoon, the judge released King on a $2,000 appeal bond. For his part, Nixon took no steps to address the controversy or assist King. Presumably, Nixon remained silent because he did not want to alienate Southern whites.

In late September, Nixon faced the charismatic John Kennedy in the nation's first televised presidential debate, a forum that exaggerated the appearance of the candidates over the substance of what they had to say. To the television audience, Kennedy appeared relaxed and suntanned from his recent open-car campaigns in California, whereas Nixon looked haggard and gaunt. Nixon had suffered a knee injury at a campaign stop several weeks previously, and he eventually spent time in the hospital with a serious hemolytic staph infection. Not even "Lazy Shave" cosmetic treatments designed to hide his five o'clock shadow worked well in the bright stage lights. Radio audiences thought Nixon won the debate, but television audiences overwhelmingly disagreed.

In the weeks leading up to Election Day, President Eisenhower finally campaigned actively for Nixon, narrowing the race. However, when a reporter asked what major idea Nixon had contributed that was adopted into policy during the eight years of the Eisenhower administration, Ike unhelpfully responded, "Give me a week and I might think of one." Kennedy won the 1960 presidential election by a margin of only 118,550 votes out of almost 69 million votes cast. The heavy turnout of black voters for Kennedy may have been decisive.

Nixon chose not to challenge the results in court. Nevertheless, he apparently believed that Kennedy's victory was fraudulent. At a party he gave in December 1960, he reportedly greeted his guests by saying, "We won but they stole it from us."[12] Be this as it may, other factors clearly came into play in Nixon's loss, including Eisenhower's tepid support, running mate Henry Cabot Lodge's weak contributions to the campaign, Nixon's poor performance in the first debate, and the recent decline in the economy. For the country itself, the close campaign laid the foundation for deepening political divisions that linger today. Nixon researchers Tom Wicker[13] and Rick Perlstein[14] have argued that the razor-thin presidential election of 1960 in conjunction with later events involving racial unrest, antiwar demonstrations, and cultural upheaval precipitated the ideological polarization of modern politics in the United States. As Wicker phrased it, "Those who voted for Nixon sought no liberation from restraints they never felt. They wanted more of the same as they understood it; more of the economic affluence, political stability, social conformity and military security that formed the even surface of the fifties, more of Eisenhowerland from which they took Richard Nixon to be in direct line of descent."[15]

John F. Kennedy's defeat of Richard Nixon in 1960 led to warm relations between Earl Warren and John Kennedy.[16] Over the years, as Warren and Kennedy's friendship grew, Kennedy publicly embraced the Court's school desegregation and civil rights decisions. Sharing an animosity toward Nixon, they closely followed Nixon's campaign for Governor of California in 1962.

Nixon's hopes for victory in California ran high. The Republican Party had done well in California statewide contests in the 1950s: Nixon had won his bid for election to the U.S. Senate in 1950, the Eisenhower-Nixon campaigns had carried California in 1952 and 1956, and Nixon took California in the 1960 presidential race. Nevertheless, incumbent Governor Pat Brown, who had trailed Nixon in the period leading up to Election Day, pulled off a surprising last-minute victory. In defeat, Nixon responded with an acrimonious statement in which he blamed his loss on the press. Nixon's remarks provide a window into his hostile relationship with those he perceived as political adversaries:

> (N)ow that all the members of the press are so delighted that I have lost, I'd like to make a statement of my own. And as I leave the press, all I can say is this: for sixteen years, ever since the Hiss case, you've had a lot of fun—a lot of fun—that you've had an opportunity to attack me, and I think I've given as good as I've taken. . . . I leave you gentlemen now, and you will write it. You will interpret it. That's your right. But as I leave you I want you to know—just think of how much you're going to be missing. You won't have Nixon to kick around anymore, because, gentlemen, this is my last press conference.[17]

THE WARREN-BRENNAN PARTNERSHIP, 1956–1964

For many, the *Brown* decision represents Earl Warren's most important contribution to American law. However, the Chief Justice disagreed with this assertion. "It seemed to me," Warren later wrote, "that accolade should go to the case of *Baker v. Carr* (1962), which was the progenitor of the 'one man, one vote' rule," a decision that Justice William Brennan wrote.[18] Like John Marshall and Joseph Story before them, the Warren-Brennan partnership featured a Chief Justice who had a keen sense of the political needs of his time and a trusted lieutenant whose knowledge of the law provided the technical skills to accomplish the goals that the Chief Justice had in mind.

Brennan joined the Court in 1956 after a successful career as a judge in New Jersey. His Catholic background and northeastern roots brought political advantages to Eisenhower in a presidential election year. Broad minded and liberal, Brennan shared Warren's strong sense of fairness. Although he exhibited many of the same values as Justices Black and Douglas, Brennan's practicality and lack of dogmatism gave him the advantage of diplomacy when it came to modifying draft opinions in order to attract the support of wavering justices.

Brennan and Warren soon became the closest of colleagues. Often, Warren would visit Brennan in chambers, where they would discuss pending cases, formulate strategies for the Court's weekly conferences, and reflect on opinion-writing assignments. Warren's intellectual partnership with Brennan led to expansion of protections for political dissidents in the McCarthy years as well as the development of a new concept of citizenship in American constitutional democracy. With supplemental leadership and cooperation from Justices Black and Douglas, they forged many of the signature decisions of the Warren Court.

The constitutional approach that Warren and Brennan devised featured an expansive role for the Supreme Court in broadening the power of the federal government to protect the rights of citizens in the democratic political order. Since the time of the framers, America had been a protective democracy that featured limited voting rights and safeguards to protect elite property holders from the tyranny of the majority. The design of the federal government, as laid out in the Constitution, stressed structural safeguards such as the separation of power, indirect and staggered election of Senators, and the Electoral College. The framers devised these procedures to make it difficult for political movements to gain majority support in the nation's capital.

Under the framer's design, as reflected in the U.S. Constitution, there is no federal right to vote. Instead, states address voting rights in their own constitutions. For much of American history, the states placed severe restrictions on the franchise rights of women, blacks, and those who did not own real property. As a result, political insiders froze disfavored groups out of the power structure. The undemocratic consequences of this system may have been compatible with the intentions of the founding fathers, who feared the so-called tyranny of the majority. But the persistent and structural dynamics of stratification ultimately deprived the American Republic of any footing in the bedrock of popular sovereignty. By insisting that structural inequality must be squared with the precepts of modern democracy, Warren and Brennan appealed to the underlying values of citizenship, equality, and natural rights democracy that lay at the core of the Declaration of Independence.

Perhaps the most blatant example of the problem lay in the Jim Crow system that the Court had confronted in *Brown*. Just as the scope of white supremacy reached far beyond the public schools into segregated restaurants and the exclusion of blacks from the polls, the problem of political inequality led to unreasonable restrictions on freedom of expression and flaws in the structure of the representation system itself.

On all of these matters, the proponents of judicial restraint bitterly opposed Warren's designs. Yet with the help of Brennan and, belatedly, the political branches, Warren forged a new set of citizenship rights, grounded in the federal constitution, which ensured greater levels of political equality in American government. In so doing, he embraced all three prongs of Justice Stone's footnote four from the *Carolene Products* case: he took the Bill of Rights seriously, ensured judicial protection of minorities, and refereed the fairness of political structures.

Warren's vision of democracy included the idea that the Supreme Court had a legitimate responsibility to regulate the electoral process to assure meaningful equality and fairness in the democratic order. Attaining this vision fractured Warren's relations with Felix Frankfurter. Unlike Warren, Frankfurter resisted any prospect of unelected judges resolving disputes in the "political thicket," and he trusted the legislature to provide reasoned and unbiased consideration of political questions. In contrast, Warren's experience with the California legislature led him to distrust the integrity of the legislative process.

Warren's break with Frankfurter occurred even as the former Harvard law professor effusively praised Warren's decisions, as he had following release of the first *Brown* opinion. Gradually, Warren became distrustful of Frankfurter's ingratiating comments, which began to seem patronizing. Warren suspected that Frankfurter sought to manipulate him into taking sides against Justice Black in Frankfurter and Black's longstanding dispute over judicial restraint. Frankfurter had a pattern of trying to woo new justices toward his position, especially if he perceived them as unschooled or intellectually weak.

During the Court's weekly conferences, Warren chafed at Frankfurter's lengthy lectures and his intemperate outbursts. Warren eventually confided, "All Frankfurter does is talk, talk, talk. He drives you crazy."[19] For Frankfurter, questions of jurisdiction, justiciability[20] (ripeness, standing, mootness, political questions and the like), and precedent assumed great importance. While he did not ignore these considerations, Warren focused more on the facts of a case and their broader social and equitable implications. This gave rise to memorable debates in conference. In one of their more famous quarrels from the late spring of 1957, Frankfurter yelled at the Chief, "God damn it, you're a judge! You don't decide cases by your sense of justice or your personal predilections."

"Thank heaven, I *haven't* lost my sense of justice," Warren replied.[21]

POLITICAL DISSIDENTS AND THE RED SCARE, 1954–1962

The massive campaign to expose and exclude communists from American society known as McCarthyism began long before Senator Joseph McCarthy entered the U.S. Senate in 1950. The anticommunist movement had a number of roots in both international and domestic politics. Communist ideology called for the working class to overthrow capitalist nations, and the successful Russian Revolution of 1917 gave the international communist movement a base from which to operate. Although the Soviet Union and the United States became allies in World War II, a number of events in the postwar era caused their relationship to deteriorate. These included Soviet subjugation of Eastern Europe at the end of the war, the fall of China to the communists in 1948, and the unexpected development of a Soviet nuclear bomb in 1949.

Domestically, the Cold War had a number of implications. Political forces on the American right, including many leaders of the Republican Party, exaggerated the dangers of communism in a successful effort to contain Franklin Roosevelt's New Deal policies. During the depths of the Great Depression, many disillusioned Americans briefly had flirted with the American Communist Party, including young intellectuals who later obtained prominent positions in government, labor, and the film industry. As officials exposed Alger Hiss, Julius and Ethel Rosenberg, and Klaus Fuchs as alleged Soviet agents, Richard Nixon and Joseph McCarthy gained political advantages by attacking the loyalty of largely innocent "fellow travelers." Many prominent and law-abiding citizens suffered firings, black listings, and ostracism. They included physicist Robert Oppenheimer, actor Zero Mostel, singer Paul Robeson, and playwright Lillian Hellman.

The government's strategy against the communists featured the Alien Registration Act, passed in 1940 under the popular name of the "Smith Act." This Act made it unlawful to knowingly advocate or teach the overthrow of the government or participate in an organization dedicated to this purpose. Another law, the McCarran Act, required every communist to register with the Subversive Activities Control Board, a process that resulted in the banning of persons from employment in government, defense, or labor positions.

Although the U.S. Department of Justice prosecuted several hundred people using the criminal provisions of the Smith Act, the government's most far-reaching tactic involved legislative committees such as the House Un-American Activities Committee (HUAC) and the Senate Internal Security Subcommittee (SISS). These committees conducted investigations of individual citizens in an effort to label them as communists and thus either directly or indirectly deprive them of employment. The famous question posed in the hearings was: "Are you now or have you ever been a member of the Communist Party?" If the witness falsely answered no, s/he could be prosecuted for perjury; if the individual answered yes, he or she could be dismissed from employment; and if the individual asserted the Fifth Amendment privilege against self-incrimination and refused to testify, the s/he would be dismissed anyway, based on the dubious inference that the person had something to hide.

In the period before Earl Warren joined the Supreme Court, the justices sustained the constitutionality of the Smith Act in *Dennis v. United States* (1951). *Dennis* involved the prosecution of eleven leaders of the American Communist Party for advocating the violent overthrow of the federal government. Chief Justice Fred Vinson wrote a plurality opinion that three other justices joined. Vinson sustained the convictions by balancing the individual's right to freedom of expression against the government's interest in protecting itself from violent overthrow. He reasoned that since the government's very existence was at stake, it should not have to wait until its enemies presented a "clear and present danger" in order to defend itself. Vinson wrote:

> Overthrow of the Government by force and violence is certainly a substantial enough interest for the Government to limit speech. Indeed, this is the ultimate value of any society, for if a society cannot protect its very structure from armed internal attack, it must follow that no subordinate value can be protected.
>
> . . . Obviously, the words ("clear and present danger") cannot mean that before the Government may act, it must wait until the *putsch* is about to be executed, the plans have been laid and the signal is awaited. If Government is aware that a group aiming at its overthrow is attempting to indoctrinate its members and to commit them to a course whereby they will strike when the leaders feel the circumstances permit, action by the Government is required.[22]

Justices Frankfurter and Jackson filed concurring opinions in the case. Frankfurter argued that in striking a balance between free speech and national security, the Court should defer to the legislature:

> The demands of free speech in a democratic society as well as the interest in national security are better served by candid and informed weighing of the competing interests, within the confines of the judicial process, than by announcing dogmas too inflexible for the non-Euclidian problems to be solved.

> But how are competing interests to be assessed? Since they are not subject to quantitative ascertainment, the issue necessarily resolves itself into asking, who is to make the adjustment?—who is to balance the relevant factors and ascertain which interest is in the circumstances to prevail? Full responsibility for the choice cannot be given to the courts. Courts are not representative bodies. They are not designed to be a good reflex of a democratic society. . . .
>
> Primary responsibility for adjusting the interests which compete in the situation before us of necessity belongs to the Congress. . . . We are to set aside the judgment of those whose duty it is to legislate only if there is no reasonable basis for it. . . . Above all we must remember that this Court's power of judicial review is not "an exercise of the powers of a super-legislature." (internal citations deleted). [23]

Justices Black and Douglas dissented in *Douglas*, arguing that the First Amendment should be assigned a "preferred position" over the government's transient national security interests, especially in situations where no proof of overt action beyond mere discussion of abstract ideas had been presented at trial.

During his initial years on the Court in 1954 and 1955, Warren sided with Justice Frankfurter in domestic security cases. For example, in *Galven v. Press* (1954), he joined Frankfurter's majority opinion in holding that the McCarran Act did not require the government to prove that a member of a communist organization must have known about and supported the purposes of the organization in order for a successful prosecution to take place.

The first major shift in Warren's voting patterns cases came in *Pennsylvania v. Nelson* (1955), in which Warren held that federal laws concerning communist subversives were so extensive that states could not supplement them. Writing for the majority, Warren noted that state sedition laws "present(ed) a serious danger of conflict with the administration of the federal program" and thus federal law preempted them. His decision invalidated the sedition laws of 42 states.

Nelson sparked resistance in Congress. Dixiecrats who earlier had opposed the school desegregation decisions now seized the opportunity to gain allies in criticizing the Warren Court. They used the violation of states' rights as ammunition. In a hearing before the Senate Judiciary Committee, Senator Eastland had the following staged exchange with Senator Joseph McCarthy:

> "You have heard one communist after another come before this committee and take the position that the Communist Party was just another political party; in fact, that is the Communist line, is it not?" Eastland asked.
>
> "That is strictly the Communist line," McCarthy responded.
>
> "Is not that the line that the Chief Justice of the United States takes?"

> "Unfortunately, yes, Mr. Chairman," said McCarthy. "And I may say that I follow what is said in communist publications, to follow their line, rather closely. And the communist *Daily Worker* applauded this decision, the *Nelson* decision, and other decisions of the Supreme Court. In their book Earl Warren is a hero."[24]

In the privacy of his Supreme Court chambers, Warren responded that Senator McCarthy was a "querulous, disreputable liar."[25]

The next term, following the appointment of Justice Brennan, the Court issued twelve decisions in domestic security cases, and it decided all of them against the prosecution. Nearly all of the decisions featured narrow rulings, based on technicalities that avoided broad interpretations of the Constitution. In the most important of these, the Court spoke either unanimously or with only one or two dissents.

On June 17, 1956, a date that later became known in the press as "Red Monday," the Court issued four domestic security decisions. *Yates v. United States* (1957) involved Smith Act prosecutions against mid-level Communist Party leaders. Writing for a unanimous Court, Justice Harlan reversed the defendants' convictions based on a narrow interpretation of the *Dennis* decision. Harlan held that under *Dennis*, the Smith Act could only reach incitement to illegal action, not advocacy of violent revolution in the abstract.

Chief Justice Warren wrote two of the other decisions announced on Red Monday, both of which concerned legislative investigations of alleged communists. In *Watkins v. United States* (1957), he used the concept of separation of power to criticize legislative investigations that focused more on individual conduct than on gathering evidence for the purpose of legislation. Although Warren refrained from grounding the decision in the First Amendment, he implied that Congress had exceeded its constitutional powers during the McCarthy era hearings. He wrote, "No inquiry is an end in itself; it must be related to, and in furtherance of, a legitimate task of the Congress. Investigations conducted solely for the personal aggrandizement of the investigators or to 'punish' those investigated are indefensible."[26]

Reaction to the Red Monday decisions was swift. The *New York Times* applauded the decisions, saying: "The Supreme Court has shown itself by far the most courageous of our three branches of Government in standing up for basic principles."[27] However, official Washington responded with hostility. Speaking off the record at the White House in front of guests, President Eisenhower said that he had "never been as mad" as he was when he read the *Jencks* opinion. Eisenhower's own appointees—Justices Warren, Harlan, Whittaker, and Brennan—had voted to give defendants access to government security files so that they might impeach the credibility of adverse government informants who had been paid to testify against them.

FBI Director J. Edgar Hoover testified in a House Appropriations Committee hearing that one "top Communist functionary" called the Supreme Court's *Yates* decision "the greatest victory the Communist Party in America has ever received. The decision will mark a rejuvenation of the party in America."[28] The real rejuvenation, of course, occurred within Hoover's own Bureau, since the controversy triggered more funding for the expansion of counter-insurgency and espionage activities. The incident marked the end of cordial relations between Hoover and Warren.

The most formidable opposition to the Red Monday decisions came in the House of Representatives in the form of the Jenner-Butler Bill. The bill sought to reverse the Court's Red Monday decisions, reasserting the investigatory authority of congressional committees, authorizing states to enforce anti-sedition laws, and extending the Smith Act to make advocacy of the overthrow of the government a crime. Another section of the bill directly challenged the authority of the Supreme Court itself. It used Congress' power under Article III of the Constitution to limit the appellate jurisdiction of the Supreme Court, stripping the Court's power to hear national security cases. In the fall of 1957, the House of Representatives passed the Jenner-Butler Bill and sent it to the Senate for further consideration.

During the Senate's deliberations that December, a little-known former clerk of Justice Robert Jackson by the name of William Rehnquist published an essay in *U.S. News & World Report* under the title, "Who Writes Decisions of the Supreme Court?"[29] In an obvious effort to ignite further criticism of the Warren Court, Rehnquist accused the other law clerks of exerting an unconscious liberal bias in making recommendations about which cases to add to the Court's docket. As a group, Rehnquist wrote, the law clerks exhibited "extreme solicitude for the claims of Communists and other criminal defendants." They sought "expansion of federal power at the expense of State power," and tended to exert "great sympathy toward any government regulation of business." Their ideas reflected "the political philosophy now espoused by the Court under Chief Justice Earl Warren." After his own appointment to the Court in 1972, Rehnquist would seek to reverse these trends.

Senate Majority Leader Lyndon Johnson opposed the Jenner-Butler Bill and implored his colleagues to defeat it. In the fall of 1958, the Senate did exactly that, rejecting the bill by a 49–41 vote. If the bill had passed, it would have led to the most significant reduction in the Court's jurisdiction since the Civil War.

The Supreme Court narrowly escaped the wrath of its Congressional critics. In response, however, the Court's most conservative members, Justices Harlan and Frankfurter, now shifted sides to support the government in the next series of national security cases. In *Konigsberg v. State Bar of California II* (1961), Justice Harlan upheld the State of California Bar

Association's power to require an applicant for the bar to answer questions concerning his alleged communist background. In *Scales v. United States* (1961), Harlan ignored the principles of his own *Yates* decision in upholding the conviction of two communist leaders under the Smith Act. In *Communist Party v. Subversive Activities Control Board* (1961), Justice Frankfurter upheld the McCarran Act's provisions requiring the registration of members of the Communist Party. In each of these cases, Chief Justice Warren joined Justices Brennan, Black, and Douglas in dissent.

In the summer of 1962, Justice Frankfurter suffered a debilitating stroke and retired from the bench. President Kennedy replaced him with Arthur J. Goldberg, an attorney from the West Side of Chicago who had served as Secretary of Labor in the first two years of the Kennedy administration. Goldberg firmly endorsed Earl Warren's social values. He later reported that he met daily in conferences with Warren, noting "There is nobody I felt closer to than Warren."[30]

Goldberg's appointment marked the end of the first, more conservative stage of the Warren Court. For the next seven years, Goldberg, or at a later point Justices Abe Fortas or Thurgood Marshall, would join the four liberals to support the philosophical approaches of Warren, Black, Douglas and Brennan.

In cases involving political dissidents and national security, the new liberal majority gradually restored civil liberties and ended the repression of the McCarthy period. In *Albertson v. Subversive Activities Control Board* (1965), it reversed Frankfurter's decision in *Communist Party v. Subversive Activities Board* (1961). The Court used the Fifth Amendment privilege against self-incrimination to strike down the McCarran Act's requirement that members of the Communist Party must register with the federal government. The Warren Court's other major First Amendment decisions from Earl Warren's final few years on the Court will be discussed in Chapter 13.

"LEGISLATORS REPRESENT PEOPLE, NOT TREES"

The case that Warren considered the "most important of (his) tenure on the Court," involved the problem of legislative apportionment. State laws required legislatures to make periodic adjustments in voting districts so that the districts remained equal as the population changed over time. Article I, Section 2 of the U.S. Constitution also required that members of the House of Representatives be apportioned among the states based on their respective numbers and that the voting districts be reapportioned every ten years. During the twentieth century, as the population of the United States grew and people moved from rural to urban areas, many state legislatures refused to reapportion themselves.

The *Baker* case arose in Tennessee. Between 1900 and 1960, the state's voting-age population increased from 487,380 to 2,092,891. Yet the Tennessee legislature failed to reapportion itself. The dominant demographic trend involved persons moving from farms to cities. As a result, overrepresented rural districts sent too many representatives to the legislature and underrepresented urban districts sent too few. For example, in 1950, Memphis had a population of 312,000 voters and had seven representatives in the legislature; the twenty-four counties surrounding the city had a similar population and twenty-six representatives.[31] Legislators from rural districts predominated, and they declined to vote themselves out of office.

Other states faced similar problems. In his analysis of the issue, Professor Morton Horwitz found that at the time of the *Baker* decision, "in eleven states, a voting majority could be elected by less than 20 percent of the population, including California (10.7%), Florida (14.1%), and Nevada (8%)."[32] Although this situation posed a significant problem of political inequality, federal courts repeatedly had refused to intervene. In *Colegrove v. Green* (1946), the Supreme Court rejected a challenge against the malapportioned congressional districts in Illinois.

The *Colegrove* decision illustrates Justice Frankfurter's intense opposition to the notion that federal courts should intervene in issues of political apportionment. Likewise, the case foreshadows the tension that arose nearly fifteen years later when a majority of the Court rejected his point of view. Writing for two other justices in *Colegrove*, Frankfurter held that malapportionment actions were not judiciable in federal court because they raised political questions. Frankfurter reasoned that the Constitution gives Congress the power to alter the way states select representatives to the House of Representatives[33] and that Courts could not redraw the district boundaries by themselves. He continued:

> (D)ue regard for the effective working of our Government reveal(s) this issue to be of a peculiarly political nature and therefore not meet for judicial determination.
>
> . . . (N)othing is clearer than that this controversy concerns matters that bring courts into immediate and active relations with party contests. From the determination of such issues, this Court has traditionally held aloof. It is hostile to a democratic system to involve the judiciary in the politics of the people. And it is not less pernicious if such judicial intervention in an essentially political contest be dressed up in the abstract phrases of the law.
>
> . . .To sustain this action would cut very deep into the very being of Congress. Courts ought not to enter this political thicket.[34]

Perhaps more than any other single decision, Justice Frankfurter's *Colegrove* opinion reflected his philosophy of judicial restraint. While he acknowledged the unfairness of malapportionment, Frankfurter believed it was the duty of elected officials in either the states or the Congress to remedy the problem. Frankfurter placed his faith in the integrity of democratically elected legislators and deeply distrusted unelected judges.

Earl Warren vehemently disagreed. To him, legislative malapportionment and the Jim Crow system went hand-in-hand. Warren once said:

> If *Baker v. Carr* had been in existence fifty years ago, we would have saved ourselves acute racial troubles. Many of our problems would have been solved a long time ago if everyone had the right to vote, and his vote counted the same as everybody else's. Most of these problems could have been solved through the political process rather than through the courts. But as it was, the Court had to decide.[35]

Warren had not always opposed malapportionment. As Governor of California, he presided over one of the most malapportioned states in the union. In the 1920s, when the population of Los Angeles boomed, reformers placed an initiative on the ballot that changed the structure of the California Senate. Instead of a representation system based on population, they sought a so-called "federal model" that prohibited a single county from having more than one senator. The proposal also provided that no senatorial district would contain more than three counties. The initiative passed into law, even though it blatantly discriminated against urban areas and gave disproportionate power to rural and agricultural interests.

As the population of California's urban areas mushroomed over the next forty years, the situation became more unfair. Yet when another group of reformers sought to change this system in 1948, Governor Warren resisted them. In his *Memoirs*, he later described his opposition to the newly proposed reform as "a matter of political expediency."[36]

In October 1961, during one of the oral arguments in *Baker v. Carr*, Chief Justice Warren raised a question that showed how far he had progressed from his days as a politician. He asked Jack Wilson, the Assistant Attorney General of Tennessee, about those who suffered from the dilution of their voting power as a result of malapportionment: "Is there any remedy in the courts of Tennessee for these people—if they are, as they say now, at the end of the road—if we don't take this case?"

Wilson responded, "I would say, may it please the Court, that on the present status of the case law in Tennessee and of the views held as to the constitutional law in Tennessee, that this right, alleged right, is not enforceable in *any* of the courts of Tennessee to *any* degree whatsoever."[37]

This frank but distressing answer persuaded moderates such as Justice Potter Stewart to vote in favor of accepting jurisdiction in the case. At the conference of the justices after the oral argument, Warren began by laying out his position on the merits. He believed that Tennessee's failure to reapportion its legislature denied the equal protection rights of the plaintiffs. Justices Black, Brennan, and Douglas also shared this point of view. Warren recommended that the Court should simply announce that federal courts would now have jurisdiction to decide legislative apportionment cases. The question of determining whether a legal violation had occurred and, if so, of fashioning a remedy, could be addressed in the lower courts, subject to later review, if necessary. Justice Stewart agreed with Warren, and in the coming weeks, Justice Clark also joined with them. Thus, six justices favored accepting jurisdiction and two—Justices Frankfurter and Harlan—opposed it.

The two-stage process that Warren proposed in *Baker* resembled but did not mirror the strategy he used in *Brown*. There, the Court reached the merits of the constitutional question in its initial decision and resolved it in favor of the black plaintiffs. It reserved the question of the remedy, which it addressed by means of the "all deliberate speed" principle in the *Brown II* decision one year later. In contrast, Justice Brennan's decision in *Baker* only addressed the jurisdictional question and did not reach a decision on the merits.

The Court's lengthy internal deliberations over the *Baker* case became highly stressful. In the spring of 1962, Justice Charles Evans Whittaker waffled between the opposite poles that Warren and Frankfurter had staked out, and when Frankfurter learned that Whittaker might cast his vote with Warren, he exerted unrelenting, full-court pressure on his uncertain colleague.

A former corporate lawyer with political ties to the Republican Party in Missouri, Whittaker often had difficulty making decisions on the Court. Prior to joining the Supreme Court, his judicial experience consisted of less than one year on the Eighth Circuit Court of Appeals. He found himself adrift between two warring sides on the Court without a firm sense of where he stood.

Whittaker suffered a nervous breakdown and entered the hospital during the first week of March, 1962. Citing his medical problems, he announced that he would retire from the Court at the end of June. Then, on March 26, a mere ten days after the release of the *Baker* decision, Justice Frankfurter suffered a major stroke in his chambers and was rushed to the hospital. Paralyzed, he could barely speak. At the end of August, after twenty-eight years of service, Frankfurter also resigned from the Court.

President Kennedy nominated Deputy Attorney General Byron White to replace Whittaker and Secretary of Labor Arthur J. Goldberg to replace Frankfurter. White had served as a leading figure in President Kennedy's election campaign in 1960, and he had represented the administration in tense negotiations with Southern politicians during the Freedom Rides in the summer of 1961. His background also included a stellar career in football. Known as "Whizzer White," he was an All-American halfback at the University of Colorado in the 1930s and later played successfully for the Chicago Bears and (then) Pittsburgh Pirates in the NFL. In the Kennedy administration, White had the reputation as a conservative who resented having to solve the legal problems of civil rights demonstrators. In 1962, he authorized FBI surveillance of one of Dr. Martin Luther King, Jr.'s principal aides, Stanley Levison, on suspicion that Levison had ties to the Communist Party.

Of Jewish background, Arthur Goldberg had grown up in poverty in inner-city Chicago. After earning his law degree from Northwestern University, Goldberg worked for the secretive Office of Strategic Services during World War II. Following the war, he returned to Chicago and specialized in labor law, representing the United Steelworkers of America. A gifted intellectual with a sharp mind and liberal political views, he provided the fifth crucial vote for the liberal wing of the Court—Warren, Brennan, Black, and Douglas. Goldberg's appointment represented a milestone for the Warren Court: in the previous period (1953–1962) the Court often found itself split between liberal and conservative factions, whereas in the subsequent period (1963–1969) its decisions became considerably more liberal.

The *Baker* decision reflected Warren's developing view that voters deserved to be treated equally in the American political process. As Warren saw it, if democratic society contained a core principle of equality in the political order, and if courts had a legitimate role to play in ensuring voter equality in electoral process, it made little sense to proceed gradually. He wrote,

> In the Supreme Court, the basic ingredient of decision is principle, and it should not be compromised and parceled out a little in one case, a little more in another. . . . If the principle is sound and constitutional, it is the birthright of every American, not to be accorded begrudgingly or piecemeal or to special groups only, but to everyone in its entirety whenever it is brought into play.[38]

Warren's experiences with elected officials in Oakland and the California General Assembly convinced him that politicians acted out of self-interest and tended to favor the special interests that helped to assure their reelection. Just as he fought graft as a District Attorney, he now fought a lopsided electoral system in which a small number of rural voters could control the state legislative process. Warren fashioned a constitutional doctrine that protected political outsiders from the machinations and intransigence of political insiders. In his groundbreaking opinion in *Reynolds v. Sims* (1964), Warren found grist for his constitutional mill.

In the aftermath of the *Baker* decision, attorneys filed many challenges against state legislative malapportionment, and the Supreme Court resolved the *Reynolds v. Sims* case. The principle of "one person, one vote" that the

Court announced in *Reynolds* meant that urban residents—both those in inner-cities as well as those in the suburbs—would enjoy increased political power in direct proportion to their numbers in the state population. The tyranny of rural legislators came to an end.

The *Reynolds* case involved Alabama's system of electing state legislators. Under this system, each county regardless of its population sent at least one representative to each of the two houses in its legislature. As with the State of Tennessee in *Baker*, the Alabama legislature had refrained from conducting any redistricting over the span of sixty years. Given the significant population growth during that time and the demographic shift in favor of urban areas, an acute apportionment problem arose.

In his opinion for an eight-member majority, Chief Justice Warren accepted the trial court's finding that population-variance ratios of up to 41:1 existed in the Alabama Senate and of up to 16:1 in the Alabama House. In Bullock County, two elected officials represented a population of 13,462 whereas in Mobile County, three officials represented 314,301 people. In the state senate, the situation was even worse. Lowndes County—which would later become a battleground in civil rights movement—had one state senator for a population of 15,417, whereas Jefferson County's population of 600,000 also had just one senator.

In analyzing these facts, Warren stated, "Legislators represent people, not trees or acres. Legislators are elected by voters, not farms or cities or economic interests. As long as ours is a representative form of government, and our legislatures are those instruments of government elected directly by and directly representative of the people, the right to elect legislators in a free and unimpaired fashion is a bedrock of our political system."[39]

Perhaps the most important portion of the *Reynolds* decision involved the Court's reasoning: the right to participate an equal basis in the franchise now had become fundamental, and restrictions on voting rights potentially could trigger strict scrutiny. As Warren phrased it, "(T)he right of suffrage is a fundamental matter in a free and democratic society. Especially since the right to exercise the franchise in a free and unimpaired manner is preservative of other basic civil and political rights, any alleged infringement of the right of citizens to vote must be carefully and meticulously scrutinized."[40] This language launched the Court into a stalwart defense of voting rights that would last well into the early years of William Rehnquist's tenure as Chief Justice. Later, it served as the basis for the Court's controversial *Bush v. Gore* decision, which resolved the 2000 presidential election.[41]

Critics of *Reynolds* argued that the Court had no basis for imposing its "one person, one vote" rule on the states since the founding fathers themselves did not follow this principle in the design of the U.S. Senate. Warren anticipated this argument and met it head-on: "Attempted reliance on the federal analogy appears often to be little more than an after-the-fact rationalization offered in defense of maladjusted state apportionment arrangements," he wrote. Noting that the constitutions of 36 states required that representation in *both* houses of the state legislatures be based wholly or at least partially on population, he concluded that the framers of the Constitution did not seek to impose the U.S Senate formula on the states.

In *Westberry v. Sanders* (1964), the Court later extended the principle of "one person, one vote" to congressional elections. As a result, the only national officials not selected according to population are those in the U.S. Senate and the White House.

The Warren Court's sweeping legislative apportionment decisions did not prove as controversial as its decision in *Engel v. Vitale* (1962). *Engel* involved a public school district on Long Island that began the class day with a nonsectarian prayer. The New York Board of Regents had approved the prayer for use in state schools, and its recommended language read, "Almighty God, we acknowledge our dependence upon Thee, and we beg Thy blessings upon us, our parents, our teachers, and our country. Amen."[42]

Five sets of parents challenged the Board of Regents' prayer under the First Amendment Establishment Clause, and in June 1962, the Supreme Court issued a 5-1-1 decision striking it down. Although the prayer was voluntary, Justice Black held that the involvement of state officials in composing the prayer violated the "wall of separation between church and state" that he saw as the core principle behind the Establishment Clause.

Both conservative and liberal religious leaders denounced the decision. Evangelist Billy Graham derided *Engel* as "another step toward the secularization of the United States," and Francis Cardinal Spellman, the Archbishop of New York, said that the decision struck "at the very heart of the Godly tradition in which America's children had so long been raised." Warren himself recalled a bold newspaper headline that appeared the day the Court released its opinion: "Court Outlaws God."[43]

Politicians quickly took up the cause. Congressman Frank Becker of Long Island, where the *Engel* case arose, accused the Court of issuing an illegitimate decision. "This is not the first tragic decision of the Supreme Court, but I would say it was the most tragic decision in the history of the United States," he asserted.[44]

Southern politicians, who had long been bitter about the school desegregation decisions, joined with rural legislators in fomenting a rebellion against the Warren Court using the rubric of states' rights. Right-wing conservatives from the John Birch Society called for the impeachment of Earl Warren, and they began a nationwide movement featuring anti-Warren billboards along the nation's highways.

In one of his "Washington Merry-Go-Round" broadcasts, Drew Pearson reported on Earl Warren's reaction to the John Birch Society impeachment campaign. The campaign offered $2,300 in prizes for the best essay written by a college student concerning why Warren should be impeached. When officials in Norway quizzed Warren about the contest, he laughed. "I'll have to get Mrs. Warren to enter the contest," he said. "She knows more of my faults than anyone else—unless it's my three boys. Maybe she could win first prize and my boys could win the other prizes. Then we could keep the money in the family."[45]

The Council of State Governments did not take the matter so lightly. It drafted a series of constitutional amendments that sought to strengthen the power of states in their relations with the U.S. Supreme Court. The draft amendments contained three propositions. First, they would alter the provisions of Article 5 of the U.S. Constitution governing the process for amending the Constitution. Under the proposal, the affirmative vote of two-thirds of the states would be sufficient to amend the Constitution without any requirement that the Congress agree to propose the amendment with its own two-thirds vote. Second, they proposed that the Court's decision in *Baker v. Carr* be overturned. Finally, they would create a new Court of the Union, consisting of the chief justices of the fifty states, that would have the power to overturn U.S. Supreme Court decisions.[46]

The proposal met with widespread approval among state legislatures. Of course, the Court's decisions in *Baker v. Carr* and *Reynolds v. Sims* placed the seats of many state legislators in jeopardy. From his vantage point in Washington, D.C., Warren viewed the firestorm with concern. "Those things went through Legislature after Legislature till almost two-thirds of them passed some kind of resolution on them, and there was no debate of any kind on the part of the bar in the country," he said in a later interview. "To think of coming that close to a constitutional amendment on important issues of that kind without the bar taking an interest is almost a frightening thing."[47]

By 1967, state legislatures came close to the number of votes needed for a constitutional convention. However, as Professor Ward Elliott[48] has argued, compliance with the *Baker* and *Reynolds* decisions occurred very rapidly, and the movement in opposition to the Warren Court came rather late. Urban and suburban political interests organized and responded to the opening that the Court provided, and by the time the last few votes took place, the state legislatures already had been re-apportioned. The 2% of the American population that the rural politicians represented no longer dominated state politics, and more state tax revenue started to flow into urban and suburban areas. The crisis passed, and both the Warren Court and the structure and appellate jurisdiction of the Supreme Court survived intact.

The controversy of the school prayer decisions notwithstanding, most Americans supported the Warren Court's legislative apportionment reforms for one simple reason: the country needed them. Self-serving politicians and their special interests represented a problem that voters could readily perceive, and in many parts of the nation, the existing political structures severely diluted the voices of the people. As he did in the *Brown* decision, Warren highlighted a social inequity that arose because insiders excluded outsiders from the political process.

The Court's achievements in the legislative malapportionment cases brought it to the brink of constitutional crisis. State legislators from malapportioned rural districts—whose jobs the Court's reforms threatened—joined forces with the John Birch Society in calling for Warren's impeachment. Congressional opponents of the Warren Court sought to curb the Court's jurisdiction over national security and legislative apportionment cases. They came close to succeeding. Yet even in the face of intense political controversy, Warren decided cases based upon Constitutional principle and his own conscience. He showed particular courage in the fight over legislative apportionment, and he regarded his decisions in this area as his most important contribution to American law.

In the matter of freedom of expression for political dissidents, Warren also stood on principle. A good example of Warren's stance comes in the *Konigsberg v. State Bar* (1957; 1961) decisions. In the first of these, Warren sided with the majority in holding that Konigsberg's alleged involvement in the Communist Party, standing alone, did not constitute evidence of bad moral character sufficient to warrant Konigsberg's exclusion from the practice of law. In the second appeal, which followed a tempest of criticism directed against the Supreme Court's "Red Monday" decisions, a majority of the Court sustained California's second decision to bar Konigsberg from the practice of law. The majority reasoned that Konigsberg's refusal to answer questions about his alleged communist associations obstructed the investigation into his qualifications for the bar. Warren, joined by Justices Black, Douglas, and (writing separately) Brennan dissented. The dissenting justices criticized the Court for adopting a watered-down, balancing test for First Amendment protection. Several members of the majority in *Konigsberg II* shifted their views of constitutional protection with the political winds. To his credit, Warren did not. In taking consistent positions on these constitutional questions and deciding the cases based on principle and not politics, Warren showed integrity.

The decisions that Warren reached in the legislative apportionment and Red Scare decisions should not obscure the underlying truth that the stances he took in these cases conflicted with positions he adopted on similar questions at earlier stages in his career. As noted, in 1948 as Governor of California, Warren opposed a state constitutional amendment that would have abolished the selection system for the California state senate. He did so because of political expediency. Likewise, in the 1920s and 1930s, District Attorney Warren prosecuted people for advocating communist revolution, and in Frank F. Merriam's 1934 gubernatorial campaign, Warren, as Chair of the California Republican Party, denounced Upton Sinclair for advocating socialist policies.

Yet Warren hardly stands alone among the ranks of leading American politicians who acted inconsistently on matters of public policy. Just as Jefferson violated his democratic principles when he exercised executive authority in making the Louisiana Purchase and Lincoln took hypocritical positions on the issue of slavery, Warren, too, had his contradictions. However, in the circumstances that mattered most, those arising out of his position as Chief Justice, Warren took a clear and principled stand on issues of great constitutional importance, and his actions changed American history.

NOTES

1. Quoted in Simon, *In His Own Image*, 55 (see chap. 2, n. 10).

2. Earl Warren, "The Law and the Future," published in the November 1955 edition of *Fortune Magazine*, in *The Public Papers of Chief Justice Earl Warren*, ed. Henry M. Christman (Westport, Conn.: Greenwood Press, 1974), 111.

3. Container 56, India 1956 Correspondence, Personal File, Earl Warren Papers, Manuscript Division, Library of Congress, Washington, D.C. See also "Chief Justice Warren in India," *The Sun* (Baltimore) October 1, 1956.

4. The article, "Jurist's Joyful Junket," from the September 17, 1956 issue of *Life*, is available online at http://books.google.com/books.

5. One of these reforms, "The Untouchability Offences Act of 1955," guaranteed access to religious shrines, wells, and educational institutions.

6. Warren, *Memoirs*, 343.

7. Ibid.

8. Drew Pearson, Washington Merry-Go-Round, March 16, 1966, available at http://www.library.american.edu/pearson/biography.html.

9. Cray, *Chief Justice: A Biography of Earl Warren*, 363–64.

10. Ibid., 340.

11. Richard Nixon, "The Need for Leadership: An Address in Greensboro, North Carolina," August 17, 1960, courtesy Gerhard Peters and John T. Woolley, The American Presidency Project, Santa Barbara, CA, available at http://www.presidency.ucsb.edu/ws/?pid=25385.

12. Reported in William B. Ewald, Jr., *Eisenhower the President: Crucial Days, 1951–1960* (Englewood Cliffs, N.J.: Prentice Hall, 1981), 313; see also Tom Wicker, *One of Us: Richard Nixon and the American Dream* (New York: Random House, 1991), 256.

13. Ibid.

14. Rick Perlstein, *Nixonland: The Rise of a President and the Fracturing of America* (New York: Schribner, 2008).

15. Ibid., 260.

16. Nationwide, Kennedy defeated Nixon by 112, 827 votes, but the margin in the Electoral College was not nearly so close. There, Kennedy won by a vote of 303 to 219.

17. See *Richard Nixon: Speeches, Writings, Documents*, ed. Rich Perlstein (Princeton, New Jersey: Princeton University Press, 2008), 106–12; see also Gladwin Hill, "Nixon Denounces Press as Biased," *New York Times*, November 8, 1962, A-1); and Stephen E. Ambrose, *Nixon: The Triumph of a Politician, 1962–1972* (Los Angeles: Premier Digital Publishing, 1989), 1.

18. Warren, *Memoirs*, 306.

19. Quoted in Peter Irons, *A People's History of the Supreme Court* (New York: Viking, 1999), 328.

20. Justiciability refers to limitations on a federal court's ability to adjudicate cases, including rules that block subject matter jurisdiction in unripe cases, moot cases, cases in which parties lack standing, or cases presenting political questions.

21. Quoted in Cray, *Chief Justice: A Biography of Earl Warren*, 356.

22. 341 U.S. at 509.

23. 341 U.S. at 524 (Frankfurter, J., concurring).

24. Quoted in Cray, *Chief Justice: A Biography of Earl Warren* (1997), 322.

25. Ibid.

26. 354 U.S. at 187.

27. *New York Times*, June 18, 1957, 32.

28. Quoted in Cray, *Chief Justice: A Biography of Earl Warren* (1997), 354.

29. William H. Rehnquist, "Who Writes Decisions of the U.S. Supreme Court?" *U.S. News & World Report*, December 13, 1957.

30. On an NET Journal Documentary on Earl Warren, dated July 7, 1969, former Justice Goldberg confirmed that he met daily in conferences with Chief Justice Warren. For further information, see Sheldon Goldman and Thomas P. Jahnige, *The Federal Courts as a Political System*, 2nd ed. (New York: Harper & Row, 1976). For Goldberg's statement about being close to Warren, see Cray, *Chief Justice: A Biography of Earl Warren*, 386.

31. Ibid., 378.

32. Morton J. Horwitz, *Warren Court and Pursuit of Justice*, 83 (see chap. 1, n. 28).

33. U.S. Const. art. I, §4, cl. 1.

34. 328 U.S. at 553–6.

35. Quoted in Pollack, *Earl Warren: The Judge Who Changed America*, 209.

36. Warren, *Memoirs*, 310.

37. A recording of the oral argument is available online at http://www.oyez.org/cases/1960–1969/1960/1960_6.

38. Warren, *Memoirs*, 6.

39. 377 U.S. at 562.

40. Ibid., 561–62.

41. For further analysis of the *Bush v. Gore* decision, see Richard B. Saphire and Paul Moke, "Litigating *Bush v. Gore* in the States: Dual Voting Systems and the Fourteenth Amendment," 51 *Villanova L. Rev.*, 229 (2006).

42. 370 U.S. at 422.

43. Warren, *Memoirs*, 315–16.

44. Quoted in Cray, *Chief Justice: A Biography of Earl Warren*, 387.

45. Drew Pearson, "Washington Merry-Go-Round" August 18, 1961.

46. For a summary of the Council of State Governments' proposal, see Cray, *Chief Justice: A Biography of Earl Warren*, 390–1. See also Warren, *Memoirs*, 310–11.

47. Warren interview with Anthony Lewis, *New York Times Magazine*, October 19, 1969, 133.

48. Ward Y. E. Elliott, The *Rise of Guardian Democracy: The Supreme Court's Role in Voting Rights Disputes,* 1845–1969 (Cambridge, MA: Harvard University Press, 1974).

Chapter 9

The Warren Court and the Civil Rights Movement

In a memorandum to the Court in the spring of 1954, Warren shared his thoughts about the major points he proposed to make in his draft opinion in the *Brown* case. He wrote, "No section of the country and no segment of our population can justly place full responsibility for segregation on others. They must assume a measure of that responsibility for themselves."[1] Unfortunately, Warren's statement never made it into the final version of the *Brown* opinion. Had Earl Warren been President in 1954, it offers an intimation of what he might have said to the American public about the problem of racial segregation.

President Eisenhower's apparent indifference to the problem of racial injustice meant the loss of a golden opportunity. Eisenhower's silence deeply troubled Warren. In his *Memoirs*, Warren wrote:

> With his popularity, if Eisenhower had said that black children were still being discriminated against long after the adoption of the Thirteenth, Fourteenth, and Fifteenth Amendments, that the Supreme Court of the land had now declared it unconstitutional to continue such cruel practices, and that it should be the duty of every good citizen to help rectify more than eighty years of wrongdoing by honoring that decision—if he had said something to this effect, we would have been relieved, in my opinion, of many of the racial problems which have continued to plague us. But he never even stated that he thought the decision was right until after he had left the White House.[2]

Although the Warren Court made a substantial first step in its *Brown* opinions, the Court could not achieve sweeping social change on its own. Constrained by their institutional role from addressing the nation extemporaneously, the justices could only speak through their opinions in the cases that came before them. They also faced the difficult problem of how to enforce their decision. The political branches bore the responsibility of implementing *Brown*, and in significant portions of the nation, local officials simply refused to do so. Outside the world of public education, an entire set of Jim Crow practices—from segregated lunch counters and municipal parks to widespread disenfranchisement on the basis of race—still remained in place.

Squaring the ideals of justice with the pernicious racism of American society would be an arduous undertaking. The principles of *Brown* would have to be promoted and the nation's consciousness raised regarding the evils of racial segregation. Where necessary, recalcitrant white supremacists would need to be confronted and constrained. Helpful as it was, the Court's "top down" approach to reform could not accomplish these objectives alone, nor could the NAACP's repeated use of test cases in the federal courts. Although reformers had an indispensable ally in the courts—and during the 1940s and 1950s civil rights reformers had precious few allies—the revolution would have to come from below.

The familiar story of the civil rights movement embraces all of these themes. It includes articulate and charismatic Baptist ministers and their religious allies, community activists who put their lives on the line for the cause, and a handful of federal officials who issued court decisions, authorized the use of federal marshals and troops, and, eventually passed and implemented groundbreaking legislation.

As a textbook example of how to achieve sweeping change in American politics, the civil rights movement offers many lessons. Insiders worked the system from the seat of government, while outsiders confronted racism in the streets of the South. In Washington, the civil rights leadership lobbied, litigated, and organized mass rallies; in the small towns of the Deep South, like Selma, Alabama and McComb, Mississippi, everyday citizens created Freedom Schools and organized voter registration campaigns. When vigilantes retaliated against them, the civil rights activists remained faithful to the principle of nonviolence. The national media publicized their courageous stand, and the activists won public support for a goal that at one time seemed wholly unobtainable.

During most of these dramatic events, the Warren Court remained in the background, off stage. But at crucial moments along the way, the Court's decisions proved pivotal to the success of the movement.

In every major civil rights case that came before him, Earl Warren voted in favor of the extension of civil rights. Further, in nearly all of these cases, he persuaded a majority of the Court to back his position. As the experience of the United States in the period of retrenchment following the end of the first era of Reconstruction showed, the cause of racial justice during the 1950s and 60s would have been even more of an uphill battle, and perhaps would have had a very different outcome, in the absence of support from the Supreme Court.

THE BARE BONES OF THE CONSTITUTION

Several years after Warren retired from the Court, an interviewer asked him to comment on the difficult decisions the Warren Court had rendered during the civil rights era. "Did you feel isolated and exposed in some of those decisions?" the interviewer asked. Warren replied:

"We did indeed. And a lot of people are of the opinion that the Supreme Court just reached out and grabbed onto those issues and decided them in opposition to Congress. . . . But, really all the Court was doing was filling in a vacuum because Congress had *not* acted (emphasis in the original)." [3]

After reflecting more carefully on the question, Warren amended his answer. He added that it would be unfair to lay all the blame on Congress, because Congress did pass the Civil Rights Act of 1875, which guaranteed that all persons would have equal access to private businesses regardless of any condition of previous servitude. The Supreme Court itself had held this statute unconstitutional in the *Civil Rights Cases* (1883). There the Court ruled that the Fourteenth Amendment contained a state action requirement, and Congress could not use Section 5 of the Fourteenth Amendment to regulate private wrongs without violating the Tenth Amendment rights of the states.[4] In effect, this left the fate of the freedmen in the hands of the often-belligerent states.

"As a result," Warren concluded, "there was just a great gap there from that time on until the time Lyndon Johnson came on. Up until that time we just had to deal with the bare bones of the Constitution on the question of equal protection of the law, what the limits were, and due process of law; those were two things we had to be guided by as they appeared in the Fourteenth Amendment."[5]

In a set of notes that he prepared for a lecture at New York University, Warren expanded on this thesis.[6] He argued that three Supreme Court decisions from the Reconstruction Era—*United States v. Cruishank* (1876), the *Slaughterhouse Cases* (1873), and the *Civil Rights Cases* (1883)—gutted Congress' power under Section 5 of the Fourteenth Amendment. In its place, the Court reserved for itself the power to enforce the Fourteenth Amendment. Decisions such as *Yick Wo v. Hopkins* (1886), where the Court held that biased enforcement of an otherwise impartial municipal ordinance violated the Equal Protection Clause, and *Strauder v. West Virginia* (1880), where the Court struck down a state law that barred blacks from jury service, illustrate this trend.

By emphasizing federalism and the role of the states in the enforcement of civil rights, Warren continued, the Court elevated governmental form over the substance of protection that the Fourteenth Amendment promised to blacks. Then, adding insult to injury, during the *Lochner* era it construed the Fourteenth Amendment Due Process Clause into a major vehicle for the protection freedom of contract and the corporate interest in voiding government regulation, in effect abandoning the role of the Fourteenth Amendment in protecting the rights of the freedmen altogether. Thus, in Warren's estimation, the Supreme Court itself had played a major role in relegating black America to second-class status.

For Warren, the key question concerned how best to achieve racial equality. Other legal questions such as the nuances of federalism, the need for judicial restraint, or the assigning of blame between Congress and the Supreme Court in the sorry history of the Jim Crow era paled in comparison. Warren concluded his lecture notes by praising the resurgence of Congress in the enforcement of civil rights. He advocated an expansive role for the Court in issuing broad constructions of the Reconstruction Amendments and in applying civil rights laws aggressively.

The story of the Warren Court and the civil rights movement represents a case study in how Earl Warren accomplished these objectives.

DIRECT ACTION AND THE WARREN COURT, 1955–1968

The Bus Boycott Cases

In the immediate aftermath of the *Brown* desegregation cases, NAACP activists in Montgomery, Alabama organized a bus boycott to protest segregation on municipal buses. Montgomery municipal ordinances and community custom required blacks to sit at the back of the bus. For years, pastors at the Dexter Avenue Baptist Church in Montgomery had made a point of refusing to sit in the seats reserved for blacks. In their sermons, Reverend Vernon Johns and Dr. Martin Luther King, Jr. urged the congregation to join in the protests, but in the early 1950s relatively few persons did so.[7]

In December 1955, Montgomery Police arrested Rosa Parks for refusing to give up her bus seat to a white passenger in violation of local segregation laws. NAACP leaders organized a bus boycott, and Dr. Martin Luther King, Jr. sponsored mass rallies at his church, where he praised the Christian commitment of Rosa Parks. As thousands attended King's meetings and the number of boycotters reached into the tens of thousands, King convinced his audience that going to jail for a just cause represented a badge of honor. At the height of the boycott, every day between 30,000 and 40,000 persons refrained from riding the Montgomery buses.

The success of black leaders in organizing the boycott led to resistance from groups such as the White Citizens' Council and the Ku Klux Klan. Six separate bombing incidents occurred during the year-long boycott, including the bombing of King's own home. The leaders of the boycott filed suit in federal court challenging the constitutionality of bus segregation in Montgomery. In a second action, Alabama Attorney General (and later Governor) John Patterson filed suit in state court charging the NAACP with illegally organizing the Montgomery bus boycott.

These actions show the interplay between the direct action of the protestors and the court system. Repeatedly throughout the next decade, civil rights protestors filed suits in federal courts seeking orders that would strike down specific Southern segregation and voting laws. Likewise, when Southern officials used state courts against them—requesting injunctions against civil rights organizers, filing criminal actions for trespass or breaches of the peace, or seeking compensatory or punitive damages for allegedly libelous fundraising ads—the civil rights activists, as defendants in these actions, appealed to the Supreme Court. In reviewing these actions, the Warren Court linked itself inextricably to the events of the civil rights era.

Browder v. Gayle, the Montgomery bus boycott case that Dr. King and his followers filed, reached the Supreme Court in the summer of 1956. The case raised the issue of public accommodations in the context of a city-owned bus system. The Court resolved the case in favor of the plaintiffs, issuing a summary decision that cited *Brown* and four other decisions. These included decisions that struck down segregation at Baltimore's public beaches and bathhouses[8] and Atlanta's municipal golf course,[9] as well as two decisions from the 1940s prohibiting discrimination against racial minorities on the part of common carriers such as railroads that operated in interstate commerce.[10]

Attorney General Patterson's state case against the NAACP sought to cripple King and his NAACP allies financially and deprive them of legal authority to conduct business in Alabama. Patterson alleged that the NAACP had failed to comply with Alabama non-profit corporation laws and had unlawfully conspired to attack Alabama's segregation laws. Patterson convinced the trial judge to compel the NAACP to produce a variety of business records, including its membership lists. When the NAACP refused to comply on the grounds that doing so would subject its members to reprisal and attacks from white supremacists, the Alabama Supreme Court held it in contempt and fined it $100,000.

The NAACP appealed to the U.S. Supreme Court, and in 1958, the Court issued a unanimous decision reversing the contempt order. In his opinion for the Court, Justice Harlan wrote, "Freedom to engage in association for the advancement of beliefs is an inseparable part of the 'liberty' assured by the Due Process Clause."[11] Especially in situations involving unpopular organizations, individual members enjoy privacy rights in their group associations, and the government must present a compelling justification for demanding release of such sensitive information.

Patterson's next legal attack against King involved a felony action for perjury arising out of King's alleged failure to file proper Alabama income taxes. The lawsuit forced King to spend significant resources to defend himself. One of King's trusted aides, Bayard Rustin, placed a full-page ad in the *New York Times* seeking to raise funds for King's defense. The ad, entitled "Heed Their Rising Voices," praised student protestors in South Carolina and Alabama who conducted nonviolent sit-ins at segregated lunch counters. It criticized the "unprecedented wave of terror" that public officials used to stop the protestors. The ad described "truckloads of police" who "ringed the Alabama State College campus and padlocked students in a dining hall" and then accused "Southern violators" of meeting peaceful protest with "intimidation and violence." It charged the "Southern violators" with bombing King's house, arresting him repeatedly on fabricated charges, and seeking to remove him as a leader of the movement. Several names appeared at the bottom of the ad, including four SCLC ministers, Rev. Ralph Abernathy, Rev. Fred Shuttlesworth, Rev. Joseph Lowery, and Rev. S. S. Seay.

Rustin's ad generated significant contributions for the SCLC, but it also contained a number of minor factual errors. The ad outraged Governor Patterson and L.B. Sullivan, a City of Montgomery Police Commissioner. Patterson and Sullivan filed libel actions in Alabama state court against each of the four ministers and the *New York Times*, seeking over two million dollars in compensatory and punitive damages. The juries held in favor of the plaintiffs, and the Alabama Supreme Court upheld the judgments. The defendants then appealed to the U.S. Supreme Court, arguing that the civil judgments deprived them of their First Amendment right to freedom of expression.

In a groundbreaking decision (*New York Times v. Sullivan*, 1964), Justice Brennan reviewed the history of libel and sedition in America. He found in the First Amendment a "profound national commitment to the principle that debate on public issues should be uninhibited, robust, and wide-open. . . . (I)t may well include vehement, caustic, and sometimes unpleasantly sharp attacks on government and public officials."[12] Brennan held that members of the public had a constitutional right to criticize public officials and that lawsuits for defamation of character against public officials could not succeed unless the plaintiff showed that the defendant acted with knowledge that his or her remarks were false or that the defendant acted in reckless disregard of the truth. The new "actual malice" standard created a zone of freedom for critics of government and publishers who disseminated their remarks.

NAACP v. Alabama and *New York Times v. Sullivan* show the lengths to which Southern officials went in their effort to defeat the movement for racial equality. The cases also illustrate the wide array of political and legal tools that can be used to repress unpopular minority groups. By expanding First Amendment freedoms to include the right to privacy regarding organizational memberships and the right to engage in robust criticism of public officials, the Warren Court took great strides in expanding the scope of human liberty.

The Sit-In Cases

In the spring of 1960, the Southern Christian Leadership Conference (SCLC) sponsored nonviolence workshops throughout the South. A new generation of student leaders, including Robert Moses, Diane Nash, and John Lewis, attended these workshops and then formed a new organization, the Student Nonviolent Coordinating Committee (SNCC). Focusing on a strategy of direct action, the students confronted white supremacists face-to-face and bore the risk of violent reprisal. The students embraced a militant political ideology that differed from the more moderate approach of Dr. King and the SCLC. They relied upon local community organizing to galvanize opposition to the Jim Crow system.

The activists who endured the savagery of the Ku Klux Klan and sometimes died in the cause of freedom lacked the sophistication and oratory skills of Dr. King. They were sharecroppers, maids, and students, and they spoke by putting their lives on the line. While Dr. King emerged as the voice of the civil rights movement, the image of civil rights activists standing up to vicious police dogs, fire hoses, and brutal beatings convinced the nation of the righteousness of the civil rights cause.

The first of the famous sit-in demonstrations occurred in February of 1960 when students at North Carolina A & T College in Greensboro, North Carolina conducted a silent protest at a Woolworth's lunch counter. In rapid succession, protests spread to dozens of other cities. In Nashville, SCLC activist James Lawson organized nonviolent sit-in demonstrations at downtown five-and-dime stores. One of his apprentices, Diane Nash, emerged as a local leader of SNCC. Lawson, Nash, and their colleagues organized hundreds of middle-class college students to conduct the sit-ins. Dressed in their Sunday best, wave after wave of students entered the lunch counters and silently refused to comply with segregation laws. When police arrested one group, a second would take its place at the counters, until finally the jails were overflowing with students.

As a matter of constitutional law, the sit-in cases posed difficult questions. On one hand, private property owners claimed that they had a legal right to exclude unwanted customers, and under existing precedents, their argument had force. On the other hand, racial minorities asserted that they had a fundamental right to be treated equally with whites in places of public accommodation.

In the period between 1960 and 1966, the Warren Court reviewed scores of sit-in cases, and in nearly all of them, it sided with the demonstrators. Earl Warren brought unusual care and concern to the review of these cases. In a memorandum for the conference in the spring of 1962, he summarized the constitutional arguments presented in eighteen of the Court's then pending sit-in cases and suggested how the Court might resolve each.[13] According to Warren, four basic constitutional arguments applied to the cases: (1) the "equal protection" argument that the discriminatory purpose of private individuals should be attributed to the state since in some way the state had participated in the discrimination; (2) the "void for vagueness" argument that the state trespass and breach of the peace statutes used in the cases did not give adequate notice of the acts they prohibited; (3) the "free speech" argument that the protestors' words did not represent a clear and present danger; and (4) the "no evidence" argument that the actions of the protestors—which typically involved "just peaceably sitting there"—did not rise to the level of a breach of the peace.[14]

Over the next several terms, the Court issued unanimous or nearly unanimous decisions vindicating the rights of civil rights protestors on each of these grounds. *Burton v. Wilmington Parking Authority* (1961) illustrates the first of Warren's four basic arguments. There, the Court decided that a private restaurant operating in a municipal parking garage was the functional equivalent of a publicly owned enterprise and therefore had to comply with the Fourteenth Amendment. In this case, the City of Wilmington, Delaware erected and maintained the building using public funds, and it indirectly received profits from the private restaurant on the property.

Warren's second and third arguments, involving "void for vagueness" and "freedom of speech," found application in *Cox v. Louisiana* (1965). Prosecutors charged Cox with breach of the peace arising out of a large demonstration he led on the steps of a local courthouse to protest the arrest of students at segregated lunch counters in Baton Rouge, Louisiana. Cox did not obtain a permit from city officials authorizing the march. At the height of the demonstration, as hundreds of protestors stood on a public sidewalk, Cox urged his fellow students to go back to the segregated lunch counters to conduct further protests. Police officers found these remarks incendiary and arrested Cox.

In his opinion for the Court, Justice Goldberg reversed Cox's conviction. Reviewing the trial record independently, he rejected the trial court's factual findings that Cox and the student demonstrators behaved in a disruptive and overly aggressive manner. Cox's remarks, while disquieting and unpopular, were protected under the First Amendment. Nor could the nature of Cox's remarks serve as a basis for his conviction. Quoting from Justice Douglas' opinion in *Terminiello v. Chicago* (1949), Goldberg ruled:

> (A) function of free speech under our system of government is to invite dispute. It may indeed best serve its high purpose when it induces a condition of unrest, creates dissatisfaction with conditions as they are, or even stirs people to anger. Speech is often provocative and challenging. It may strike at prejudices and preconceptions and have profound unsettling effects as it presses for acceptance of an idea. That is why freedom of speech . . . is . . . protected against censorship or punishment . . . . There is no room under our Constitution for a more restrictive view. For the alternative would lead to standardization of ideas either by legislatures, courts, or dominant political or community groups.[15]

Goldberg attacked the second prong of Cox's breach of the peace conviction—that involving failure to secure a permit for the demonstration—using the "void for vagueness" doctrine. He challenged the discretionary nature of the permit-granting process and noted that applicable laws provided no standards to guide local officials in deciding which applications to grant and which to deny. This fatally vague approach gave police too much discretion to disapprove unpopular ideas.

Warren's fourth approach—that the state presented "no evidence" of a breach of the peace—appeared in *Garner v. Louisiana* (1961). There, students conducted a sit-in at a Kress department store and refused to leave a "whites only" seating area. Prosecutors charged them with breaching the peace. Writing for a unanimous court, Chief Justice Warren found no evidence that the students did anything other than sit peacefully in a prohibited place:

> (H)aving shown that these records contain no evidence to support a finding that petitioners disturbed the peace, either by outwardly boisterous conduct or by passive conduct likely to cause a public disturbance," he wrote, "we hold that these convictions violated petitioners' rights to due process of law guaranteed them by the Fourteenth Amendment to the United States Constitution.[16]

In each of these early sit-in cases, the Supreme Court avoided the underlying issue of whether the human rights of black Americans outweighed the property rights of business owners. In the 1963 term, five new cases squarely raised this difficult question.[17] By that time, America had endured three long years of civil strife. The freedom rides, Sheriff "Bull" Connor's attacks on unarmed demonstrators, the assassination of NAACP leader Medgar Evers, and the deaths of four teenage girls in the bombing of Sixteenth Street Baptist Church in Birmingham provided a compelling context for the Court's decisions in the new cases.

On the merits, the Court struggled to strike a balance between the equal protection, freedom of association, and private property interests the new cases presented. In addition, the justices disagreed about what role, if any, pending civil rights legislation in Congress should play in the Court's resolution of the cases. In the wake of John F. Kennedy's assassination, President Lyndon Johnson pressed Congress to pass a comprehensive civil rights bill in Kennedy's honor, and several justices, including Justice Brennan, did not want to do or say anything that might prevent Congress from resolving the policy questions at stake. On the other hand, Justices William O. Douglas and Arthur Goldberg thought it was the Court's responsibility to reach the merits of the constitutional questions and resolve them in favor of the civil rights demonstrators. The more conservative members of the Court, Justices John Marshall Harlan, Potter Stewart, and Byron White, opposed the erosion of the property rights of private business owners, and Justice Hugo Black joined them. Justice Tom Clark waivered in the middle. For his part, Chief Justice Warren diplomatically sought to present "as united a front as possible" in the Court's resolution of the cases. Eventually, Warren's strong feelings on the issue of racial equality came to the forefront.

A relatively unrecognized sit-in case from the 1963 term illustrates the depth of Warren's concern. *Barr v. City of Columbia* (1964) involved breach of the peace and criminal trespass convictions of several civil rights protestors who conducted a sit-in at a private lunch counter in Columbia, South Carolina. The five-and-dime store in question permitted blacks to enter the front of the store in order to purchase items for sale, but they could not take seats in the luncheonette at the back. Instead, they could only make carry-out orders for food. During the Court's internal deliberations, a majority of the justices appeared poised to uphold the defendants' convictions. Warren wrote a draft dissent, which Justices Brennan, Goldberg, and Douglas joined, but at a later point, when the remaining justices agreed to issue a *per curiam* (by the entire court) opinion on behalf of the defendants, he withdrew the dissent. Warren's opinion, available only in his papers in the Library of Congress, contained the following observation:

> (T)he arrest, although technically for the crime of trespass, can solely be justified as for the purpose of enforcing the store's policy, . . . which was founded on a right to compel Negroes to stand up to buy their food solely for the reason that they were Negroes. The store might as well have offered to feed only Negroes who would crawl in on their hands and knees, or, as in other caste systems, who would purchase food under conditions that would not cause their shadow to fall on the food of whites. It saddens me deeply to think that this Court, which has so far advanced the notion of the equal dignity of all men before the law, would sanction the right so publicly to first shame and then punish one who merely seeks that which any white man takes for granted. Irrespective of the activity

of other branches of our Government, the courts, and particularly this Court, cannot escape the responsibility imposed by the Constitution to assure to all Americans the basic rights of equal protection under the laws.[18]

Warren's reference to the caste system of India and to rules prohibiting Dalits (untouchables) from casting their shadows on the food of Brahmins provided a potent means of presenting the issues of the sit-in cases in international context. In his trips to India, Warren had encountered traditional Hindu prohibitions on social interaction between members of different castes, rules that extended to matters of religious worship, meals, food, and water, employment, and marriage. Traditionally, untouchables had to drag thorny branches behind them to wipe out their own footprints and then lie face-down on the ground some distance away as Brahmins passed, so as not to defile the holy Brahmins with impurities.[19] The implications of Warren's assertion, left tacit, concerned the extensive similarities between the norms of the Jim Crow system and those of the traditional Hindu castes. In both cases, the community enforced prohibitions through legal and extralegal channels, and in both the norms triggered social and economic exclusion, endogamy, and bitter injustice. The mirror that Warren proposed to hold up before the American people presented an unfavorable image to the world, and the conservatives on the Court apparently wanted to avoid that outcome. In an unusual turn of events, Justice Black delivered the *per curiam* opinion of the Court holding that the defendants' breach of the peace convictions lacked an evitendiary foundation and could not stand. A majority of the Court then voted to reverse the defendants' criminal trespass convictions, but Justice Black, writing on behalf of justices Harlan and White, dissented from this portion of the case, arguing that the conduct of police in arresting the defendants for trespassing on private property did not rise to the level of "state action" under the Fourteenth Amendment and that the defendants' criminal trespass convictions should be upheld. In effect, Black dissented from his own *per curiam* opinion in exchange for the dropping of Warren's controversial dissent.

Another more famous sit-in case from the 1963 term, *Bell v. Maryland*, provided a more extensive forum for the resolution of the competing constitutional issues before the Court. The case concerned Robert Mack Bell, a 16-year-old high school student, who joined a mass sit-in at a segregated restaurant in Baltimore. A local court found the students guilty of criminal trespass, and the Maryland Supreme Court affirmed their convictions.

In the Supreme Court's conference, Chief Justice Warren highlighted the moral dimension of the case. He wanted the Court to get to the "raw"' of the problem and reach the basic questions. To him, this meant that those who opened their restaurants to the public "abandon private choice" in determining which customers to serve. In an apparent reference to the Vinson Court's housing discrimination decision, *Shelley v. Kraemer* (1948), Warren argued that as long as the black customers "behave themselves, the owner can't have police to help to throw them out. The state then unconstitutionally enforces discrimination." Justice Black, who had been a steadfast leader of the cause of free speech and racial justice on the Court for many years, now voiced concern about the disruptive actions of the protestors.[20] Referring to his own father who ran a general store in rural Alabama, he said, "I don't think the Constitution forbids the owner of a store to keep people out."[21]

Initially, the Court decided to uphold Bell's conviction by a vote of 5–4. Justice Brennan worked behind the scenes to postpone final judgment in the case. Knowing that Congress soon would vote on a new Civil Rights Bill, which would resolve the conflict between property rights and human rights without the Court having to do so, Brennan sought additional time. He persuaded five justices to ask the U.S. Solicitor General to file a brief addressing the broader constitutional issues in the case.

Eventually, Brennan convinced Justices Clark and Stewart to change their votes on the merits. The three justices filed an opinion emphasizing that Maryland had recently passed a law prohibiting segregation in restaurants, and, accordingly, the Court should send the *Bell* case back to the Maryland state courts for further consideration. In a separate concurrence, Warren joined Justices Goldberg and Douglas in arguing that racial segregation in private businesses was unlawful. Warren and Goldberg found a basis for this conclusion in the Fourteenth Amendment Equal Protection Clause, while Douglas found it in the common law. The remaining justices joined Black in dissent. Thus, the Court split 3-3-3 in a plurality judgment that reversed Bell's conviction. Ten days after the Court released its decision, the Senate voted in favor of the Civil Rights Act, and President Johnson signed it into law.

The Civil Rights Act of 1964 helped to resolve the fight over racial segregation. Grounded in Congress' power to regulate interstate commerce, the Act prohibited racial discrimination in places of public accommodation, such as restaurants, hotels, and gas stations. In the coming years, the Warren Court would address charges that the Act unconstitutionally regulated intrastate conduct and usurped powers that the founding fathers had reserved to the states under the Tenth Amendment. These matters will be addressed in Section 3, below.

Voting Rights

The 1964 Civil Rights Act could not have become law without the vision, organizational skill, and sacrifice of the civil rights movement. For nearly ninety years, Congress did nothing to safeguard the human rights of black

Americans. In the relatively short span of ten years, significant social and political change took place, albeit in symbolic areas of American life that did not involve a redistribution of political or economic power. Challenges against voting discrimination represented a different order of magnitude since they raised the issue of how readily minority whites would grant voting rights to blacks in parts of the country where blacks comprised the numerical majority. In the rural counties of the Black Belt and inner city precincts throughout the South, the challenges focused attention on the lengths to which whites would go to exclude blacks from the political power structure. Forty persons are known to have been murdered as a result of protest activities in the South during the civil rights movement, and the circumstances of another 75 victims still are under investigation.[22]

In the half-century leading up to the civil rights era, the Supreme Court issued numerous decisions protecting the voting rights of black citizens. These included decisions prohibiting the grandfather clause,[23] white primaries,[24] racial gerrymandering,[25] and arbitrary administration of literacy tests.[26] Nevertheless, the federal effort proved inadequate. Throughout the Deep South, state and county officials adopted an array of policies to prevent blacks from voting, such as poll taxes, literacy tests, and good morals requirements. The most effective restrictions enhanced the discretionary judgments of county elections officials, and in several rural counties of Alabama and Mississippi, no blacks had ever exercised the franchise in living memory. In 1956, the percentage of voting-age blacks who had registered in Louisiana was 31.7%, whereas in Alabama it was 14.2%, and in Mississippi, 4.4%.[27] Another strategy to prevent blacks from voting involved the blocking of reform legislation in Congress. Senators from the Deep South, including Senator James Eastland of Mississippi, used their seniority to block civil rights bills in committee. When that tactic failed, they successfully filibustered. Between 1954 and 1964, over 121 civil rights bills died in Congress.[28]

In 1957, the Eisenhower Administration succeeded in getting a diluted civil rights bill through Congress. The 1957 Civil Rights Act gave the attorney general the power to seek injunctive relief against persons who interfered with voting rights on the basis of race. Assembling evidence for injunctive relief under the Act proved daunting. John Doar and other highly committed attorneys in the Civil Rights Division of the U.S. Department of Justice examined registration records meticulously for thousands of hours in order to develop enough evidence to obtain injunctive relief. Even then, the defendants often responded by inventing new ways to discriminate, such as by redrafting literacy tests or simply closing registration offices. On the eve of the adoption of the 1965 Voting Rights Act, federal officials had made only modest improvements in the percentage of voting-age blacks who successfully registered in the Deep South.

The Student Nonviolent Coordinating Committee (SNCC) challenged voting discrimination by taking direct action at the grassroots level. Following its success in the freedom rides of 1960 and 1961, SNCC made voter registration its top priority. It sent organizers such as Bob Moses into rural Mississippi to increase the number of registered voters and to build a base of political support in the black community.

Organizing voter registration in rural Mississippi and Alabama was a life-threatening enterprise. Vigilantes firebombed churches that sponsored voting rights meetings, and they murdered civil workers with impunity. According to FBI records, during the five-year period between 1963 and 1968, the White Knights of the Ku Klux Klan committed nine murders, seventy-five church burnings, and over three hundred bombings and assaults.[29] The fallen include Vernon Dahmer, Herbert Lee, Louis Allen, and Viola Liuzzo.[30] Selflessly, they gave their lives to win voting rights for black citizens.

Historians of the civil rights movement also credit SNCC with pushing the SCLC to take a more militant stance in support of voting rights in the crucial period between 1963 and 1965.[31] In this period, Dr. King focused on large-scale media events such as the March on Washington and the lengthy struggle to desegregate downtown stores in Birmingham, Alabama. He resisted spending finite resources on voter registration initiatives in small towns such as Selma, Alabama. However, in January of 1965, King and the SCLC agreed to work with SNCC in Selma to address the voting rights issue.

The famous protests at Edmund Pettus Bridge in Selma and the subsequent march to Montgomery brought national attention to the problem of disenfranchisement in the South. The route of the march took protestors through Lowndes County, where blacks comprised over 80% of the local adult population but could not register to vote. Over 25,000 protestors marched triumphantly into Montgomery for a rally. That evening, Viola Liuzzo, a white mother from Detroit, was shot to death in Lowndes County as she attempted to drive a civil rights worker back to Selma.

President Johnson addressed the nation on March 15. He announced his plan to present a voting rights bill to Congress and in strong language endorsed the goals and sacrifice of the protestors in Selma. Later that spring, Johnson's allies in the Senate overcame a filibuster, and in early summer, the House of Representatives passed its version of the bill. On August 6, 1965, the President signed the historic Voting Rights Act of 1965 into law. The Act made it unlawful to deny or abridge the right to vote on the basis of race, outlawed literacy tests, and required jurisdictions with a history of voting discrimination to "clear" proposed changes in voting policies with the U.S. Department of Justice or a federal court before they could take effect.

Unlike the Civil Rights Act of 1957, which featured a litigation-based approach to social change, the new law incorporated administrative strategies by authorizing the use of federal examiners and observers to oversee the registration of hundreds of thousands of black citizens across the South. Within two years, voter registration among blacks in Alabama increased from 19% to 52% and in Mississippi from 7% to 60%.[32]

THE WARREN COURT AND CIVIL RIGHTS

The landmark legislation of the civil rights era offered the Supreme Court political and legal cover for the fight against racial discrimination. During the period between 1954 and 1964, the judiciary had stood alone among the three branches of the federal government in attacking the racial caste system. Now the three branches stood united, and the powerful arm of the federal executive branch ensured greater levels of compliance with school desegregation and voting rights laws.[33] Legally, the Commerce Clause provided a constitutional predicate for the exercise of congressional authority in the civil rights arena, and the enforcement clauses of the Reconstruction Amendments offered a new basis for the assertion of Congressional power to fight racial discrimination. Table 9.1 displays the Warren Court's record in civil and voting rights cases. Consistently, supermajorities among the justices voted to sustain the constitutionality of civil rights legislation.

Relying on federal marshals to protect voting rights under the 1965 Voting Rights Act proved far more successful than the previous case-by-case litigation strategy. It also assured greater levels of fairness in the criminal justice system by placing more blacks on the voting rosters from which jury commissioners selected prospective jurors. Together, the Supreme Court and the Congress expanded the concept of citizenship and transformed the role of federal law in the elections process. In so doing, they substantially fulfilled the promise of the Fifteenth Amendment.

In the final three years of the Warren Court, a majority of the justices twice rejected the appeals of civil rights demonstrators. The first of these decisions occurred in *Adderley v. Florida* (1966), where the Court ruled by a vote of 5–4 that the First Amendment rights of protestors did not extend to protests conducted on the grounds of a jail. In the second case, *Walker v. Birmingham* (1967), the Court ruled 5–4 that the City of Birmingham could hold Martin Luther King Jr. in contempt for failure to obey an injunction that required him to refrain from organizing street demonstrations without a permit.

Warren dissented in both cases. In *Walker*, he wrote the dissenting opinion. The *Walker* case involved the famous Easter 1963 protests against segregation in the commercial establishments of downtown Birmingham. By ordinance, the city required a permit for demonstrations, and the permit process gave city officials great discretion to approve or disapprove permit

Table 9.1 Cases Involving Civil or Voting Rights, 1964–1968

Case	*Issue*	*Holding*
Heart of Atlanta Motel v. U.S. (1964) (Clark, J.) (decision: 9-0); *Katzenbach v. McClung* (1964) (Clark, J.) (decision: 9-0).	Does the 1964 Civil Rights Act unconstitutionally infringe upon the power of local hotels or restaurants to refuse accommodations and service to African American guests?	No. The 1964 Civil Rights Act is a valid exercise of Congress' power to regulate interstate commerce. The flow of persons from one state to another is "commerce" for purposes of constitutional analysis. Where a substantial portion of food served comes from out-of-state sources, a local business operates in interstate commerce.
South Carolina v. Katzenbach (1966) (Warren, C.J) (decision: 8-1).	Does Congress have the power to suspend literacy tests and authorize federal examiners to register voters in areas of the country where voting discrimination has been common?	Yes. Section 2 of the Fifteenth Amendment authorizes Congress to enforce the right of citizens to be free from voting discrimination on the basis of race, and this authority supersedes the reserved powers of the states. Congress is free to use whatever means are appropriate to carry out the objects of the Constitution.
Harper v. Virginia State Board of Elections (1966) (Douglas, J.) (decision: 6-3).	Does the Virginia poll tax violate the Fourteenth Amendment Equal Protection Clause?	Yes. Classifications that impinge upon the fundamental right to vote must be closely scrutinized. Fee payments are unrelated to a citizen's ability to participate intelligently in the electoral process.
Katzenbach v. Morgan (1966) (Brennan, J.) (decision: 7-2).	Does Section 4(e) of the Voting Rights Act, which prohibits states from denying certain citizens the right to vote because of an inability to read or write English, violate states' rights under the Tenth Amendment?	No. Section 4(e) is appropriate legislation to enforce the requirements of the Fourteenth Amendment. Section 5 of the Fourteenth Amendment grants Congress the independent power to enforce the provisions of the Amendment by appropriate legislation, trumping the reserved powers of the states.
Jones v. Alfred H. Mayer Co. (1968) (Stewart, J.) (decision: 7-2).	Does Congress have the power to authorize private individuals to sue for housing discrimination without the need to show state action?	Yes. Section 2 of the Thirteenth Amendment authorizes Congress to bar discrimination that is based on the badges and incidents of slavery. Federal housing laws prohibit *all* discrimination against blacks in the sale or rental of property.

applications. In this instance, the city summarily rejected the application, and just days before the planned protest, it sought an *ex parte* temporary restraining order prohibiting the demonstration. Attorneys for the city included the text of the city ordinance into the court's decree and persuaded the court to include a warning in its decree that violation of the decree might result in a finding of contempt. Objecting to this legal process, Warren wrote:

> The Alabama Circuit Court did not issue this temporary injunction to preserve existing conditions while it proceeded to decide some underlying dispute. There was no underlying dispute before it, and the court, in practical effect, merely added a judicial signature to a preexisting criminal ordinance. Just as the court had no need to issue the injunction to preserve its ability to decide some underlying dispute, the city had no need of an injunction to impose a criminal penalty for demonstrating on the streets without a permit. The ordinance already accomplished that. In point of fact, there is only one apparent reason why the city sought this injunction and why the court issued it: to make it possible to punish petitioners for contempt, rather than for violating the ordinance, and thus to immunize the unconstitutional statute and its unconstitutional application from any attack. I regret that this strategy has been so successful.[34]

Warren's position in the case illustrates his willingness to use heightened scrutiny to expose discriminatory conduct on the part of public officials as well as the depth of his efforts to protect civil rights demonstrators from abusive legal procedures.

THE IMPACT OF THE WARREN COURT'S CIVIL RIGHTS REFORMS

School Desegregation and Civil Rights

The Warren Court's civil rights jurisprudence highlights the importance of constitutional interpretation in the protection of controversial minority groups who otherwise find themselves at the mercy of powerful political majorities. In the period before the adoption of key civil rights legislation in the summer of 1964, the Court used heightened scrutiny under the First Amendment and innovative extensions of the state action and void for vagueness doctrines to protect civil rights protestors from repression.

Following the adoption of the 1964 Civil Rights Act and the 1965 Voting Rights Act, the Court shifted its attention to the constitutionality of the new legislation. It used the commerce clause and the enforcement clauses of the Reconstruction Amendments to sustain the constitutionality of these landmark civil rights laws. The Warren Court's interpretations of the enforcement clauses in the Reconstruction Amendments proved significant. The legal argument about these clauses—Section 2 of the Thirteenth Amendment, Section 5 of the Fourteenth Amendment, and Section 2 of the Fifteenth Amendment—centered on whether Congress has the power to determine the scope and application of rules *enforcing* the Reconstruction Amendments or whether the judicial branch, using its authority to interpret the meaning of the Amendments themselves, has the exclusive power to do so. In *Katzenbach v. Morgan*, Justice Brennan addressed this question in the context of Section 4 (e) of the Voting Rights Act:

> (The State of New York) urges that § 4(e) cannot be sustained as appropriate legislation to enforce the Equal Protection Clause unless the judiciary decides—even with the guidance of a congressional judgment—that the application of the English literacy requirement prohibited by § 4(e) is forbidden by the Equal Protection Clause itself. We disagree. Neither the language nor history of § 5 supports such a construction. As was said with regard to § 5 in *Ex parte Virginia*, "It is the power of Congress which has been enlarged. Congress is authorized to enforce the prohibitions by appropriate legislation. Some legislation is contemplated to make the amendments fully effective."
>
> A construction of § 5 that would require a judicial determination that the enforcement of the state law precluded by Congress violated the Amendment, as a condition of sustaining the congressional enactment, would depreciate both congressional resourcefulness and congressional responsibility for implementing the Amendment. It would confine the legislative power in this context to the insignificant role of abrogating only those state laws that the judicial branch was prepared to adjudge unconstitutional. (Internal footnotes and citations deleted).[35]

By broadly interpreting Congress' power under the enforcement clauses, the Warren Court created a compound system of civil rights protection. Under this system, if Congress becomes unhappy with judicial interpretations of the Reconstruction Amendments, it can pass broad enforcement legislation in order to protect additional rights. Conversely, if the Supreme Court becomes impatient with Congress' failure to adopt new legislation to enforce existing constitutional rights, it may issue more expansive interpretations of specific clauses of the Constitution.

Apart from the many modifications of constitutional doctrine that the Warren Court's racial justice decisions spawned, its reforms also raised broader questions about the efficacy of the Supreme Court in precipitating social change. Critics such as Gerald Rosenberg[36] and Donald L. Horowitz[37] have argued that the Supreme Court is an ineffective vehicle for the achievement of sweeping social change. Rosenberg uses the school desegregation and civil rights movements as a case study to test the proposition that the Court, as a dynamic institution, played a direct role in ending discrimination in education. He notes that the Court lacks budgetary and coercive power to enforce its decisions, and it depends upon the support of the parties, public officials, and citizens to accomplish its objectives.

Rosenberg explores several alternative paths by which the Court may have accomplished the goal of school desegregation. He examines the possibility of enhanced media coverage of school segregation issues, the Court's ability to exert political pressure on the legislative or the executive branches of government, and its influence on black activists, who may have pressured white elites to act. On all fronts, he finds the Court ineffective. Press coverage in both nonelite and elite publications remained relatively low through the 1950s, and Senate filibusters blocked civil rights legislation in the late 1950s and early 1960s. Black activists like Dr. Martin Luther King Jr. expressly rejected litigation as the principal means of attacking the white power structure since ordinary persons function only as "passive spectators."

Rosenberg concludes that the *Brown* decision produced virtually no change for black students attending segregated schools in the South during the ten-year period between 1954 and 1964 and that it was only after the political branches became involved in the passage of the 1964 Civil Rights Act that meaningful change occurred. Thus, according to Rosenberg, *Brown* stands for the proposition that "courts are impotent to produce significant social reform."[38]

The hypothesis that the Supreme Court is a constrained institution incapable of precipitating meaningful social change has been influential in American law and politics. Nevertheless, as it applies to the civil rights movement in the postwar era, the theory has several shortcomings. Rosenberg's analysis begins at an arbitrary point in the litigation process, the announcement of a decision by the U.S. Supreme Court. With that as a first cause, he then explores the effect of the Court's decision. Absent in his model is the role of the plaintiffs who brought the litigation in the first place. Students of the Court know that the justices, unlike their counterparts in the legislative and executive branches, cannot initiate policy on their own. As reactive institutions, courts can only speak through the cases that parties bring before them. The parties to litigation shape the contours of judicial rulings through the legal theories they develop and the witnesses and evidence that they bring before the court.

In his description of the school desegregation cases, Rosenberg stresses the point that the plaintiffs pursued a litigation strategy for reform as opposed to the direct action strategies of the civil rights movement. His interpretation overstates the differences between the school desegregation reformers of the 1940s and early 1950s and the civil rights activists of the 1960s. The plaintiffs in the school desegregation cases were ordinary Americans who joined the NAACP because they wanted a better life for their children. Like the activists of the 1960s, they suffered reprisals for their political activism, and they fought their battles at a local level as they tried to implement and enforce the rights that the Supreme Court and the U.S. Constitution gave them.

To speak of the *Brown* litigation and the parties who brought it as if they were functionally separate from the direct action protests of the 1960s is to misread the history of the movement. To be sure, litigation and direct action involve separate strategies for social reform, and various organizations under the broad umbrella of the civil rights movement emphasized each. Yet in key respects the NAACP litigation strategy and the direct action activities of the SCLC overlapped and were mutually reinforcing. The prototypical examples of direct action in the fight against racial oppression—the Montgomery bus boycott and the freedom rides—ended when the U.S. Supreme Court issued rulings striking down Montgomery's bus ordinance and the segregation of bus terminals used in interstate commerce. Similarly, when plaintiffs in Alabama tried to put the NAACP out of business in the legal battle over defamation in the New York Times "Heed Their Rising Voices" advertisement, the Supreme Court resolved the issue favorably for the civil rights defendants. All of these encounters involved *both* direct action *and* litigation, and in all of them, the Supreme Court played an important role. Despite their occasional disagreements, the NAACP and the direct action groups of the 1960s worked *in tandem* for social change, a fundamental truth that Rosenberg's argument overlooks.

Another weakness in Rosenberg's argument concerns his failure to consider the causal relationship between the *Brown* decisions, the rise of the massive resistance movement in the Deep South, and the savage violence directed against civil workers during the early to mid-1960s. Professor Michael J. Klarman explores this relationship in detail and finds that in the absence of the *Brown* decision, the massive resistance of the South may not have occurred. To summarize Klarman's argument, *Brown* legitimized the principle of racial neutrality and placed white supremacists in the South on the defensive. The white supremacists' vicious stance against nonviolent civil rights workers lost them public support and helped persuade Congress and the Johnson Administration to endorse key civil rights legislation.

Conservative scholars such as Donald L. Horowitz portray the *Brown* decision as the first in a series of cases that have improperly involved federal and state courts in organizational change litigation. This type of litigation seeks to use a court's equitable power to issue structural injunctions. Plaintiffs seek these injunctions in order to remedy constitutional violations in complex institutions such as public school districts, prisons, mental health hospitals, and welfare systems.

Conservatives contend that courts lack the expertise to make policy judgments involving large public institutions and that rules of evidence often make it difficult to engage in proper fact finding in matters involving statistics, research methods, or scientific testing. They question whether it is wise for courts to order the expenditure of public funds in one area of government operations since judges, unlike legislators, do not have to balance additional expenditures in one area with budget cuts in others. In recent decades, Horowitz's ideas have been influential among Republican appointees to the federal courts. As a result, institutional litigation has declined and the discretionary power of states and corporations has increased. Critics respond that complex institutional litigation is necessary to defend constitutional rights.

The Warren Court perceived that the racial caste system of the Jim Crow era led to the systematic isolation of blacks in virtually every aspect of their lives. The normal channels of the political process did not provide them a remedy, and the severity of the problem demanded judicial action. The interplay between civil rights reformers and the Warren Court illustrates both the process by which sweeping legal change took place in the 1950s and 1960s and the magnitude of the Court's accomplishments. In virtually every aspect of civil rights—schools, public accommodations, voting, and housing—the Warren Court demanded and at least partially achieved legal equality. Congress and the administrative agencies of the Executive Branch proved indispensable allies in this endeavor. Yet as Dr. King in the latter stages of his life well recognized, the extension of legal rights did not overcome the lingering effects of slavery and racial discrimination on the financial condition of black America. In the immediate aftermath of the Warren Court, the problem of economic inequality and race jeopardized the legal victories of the civil rights era.

THE RESURRECTION OF JIM CROW

The history of racial discrimination in the United States shows that the forces of racial hierarchy are readily adaptable. At the end of the Civil War, as the system of chattel slavery came to an end, radical Reconstruction policies threatened the white power structure of the former Confederacy. After a campaign of violence and terrorism directed against blacks, a new social order emerged in the South featuring a Jim Crow system of black codes, segregation laws, and economic ostracism of black Americans. Seventy-five years later, the Warren Court's school desegregation and civil rights decisions threatened the legal foundations of the Jim Crow system. In a response that in some ways echoed the history of the Reconstruction era, vigilantes in the South and in Northern "inner-ring" suburbs met civil rights protestors with violence and massive resistance. The triumph of the civil rights movement in the mid-1960s prompted white supremacists to devise new mechanisms of social and racial control.

In her recent book *The New Jim Crow*, Professor Michelle Alexander argues that in the final decades of the twentieth century a new caste system based on mass incarceration has replaced the old Jim Crow stratification system, thus maintaining and reinforcing the traditional social and economic injustices of the past. Alexander explores the process by which one system of racial subjugation replaces another throughout American history.

The rhetoric of the "new" Jim Crow includes race-neutral language intentionally designed to tap into racist attitudes. Terms such as "neighborhood schools," "welfare queens," and "criminal predators" illustrate the trend. As Alexander argues, those who opposed school desegregation and civil rights reforms in the 1960s supported conservative candidates who incorporated the new rhetoric into their campaigns. Richard Nixon successfully used this approach in his 1968 and 1972 presidential campaigns as part of a "Southern strategy" of realignment, and both Ronald Reagan and George H.W. Bush made similar appeals.

In the period since Earl Warren left the Supreme Court, conservative social policies have enhanced economic stratification and accelerated the rise of gated communities, radical individualism, and political secession among elites. Conversely, deindustrialization, globalization, and weak inner-city schools have triggered an epidemic of drugs, gangs, and street crime in inner-city neighborhoods. The crisis of unemployment among ghetto youth is stark and disconcerting. Troy Duster reports that in 1954 at the time of the *Brown* decision unemployment rates among black and white youth were about equal; thirty years later, in 1984, unemployment rates among black youth nearly quadrupled, while unemployment rates among white youth remained about the same.[39] America's postindustrial economy demanded fewer unskilled and semiskilled workers, and the burden of job displacement and downward mobility fell disproportionately on inner-city residents.

Alexander also explores the role of the War on Drugs in the creation of a new mass incarceration system. Law and order policies have targeted ghetto youth in the fight against crack cocaine, and criminal sentences for drug offenders have become more severe. After their release from prison, ex-offenders in many states continue to face debilitating sanctions that bar them from many types of employment, as well as eligibility for welfare and educational benefits and the right to participate in the franchise.

The new caste system that Alexander documents operates with the veneer of racial neutrality since it stresses individual responsibility for wrongdoing. Yet the discretionary nature of law enforcement and the targeting of persons of color in the War on Drugs have led to the marginalization and disenfranchisement of urban minorities in ways that closely resemble the outcomes of the old Jim Crow system. According to a recent article in the *New York*

Times, almost 7.7% of black Americans of voting age cannot vote because their status as ex-offenders disenfranchises them.[40] Currently, blacks represent 38.2% of the prison population, and the total number of persons under some form of correctional supervision in America has mushroomed to over 7 million.[41]

The "new Jim Crow" operates as an invisible caste system that permanently deprives poor people of color and other ex-offenders of their civil rights. In significant ways, it undermines the fundamental rights of national citizenship that the Warren Court sought to guarantee. Even as the Warren Court developed new legal doctrines in the areas of legislative apportionment, defamation, and freedom of expression to protect the rights of outsiders in the American political process, the Supreme Court in recent decades has deferred to legislative majorities and failed to respond creatively to the problem of rising inequality in American life. From gerrymandering to the debilitating legal sanctions directed against ex-offenders, the dominant trend has been to close the courthouse door to those who seek to challenge the status quo.

Viewed in historical perspective, Earl Warren and the Warren Court played an important part in the struggle for racial justice in the United States. Warren and his colleagues ended the legacy of *de jure* segregation in public schools and other fields; they found constitutional support for Congress' power to guarantee public accommodation in the Commerce Clause; and they issued precedential decisions that broadly construed Congress' powers under the enforcement clauses of the Reconstruction Amendments. Yet as Michele Alexander shows, the Warren effort also can be interpreted as another chapter in the sorry story of the unsuccessful effort to constrain and abolish the forces of racism in American life. In the nineteenth century, the Reconstruction Amendments fundamentally altered the structure of federalism in the United States in the interest of enhancing the fundamental rights of the freedmen. During the Jim Crow era, the promise of Reconstruction deteriorated in the face of violent resistance, discriminatory laws, and widespread white indifference. In the same way, the Warren Court tried to resuscitate the spirit and meaning of the Reconstruction Amendments, building into the law a set of principles consistent with the demands of racial equality. But in fundamental ways, the initiatives of the Warren Court suffered setbacks and disappointments in the period that followed. To date, the citizens of the United States have proven unable to accept the changes that the Warren Court demanded, and, as a result, the dream of racial justice remains unfulfilled.

NOTES

1. Container 574, Supreme Court File, Earl Warren Papers, Manuscript Division, Library of Congress, Washington, D.C.

2. Earl Warren, *Memoirs*, 291.

3. Joe B. Frantz, Interview with Former Chief Justice Earl Warren, 1971, Lyndon Baines Johnson Library, Austin, Texas. Available at http://glifos.lbjf.org/gsm/index.php/Warren_Earl_OHInt1_092171.

4. In *U.S. v. Guest*, 383 U.S. 745 (1966), Warren joined Justice Brennan's concurring opinion, which asserted that federal statutes passed under Section 5 of the Fourteenth Amendment can reach private action, even though Section 1 of the same amendment does contain a state action requirement. In *Jones v. Alfred H. Mayer* (1968), the Court held that Section 5 of the Fourteenth Amendment authorized Congress to prohibit all forms of housing discrimination, including those that arose between private parties.

5. Frantz, Interview with Former Chief Justice Earl Warren.

6. Container 825, Speeches and Writings File, Earl Warren Papers, Manuscript Division, Library of Congress, Washington, D.C. Warren's speech at New York University Law School, given October 4, 1968, was entitled "The Fourteenth Amendment: Retrospect and Prospect." See also, Earl Warren, "Fourteenth Amendment: Retrospect and Prospect," in *The Fourteenth Amendment Centennial Volume*, ed. Bernard Schwartz (New York: New York University Press, 1970), 212–33.

7. Reverend Vernon Johns' most famous sermon, "Segregation after Death," arose from the parable of the beggar Lazarus and the rich man Dives from Luke 16:19-31. The passage reads as follows: "There was a rich man who was clothed in purple and fine linen and who feasted sumptuously every day. And at his gate was laid a poor man named Lazarus, covered with sores, who desired to be fed with what fell from the rich man's table. Moreover, even the dogs came and licked his sores. The poor man died and was carried by the angels to Abraham's side. The rich man also died and was buried, and in Hades, being in torment, he lifted up his eyes and saw Abraham far off and Lazarus at his side. And he called out, 'Father Abraham, have mercy on me, and send Lazarus to dip the end of his finger in water and cool my tongue, for I am in anguish in this flame.' But Abraham said, 'Child, remember that you in your lifetime received your good things, and Lazarus in like manner bad things; but now he is comforted here, and you are in anguish. And besides all this, between us and you a great chasm has been fixed, in order that those who would pass from here to you may not be able, and none may cross from there to us.'" Luke 16:19-31 (English Standard Version).

In his sermon, Johns noted that Dives' fault lay not with his riches, but with the "great gulf of separation" that he imposed upon Lazarus. The "great gulf" resembled the segregation system, and God would condemn those who perpetuated it.

For his part, Dr. Martin Luther King's sermons often focused on Amos 5:24 ("But let justice flow down like water And righteousness like a mighty stream,") Isaiah 40:4 ("Every valley shall be exalted And every mountain and hill brought low; The crooked places shall be made straight And the rough places smooth,") and Luke 4:18 ("The Spirit of the Lord is upon me, because he has anointed me to preach the gospel to the poor; he has sent me to heal the brokenhearted, to proclaim liberty to the captives and recovery of sight to the blind, to set at liberty those who are oppressed").

8. *Dawson v. Mayor and City Council of Baltimore*, 350 U.S. 877 (1955).

9. *Holmes v. Atlanta*, 350 U.S. 879 (1955).

10. *Morgan v. Virginia*, 328 U.S. 373 (1946) and *Henderson v. U.S.*, 339 U.S. 816 (1950).

11. *NAACP v. Patterson*, 357 U.S. 449, 460 (1958).

12. 376 U.S. at 270.

13. Container 602, Memorandum from Chief Justice Re: The Sit-In Cases, June 11, 1962, Supreme Court File, 1930–1974, Earl Warren Papers, Manuscript Division, Library of Congress, Washington, D.C.

14. The careful attention Warren brought to the analysis of the constitutional issues raised in the sit-in cases also appears in the memoranda he prepared for the brethren in the spring of 1963. See Container 604, Memorandum from Chief Justice Re: The Sit-In Cases Remaining on the Docket of the Court, May 31, 1963 and Sit-In Cases, Opinions and Results from Associate Justices, Supreme Court File, 1930–1974, Earl Warren Papers, Manuscript Division, Library of Congress, Washington, D.C.

15. 379 U.S. at 552 (internal citations deleted).

16. *Garner v. Louisiana*, 368 U.S. 157, 174 (1961).

17. The five cases were: *Barr v. City of Columbia*, 378 U.S. 146 (1964); *Griffin v. Maryland*, 378 U.S. 130 (1964); *Robinson v. Florida*, 378 U.S. 153 (1964); *Bouie v. City of Columbia*, 378 U.S. 347 (1964); and *Bell v. Maryland*, 378 U.S. 226 (1964).

18. Container 610, *Barr v. City of Columbia* draft dissent, later withdrawn, p. 6, Supreme Court File, 1930–1974, Earl Warren Papers, Manuscript Division, Library of Congress, Washington, D.C.

19. See G. S. Ghurye, *Caste and Race in India* (London: Routledge and Degan Paul, 1932), 3, 11–12.

20. Black's opposition to the rights of political protestors reached its zenith in his dissent in *Tinker v. Des Moines School Board* (1969), in which the majority of the Court upheld a high school student's right to wear a black armband to school as a protest against the Vietnam War.

21. Peter H. Irons, *The Courage of Their Convictions: Sixteen Americans Who Fought Their Way to the Supreme Court* (New York: Penguin, 1990), 138. Professor Irons provides perceptive analysis of the *Bell* case and many of the other civil liberties cases of the Warren era.

22. See "Southern Poverty Law Center Provides List of Unresolved Civil Rights Era Deaths to FBI," available at http://www.splcenter.org/civil-rights-memorial/history, February 27, 2007.

23. *Guinn v. United States*, 238 U.S. 347 (1915).

24. *Smith v. Allwright*, 321 U.S. 649 (1944).

25. *Gomillion v. Lightfoot*, 364 U.S. 339 (1960).

26. *Schnell v. Davis*, 336 U.S. 933 (1949).

27. For further discussion of black voting registration levels in the South during the 1950s, see Chief Justice Warren's majority opinion in *South Carolina v. Katzenbach*, 383 U.S. 301, 313 (1966) and Hanes Walton, Jr., Sherman C. Puckett, and Donald R. Deskins, Jr. *The African American Electorate: A Statistical History*, vol. 1. (Thousand Oaks, CA: CQ Press, 2012).

28. Taylor Branch, *Pillar of Fire: America in the King Years,* 1963–1965 (New York: Simon & Schuster, 1998), 267.

29. Ibid., 610.

30. For further information about these individuals (and numerous others), see ibid. See also Taylor Branch, *At Canaan's Edge* (New York: Simon & Schuster, 2006).

31. See e.g., Stewart Burns, *Social Movements of the 1960s: Searching for Democracy* (Boston: Twayne Publishers, 1990).

32. J. Morgan Kousser, *Colorblind Injustice: Minority Voting Rights and the Undoing of the Second Reconstruction* (Chapel Hill, NC: The University of North Carolina Press, 1999), 55.

33. In a reciprocal sense, it also may be true that the Court provided "cover" for Congress in that the Court's constitutional interpretations required adherence to the principle of racial equality and perhaps gave legislators a reason to take constitutional rights more seriously in the drafting of legislation. However, as the history of non-enforcement of civil rights between 1954 and 1964 shows, federal courts encountered great difficulty making real the promise of racial equality in the absence of support from the political branches.

34. *Walker v. City of Birmingham*, 388 U.S. 307, 333–34 (1967) (Warren, C.J, dissenting).

35. 384 U.S. at 648–9.

36. Rosenberg, *Hollow Hope* (see chap.1, n. 34).

37. Donald L. Horowitz, *The Courts and Social Policy* (Washington, D.C.: Brookings Institution, 1977).

38. Rosenberg, *Hollow Hope*, 71.

39. Troy Duster, "Pattern, Purpose, and Race in the Drug War: The Crisis of Credibility in Criminal Justice," in *Crack in America: Demon Drugs and Social Justice*, ed. Craig Reinarman and Harry Levine (Berkeley: University of California Press, 1997); see also Alexander, *The New Jim Crow*, 218.

40. *New York Times*, July 15, 2012, "Disenfranchised Felons" (Editorial Page).

41. See U.S. Department of Justice, Office of Justice Programs, Bureau of Justice Statistics, "Correctional Population in the United States, 2010," *available at* www.bjs.gov/content/pub/pdf/cpus10.pdf.

Chapter 10

Reforming Criminal Justice

When Earl Warren first entered public service in the Prohibition era, the United States confronted an epidemic of crime arising out of the corruption and ruthlessness of organized criminal enterprises. Law enforcement officers received little or no training, and in municipal police departments graft and racial discrimination flourished. In several parts of the country, prosecutors and judges participated actively in the racial caste system, systematically excluding blacks from juries and presiding over perverse forms of due process in cases involving black criminal defendants. Non-judicial actors pursued lynching and other forms of terrorism with impunity. In these ways, the Jim Crow culture went far beyond the formal *de jure* segregation of schools and places of public accommodation, descending into a comprehensive mechanism for racial subordination and control under the discretionary auspices of the criminal justice system.

By the end of Warren's career, the nature of crime and law enforcement in the United States had changed. The explosive violence of the Prohibition era waned, and federal courts demanded that police, prosecutors, and state judges honor the due process rights of the criminally accused in all parts of the country, including the South. Slowly, the United States reformed its criminal justice system, initiating training programs for police, stamping out municipal graft, and taking steps toward the creation of a color-blind society.

Throughout his life, Warren was a leading figure in the struggle for criminal justice reform. As a young prosecutor in the 1920s and 30s, he championed the cause of "clean government," pugnaciously sent many corrupt officials to prison, and developed training programs and college instruction for police officers. In 1927, he successfully pushed for an amendment to the Alameda County Charter granting indigent criminal defendants the right to court-appointed counsel. Throughout the 1930s, he advocated the restructuring of county and state law enforcement agencies, promoting intercounty criminal investigation and forensics units and requiring the State Attorney General's Office to maintain a full-time staff.

As Governor of California in the 1940s and early 1950s, Warren initiated programs to confront the social roots of crime. He introduced a comprehensive set of juvenile justice, mental health, and adult correctional reforms. He hired a national expert, Richard A. McGee, to serve as director of California's Department of Corrections. Under McGee's leadership, the Department adopted innovative inmate classification systems, expanded rehabilitation programs, and created fire-fighting and forestry work camps. From the bench in the 1950s and 60s, Warren opposed institutionalized racism, sympathized with the problems of the urban poor, and insisted that local police honor the guarantees of the Bill of Rights. In these ways, Warren's ethical vision and humanistic values at least partially transformed an anachronistic and broken criminal justice system.

Warren believed the root causes of crime lay in poverty and the squalid conditions of ghetto life. He endorsed juvenile treatment programs as a means of fighting unemployment, illiteracy, and substance abuse. When he served as a prosecutor Warren often remarked that he took little pleasure in winning jury trials against criminal defendants. Sending guilty defendants to prison, he reasoned, imposed adverse consequences on innocent family members. This concern became even more compelling in death penalty cases. In his *Memoirs*, Warren wrote:

> I never hear the jury foreman say, 'Guilty of murder in the first degree' without having a feeling of nausea. The taking of human life, even by the law in retribution for an unlawful killing is so awesome and gruesome that it becomes a traumatic experience for any participant in the legal tragedy.[1]

During Warren's fifteen years in state government, California executed over eighty inmates, and as Attorney General and Governor, Warren had major responsibilities in the administration of the capital punishment system. Although he dutifully carried out the law, after his retirement he admitted that on a personal level he found the death penalty "repulsive."

In his years on the Supreme Court and especially in the period between 1962 and 1969, Warren joined with Justices Hugo Black, William O. Douglas, William Brennan, and either Arthur Goldberg, Abe Fortas, or Thurgood Marshall to forge a judicial majority in favor of extending the constitutional rights of suspects. In famous decisions such as *Mapp v. Ohio* (1961) and *Miranda v. Arizona* (1966) the Warren Court crafted new rules to curb police misconduct and encourage compliance with constitutional mandates. Warren perceived these rules as justifiable efforts to improve law enforcement. In an interview shortly after his retirement, he observed: "(T)he prosecutor under our system is not paid to convict people [but to] protect the rights of people in our community and to see that when there is a violation of the law, it is vindicated by trial and prosecution under fair judicial standards."[2] Although critics blasted Warren and his colleagues for being "soft" on crime and for "handcuffing police," Warren thought the reforms would strengthen law enforcement by encouraging police to avoid shortcuts in the criminal investigation process.

Warren insisted that "the police must obey the law while enforcing the law."[3] He had high ethical expectations for all government officials, and if individuals crossed the line into wrongdoing, he would react with a firm hand. Although he accepted deterrence as a justification for punishing criminals, he also endorsed rehabilitation programs for those who turned to crime out of poverty or illiteracy. He often expressed concern about the problem of recidivism, remarking on one occasion that society could not expect anything better as long as it "caged up men like animals."

THE WARREN COURT'S DUE PROCESS REVOLUTION

Overview

During Earl Warren's tenure as Chief Justice, the Supreme Court initiated significant reforms of the criminal justice system, asserting its power against state and local law enforcement agencies and state judges who had the principal responsibility for administering criminal laws in the United States. Legally, the reforms involved the question of how the federal Bill of Rights applied to state and local law enforcement. As the American political system evolved over the nineteenth century, states assumed primary responsibility for investigating and prosecuting common crimes against persons and property. Federal agencies focused on specialized crimes such as those involving interstate fraud, crimes committed by military personnel, and crimes occurring on the high seas. As the referee of America's legal system, the Supreme Court used its power of judicial review only rarely to protect human rights in criminal cases. The result was a deeply troubled legacy.

By the end of the nineteenth century, significant differences in regional justice systems arose. In the urban Northeast and North Central regions, political machines dominated law enforcement and criminal courts. A rough system of justice emerged, featuring widespread corruption and lax enforcement of criminal laws in the saloons, gambling dens, brothels, and tenements of inner-city neighborhoods. In the South, black codes and a culture of racism induced officials to ignore black-on-black crime and reserve their harshest penalties for black-on-white crimes. Vigilante justice and extrajudicial lynching occurred frequently, and rudimentary correctional systems included chain gangs and the lucrative practice of leasing prisoners to private individuals and businesses. In the West, justice systems consisted of a hybrid of the Northern and Southern models, with formal approaches to justice gradually replacing vigilantism.

The Warren Court attacked the roots of racial discrimination, economic inequality, and unprofessionalism in the criminal justice system, especially in the South, through a series of decisions grounded in the Fourteenth Amendment Due Process Clause. This clause states that a state may not deprive "any person of life, liberty, or property without due process of law." The concept of due process is deeply rooted in Anglo-American jurisprudence, yet its elements are difficult to summarize. As Justice Felix Frankfurter once observed, "Due process of law, as a historic and generative principle, precludes defining, and thereby confining, these standards of conduct more precisely than to say that convictions cannot be brought about by methods that offend a 'sense of justice.'"[4]

The due process clause places limits on government authority. It constrains both the means of government conduct and the ends of its laws. Procedural due process focuses on how the government must proceed in order to accomplish its objectives. For example, if the government accuses A of committing a crime, does s/he have the right to notice and a hearing before being sent to prison? Is there a right to counsel or the right to confront adverse witnesses before the court renders a judgment in the case? On the other hand, substantive due process focuses on the permissible goals of government action. For example, does the state have the right to criminalize the act of marrying someone of a different race? Substantive due process places an absolute limit on government authority in a free society.

The line between procedural and substantive due process sometimes is indistinct. Both forms of due process are "comprised within the term liberty."[5] Justice John Paul Stevens recently recognized the necessary overlap between procedural and substantive due process when he wrote, "Procedural guarantees are hollow unless linked to substantive interests; and no amount of process can legitimize some deprivations."[6]

In protecting the rights of criminal suspects, the Warren Court extended the reach of the due process clause in both procedural and substantive directions. Its procedural due process decisions required the states to follow nearly all of the procedural entitlements granted to criminal suspects under the federal Bill of Rights. Its substantive due process decisions provided heightened protection for fundamental rights and individual liberty interests, including the right of married persons to possess contraceptives and the right of individuals to marry a person of a different race. The Warren Court's due process reforms extended human liberty and made constitutional rights more uniform throughout the country; yet its reforms extended the Supreme Court's supervisory role over the judicial systems of the states far more than at any previous point in American history.

Toward Selective Incorporation

At the time of his appointment to the Supreme Court in 1953, Earl Warren may have had a more extensive background in law enforcement than any other justice in Supreme Court history. Nevertheless, he had been away from the practice of law for eleven years. As Attorney General, he had viewed legal issues from the point of view of the State of California, and to some extent his own stance on issues of constitutional criminal procedure remained uncertain. Now Warren had the responsibility of striking a balance between the rights of suspects and the authority of society under the Fourteenth Amendment Due Process Clause.

In the 1940s Justices Frankfurter and Black began a protracted debate over the proper interpretation of this clause. The central question in the debate concerned the appropriate level of state autonomy in the framing of criminal laws and procedures. The federal Bill of Rights set specific standards and safeguards in the first eight amendments, and the justices divided over how closely the states should follow these standards.

Justice Frankfurter argued in favor of state autonomy and a loose set of due process standards that required states to honor only fundamental liberties. Under Frankfurter's approach, states would not have to follow "jot for jot" the specific requirements that the Court demanded for federal agencies. He thought federal courts should be free to exercise their own judgment regarding which state actions ran afoul of the constitution. Frankfurter's position squared with the Court's early precedents, which held that states would be free to depart from federal practice as long as their procedures did not violate the "fundamental principle of liberty and justice which inheres in the very idea of free government."[7]

Many of the due process decisions from the period immediately preceding Earl Warren's arrival on the Court involved acts of police or prosecutorial repression against African Americans. Significant cases from the early history of the Civil Rights Movement, including *Moore v. Dempsey* (1923), *Powell v. Alabama* (1932), *Norris v. Alabama* (1935), and *Chambers v. Florida* (1940) illustrate this trend. In each of these cases, the Court reversed the conviction of one or more African American defendants, using special factual circumstances and case-by-case development of legal doctrine to avoid issuing sweeping new rules. The coming of World War II accelerated the Court's concern for the rights of suspects. The United States fought to destroy fascism and systems of "justice" that condemned people on the basis of their race or religion without any due process of law. After the war, as it became clear that the double standards of criminal justice in the Black Belt represented nearly as much of a threat to American ideals as the arbitrary justice of the Nazis, several justices began to question the wisdom of the Cardozo-Frankfurter approach to due process issues. The struggle for racial equality in the South provided an important social and political context for their initiatives.

One of the justices in question was Hugo Black. In his first year on the Court, Black joined Justice Cardozo's opinion in *Palko v. Connecticut* (1937), which endorsed the fundamental fairness approach to the Due Process Clause. By 1942, however, Black dissented from the application of the *Palko* standard in *Betts v. Brady* (1942), a right to counsel case. There, the Court decided that an indigent criminal defendant in a non-death penalty case pending in state court did not have the right to a court-appointed attorney. Black's dissent condemned the logic and fairness of the majority's position. "A practice cannot be reconciled with 'common and fundamental ideas of fairness'," he wrote, "which subjects innocent men to increased dangers of conviction merely because of their poverty."[8]

In his dissent in *Adamson v. California* (1947), Black challenged Justice Frankfurter's analytical framework for testing due process violations. Black did an extensive amount of research on the congressional debates leading to adoption of the Fourteenth Amendment. He concluded that the framers intended for all of the Bill of Rights to apply to the states, a principle known as total incorporation.[9]

Although three other justices agreed with Black's assertion that all of the Bill of Rights should apply to the states, a majority of the justices in *Adamson* adhered to the *Palko* standard. In *Wolf v. Colorado* (1949) the Court declined to apply the Fourth Amendment exclusionary rule to the states in search and seizure cases, and in *Rochin v. California* (1952), it used a "shocks the conscience" test to exclude from trial drug capsules that police pumped from the defendant's stomach without his consent.

During his first two years on the Court, Warren sided with Justice Frankfurter in criminal cases. Warren's first significant vote came in *Irvine v. California* (1954), where he joined a 5–4 majority in sustaining the admissibility of incriminating conversations police obtained by hiding microphones in the walls of a suspect's home. The police did not secure a warrant before placing the microphones in the home. Unhappy about the level of police misconduct in the case, Warren persuaded Justice Robert Jackson to include an additional sentence in his final opinion. It directed the Clerk of the Supreme Court to forward a copy of the record in the *Irvine* case, together with a copy of the Court's opinion, to the Attorney General of the United States. Although

Warren hoped to encourage the Attorney General to initiate legal proceedings against the police officers who conducted the surveillance in the case, nothing came of his efforts.

The episode had a significant influence on Warren. Since the late 1930s, he had opposed the use of unconsented, hidden microphones in criminal investigations, and the absence of a search warrant only compounded the problem. If the officers had been federal agents, the incriminating conversations would have been excluded from the evidence under the *Weeks v. U.S.* (1914) decision. In the wake of *Wolf v. Colorado*, however, the states remained free to adopt their own remedies for illegal searches and seizures. One such remedy involved the creation of special tribunals that could issue sanctions against police officers who violated suspects' rights. The Attorney General's decision not to prosecute the police officers in *Irvine* may have persuaded Warren of the futility of the tribunal remedy. Warren later revealed that if he were given the opportunity to change one vote he had cast while on the bench, it would be the vote he cast in the *Irvine* case.[10]

In an interview following his retirement, Warren explained the reason for his vote to uphold Irvine's conviction. He noted that just four years previously, in *Wolf v. Colorado* (1949), the Court had refused to impose federal Fourth Amendment requirements on the states in a similar eavesdropping case. "That having been such a very recent case and a majority of the Court having agreed not to overrule it at that particular moment, and I being a new justice on the Court still groping around in the field of due process," Warren said, "I went along with that opinion, shocked as I was at the conduct of the police."[11]

In the mid-to-late 1950s, Warren gravitated toward Hugo Black's position on civil liberties and due process issues. Although liberals on the Court lacked a solid majority for their position until Felix Frankfurter's retirement in 1962, Warren, Douglas, Black and Brennan attempted to extend the constitutional rights of the criminally accused.[12] Douglas and Black preferred a total incorporation approach that would forbid states from violating the federal Bill of Rights. Warren and Brennan took a more flexible stance on the issue and appeared to be willing to use the fundamental fairness approach as necessary to attract majority support for their positions. In the period leading up to the landmark *Mapp v. Ohio* (1961) decision, a majority of the Court continued to favor the *Palko* fundamental fairness approach to due process issues, and Black's total incorporation approach remained a minority position.

Viewed in their totality, the Supreme Court's criminal justice reforms of the 1930s, 1940s, and 1950s generated little controversy, but they also yielded little meaningful change in the Jim Crow justice system. Some defendants, such as those in the famous Scottsboro Boys cases, won reversals only to be reconvicted on remand. Others, such as those in *Chambers*, won their appeals, and prosecutors quietly dismissed the charges against them. Yet the underlying discriminatory practices continued unabated. Even in the North and the West, where state constitutions and statutes occasionally offered legal protections such as the exclusion of illegally seized evidence from use at trial or the privilege against self-incrimination, courts often gave relatively little protection to suspects. Searches without probable cause and psychologically coercive interrogation methods occurred frequently, and the trials that took place afterward represented little more than empty formalities.

The Warren Court began its due process revolution in *Mapp v. Ohio* (1961). The case arose when Cleveland police received a tip that someone living in Dolree Mapp's home had been involved in a recent bombing. They arrived at Mapp's house and demanded entry so they could search the premises. Mapp contacted her attorney, who, erroneously, advised her that police could not search her house without her consent unless they produced a valid search warrant. When she refused consent, police staked out her house for the next several hours. Then they attempted to kick in Mapp's back door, and when that failed, they broke a window and gained entry into her house. Mapp demanded to see a search warrant, the officers showed her a piece of paper, which was not a warrant. She grabbed it and stuffed it down the front of her dress. A struggle ensued, and the officers retrieved the paper, handcuffed Mapp, and conducted a thorough search for criminal evidence. They eventually found several allegedly pornographic photographs and "an obscene doodle." They arrested Mapp on the charge of knowing possession of obscene materials.

The trial court convicted Mapp of the charges, and she appealed to the Ohio Supreme Court. The state court acknowledged that the methods police used to obtain the criminal evidence might "offend a sense of justice," but the justices upheld Mapp's conviction because police did not use brutal or offensive physical force against her person. Mapp then appealed to the U.S. Supreme Court primarily on First Amendment grounds. The American Civil Liberties Union filed an amicus brief on her behalf, and the final paragraph of its brief raised the Fourth Amendment search and seizure issue. The ACLU asked the Court to overrule *Wolf v. Colorado* and adopt the exclusionary rule as a remedy for state police violation of Fourth Amendment rights. The Court's decision in *Mapp* followed this request.

Chief Justice Warren exercised diplomacy in assigning the case to Justice Tom Clark, a moderate from Texas who convinced Justice Stewart to join the majority in reversing Mapp's conviction. Clark wrote what may have been the best decision of his career. In his analysis of the case, Clark gave three reasons why the exclusionary rule should apply to the states: the success of the FBI under the *Weeks* decision in avoiding "short cut" methods of law enforcement; the deterrence of police misconduct; and the need to uphold the integrity of the judicial process. Clark's thoughts on upholding judicial integrity have become a noteworthy statement in American constitutional law:

> There are those who say, as did Justice (then Judge) Cardozo that, under our constitutional exclusionary doctrine, "(t)he criminal is to go free because the constable has blundered." In some cases this will undoubtedly be the result. But, as was said in *Elkins*, "there is another consideration—the imperative of judicial integrity." The criminal goes free, if he must, but it is the law that sets him free. Nothing can destroy a government more quickly that its failure to observe its own laws, or worse, its disregard of the charter of its own existence.[13]

The 6–3 vote in *Mapp* foreshadowed the decline of Justice Frankfurter's approach to due process issues. The *Mapp* majority perceived a trend in favor of the exclusionary rule among state supreme courts. Warren's experience with the issue in California illustrates the dynamics of this trend. In 1955, the California Supreme Court adopted the exclusionary rule in *People v. Cahan.* The decision, written by Warren's acquaintance Chief Justice Roger Traynor, reversed *People v. Gonzales* (1942). In *Gonzales* police conducted a warrantless entry into a defendant's apartment in order to obtain materials allegedly used in a fraudulent scheme to reproduce U.S. currency. As state Attorney General, Warren had argued the case on appeal, and Justice Traynor wrote a decision upholding the admission of the disputed evidence. Later Traynor overruled *Gonzales* in part because he believed alternatives to the exclusionary rule had proven ineffective in curbing illegal police search and seizure practices.

At the time of the Court's decision in *Mapp*, half of the states had adopted the exclusionary rule as a remedy for violation of search and seizure rights. To some extent, this blunted the inevitable controversy that came in the wake of the Court's decision. Nevertheless, many police chiefs, prosecutors, and conservative legal scholars rebelled at the prospect of a Court-mandated exclusionary rule.[14] They charged that the new rule focused too much attention on the activities of the police in investigating crime and too little attention on the wrongfulness of a suspect's conduct. In a series of speeches, position papers, and law review articles, they decried the prospect of "lost convictions" in search and seizure cases.

Most careful studies of the empirical evidence have not found support for the conclusion that the number of "lost convictions" under the exclusionary rule is high; perhaps the most extensive and reliable study estimates the number of lost convictions at under 1.3% of the cases in which a motion to suppress criminal evidence has been granted.[15]

The next significant decision of the due process revolution occurred in *Gideon v. Wainwright* (1963), a case that concerned an indigent criminal defendant's attempt to obtain court-appointed counsel in a state trial. Chief Justice Warren played an important role in bringing the *Gideon* case to the attention of his colleagues. From his consultations with Brennan and Black, Warren realized that the brethren might be receptive to granting certiorari in a case challenging the rule that states could initiate felony proceedings against indigent defendants without providing them court-appointed counsel. He instructed his clerks to screen certiorari petitions and give special attention to poorly written, hand-hewn appeals from inmates, looking for "appropriate" cases raising the issue that did not involve troubling facts.[16]

Progressive trends in the states also affected the Court's judgment in *Gideon*. At the time the Court accepted jurisdiction in the case, many states in the Northeast, Midwest, and West already provided court-appointed counsel to indigent defendants. Only states in the Deep South declined to do so.[17] The State of Florida reacted to Gideon's appeal by inviting attorneys general in other states to join an *amicus curiae* brief in opposition. Only North Carolina and Alabama accepted the invitation. Twenty-three other states filed an amicus brief in support of Gideon.

The composition of the *Gideon* court accelerated the trend toward reform. In *Mapp*, the three most conservative justices on due process issues—Justices Frankfurter, Harlan, and Whittaker—had dissented. Two years later, at the time of *Gideon*, Justices Frankfurter and Whittaker had retired from the Court. Their replacements, Justices Arthur Goldberg and Byron White, joined Justice Black's opinion, making it unanimous. Black's opinion avoided any discussion of his total incorporation theory and instead relied upon the *Palko* fundamental fairness test to reach his holding that the Sixth Amendment guarantee of counsel was a fundamental right. In so doing, he overruled *Betts v. Brady* (1942) and required states to provide indigent defendants with court-appointed counsel in all serious felony cases.

The compelling story of Gideon's successful appeal shows the American judicial system at its best. Several influential books and a Peabody Award-winning film helped to make *Gideon* the most popular of the Warren Court's criminal procedure reforms. Yet even today, the premise of Justice Black's opinion—that poor criminal defendants deserve professional representation on a par equal to that of the state—remains under constant challenge. Throughout the nation, public defenders struggle for adequate funds and staffing to maintain at least a reasonable quality of service for their clients.

The Court's decisions in *Mapp* and *Gideon* represented just the opening wave of the Warren Court's many opinions during the 1960s that incorporated specific elements of the Bill of Rights into the Fourteenth Amendment Due Process Clause. Table 10.1 provides a full listing of the Warren Court's incorporation decisions in the field of criminal procedure.[18]

Table 10.1 The Warren Court's Incorporation Cases Involving Criminal Procedure

Case Name	*Issue*	*Decision*
Mapp v. Ohio (1961)	May evidence seized from a home in violation of the Fourth Amendment be admitted in a state criminal trial?	No. "All evidence obtained by searches and seizures in violation of the constitution is, by that same authority, inadmissible in a state court." The Fourth Amendment exclusionary rule is incorporated.
Robinson v. California (1962)	Does a statute that prohibits being addicted to narcotics violate the cruel and unusual punishment clause of the Eighth Amendment?	Yes. The status of narcotics addiction, standing alone, is an illness analogous to disease, a mental disorder, or leprosy. The Eighth Amendment cruel and unusual punishment clause is incorporated.
Ker v. California (1963)	Should federal standards of reasonableness apply to the states in the reviewing the constitutionality of warrantless searches and seizures?	Yes. Both the Fourth Amendment and the exclusionary rule have been applied to the states. States must follow federal rules regarding search warrants, warrantless searches, and searches incident to arrest.
Gideon v. Wainwright (1963)	Does the Sixth Amendment right to counsel guarantee an indigent the right to court-appointed counsel in a state felony trial?	Yes. The right to be represented by counsel in a felony criminal proceeding is a fundamental right. "Lawyers in criminal courts are necessities, not luxuries." All poor defendants in serious criminal cases who lack the means to retain their own attorneys have the right to be represented by court-appointed counsel.
Malloy v. Hogan (1964)	Does the Fifth Amendment privilege against self-incrimination apply in state criminal proceedings?	Yes. "Governments, state and federal, are . . . constitutionally compelled to establish guilt by evidence independently and freely secured, and may not, by coercion, prove a charge against the accused out of his own mouth."
Aguilar v. Texas (1964)	Do the warrant requirements of the Fourth Amendment apply to the states?	Yes. The requirements for establishing probable cause to support an application for a search warrant are the same under the Fourth Amendment as they are under the Fourteenth Amendment.

(Cont...)

Table 10.1 The Warren Court's Incorporation Cases Involving Criminal Procedure (*Cont...*)

Case Name	*Issue*	*Decision*
Pointer v. Texas (1965)	Does the Sixth Amendment right to confront adverse witnesses apply to state criminal proceedings?	Yes. The right of cross-examination includes the right to confront the witnesses against one. It is a fundamental right essential to a fair trial in a criminal prosecution.
Washington v. Texas (1966)	Does the Sixth Amendment right to have compulsory process for obtaining witnesses apply to the states?	Yes. The right to compel the attendance of witnesses is necessary to prepare a defense. It is a fundamental element of due process of law.
Klopfer v. North Carolina (1967)	Does the Sixth Amendment right to a speedy trial apply to the states?	Yes. Indefinite postponement of a trial without consent or stated justification violates the fundamental right to a speedy trial.
Duncan v. Louisiana (1968)	Does the Sixth Amendment right to trial by jury apply to the states?	Yes. The right to trial by jury is fundamental to the American system of justice and applies to the states in cases that authorize serious criminal punishments. States are not required to follow federal rules regarding the unanimity of jury decisions or the size of juries.
Belton v. Maryland (1969)	Does the Fifth Amendment freedom from double jeopardy apply to the states?	Yes. ". . . The double jeopardy prohibition of the Fifth Amendment represents a fundamental ideal in our constitutional heritage, and . . . it should apply to the states through the Fourteenth Amendment." *Belton* overruled *Palko v. Connecticut* (1937), in part.

Table 10.2 Major Positions on the Incorporation of the Bill of Rights

Theory	*Definition*	*Representative Cases*	*Representative Justices*
Selective Incorporation	Portions of the Bill of Rights apply to the states through the Fourteenth Amendment; other rights not implicit in the concept of ordered liberty under the fundamental fairness test do not apply to the states	*Gideon v. Wainwright*; *Malloy v. Hogan*; *Duncan v. Louisiana*; *Adamson v. California* (dissenting opinion); *Griswold v. Connecticut* (concurring opinion); *McDonald v. City of Chicago* (dissents)	Hughes, Stone, Warren, Brandeis, Cardozo, Reed, Jackson, Burton, Clark, White, Blackmun, Warren, Brennan, Goldberg, Stevens, Breyer, Ginsburg, Sotomayor
Fundamental Fairness	The Fourteenth Amendment requires only that states grant procedural rights that are implicit in the concept of ordered liberty.	*Palko v. Connecticut*; *Adamson v. California*; *Duncan v. Louisiana* (dissent)	Frankfurter, Harlan, Vinson, Minton, Whittaker, Burger, Rehnquist
Total Incorporation	All portions of the Bill of Rights apply to the states through the Fourteenth Amendment Due Process Clause. Courts may not use natural law to expand due process rights beyond the scope of the first ten amendments.	*Adamson v. California* (dissent); *Duncan v. Louisiana* (concurring opinion)	Black, Douglas
Total Incorporation Plus	Incorporate all of the Bill of Rights and allow courts to extend due process rights beyond the first ten amendments as the interests of justice demand.	*Adamson v. California* (Murphy's dissent); *Griswold v. Connecticut* (majority opinion); *Bell v. Maryland* (concurring opinion).	Murphy, Rutledge, Douglas, Goldberg, Warren, Brennan

In addition to these cases, the Warren Court's substantive due process decisions also addressed the question of whether the states would have to honor federal rights guaranteed in the first ten amendments. For example, vague state laws that chilled freedom of expression or prohibited marital couples from possessing contraceptives also curtailed liberties protected under the Bill of Rights, and the Court had to decide whether states had to abide by the federal guarantees. Although the Warren Court consistently ruled in favor of the incorporation of the Bill of Rights, it did so under a variety of legal theories. Table 10.2 summarizes the major positions of the justices in incorporation cases.

As Table 10.2 indicates, the positions of some justices have been inconsistent on incorporation questions. Among them is Chief Justice Warren, who voted in favor of selective incorporation in *Gideon* but then joined Justice Goldberg's concurring opinion in *Griswold* that interpreted the due process clause as including protections outside the express language of the Bill of Rights. These themes will be explored at greater length in upcoming sections of this Chapter. The recent case *McDonald v. City of Chicago* (2010) shows that the debate over incorporation continues into the contemporary era. The case, which concerns the Second Amendment and the right to possess handguns, features an extensive discussion of incorporation, fundamental fairness, and the *Palko v. Connecticut* decision.

STATIONHOUSE INTERROGATIONS

Perhaps the most controversial of Warren's criminal justice reforms involved the problem of custodial interrogation. As former prosecutors, Chief Justice Warren and Justice Hugo Black long had been critical of police interrogation practices.[19] In the 1930s, the National Commission on Law Observance and Enforcement, informally known as the Wickersham Commission, issued a report entitled "Lawlessness in Law Enforcement," that gave voice to many of their criticisms. Law professor Zechariah Chaffee Jr. served as one of several consultants to the Commission and analyzed appellate court opinions involving police use of coercive methods to obtain confessions from suspects. Chaffee's report highlighted the history and then-current practice of police interrogation in the United States and issued recommendations concerning appropriate policy responses to the problem.

In reviewing the history of custodial interrogation, Chaffee found that the earliest documented cases of involuntary confessions arose during the Civil War, when officials used "sweat boxes" during detentions. This method of torture involved placing the accused in a cell in close proximity to a hot stove filled with bones, rubber shoes, or other materials emitted noxious odors.

Prolonged exposure to the heat and bad odors often led the inmate to confess in order to gain release. In time, the term "sweating" came to denote any one of a wide variety of measures designed to induce an individual to admit wrongdoing. According to Chafee's research, by the 1920s, common methods of "sweating" involved whipping, beating with rubber hoses, or making threats or promises. Police shined spotlights into the suspect's face, or made suspects sit in (mildly) electric chairs. The most successful method featured "persistent questioning, continuing hour after hour, sometimes by relays of officers. It has been known since 1500 at least that deprivation of sleep is the most effective torture and certain to produce any confession desired."[20]

In his examination of appellate records, Chafee stressed the extreme measures that police used to elicit confessions. In one Texas murder investigation, police subjected recalcitrant black witnesses to water torture. "In the jail," the appellate judge wrote, "Negroes were severely and cruelly whipped by the sheriff. One of them was put in water and his head held in water until he was almost drowned. Another, a woman, was stripped of her clothes, laid on the floor, and severely whipped and strapped."[21]

Chaffee's report to the American Bar Association reached a sobering conclusion. He stated, "The boldness with which the sheriffs, police, and States' attorneys practice this lawlessness is astonishing and goes on in spite of protests and rebukes from the courts. Indeed no other fact more clearly demonstrates the feebleness of our courts than their inability, or at least their failure, to compel officers to obey the law in this respect."[22] Chaffee's report stopped short of calling for new legislation: "(T)he law as it now stands is sufficient. The difficulty is that it is either not enforced or is deliberately disobeyed—and by the very persons charged with its enforcement . . . .The real remedy lies in the will of the community."[23]

The Wickersham Commission Report yielded only modest changes in police interrogation practices. In 1936, the Supreme Court outlawed the use of physical force in beating confessions out of suspects,[24] and in 1940 it also prohibited psychologically coercive methods.[25] On the federal level, by the early 1950s both the Federal Bureau of Investigation and the U.S. Code of Military Justice required law enforcement officials to issue warnings to suspects prior to initiation of custodial interrogations. The warnings informed suspects of their constitutional right to remain silent, told them any statement given could be used against them in court, and advised them of their right to counsel.[26] Yet at a state and local level, police abuses of the interrogation process remained common.

In the period before *Miranda*, the Warren Court used a voluntariness test to review allegations of impropriety in custodial interrogations. Under this test, if the facts showed that the police coerced a confession out of a suspect, the Court would exclude the confession from trial. In a handful of cases decided in the late 1950s and early 1960s, it reversed criminal convictions. For example, in *Spano v. New York* (1959) the Court condemned the post-indictment interrogation of a semiliterate immigrant because police used psychological manipulation and fatigue to secure Spano's confession. In his majority opinion in the case, Chief Justice Warren wrote:

> The abhorrence of society to the use of involuntary confessions does not turn alone on their inherent untrustworthiness. It also turns on the deep-rooted feeling that the police must obey the law while enforcing the law; that in the end life and liberty can be as much endangered from illegal methods used to convict those thought to be criminals as from the actual criminals themselves.[27]

Likewise, in *Townsend v. Sain* (1963), Warren's majority opinion ruled a confession inadmissible because police induced it by means of a "truth serum." Despite the Court's concerns about the unreliability and unfairness of many custodial interrogation techniques, law enforcement officials continued to rely heavily on confessions in serious criminal cases. In the mid-1960s, New York City prosecutors introduced confessions in approximately 50% of their homicide cases.[28] The gap between the expectations of the Warren Court and the behavior of state and local police in custodial interrogations appeared to be widening.

The Warren Court's first serious effort to move beyond the limitations of the voluntariness standard occurred in *Escobedo v. Illinois* (1964). The case arose when Chicago police arrested Danny Escobedo and interrogated him for involvement in the murder of his brother-in-law. During the interrogation, Escobedo asked to consult with his attorney. Police repeatedly denied his requests even though the attorney was at the station house, trying in vain to consult with his client. During the interrogation, Escobedo inadvertently told police that he had been involved in the crime, and prosecutors used his statement to secure his conviction at trial.

On appeal, Justice Goldberg's majority opinion overturned Escobedo's conviction because Chicago police denied him the right to counsel during the interrogation. Goldberg's opinion extended the right to counsel into pretrial, "critical stages" of the criminal process. But the unique facts of *Escobedo*—in which both the client and the attorney wanted to consult with each other at the station house—arguably made the case distinguishable from most other situations. Four justices—White, Stewart, Harlan, and Clark—issued dissents in *Escobedo*. The absence of clear guidelines in Goldberg's opinion and the harsh criticism of the dissenting opinions left law enforcement officials guessing.

Within one year, the Court accepted jurisdiction in several other custodial interrogation cases, apparently selected by lottery, and then consolidated them into the *Miranda* decision. *Miranda* itself involved a young male of Mexican background whom prosecutors accused of raping a young Phoenix woman. After a lengthy interrogation in which he was not told about his right to counsel or his right to remain silent, Miranda signed a confession, which prosecutors used to convict him. Miranda's attorneys appealed, challenging the problems of ignorance and inequality during custodial interrogations. They argued that well-educated and well-connected suspects knew about their constitutional rights and had access to legal professionals. In contrast, poor suspects or those with little formal education remained ignorant about their rights and susceptible to police manipulation.

In its amicus brief in *Miranda*, the American Civil Liberties Union used quotations from police training manuals to inform the Court about police manipulation of unschooled suspects during custodial interrogations. In another amicus brief, attorneys general from twenty-six states asked the Court to refrain from announcing new constitutional rules about pretrial interrogations until state courts and legal experts had an opportunity to address the issue. The decline in the number of states that supported an expansion of suspects' rights—from 23 in *Gideon* to 0 in *Miranda*—portended the coming controversy.

The Court's internal deliberations in *Miranda* reflected the tensions of the *Escobedo* decision. The newest member of the Court, Abe Fortas, became crucial to the outcome of the case. Fortas replaced Justice Arthur Goldberg, who had resigned from the Court in 1965 in order to serve as U.S. Representative to the United Nations. Goldberg's departure from the Court meant that the two sides from *Escobedo* were evenly split at four justices apiece. Warren's draft opinion in *Miranda* stressed an argument calculated to win Justice Fortas' support. Warren emphasized the problems of ignorance and poverty among suspects facing custodial interrogations, thus extending an argument that Fortas had presented to the Court in *Gideon v. Wainwright* just a few years before.

In his majority opinion, Warren stressed the unethical nature of common police custodial interrogation practices, the inadequacies of the Supreme Court's previous voluntariness standard, and the new rules the Court now required. Warren argued that in the absence of warnings, a suspect's real trial took place at the stationhouse where professional police took advantage of the unwary and legally ignorant. In order to make constitutional rights meaningful at the stationhouse, he contended, the police needed specific rules and guidance. Relying on quotes from the police manuals that the ACLU amicus brief had presented, Warren criticized the lengths to which police went to manipulate suspects into making confessions.

Warren required police to issue a familiar four-part warning to suspects before they conducted a custodial interrogation. The warning required police to inform suspects of their right to counsel, their right to a court-appointed attorney if they were too poor to retain their own counsel, their right to remain silent, and a statement that anything said could be used against them in court. Warren couched the new rules as safeguards of core Fifth and Sixth Amendment rights. He invited Congress to adopt an alternative approach to the problem as long as the alternative remained consistent with the standards he announced in his opinion. In the charged atmosphere that surrounded the *Miranda* decision, Congressional cooperation appeared highly unlikely.

On June 13, 1966, Warren read his 63-page opinion from the bench, his voice often trembling with emotion. In a rare move that symbolized the depth of division within the Court, Justice Tom Clark also read his dissent from the bench. Clark's dissent, joined by Justices Harlan, Stewart, and White, criticized the Court for assuming the worst about police and for constructing new rules of constitutional law seemingly out of whole cloth without textual or case law support. Only three states had rules excluding evidence from custodial interrogations whenever police failed to warn suspects of their constitutional rights, and the Court's decision would require significant changes in police procedure.[29]

The final vote in *Miranda* split the justices along class lines. Those with backgrounds of poverty or working-class life—Warren, Black, Douglas, Brennan, and Fortas—voted to place limits on police custodial interrogation. These justices were familiar with the many ways that government officials took advantage of the poor, the ignorant, the uncounseled, and the friendless. Those justices from privileged backgrounds—Harlan, Stewart, White, and Clark—saw the warnings as unjustified intrusions into the prerogatives of police and as a threat to law and order. The presence of so many justices from relatively humble backgrounds represented a distinctive feature of the Warren Court,[30] and it serves as one of the leading explanations for why Warren and his colleagues issued so many groundbreaking civil rights, civil liberties, and criminal justice reforms.

Chief Justice Warren's opinion in *Miranda* illustrates his tendency to issue broadly based decisions to announce the constitutional requirements the Court expected the law enforcement community to follow. Although conservatives have criticized the Warren Court for "legislating" from the bench, Warren's opinions provided clear guidance regarding future expectations. Recent Supreme Court decisions exhibit just the opposite problem. In leading cases such as the *Crawford v. Washington* (2004), *District of Columbia v. Heller* (2008), and *McDonald v. Chicago* (2010), the Court has deliberately refrained from providing a clear discussion of the parameters of its new rules, leaving the matter up to the lower courts and future litigation to resolve. Whether the issue involves the scope and definition of "testimonial hearsay" or the constitutional right to bear arms outside the home, the Court's more restrained approach has also led to confusion.

The *Miranda* decision unleashed a storm of criticism. Police chiefs issued public statements denouncing the opinion, and rank and file officers expressed outrage at what they perceived as unwarranted attacks against them on the part of liberal federal judges. Many police departments evaded both the letter and the spirit of the Court's opinion. Empirical studies of the impact of *Miranda* on police behavior during its first year showed that the decision had relatively little effect on police. One study of the New Haven, Connecticut police department showed that officers paid lip service to the requirements but then encouraged suspects to talk. Two particularly clever devices involved modifications of the warning. Police told suspects, "Whatever you say may be used *for or against* you in a court of law," and "You don't have to say a word, but you ought to get everything cleared up."[31] Other early studies, including those of police in Washington, D.C., showed that officers gave incomplete and inaccurate warnings between one-third and one-half of the time.[32]

In many ways, the timing of the *Miranda* decision could not have been worse. Throughout the 1950s and 1960s, the number of serious felonies increased precipitously nationwide. According to the *Uniform Crime Reports*, between 1961 and 1962, the rate of serious crime increased by 6%; in 1963 the rate increased by 10% over the 1962 levels, and again by 13% between 1963 and 1964. In 1966, the year the Court issued the *Miranda* decision, the serious crime rate increased another 6% over the 1965 rate.[33] By 1968, riots and disturbances in inner-city neighborhoods and university campuses made average citizens uneasy about the threat to law and order. For many Americans, the Supreme Court's procedural reforms seemed to coddle criminals and unduly constrain police. To them, the Court appeared indifferent to the real fear average citizens felt on the streets of America. Gradually, the public mood turned hostile toward the Supreme Court's liberal majority.

Conservative politicians exploited the shift in public opinion. In 1968, Congress responded to *Miranda* by passing the Omnibus Safe Streets and Crime Control Act. The Act authorized federal prosecutors to return to the pre-*Miranda* voluntariness standard, in effect inviting prosecutors to ignore the Court's *Miranda* decision. While prosecutors declined the invitation out of fear that federal courts would rule the new provision unconstitutional, Congress's political point had been made. On the presidential campaign trail, former vice president Richard Nixon and independent candidate George Wallace repeatedly attacked the *Miranda* decision and the liberals on the Warren Court who issued it. In a position paper written in the summer of 1968, Nixon said:

> The obvious underpinning of the Court's decision is a deep-seated distrust of all confessions . . . the result adds up to a judicial judgment that evidence from the accused should not be used against him in any way, whether compelled or not. This is the not so subtle overtone of the opinion—that it is inherently wrong for the police to gather evidence from the accused himself.
>
> From the point of view of the criminal forces, the cumulative impact of these decisions has been to set free patently guilty individuals on the basis of legal technicalities.
>
> The tragic lesson of guilty men walking free from hundreds of courtrooms across the country has not been lost on the criminal community.[34]

Ever attentive to public opinion, Earl Warren took umbrage at this criticism. It frustrated him that he had a responsibility to remain silent. His instincts, honed from years as an elected public official, urged him to defend the integrity of his positions before the public. As Chief Justice, his role called for precisely the opposite response. Those close to him knew this tension took its toll. His colleague Justice Arthur Goldberg once observed, "Like Abraham Lincoln, the Chief Justice was subjected to unparalleled abuse in the conduct of his office. Being a warm and very human person, these attacks must have made his heart ache." It was precisely Warren's willingness to accept hard constitutional cases and issue unpopular decisions, like those in *Miranda*, that won Justice Goldberg's praise. The former justice continued, "In my view, Chief Justice Warren will be remembered not primarily for any particular decision, but for his steadfast view that the least possible justification for the Court to avoid deciding a citizen's substantial claim of constitutional rights is that the Court may injure itself if it decides that case and vindicates those rights. . . . (T)he Court should not avoid unpopular decision . . . (but should) abjure popularity in decision making."[35]

Shortly after his retirement, Warren gave an interview with *New York Times* reporter Anthony Lewis in which he finally responded to the critics. He said: "If anybody could show me anything that we have done in the time that I have been on the Court other than to insist that a man is entitled to counsel at all times after he has been put upon by the Government in a criminal case, and entitled to fair treatment to due process in the trial of his case, I would concede that we had perhaps done something wrong. I can't think of any such thing."[36]

Although no one in the *Miranda* majority had a change of heart on the question of custodial interrogation, Warren's later criminal justice decisions exhibited greater deference toward the law enforcement community. In *Terry v. Ohio* (1968) Warren announced a new approach to informal encounters between police and suspects on the beat. Under the new standard, if officers could articulate a reasonable basis for their suspicion, they would be permitted to conduct a brief stop and frisk of suspects in order to determine if weapons were present that might pose a danger to the officer or the public. Warren's decision split the liberal majority from *Miranda*, and Justice Douglas dissented. The *Terry* reasonable suspicion standard later became an important factor in the erosion of Fourth Amendment rights in the Burger and Rehnquist Courts.

The Warren Court's procedural due process reforms undermined the legal foundations of the Jim Crow justice system and ended many egregious law enforcement practices. The Court forced state officials to take constitutional rights more seriously. As the administrative leader of the Warren Court, Earl Warren deserves credit for initiating necessary change. He believed that neutral law enforcement professionals could end a political culture of corruption through enlightened management, efficiency, and ethics in public administration.

Yet many of the Court's procedural due process reforms also proved politically unpopular. By 1969, only about one-third of the American people reported having a great deal or quite a lot of confidence in the Supreme Court.[37] In the late 1960s and throughout the next several decades, conservatives challenged and then successfully undercut the social justice initiatives of the Warren era. The resulting legal and political backlash restricted federal court intervention in the state criminal process and increased state criminal penalties. Today, criminal laws in the United States are among the harshest and most repressive in the world. With 5% of the world's population, the United States holds 25% of the world's prisoners, over half of whom serve time for nonviolent offenses. At this writing, 2.3 million Americans are behind bars.[38]

SUBSTANTIVE DUE PROCESS AND THE CRIMINAL LAW

The second prong of the Warren Court's criminal justice reforms occurred in the context of substantive due process. In decisions such as *Griswold v. Connecticut* (1965), *Loving v. Virginia* (1967), and *Shapiro v. Thompson* (1969), the Court limited the reach of state power. *Griswold* and *Loving* arose in the context of criminal justice system, and *Shapiro* concerned the right to travel and eligibility for welfare. All three cases illustrate the Warren Court's approach to substantive due process, and all helped to shape the doctrinal framework for *Roe v. Wade* (1973), a Burger Court decision that curtailed the power of state legislatures to criminalize abortions in the United States.

The doctrine of substantive due process reflects the view that individuals enjoy certain natural rights that the government cannot impair. The doctrine has its roots in the Magna Carta[39] and in the political philosophy of John Locke.[40] Despite this pedigree, substantive due process also has a long and troubled history in Anglo-American law. The scope of natural rights is nebulous, and their uncertain parameters have given courts great discretion and power in constitutional interpretation.

Early substantive due process cases include Chief Justice Roger Taney's decision in the *Dred Scott* (1857) case.[41] Taney held that the Constitution did not grant Congress the power to prohibit slavery in the territories and that the Missouri Compromise, which prohibited slavery in the Iowa Territory, deprived owners of their "natural right" to hold slaves.

The adoption of the Fourteenth Amendment in 1868 seemingly lay to rest Chief Justice Taney's controversial interpretations of the Fifth Amendment Due Process Clause. Nevertheless, the doctrine of substantive due process survived. The industrial revolution of the final three decades of the nineteenth century substantially increased the influence of American corporations, and corporate leaders used the idea of substantive due process to obtain protection from unwelcome governmental regulation. They successfully asked the Supreme Court to protect freedom of contract and the free market system from state regulations that protected the health, safety, and welfare of citizens. Striking a balance between these two interests was a subjective process that resulted in unprincipled and inconsistent decisions.[42] When the Court later used substantive due process as part of its attack against Franklin Roosevelt's New Deal, its rulings proved unpopular and triggered political and legal change. Roosevelt's new appointees to the Court repudiated the use of natural law and substantive due process and deferred to Congress in the interpretation of social and economic legislation.

In the area of individual rights, the Court occasionally issued decisions that appeared to use natural law as a basis for limiting government authority. Two decisions in the 1920s, *Meyer v. Nebraska* (1923) and *Pierce v. Society of Sisters* (1925), recognized the right of parents to make educational decisions concerning their children.[43] Later, in *Skinner v. Oklahoma* (1942), the Court struck down an Oklahoma statute that sanctioned the sterilization of persons convicted of three or more felonies involving moral turpitude. The Oklahoma statute exempted persons convicted of embezzlement, violation of revenue laws, and a short list of other designated offenses from the sterilization punishment.

Justice Douglas' majority opinion in *Skinner* carefully avoided any open discussion of natural law or substantive due process. Instead, Douglas stressed the equal protection clause and the unequal treatment of similarly situated persons who also had committed theft crimes. In a concurring opinion, Justice Robert Jackson did reach the substantive due process question. Jackson implied that procreation was a fundamental right that might trigger strict scrutiny. He wrote, "There are limits to the extent to which a legislatively represented majority may conduct biological experiments at the expense of the dignity and personality and natural powers of a minority."[44]

The Warren Court's first occasion to address the issue of substantive due process occurred in *Griswold v. Connecticut* (1965). A Connecticut law prohibited married persons from using contraceptives, and Justice Douglas, again writing for the majority, struck down the law. He based his opinion on an implied fundamental right of privacy, which he found anchored in "penumbras" of the First, Third, Fourth, and Fifth Amendments. By this term, Douglas meant that several of the Court's previous decisions interpreting these amendments had explicitly recognized privacy rights. For example, its First Amendment decisions protected the privacy of membership in political organizations, and its Fourth and Fifth Amendment cases gave individuals a zone of privacy that the state could not invade at will. Chief Justice Warren joined Justices Brennan and Goldberg in a concurring opinion written by Justice Goldberg. They argued that the Ninth Amendment protected unenumerated rights that reflected the "traditions and conscience" of the nation. These included the right to privacy in matters involving procreation.

Although both Justice Douglas and Justice Goldberg offered a plausible basis for recognizing a constitutional right to privacy, other justices found their approaches subjective. In a separate concurring opinion, Justice Harlan argued in favor of a return to a natural law framework in substantive due process cases. Harlan believed that the justices legitimately could protect certain values the American people historically had shielded from legislative encroachment. Justice Black wrote an important dissent in which he assailed his colleagues for embracing the discredited natural law doctrines of the *Lochner* era. His dissent in *Griswold* foreshadowed the criticism of the implied constitutional right to privacy and reproductive freedom that raged across the country in the wake of the Burger Court's *Roe v. Wade* (1973) decision.

Black strongly advocated literalism in constitutional interpretation, and he criticized the freewheeling power that the doctrine of substantive due process bestowed upon unelected courts. He objected to the use of natural law in constitutional cases, a practice he believed gave judges too much power to shape constitutional rules on the basis of their own subjective appraisal of the wisdom or reasonableness of the law. He wrote:

> My point is that there is no provision of the Constitution which either expressly or impliedly vests power in this Court to sit as a supervisory agency over acts of duly constituted legislative bodies and set aside their laws because of the Court's belief that the legislative policies adopted are unreasonable, unwise, arbitrary, capricious or irrational. The adoption of such a loose, flexible, uncontrolled standard for holding laws unconstitutional, if ever it is finally achieved, will amount to a great unconstitutional shift of power to the courts which I believe and am constrained to say will be bad for the courts, and worse for the country.[45]

The novel substantive due process issues in *Griswold* split both the liberal majority and the conservative minority on the Warren Court. Justice Black left his liberal colleagues over the issue of an implied constitutional right of privacy; conversely, Justices Clark, White, and Harlan abandoned Justice Stewart, who also dissented in the case. *Griswold* stands for the proposition that the Warren Court actively enforced values that did not appear in the express provisions of the Constitution. In this sense, the Court followed the behavior of earlier justices in the seemingly discredited *Lochner* era.

The next significant substantive due process case of the Warren era occurred two years later in *Loving v. Virginia* (1967). As in *Skinner v. Oklahoma*, the issues in *Loving* raised both substantive due process and equal protection concerns. The presence of less controversial equal protection problems in the fact pattern enabled the justices to reach a unanimous decision in the case.

Loving involved a challenge against Virginia's antimiscegenation law. Adopted in 1923, the Racial Integrity Act sought to preserve the purity of the races and enhance the interest of white supremacy by criminalizing interracial marriage. The *Loving* case arose when an interracial couple, Richard and Mildred Loving, got married in Virginia and spent the night at a local motel. At 2 a.m. police broke into the couple's motel room and arrested them. The Lovings pleaded guilty to the charges, and the trial judge sentenced them to one year in jail. The judge later suspended the sentence for a term of 25 years on the condition that the defendants leave Virginia and not return for a period of 25 years. They appealed their conviction to the U.S. Supreme Court.

Chief Justice Warren assigned the case to himself and ruled the Virginia statute unconstitutional. Warren wrote: "Under our Constitution, the freedom to marry, or not marry, a person of another race resides with the individual and cannot be abridged by the State."[46] Like Douglas in the involuntary sterilization case, Warren based his holding on both an equal protection and a due process analysis. The equal protection portion of the decision stressed the invidious nature of racial discrimination, and the due process analysis emphasized the fundamental right to marry. Warren's decision recognized that individuals enjoy a zone of autonomy regarding intimate and marital relations and that society acts illegitimately when it seeks to condemn individual freedom of action under the auspices of racial orthodoxy. In slightly different form, this principle may come into play in the Court's future consideration of the constitutionality of laws prohibiting same sex marriage.

In many respects, Warren's opinion resembled the decision he wrote in *Brown v. Board of Education*. Here, as in *Brown*, he did not accept as dispositive the views of the framers of the Fourteenth Amendment on the question of racial integration. At the time of the ratification debates, several Congressmen had argued that the new amendment would not deprive the states of the power to proscribe interracial marriage. Deferring to their views on the question would have led to a decision in favor of the State of Virginia. Instead, Warren grounded his interpretation in the principle that government racial classifications ran afoul of equal protection of the law. As in *Brown*, Warren composed his opinion using plain and simple language. He wrote for a supermajority of his colleagues,[47] and his opinion struck down the discriminatory laws of many states.[48] Likewise, by sanctioning interracial social ties, his decisions sought to reduce the social isolation of African Americans, thereby increasing the likelihood of their upward mobility in American society.

The last major substantive due process case of the Warren Court involved a challenge against welfare laws in two states and the District of Columbia. The laws in question required new residents to wait one year before becoming eligible for welfare benefits. In *Shapiro v. Thompson* (1969), the Court ruled that the state laws violated the Fourteenth Amendment Equal Protection Clause and the District law violated the Fifth Amendment Due Process Clause. Justice Brennan's majority opinion held that the government defendants could not discriminate between old and new residents in the allocation of welfare benefits in a manner that compromised the constitutional right to travel. His opinion refined the framework for analyzing equal protection issues. Under the new framework, rights expressly or impliedly recognized in the Constitution would be considered "fundamental" and would trigger strict scrutiny. The government would have to demonstrate a compelling interest for its law and show that it used the least drastic means to accomplish its objectives. Rights not considered fundamental would be subject to the Court's less rigorous rational basis standard, which requires only a showing of a rational relationship between the means and ends of a given governmental initiative. Using the new framework, Brennan concluded that the government interest in preventing fraud and discouraging the in-migration of needy people did not represent compelling interests and did not justify the infringement of the right to engage in interstate travel.

The right to travel is not expressly recognized in the Constitution. However, the Articles of Confederation did acknowledge the right,[49] and in The *Slaughter-House Cases* (1873) the Supreme Court recognized the right to travel as one of the privileges and immunities of federal citizenship. Chief Justice Warren and Justices Black and Harlan filed dissenting opinions in *Shapiro*. Warren argued that the Commerce Clause gave the Congress power to authorize the states to set reasonable residency requirements of up to one year for welfare programs. He relied heavily on the legislative history of the Social Security Act and noted Congress' desire during the height of the Great Depression to encourage the states to enhance their welfare benefits. A state's ability to adopt a residency requirement of up to one year increased the likelihood that it would adopt expanded welfare benefits.

Warren's opposition to the *Shapiro* majority reflected the political lessons he learned in California during the 1930s. Of particular relevance was *Edwards v. California* (1941), a case the Supreme Court decided when he was Attorney General of California. In *Edwards*, the State of California prosecuted the defendant for violating its "Okie Law," which prohibited persons from assisting paupers in gaining entry into California. The Supreme Court struck down the California law as a violation of the constitutional right to travel. As a state official during the Great Depression and head of the Republican Party during the controversial 1934 gubernatorial campaign, Warren well knew the politics behind the Okie law. He wanted to preserve state power to issue year-long residential requirements as a *quid-pro-quo* for expanding state welfare programs. Warren's opinion also recognized that the Court's decision in *Shapiro* would have important implications for residency requirements in state elections laws. In this sense, he anticipated the Court's decision in *Dunn v. Blumstein* (1972), which struck down year-long residency requirements as a precondition for the right to vote.

The Warren Court's substantive due process decisions played an important role in the Burger Court's subsequent *Roe v. Wade* (1973) decision. The right to privacy with respect to matters of procreation and marriage assumed the status of a fundamental right, which under the *Shapiro v. Thompson* (1969) precedent, triggered strict scrutiny and the compelling state interest test. Although *Roe* and its progeny have proven controversial, a majority of the American public has accepted the legitimacy of the underlying right of privacy recognized in *Griswold* and *Loving*. For this reason, the Warren Court's substantive due process decisions in the field of criminal justice have made a positive contribution to American constitutional law.

THE SOCIAL IMPACT OF WARREN'S CRIMINAL JUSTICE REFORMS

The Warren Court's major criminal justice reforms have had a mixed social impact. On the positive side of the ledger, in a relatively short period Warren and his colleagues ended many of the more egregious abuses of the criminal justice system and mandated conformity with most of the federal Bill of Rights throughout the nation. Indigent defendants received the right to court-appointed counsel; courts excluded evidence seized in violation of the Fourth, Fifth, and Sixth Amendments; and police issued *Miranda* warnings before conducting custodial interrogations. On the downside, the Warren Court's due process revolution triggered the perception (some would say misperception) that the Court sided with criminals and against police in the battle to maintain public safety. Critics contended that a deep, counter-majoritarian tension existed between the Court's own policy preferences and the predilections of the majority of the American people.

Most scholars dispute the thesis that the Warren Court's criminal justice decisions were radically counter-majoritarian. In a study of the Warren Court's signature *Mapp*, *Gideon*, *Miranda*, *Katz*, and *Terry* decisions, Corinna Barrett Lain persuasively argues that the Court reflected public opinion and merely endorsed and extended policies that already had been adopted successfully in liberal states and at the federal level.[50] In her words, the Court "stayed with favorable sociopolitical conditions and within the parameters of publicly acceptable policy positions."[51] The Court followed a trend toward the nationalization of public policy in the postwar era that extended from national security to highways, higher education, exploration of outer space, and urban renewal.

Recent critical scholarship concerning the Warren Court's criminal justice reforms includes the work of the late Professor William J. Stuntz.[52] In his influential book *The Collapse of American Criminal Justice* (2011) Stuntz argues that the Warren Court displaced the informal, jury-based systems of the late nineteenth and early twentieth centuries with rigid procedural requirements from Madison's Bill of Rights. Stuntz criticizes Warren for turning to law as a means of solving human problems. As Stuntz phases it, "Too much law amounts to no law at all; when legal doctrine makes everyone an offender, the relevant offenses have no meaning independent of law enforcers' will. The formal rule of law yields the functional rule of official discretion."[53]

In Stuntz's view, Progressive reformers like Warren expanded the power of appellate judges over juries, creating a "centralized, bureaucratic, and legalized system" that replaced the lenient, sympathetic, and working-class juries of the Gilded Age. In the traditional jury system, which lasted from the end of Reconstruction until the beginning of the Great Depression, jurors had the authority to determine both the facts of a case and the moral implications of the defendant's conduct. Under the reformed system currently in place, relatively few jury trials occur, and when they do, jurors simply make determinations about credibility. To be sure, in some states jurors render decisions about punishment. Nevertheless, common legal loopholes that defense attorneys once used as a means of reducing or eliminating criminal liability—such as self-defense, temporary insanity, or manslaughter—have been tightened. Juries no longer base their verdicts on moral judgments about defendants, and in many jurisdictions courts explicitly prohibit such verdicts.

Stuntz's praise for the neighborhood jury systems of the Gilded Age overlooks their many shortcomings. A careful review of the historical record shows that unbridled and often corrupt juror discretion triggered mass violence in the North during the 1880s. In 1884, for example, Cincinnati residents became upset at what they perceived to be a pattern of jury tampering and excessive leniency. Following a murder trial against William Berner and Joe Palmer, in which the jury convicted the two defendants of the lesser charge of manslaughter, a mob of 10,000 persons attacked the Hamilton County Courthouse over three days and burned it to the ground. In the two years before the case came to trial, there had been only four murder convictions out of fifty murder cases. This prompted a local newspaper to proclaim that "trials of murders are made mockeries of law and justice. . . ."[54] On the third day of deadly rioting, national guardsmen and police restored order by turning Gatlin guns on the unruly crowd, killing 56 persons and wounding over 200.[55]

A second problem in Stuntz's argument concerns his support for the pro-defendant leniency of local juries during the Gilded Age. The validity of Stuntz's argument on this point is not self-evident. When one explores the historical record to determine who received little or no police or jury protection from crime during the late nineteenth and early twentieth centuries, the list of victims is troubling. Ward bosses and their partners in corrupt urban machines controlled the enforcement of law in ethnic neighborhoods, often yielding biased and unjust outcomes. In Chicago, for example, the history of homicide shows a pattern of under-enforcement of law in each of three waves of homicidal violence that afflicted the city between 1870 and 1930.[56]

In the first wave, which extended from 1870 until 1890, unmarried men fought deadly drunken brawls in saloons. Available evidence shows that police often overlooked such homicides altogether, leaving the perpetrators free to kill again in the future.[57] When prosecutors did file criminal charges, defendants with connections to ward bosses often could avoid harsh penalties by means of lenient juries.

In the second wave, which extended from 1890 until 1920, urban immigrants married and violence took on a domestic face, often to the detriment of African Americans, women, and children. Police systematically under-enforced domestic violence laws in the black South Side ghetto. As the population of African Americans in Chicago increased from 14,271 to 109,458 during this period, no other group of Chicagoans experienced a higher rate of homicide. Adler (2006) reports, "From 1875 to 1920, African American Chicagoans killed and died from criminal violence at more than seven times the rate of white Chicagoans."[58]

Other victims of Gilded Age justice during this period included sick children and the husbands of women who killed. In the absence of supportive programs for the provision of health care, child support, and legally enforceable restraining orders, women with seriously ill infants or those facing abusive husbands turned to infanticide and spousal homicide to solve their problems.[59] Stuntz's praise for the tendency of police, coroners, prosecutors, and juries to overlook and drop charges against white women in these situations raises the question of why infants remained unprotected, why prosecutors singed out similarly situated black women for prosecution, and why a presumption existed that married women could gun down their (allegedly abusive) husbands with little or no scrutiny from law enforcement officials.

The third of Chicago's crime waves, which overlaps somewhat with the other two, occurred during the first three decades of the twentieth century. In this period, significant increases in homicide rates occurred as a result of commercial development. Robbery homicides and gangster activity led to over 400 unsolved murders in Chicago during the Prohibition era alone. In their fight against urban corruption, progressive reformers like Warren sought to expand the responsibility of public officials in the protection of citizens. In contrast, the discretionary justice that Stuntz advocates left many persons vulnerable and defenseless. His romanticized portrait of criminal justice in the Gilded Age does not provide a persuasive basis for attacking the efficacy of Warren's reforms.

Stuntz concludes his critique of Warren by stressing the harsh criminal penalties that external populations currently impose upon inner-city residents. He blasts the Warren Court for launching its reforms in the middle of a crime wave, thus precipitating a harsh backlash against the very urban minorities that the Court sought to protect. Stuntz highlights the increase in violent crime that began during the early 1950s, as unskilled and semiskilled Americans gradually lost positions in manufacturing. In the 1960s, unemployment levels increased precipitously in inner-city neighborhoods, and as a result, criminal activity mushroomed. Nationwide, during the two decades between 1950 and 1970, the murder rate doubled.[60] Although no causal nexus existed between the Warren Court's decisions and the rising crime rate, public concern over the problem of crime made the Court a convenient scapegoat.

Suburban voters supported a series of repressive measures directed against inner-city communities. As a result, during the past four decades sentencing laws in the United States have become among the harshest in the world. Stuntz denounces the loss of neighborhood autonomy in inner-city America as well as the imposition of draconian criminal policies by county prosecutors, state legislators, and nonlocal jurors. As Stuntz notes, the current incarceration rate among white men hovers just slightly below 500 per 100,000 persons, the highest rate of incarceration in American history. Conversely, for black men, the incarceration rate exceeds 3,000 per 100,000 persons, and for black males in their twenties and thirties, the rate exceeds 7,000.[61] Stuntz condemns the injustice that these statistics reveal, and he blames Earl Warren for the outcome.

Other critics, who occupy positions far to the right of Stuntz, assert that the Warren Court's due process revolution caused an increase in crime. Scholars in the field of law and economics, for example, contend that the *Gideon*, *Mapp*, and *Miranda* decisions offered criminals new opportunities to avoid police apprehension. As a result, they contend, crime rates increased during the 1960s, especially in small towns.[62] Generally speaking, such studies rest on a number of dubious assumptions and methodological shortcomings. These include the assumption that criminals logically calculate the costs and benefits of crime before they act (even though many are drunk, high on drugs, or behaving illogically at the time of their crimes); the failure to include warrantless searches and seizures in the specification of variables in studies on the impact of the exclusionary rule; and the adoption of research designs that incorporate large numbers of independent variables in multiple repression equations, a practice that makes it difficult to construct parsimonious explanations of the relationships between the variables under study. Most comprehensive studies, which have focused on the trial process where convictions actually are "won" or "lost" rather than on the less certain conduct of police in the field, have reached the conclusion that the number of "lost" convictions as a result of the exclusionary rule is below 2%.[63]

As a matter of empirical evidence, critics have not been persuasive in their contention that the liberal decisions of the Warren Court caused an increase in crime. Indeed, high levels of crime continued to occur even in the decades after the conservative Burger and Rehnquist Courts replaced the liberal Warren Court. Even though harsh criminal policies have superseded the relatively lenient sentencing laws of the Warren era, high rates of violent crime persisted well into the 1980s and 1990s. Only when large segments of the U.S. population outgrew criminal lifestyles through maturation did the crime rate decline. In addition, the Warren Court's reforms triggered a significant increase in the number of criminal appeals and petitions for post-conviction relief and thereby increased the quality of justice in America. In state supreme courts, a 73.5% increase in the number of criminal cases involving constitutional issues occurred between 1960 and 1970;[64] the lower federal courts also experienced a major change in the nature of cases on their dockets. Thus, the Warren Court's push for uniformity in the rights of suspects required criminal justice personnel to take constitutional rights more seriously.

The critics' case may be marginally stronger when it comes to the public relations dimension of the Warren Court's due process revolution. Richard Nixon won the 1968 presidential election in part because the majority of American voters perceived that the Warren Court's decisions hamstrung police in the fight against crime. Yet any reasonable effort to gauge Warren's legacy must ask whether Nixon and the public got it right. For several reasons, one must question whether Nixon's supporters reached the proper conclusion. Like many liberal leaders of his day, Warren favored public policies that addressed the social roots of crime. Such policies take sustained financial support, time, and public patience to work. The conservative public policy agenda of the 1970s and 1980s cut against all three of these preconditions. Reducing taxes, de-industrializing the national economy, and abandoning inner-city America became the rallying cry, and as a result, criminogenic conditions proliferated. Tragically, the public rarely saw the personal side of Warren's commitment to community and personal rehabilitation as a response to crime. Warren's own father lost his life at the hands of a criminal, but Warren's faith in community development and professionalism in law enforcement remained steadfast. He did not so much coddle criminals as insist that segregated schools blocked economic opportunity and unreliable interrogation methods often led to false positives. He demanded greater levels of forensic investigation and an end to "short cuts" in police investigations. Over time, his arguments have proven correct.

Although the Supreme Court often has expressed doubts about the wisdom of the Warren Court's criminal justice reforms during the past fifty years, it has not overruled them. Today, the Fourth Amendment exclusionary rule and the *Miranda* custodial interrogation safeguards may be riddled with good faith and public safety exceptions, but the core holdings of *Mapp* and *Miranda* remain intact. Despite frequent invitations to do so, the Court has declined to overturn the Warren Court's due process revolution. Likewise, although critics like Stunz legitimately decry the racist overtones of America's thirty-year war on crime, in fairness, one wonders how long Warren can be held responsible for events and policy pronouncements that have taken place long after his passing.

As he did with many social and political issues of his day, Warren viewed the fight against crime as a matter of collective responsibility. He called for the strengthening of understaffed and inadequately trained police departments, improving conditions in low-income neighborhoods, and encouraging personal "introspection" about the steps that might be taken on an individual level to reduce crime. "To have an ordered society, free from crime," Warren wrote in *A Republic if You Can Keep It*, "we must have order and wholesomeness in the home, in the neighborhood, on the streets, in business, and in government. . . ." His words contain the ring of truth.

NOTES

1. Earl Warren, *Memoirs*, 119.
2. Quoted in Lewis, "A Talk with Warren on Crime, the Court, the Country," *New York Times Magazine*, October 19, 1969; see also G. Edward White, *Earl Warren: A Public Life*, 271.
3. In his opinion in *Spano v. New York* (1959), Warren wrote, "The abhorrence of society to the use of involuntary confessions does not turn alone on their inherent

untrustworthiness. It also turns on the deep-rooted feeling that the police must obey the law while enforcing the law; that in the end life and liberty can be as much endangered from illegal methods used to convict those thought to be criminals as from the actual criminals themselves." 360 U.S. at 320–21.

4. *Rochin v. California*, 342 U.S. 165, 173 (1952).

5. *Whitney v. California*, 274 U.S. 357, 373 (1927)(Brandeis, J., concurring).

6. *McDonald v. City of Chicago*, 561 U.S. 742, 862(Stevens, J., dissenting).

7. *Twining v. New Jersey*, 211 U.S. 78, 106 (1908).

8. 316 U.S. 455, 476 (1942) (Black, J., dissenting).

9. Justice Douglas joined Black's dissenting opinion. The two other dissenters in *Adamson*, Justices Murphy and Rutledge, agreed with Black's total incorporation position but also wanted to give courts the flexibility to interpret the due process clause in ways that went beyond the specific entitlements of the Bill of Rights.

As part of his dissent, Justice Black offered an Appendix in which he elaborated on the historical evidence that supported his argument. He emphasized minutes from the deliberations of the Joint Committee on Reconstruction and Ohio Representative John Bingham's thoughts on the purpose of what would eventually become Section One of the Fourteenth Amendment. In the period after release of the *Adamson* decision, several scholars took issue with Justice Black's reading of the congressional history. Foremost among them was Professor Charles Fairman of Stanford Law School, who stressed the absence of similar remarks in the debates that occurred in state legislatures during the ratification process. The debate between advocates of these two positions lingered indecisively in academia for many years.

10. Schwartz, *Super Chief*, 134 (see chap. 1, n. 15).

11. Simon, *In His Own Image*, 62 (see chap. 2, n. 10).

12. Author Liva Baker has noted that one of the ways the Warren Court made the transition between its early decisions allowing states to depart from the requirements of the Bill of Rights under the fundamental fairness framework and its later opinions requiring states to follow the Bill of Rights was by gradually voting to reverse convictions in right to counsel and custodial interrogation cases. "Between 1940 and 1954," she writes, "the Court's rate of affirmance of convictions in right to counsel cases was 36%. Between 1954 and 1962 the rate of affirmance had dropped to 14%. No convictions in right to counsel cases were affirmed after 1958." A similar trend occurred in custodial interrogation cases. Baker continues, "Between 1940, when (Justice Hugo Black) wrote the Court opinion in *Chambers*, and 1964, when Danny Escobedo's murder conviction was reversed, the U.S. Supreme Court decided thirty-six state cases involving confessions. In twenty-six, or nearly three-quarters, the Court decided in favor of the criminal defendant. Hugo Black either wrote the Court opinion, wrote a concurring opinion, or silently joined the majority in all twenty-six. In ten cases the Court decided against the criminal defendant; Hugo Black dissented in nine of them and did not participate in one." Liva Baker, *Miranda: Crime, Law, and Politics* (New York: Atheneum Books, 1983), 74.

13. 367 U.S. at 659.

14. Not all police officials reacted negatively to the *Mapp* decision. For example, Deputy New York Police Commissioner Reisman noted in an interview that many departments responded by expanding their training programs. "The *Mapp* case was a

shock to us," he said. "We had to reorganize our thinking, frankly. Before this, nobody bothered to take out search warrants. Although the U.S. Constitution requires warrants in most cases, the U.S. Supreme Court had ruled that evidence obtained without a warrant—illegally, if you will—was admissible in state courts. So the feeling was, why bother? Well, once that rule was changed we knew we had better start teaching our men about it." *New York Times*, Apr. 28, 1965; also quoted in *U.S. v. Leon*, 468 U.S. 897, 951 n. 13 (1984)(Brennan, J., dissenting).

15. Comptroller General of the United States, *Impact of the Exclusionary Rule on Federal Criminal Prosecutions* (Washington, D.C.: Government Printing Office, 1979).

16. Although one of Earl Warren's law clerks, Henry Steinman, has denied that Warren issued instructions for his law clerks to look for cases that could be used to overturn precedents denying indigents the right to court appointed in noncapital cases, the majority of scholars who have examined this question have come down on the other side of the issue. See e.g., Schwartz, *Super Chief*, 404.

17. At the time of the appeal in *Gideon*, only five states (Alabama, Florida, Mississippi, North Carolina, and South Carolina) did not provide some form of court-appointed counsel for indigent criminal defendants.

18. By the end of the Warren era, only the Second Amendment, the Third Amendment, the Fifth Amendment indictment clause, the Seventh Amendment right to a jury selected from the district where the crime arose and right to jury in civil cases, and the Eighth Amendment excessive bail and fines clauses had not been incorporated. In subsequent years, the Second Amendment and in one judicial circuit, the Third Amendment have been incorporated.

19. During his years as a prosecutor in Jefferson County Alabama, Black received complaints that the Bessemer Police Department used coercive tactics during custodial interrogations at the city jail. Black conducted an investigation and issued a report on the matter. In his report, Black stated: "We find that a uniform practice has been made of taking helpless prisoners, in the late hours of the night, into a secluded room and there beat them until they were red with their . . . own blood, in the effort to obtain confessions. We find that this cowardly practice, in which four big officers with pistols safely strapped on their bodies, would thus take advantage of ignorance and helplessness, has been continuously in operation for a long number of years." Quoted in Baker, *Miranda: Crime, Law and Politics*, 73. Although Black's investigation led to no convictions or changes in police practices, it left an indelible mark on his own thinking, as shown in the critique of such practices in his opinion for the Court in *Chambers v. Florida*, 309 U.S. 227 (1940).

20. National Commission on Law Observance and Law Enforcement, Report on Lawlessness in Law Enforcement (Washington, D.C.: Government Printing Office, 1931), 47.

21. *Williams v. State of Texas*, 88 Tex. Cr. Rep. 87, 225 S.W. 177 (1920).

22. National Commission on Law Observance and Law Enforcement, 47.

23. Ibid., 191.

24. *Brown v. Mississippi*, 297 U.S. 278 (1936).

25. *Chambers v. Florida*, 309 U.S. 227 (1940).

26. See *Miranda v. Arizona*, 384 U.S. 436, 484–486, n. 54 (1966).

27. *Spano v. New York*, 360 U.S. 315, 320–1.

28. Baker, *Miranda: Crime, Law, and Politics*, 48.

29. The three states were California, Oregon, and Rhode Island.

30. Studies of the economic backgrounds of Supreme Court justices have found that about 90% of the justices in U.S. history have come from affluent families. See e.g., John R. Schmidhauser, *The Supreme Court: Its Politics, Personalities, and Procedures* (New York: Hold Rinehart, and Wilson, 1960), 31–32.

31. Quoted in Baker, *Miranda: Crime, Law, and Politics*, 178. For more detail on the New Haven study, see "Interrogations in New Haven: The Impact of *Miranda*," 76 *Yale L. J.* 1519 (1967).

32. Baker, *Miranda: Crime, Law, and Politics*, 179–80.

33. Although it is clear that the number of serious crimes escalated during the 1960s, the data presented in the Uniform Crime Reports for the 1960s must be viewed with caution due to inconsistencies in the number of jurisdictions that submitted data to the federal government.

34. Richard M. Nixon, *Toward Freedom from Fear: A Statement* (New York: Nixon for President Committee, 1968).

35. Arthur J. Goldberg, "Earl Warren: The Flame Burned Bright," *The Virgin Island Daily News*, September 30, 1974, 19. Available at *news.google.com/newspapers?nid=757&dat=19740930.*

36. Quoted in Lewis, "A Talk with Warren on Crime, the Court, the Country," *New York Times Magazine*, October 19, 1969.

37. Gallop Poll 3 (1935–1971), reported in Lee Epstein and Jeffrey A. Segal, *The Supreme Court Compendium: Data, Decisions, and Developments*, 5th Ed., (Thousand Oaks, CA: CQ Press, 2012), 777.

38. See Adam Liptak, "Inmate Count in U.S. Dwarfs Other Nations," *New York Times*, April 23, 2008.

39. The Magna Carta provided that freemen could not be imprisoned in violation of the law of the land. Arguably, this clause meant that the sovereign could not run roughshod over the customary and natural rights of the people.

40. Natural rights democrats such as John Locke argue that if the legislature passes laws that restrict vested rights protected by natural law, it violates the social contract. Courts then have a duty to strike down such laws as unconstitutional.

41. 60 U.S. (19 How.) 393 (1857).

42. Compare *Muller v. Oregon*, 208 U.S. 412 (1908) (upholding the power of states to regulate the wages of female workers) with *Lochner v. New York*, 198 U.S. 45 (1905) (striking down state regulation of working hours in the baking industry).

43. *Meyer v. Nebraska*, 262 U.S. 390 (1923) and *Pierce v. Society of Sisters*, 268 U.S. 510 (1925).

44. Ibid., 546 (Jackson, J. concurring).

45. *Griswold v. Connecticut*, 381 U.S. 479, 520–21 (Black, J. dissenting).

46. 388 U.S. at 12.

47. Justice Potter Stuart filed a concurring opinion in the case, in which he argued that under the Equal Protection Clause, states cannot make the criminality of an act depend upon the race of the actor. Thus he distanced himself from the substantive due process aspect of Warren's opinion.

48. The *Loving* decision struck down the antimiscegenation laws of 16 states.

49. Article IV of the Articles of Confederation stated: "[T]he free inhabitants of each of these States, paupers, vagabonds and fugitives from justice excepted, shall be entitled to all privileges and immunities of free citizens in the several States; and the people of each State shall have free ingress and regress to and from any other State, and shall enjoy therein all the privileges of trade and commerce, subject to the same duties, impositions and restrictions as the inhabitants thereof respectively. . . ."

50. See Corinna Barrett Lain, "Countermajoritarian Hero or Zero?" 152 U. Pa. L. Rev. 1361 (2004).

51. Ibid., 1451.

52. Stuntz died of cancer in March 2011.

53. William J. Stuntz, *The Collapse of American Criminal Justice* (Cambridge: Belknap Press of Harvard University Press, 2011), 3.

54. *The Cincinnati Commercial Gazette*, Tuesday March 25, 1884.

55. Ibid.

56. The foregoing discussion of the history of homicide in Chicago is based on the research of Jeffrey S. Adler, *First in Violence, Deepest in Dirt: Homicide in Chicago 1875–1920* (Cambridge, Harvard University Press, 2006). Adler's methodology focuses on a dataset of 5,645 homicide cases, which represents every homicide reported to the Chicago police from 1875–1920.

57. Ibid., 126.

58. Ibid.

59. "Chicago women killed sixty-seven (non-newborn) children between 1875 and 1920; in 97 % of these deaths, a mother killed her child, making child killing the second largest category of homicide by women, trailing only husband killing." Ibid., 92. "Every white woman who killed her husband between August 1905 and October 1918 was exonerated or acquitted, totaling thirty-five consecutive cases." Ibid., 113.

60. See generally, Stuntz, *The Collapse of American Criminal Justice*, 5, 14n. and the sources sited therein.

61. Ibid., 34.

62. See Raymond A. Atkins and Paul H. Rubin, "Effects of Criminal Procedure on Crime Rates: Mapping Out the Consequences of the Exclusionary Rule," *Journal of Law and Economics* 46, no. 1 (April 2003):157–79. Also available at http://www.independent.org/pdf/working papers/09 effects.pdf.

63. For a thorough review of the empirical studies on the exclusionary rule and analysis of the number of "lost cases" in seven comparison cities, see Craig D. Uchida and Timothy S. Bynum, "Search Warrants, Motions to Suppress, and 'Lost Cases:' The Effects of the Exclusionary Rule in Seven Jurisdictions," *Journal of Criminal Law and Criminology* 81, no. 4 (Winter, 1991): 1034–66. Uchida and Bynum conclude that when police obtain search warrants, the "social cost" of the exclusionary rule is slight. They also find that when criminal defendants are freed as a result of police violations of the Fourth Amendment, usually their crimes are not serious. Ibid., 1066.

64. See Robert A. Kagen, Lawrence M. Friedman, and Stanton Wheeler, "The Business of State Supreme Courts, 1870–1970." 30 *Stanford L. Rev.* 121 (1977).

Part IV

EARL WARREN OFF THE BENCH

Chapter 11

An Incident in Dallas

In the early afternoon of Friday November 22, 1963, the justices met in conference, as was their custom, to discuss the cases on their docket. Suddenly they heard a soft knocking on the door. Chief Justice Warren's Secretary, Mrs. Margaret McHugh, handed the Chief a typewritten note. After glancing at the message, Warren's face paled. In a quivering voice, he stated: "President Kennedy has been shot in Dallas. It is unknown how badly he has been injured." The justices absorbed the shocking news in silence. Just two days before, they had attended the annual White House party for the Supreme Court, and the memory of the vibrant young president must have been fresh on their minds. The Court adjourned its conference, and the justices returned to their offices to follow the news from Dallas. A short time later came word that John F. Kennedy, the thirty-fifth president of the United States, had died.

In the late afternoon, Warren issued a press release that stated, "A great and good President has suffered martyrdom as a result of the hatred and bitterness that has been injected into the life of our Nation by bigots." His words, spoken in the stress and anger of the moment, vented his inner thoughts and feelings. Warren's suspicions reflected the many death threats he himself had received over the previous ten years in the wake of the *Brown* decision. At 6 p.m. the Warrens drove to Andrews Air Force Base outside of Washington, D.C. to greet Air Force One as it arrived. They watched helplessly as Jackie Kennedy descended from the plane in her bloodstained dress and soldiers placed the president's remains in a waiting ambulance.

When doctors completed Kennedy's autopsy around midnight,[1] officials took Kennedy's body to the East Room of the White House, where it lay in state. On Saturday morning, the justices came to the White House to pay their last respects. A distraught Earl Warren returned home, and at 9 p.m., the telephone rang. It was Jackie Kennedy, calling to see if he would offer a eulogy for the fallen president at the Rotunda of the U.S. Capitol on Sunday afternoon.

Warren readily agreed but then struggled over the assignment. For hours, he attempted to sketch out his thoughts, but the words would not come. The sudden shock of the assassination may well have reminded him of his father's own violent death. Warren resolved to wake up early on Sunday to finish his remarks. On Sunday morning, after learning that the principal suspect, Lee Harvey Oswald, had himself been shot down, Warren completed his statement. As thousands lined the streets of Washington for the funeral procession, the Warrens rushed to the Capitol. In his remarks, Warren did little to hide the bitterness he felt about the events of the weekend. He stated:

> What moved some misguided wretch to do this horrible deed may never be known to us, but we do know that such acts are commonly stimulated by forces of hatred and malevolence as today are eating their way into the blood stream of American life. What a price we pay for this fanaticism!
>
> . . . If we really love this country; if we truly love justice and mercy; if we fervently want to make this Nation better for those who are to follow us, we can at least abjure the hatred that consumes people, the false accusations that divide us and the bitterness that begets violence.[2]

Warren's words revealed both the profound grief he felt at the passing of the President and his initial views of the assassination. In veiled language, he restated his allegation that a fanatic had killed Kennedy. Using phrases such as "the hatred and malevolence such as today are eating their way into the blood stream of American life," he implied that a right-wing extremist assassinated Kennedy. On the very day he delivered the eulogy, Warren received an anonymous threat that if he walked behind Kennedy's casket during the funeral march to Arlington National Cemetery, he would be killed.[3] Symbolically, a bitter Jackie Kennedy mirrored Warren's views. On the flight back to Washington, she chose to remain in her pink, bloodstained dress. When White House physician Admiral George Burkley suggested that she change her clothes before their arrival, she responded, "No. Let them see what they've done."[4]

THE GENESIS OF THE WARREN COMMISSION, NOVEMBER 22–29, 1963

As the nation honored its fallen president, law enforcement officials focused their attention on Lee Harvey Oswald, an unskilled worker at the Texas School Book Depository. A former Marine who had defected to the Soviet Union in 1960, Oswald returned to the United States in the spring of 1962 with his Russian wife and young daughter. On the afternoon of the assassination, Dallas police arrested Oswald and interrogated him throughout the weekend.[5] The interrogations took place in a small office on the third floor of the Dallas police station, with over one hundred reporters crowded into the hallways immediately outside. In the midst of this chaotic and unprofessional atmosphere, Oswald steadfastly denied any involvement in the shooting. At various points he stated, "I don't know what this is all about," "I didn't even know the president was killed until newsmen told me in the hall," and "I'm just a patsy."[6] On Sunday morning November 24, as police attempted to move Oswald from the stationhouse to the county jail, Dallas nightclub owner Jack Ruby gunned him down. A short time later, doctors at Parkland Hospital pronounced Oswald dead.

In the meantime, officials in Washington worked overtime to manage the politics of the investigation. On Saturday November 23, CIA Director John McCone twice met with President Johnson to review details of Oswald's trip to Mexico City, which had taken place in late September and early October 1963. McCone alleged that Oswald had made contact with the Soviet and Cuban embassies and later met with Valery Kostikov, a KGB agent who specialized in assassinations. In making these allegations, McCone laid the groundwork for the hypothesis that the Soviet Union had masterminded the assassination of Kennedy in retaliation for its humiliation during the recent Cuban missile crisis.[7] This disturbed President Johnson, who suspected that members of his own national security team wanted to coerce him into war.

On the afternoon of Friday November 22, J. Edgar Hoover conducted a preliminary analysis into Oswald's background and then framed a theory of the case: Oswald, "a nut of the extreme pro-Castro crowd," acting alone, committed the assassination. That very evening, President Johnson placed the FBI in charge of the investigation, and he insisted that a report of the FBI's findings be on his desk by Tuesday November 26.

On a number of levels, Johnson's move was cynical. Legally, the federal government had no jurisdiction to conduct the investigation because the United States Code contained no provision making the assassination of the president a federal crime. Thus, the State of Texas had primary responsibility for investigating the assassination. Yet President Johnson authorized the removal of Kennedy's body from Texas and then ordered the FBI to undertake an investigation and hurriedly assemble a report blaming the tragic events on Oswald alone. Professor Gerald McKnight argues that Johnson's acceptance of Hoover's hypothesis made Hoover's views the "official solution" to the assassination.[8] Hoover and Johnson conceived and then agreed upon this solution before appropriate experts had an opportunity to assemble and examine the forensic evidence.

On the evening of November 22, Hoover wrote a memo to his senior staff. In it, he related the substance of his phone conversation with Attorney General Robert Kennedy that had taken place earlier in the day. Hoover wrote that he told Kennedy, "I thought we had the man who killed the President down in Dallas at the present time. I stated the man's name is Lee Harvey Oswald, that he was working in the building from which the shots were fired that hit the president and governor, that apparently he left the building and a block or two away ran into two police officers and, thinking they were going to arrest him, shot at them and killed one of them with a side arm; that the rifle had been left in the building."[9] Hoover also indicated that FBI records showed Oswald had been involved in a pro-Castro organization known as the Fair Play for Cuba Committee.[10]

Hoover agreed to do his utmost to meet the president's deadline for completion of the report, and he ordered the Bureau's General Investigation Division to "wrap up investigation; seems to me we have the basic facts now."[11] The FBI completed its initial report and delivered it to the President on December 9.

In demanding such an unreasonable deadline, Johnson sought to shape public opinion and allay fears of foreign conspiracy, acting on the advice of his friend and former attorney, Abe Fortas.[12] White House advisor Bill Moyers articulated Johnson's concerns in a memo to Deputy Attorney General Nicholas D. Katzenbach, dated November 25, 1963:

1. The public must be satisfied that Oswald was the assassin; that he did not have confederates who are still at large; and that the evidence was such that he would have been convicted at trial.
2. Speculation about Oswald's motivation ought to be cut off, and we should have some basis for rebutting the thought that this was a Communist conspiracy.

   . . . I think this objective may be satisfied by making public as soon as possible a complete and thorough FBI report on Oswald and the assassination. . . .

   The only other step would be the appointment of a Presidential Commission of unimpeachable personnel to review and examine the evidence and announce its conclusions.[13]

Initially, both Johnson and Hoover disapproved the idea of an independent commission investigating the assassination,[14] but events on Capitol Hill forced their hand. In the days following Kennedy's funeral, Senator James O. Eastland, the powerful chair of the Senate Judiciary Committee, demanded that the Senate undertake its own investigation. A similar movement took place in the House of Representatives, and Texas officials organized a Court of Inquiry under the direction of Texas Attorney General Wagoner Carr. By November 29, President Johnson became convinced that only by appointing a special commission could he prevent multiple investigations that might reach inconsistent results.[15]

Later that same day, Assistant Attorney General Nicholas D. Katzenbach and Solicitor General Archibald Cox visited Chief Justice Warren in his chambers. On behalf of the President, they requested that Warren head the new commission. Warren rejected them outright, citing the unhappy history of the Justices' involvement in special, nonjudicial assignments. Warren believed that the principles of separation of power and judicial independence should impel justices to refrain from performing executive functions while they served on the bench. In his meeting with Katzenbach and Cox, he pointed to the controversial history of these projects, referencing the Hayes-Tilden Commission that resolved the disputed presidential election of 1876, the Roberts Commission investigation into the attack on Pearl Harbor, and Justice Jackson's service at Nuremburg. Warren noted that in 1946, when Justice Robert Jackson took a leave of absence from the Supreme Court to serve as presiding judge of the Nuremburg War Trials, the brethren had resented the increased caseload and the compromise in judicial neutrality that Jackson's activities represented.

At the end of the meeting, Warren believed that his objections had put an end to the proposal. Later that afternoon, however, the White House called requesting that he attend an urgent meeting with the President, and Warren hurried to the White House. Johnson began the meeting by noting that Oswald's murder meant that there would be no criminal trial and that an objective, bipartisan inquiry into the assassination might shore up Johnson's public legitimacy and support. When Warren repeated the reasons for declining the invitation, Johnson invoked his role as commander-in-chief. Recalling Warren's service to the country during World War I, he said, "You were a soldier in World War I, but there was nothing you can do in that uniform comparable to what you can do for your country in this hour of trouble." Johnson ominously warned that rumors of Soviet involvement in the assassination might lead to war. A first nuclear strike, he said, would lead to the loss of forty million people.[16]

In tears, Warren responded, "Mr. President, if the situation is that serious, my personal views do not count. I will do it."[17]

When Warren returned to the Supreme Court, Justices Hugo Black and William O. Douglas attempted to dissuade him from chairing the new Commission. "Hugo Black and I expressed to Warren our misgivings," Douglas later wrote. Black and Douglas argued that the Court's burgeoning docket warranted Warren's full-time attention. Warren rejected their protests, saying, "I just couldn't turn the President down."[18] Warren would pay a heavy personal price for acceding to President Johnson's demands.

Following his meeting with Warren, President Johnson issued Executive Order 11130, in which he formally appointed a Commission to evaluate and report upon the facts relating to Kennedy's assassination.[19] Johnson handpicked the remaining members of the Commission, naming Senator Richard B. Russell Jr. (D-Ga.), Senator John Sherman Cooper (R-Ky.), Representative Hale Boggs (D-La.), Representative Gerald Ford (R-Mi.), former CIA director Allen Dulles, and former Assistant Secretary of War (during World War II) and former president of the World Bank John J. McCloy. All were white males over fifty years of age. The most controversial of Johnson's appointments, Allen Dulles, fueled speculation that the Commission would cover up possible government involvement in Kennedy's assassination. The bipartisan Commission primarily included "Dixiecrats" and Republican legislative leaders, and relatively few of its members had backgrounds in the military or in national security work.

As Chair of the Commission, Warren refused to serve on a full-time basis. Heavily burdened with other responsibilities, the other Commissioners followed suit. At the time of his involvement with the Commission, Senator Russell organized the filibuster of the 1964 Civil Rights Act, then pending in the Senate. For his part, John McCloy served as Chairman of the Ford Foundation. Such responsibilities meant that many Commission members attended its hearings only on an irregular basis.[20]

Johnson's decision to charter the Warren Commission was deeply flawed. The leading politicians and public figures he chose as Commissioners lacked the time and expertise to conduct a meaningful investigation. Only one member of the Commission, Allen Dulles, had expertise on the covert activities of national security organizations, and he did not disclose to his fellow Commissioners what he knew about the CIA's program to assassinate Castro. Institutional arrangements for the inquiry also proved problematic. The Commission and its staff lacked the technical resources and personnel to undertake an independent investigation of this magnitude. Of necessity, they depended upon the FBI for witness interviews, laboratory testing, and expert witnesses. This enabled FBI Headquarters to share or withhold crucial evidence almost at will.

The Commission's mandate also included an unreasonable deadline for the completion of the investigation. In his meetings with Warren, President Johnson made it clear that he expected the Commission to reach its conclusions before the upcoming presidential campaign got underway.[21] Dutifully, Warren set the preliminary deadline for completion of the Commission's work at June 1, 1964. This left little room for flexibility, especially if the investigation uncovered new or troubling evidence that would take more time to address.

THE FBI'S INVESTIGATION AND HIDDEN AGENDA

In the period before the Warren Commission began and then throughout its investigation, the FBI functioned as the nerve center of the inquiry. The FBI had an institutional interest in "managing" the investigation so that controversies and potential criticisms of the agency could be vitiated and its public image remain untarnished. Several such controversies loomed large, including the question of why the FBI failed to put Oswald on its Security Index after he had defected to the Soviet Union and, upon his return to the United States, after he continued to make contact with the Soviet embassy and pro-Castro organizations.[22] In addition, although the FBI had interviewed Oswald's wife, Marina, and her friend, Ruth Paine, in the weeks leading up to the assassination, its agents had failed to warn the Secret Service that the President's motorcade would pass Oswald's place of employment. Eventually, the FBI disclosed both of these omissions to the Warren Commission.

But FBI Headquarters did not reveal a third troublesome fact until after release of the final Warren Commission report in September 1964. Sometime between November 2 and November 9, 1963, Oswald had hand-delivered a note to the FBI office in Dallas. He came into the building and asked receptionist Nannie Lee Fenner if he could speak with Agent James P. Hosty, the agent who on two occasions had interviewed him and his wife's friends in Dallas. Informed that Hosty was not in the building at the time, Oswald angrily threw an envelope down on the desk, snarled, "This is for Special Agent Hosty," and then charged off. Ms. Fenner later indicated that the note read, "Let this be a warning. I will blow up the FBI and the Dallas Police Department if you don't stop bothering my wife." It was signed Lee Harvey Oswald.[23]

After Oswald's murder, FBI Headquarters ordered Special Agent Shanklin, Supervisor of the Dallas office, to destroy the note, which was criminal evidence in an active assassination investigation. Shanklin told Hosty "to get rid of it. Get it out of here."[24] Hosty flushed the note down the toilet. It is likely that the order to destroy the note came from Assistant Director Alan H. Belmont or Assistant to the Director for Administrative Affairs, John P. Mohr. Given the way Hoover micromanaged the Bureau, it is highly unlikely the order came without his direct knowledge.

In this way, the FBI sought to cover up a highly damaging aspect of its own prior relationship with Oswald. Professor Gerald McKnight argues that the note itself raises important questions about Oswald's culpability in the assassination. Why, just days before a planned crime, would a killer seek to draw attention to himself in this manner? Assuming that Oswald was the calculating killer that both the FBI and the Warren Commission versions of the assassination portray him to have been, this conduct simply does not make sense. By suppressing this fact and leaking key aspects of its own report to the press in early December, FBI Headquarters sought to control the substantive results of the Warren Commission's investigation.[25]

The delicate question of the FBI's failure to warn the Secret Service about Oswald placed Hoover on the prongs of a dilemma. If Hoover asserted that the FBI did not consider Oswald—a known defector to the Soviet Union—a potential threat to national security, the agency would appear negligent. On the other hand, if Hoover contended that the FBI realized Oswald was a threat but then failed to alert the Secret Service that Oswald worked at a business on the president's motorcade route, the FBI would appear inept and incompetent. Hoover resolved this dilemma by arguing that the FBI in fact did perceive Oswald as a threat to national security. In fact, when Oswald returned from the U.S.S.R. to the U.S. in the early 1960s, it investigated him. Hoover asserted, however, that Oswald was just one of thousands of potential threats to national security at this time, and the FBI lacked the resources to keep track of all of them. As for Hosty and Curry, the director and his upper-level staff simply strong-armed both into silence.[26]

On the day after the assassination, Hoover ordered an internal probe to determine if the FBI had been negligent in its relations with Lee Harvey Oswald during the period prior to the assassination. The Assistant Director of the Inspection Division, James Gale, concluded that "a number of investigative and reporting delinquencies in the handling of the Oswald case" had taken place, and he recommended disciplinary action against seventeen agents. "Oswald should have been on the Security Index (and thus shared with the Secret Service), his wife should have been interviewed before the assassination, and investigation intensified—not held in abeyance—after Oswald contacted Soviet Embassy in Mexico."[27] Hoover approved the recommendation that the seventeen agents be disciplined, but he did so secretly, without sharing this information with the Warren Commission. Publicly, he staunchly denied that the FBI had been negligent in any manner in its failure to investigate Oswald more thoroughly. In a letter to J. Lee Rankin dated April 6, 1964, Hoover wrote, "I wish to emphasize that the facts available to the FBI concerning Lee Harvey Oswald prior to the assassination did not indicate in any way that he was, or would be, a threat to President Kennedy; nor were they such to suggest that the FBI should inform the Secret Service of his presence in Dallas or his employment at Texas School Book Depository."[28]

In November and December 1963, Hoover assigned 150 agents to work full-time on the Kennedy investigation. During the investigation, which lasted well into 1964, the Bureau conducted 25,000 interviews, and its laboratory technicians in the General Investigation Division performed extensive tests of the ballistic, photographic, and documentary evidence. The Domestic

Intelligence Division oversaw the investigation into Oswald's associations and activities, including all analysis of whether a conspiracy existed to kill the president. Assistant Director Al Belmont assumed primary responsibility for the FBI's investigation into the assassination, and Deputy Director Cartha DeLoach and Assistant Director Alex Rosen also played important roles in monitoring relations with the Warren Commission and its staff.

III. THE FBI'S ASSASSINATION REPORT AND ITS RELATIONS WITH THE WARREN COMMISSION

In the period following the assassination, the FBI placed a high priority on gathering information about Oswald. Nearly 90% of its 833-page December 1963 report is devoted to him. Consistent with J. Edgar Hoover's theory of the assassination, the report concluded that Oswald, acting alone, fired three shots at the motorcade, and all three shots hit their intended targets, President Kennedy and Governor Connally. The FBI assembled its report without having access to three important pieces of evidence: the autopsy report,[29] information about Oswald's trip to Mexico City, and bystander James T. Tague's report that he had been hit by a stray bullet as he stood along the curb of Elm Street while watching the motorcade. Shortly before the FBI presented the report to the Warren Commission and the President, FBI Headquarters leaked its essential findings to the press. This assured that the public already had a detailed picture of the assassination as seen through the lens of FBI Headquarters before the Warren Commission had a meaningful opportunity to meet.

President Johnson's decision to charter a blue-ribbon commission to draw conclusions about the assassination placed J. Edgar Hoover on the defensive. His organization had been designated the lead agency of the investigation, and Hoover, as the agency head, refused to be second-guessed. Throughout the investigation, his relations with Earl Warren and the Warren Commission remained strained. Although Hoover and Warren had a cordial friendship during the 1930s and early 40s, the Warren Court's decisions in the Red Monday cases soured Hoover on Warren. The tension in their relationship during the Commission's investigation is one of the most important details that has emerged from the recent release of FBI Headquarters records under the JFK Assassination Records Collection Act.

Hoover refused to volunteer information known to him that may have altered the Commission's substantive conclusions. For example, the FBI controlled the scientific tests that technicians used to examine the forensic evidence from the crime scene. FBI Headquarters determined which pieces of evidence technicians would examine by means of highly sophisticated Nuclear Activation Analysis[30] and which items they would not. In other instances, the FBI had exculpatory information that would have been useful to Oswald's defense that it did not share with the Warren Commission staff.[31] Hoover and his staff assumed a guarded posture in their relations with the Commission, adopting the position that if the Commission wanted information, they had to ask specifically for it. FBI Headquarters only responded to what they were asked for, and then, they only answered narrowly.

At the same time, the FBI worked assiduously to monitor the activities of the Warren Commission and its staff. The Bureau assembled dossiers on each Commissioner and employee. Two leading members of the FBI Headquarters staff, Special Agent James R. Malley and Assistant Director Cartha "Deke" DeLoach, maintained close ties with several members of the Commission, especially Representative Gerald Ford, as well as upper-level personnel within the Department of Justice, including Deputy Attorney General Nicholas D. Katzenbach. Ford and Katzenbach leaked information to FBI agents on a frequent basis, relating what took place in executive sessions, disclosing the views of key actors within the Commission and the projects that staff members worked upon, and leaking advance copies of various chapters of the Warren Commission Report to FBI Headquarters. Throughout the investigation, Hoover "managed" and outmaneuvered Earl Warren and the Warren Commission much more than they controlled him.[32]

Notwithstanding his many years of experience as Governor of California, Warren entered his conflict with J. Edgar Hoover as a relative neophyte. As chief executive officer, he understood the problem of bureaucratic inertia and resistance, but his position on the Supreme Court left him with little direct knowledge of federal executive agencies and the arcane world of the national security state. His temporary assignment as Chair of a blue-ribbon presidential commission gave him no institutional power base, and the diverse ideological and partisan disposition of his fellow Commissioners made it difficult to develop a united front in the face of Hoover's overt and covert manipulation. In Hoover, Warren faced a consummate Washington insider and one of the most powerful persons in the federal government in 1964. Hoover correctly perceived that the FBI had much to lose in a broad-ranging investigation of the assassination. He responded by spinning a web of control that Warren and the Commission found difficult to escape.

NOTES

1. On the flight from Dallas to Washington, Admiral George G. Burkley, the President's personal physician, suggested that because Kennedy had served in the Navy during World War II, the autopsy should take place at Bethesda Naval Medical Center in Bethesda, Maryland. The Kennedy family accepted this plan. Unfortunately,

Bethesda was primarily a teaching hospital, and it lacked experienced pathologists to undertake a complex forensic autopsy. The Bethesda doctors selected for the assignment, Lieutenant Commander James J. Humes and Lieutenant Commander J. Thornton Boswell, had virtually no training in forensic pathology and had never performed an autopsy on a gunshot victim. They acted under the direct command of their superior officers, Captain John H. Stover and Admiral George G. Burkley (the White House physician). This may have compromised the independence of their work.

2. Warren, *Memoirs*, 353–54.

3. Pollack, *Earl Warren: The Judge Who Changed America*, 224.

4. Quoted in Vincent Bugliosi, *Reclaiming History: The Assassination of President John F. Kennedy* (New York: W.W. Norton & Co., 2007), 119.

5. The interrogators did not inform Oswald of his right to counsel or of his privilege against self-incrimination before the interrogation took place. Although these events occurred prior to the Supreme Court's decision in *Miranda v. Arizona*, both the policies of the FBI and the law of the State of Texas required such warnings in order for any evidence from the interrogation to be admissible at trial. At a later point in the interrogation, Chief Curry of the Dallas Police asked Oswald if he wanted to arrange to talk to counsel and an effort was made to contact an attorney in New York. In addition, the local chapter of the ACLU offered to provide Oswald with counsel.

6. Oswald claimed that he was eating lunch on the second floor of the Book Depository at the time of the assassination and, following the assassination, that he spoke with his supervisor for a few minutes before going home early. See United States Warren Commission, *Report of the President's Commission on the Assassination of President John F. Kennedy* (Washington, D.C.: USGPO, 1964), 35.

7. Later in the weekend, FBI Director J. Edgar Hoover reported to the president that while Oswald indeed had visited Mexico in late September and had met with Cuban Embassy officials there, someone impersonating Oswald had visited the Soviet embassy. Unlike Oswald, this individual was fluent in Spanish. While the Warren Commission conducted a careful investigation into the details of Oswald's journey from the United States to Mexico City, it was largely silent about his activities once he arrived there.

8. For a full discussion of Johnson's "official solution" to the assassination, and the successful movement to overcome alternative theories of the assassination—centered principally in the CIA—that stressed foreign involvement in the crime, see Gerald D. McKnight, *Breach of Trust: How the Warren Commission Failed the Nation and Why* (Lawrence, KS: University Press of Kansas, 2013), 8–29.

9. Hoover's reference to the shooting of the police officer near the Book Depository was in error. Apparently, he was referring to the shooting of Officer J.D. Tippit, but this occurred in nearby Irving, Texas, about ten miles from the Texas Book Depository. For analysis of the Tippit shooting and the arrest of Lee Harvey Oswald, see Sylvia Meagher, *Accessories after the Fact: The Warren Commission, the Authorities, and the Report* (New York: Vintage Books, 1967), 253–82.

10. Hoover to Tolson et al., 11/22/1963, The National Archives (TNA): Public Record Office (PRO), FBIHQ JFK Assassination File, 62-109060-59.

11. Belmont to Evans, 11/26/1963 (containing J. Edgar Hoover's handwritten comments), TNA:PRO, FBIHQ JFK Assassination File, 62-109060-1490; See also Hoover to DeLoach, 11/22/1963 FBIHQ JFK Assassination File, 62-109060-59.

12. See Pollack, *Earl Warren:* The *Judge Who Changed America*, 228. Fortas later became an Associate Justice of the U.S. Supreme Court.

13. Memorandum to Mr. Moyers from Mr. Katzenbach, 11/25/1963, in Evans to Belmont, 11/25/1963, TNA:PRO, FBIHQ JFK Assassination File, 62-109060-1399.

14. See e.g., Hoover's memo to his senior staff, dated November 25, 1963, in which he states, "President Johnson called and stated apparently some lawyer in justice is lobbying with the (Washington) Post because that is where the suggestion came from to form a Presidential Commission which the President thinks would be very bad. I said that I, too, thought this would be bad." Hoover to Tolson, et al., 11/25/1963, TNA:PRO, FBIHQ JFK Assassination File, 62-109060-63.

15. See report from FBI Special Agent C.A. Evans to Assistant Director Alan H. Belmont, dated November 29, 1963, reporting the details of Katzenbach's meeting with Evans. In his report, Evans quoted Katzenbach as saying, "(T)he President came to the conclusion he would have to appoint a Commission in this matter because Senator Eastland was adamant in the Senate Judiciary Committee going forward with its own investigation. It was only a Presidential Commission that could forestall action by the Senate Judiciary Committee." Evans to Belmont, 11/29/63, TNA:PRO, FBIHQ Liaison with Commission File, 62-109090-2.

16. National Archives and Records Administration, John F. Kennedy Assassination Related Recordings and Transcripts, 11/22/1963–3/28/1967, LBJ Recording of Telephone Conversation, K Series, Richard Russell, 8:55 p.m., 11/29/1963, LBJ Recording, 187355. A recording of the conversation is available at http://www.historymatters.com/archive/jfk/lbjlib/phone_calls/Nov_1963/audio/LBJ-Russell_11–29-63_2nd.htm; and at https://www.youtube.com/watch?v=YE6i2vYbY3I.

17. Ibid.

18. Quoted in Pollack, *Earl Warren: The Judge Who Changed America*, 230.

19. Two weeks later, Congress responded by granting the Commission power to issue subpoenas, hear witness testimony, and accept evidence. P.L. 88–202.

20. Although Warren attended all or part of the 94 Warren Commission hearings, Senator Russell attended only six.

21. McKnight, *Breach of Trust*, 35, 13n.

22. When Oswald returned to the United States in 1962, he subscribed to several left-wing newspapers and magazines and wrote numerous letters to the Soviet embassy, the Fair Play for Cuba Committee, and the Socialist Workers Party. The FBI secretly opened his mail before it left the Dallas Post Office and likewise intercepted and read mail going to the other named organizations as well. For details on these matters, see John Newman, *Oswald and the CIA* (New York: Carroll & Graf, 1995).

23. See McKnight, *Breach of Trust*, 254–60 and the notes contained therein.

24. Ibid., 259, 32n.

25. Several of Hosty's other actions threatened Hoover's grand strategy. On the afternoon of Oswald's arrest, Hosty informed two Dallas police officers that the FBI had known about Oswald and his communist connections before the assassination.

For further analysis of this conversation, see Meagher, *Accessories After the Fact*, 91–93, 227. Later that same day, when Hosty attempted to interrogate Oswald in the presence of Dallas Chief of Police Jesse E. Curry, Oswald angrily confronted him and refused to answer any questions. From this Curry correctly inferred that the FBI either knew Oswald or had him under surveillance in the period leading up to the assassination. Thus, either Curry or Hosty himself could have undermined the FBI Headquarters strategy by disclosing this damaging fact to the press.

26. When Chief Curry gave a televised interview on November 23 alleging that prior to the assassination the FBI had placed Oswald under surveillance without informing the Dallas police, FBI Headquarters ordered him to retract the statement. If he refused to do so, the FBI would issue a press release "putting the lie to his false statements." See DeLoach to Mohr, 11/23/1963, TNA: PRO, FBIHQ JFK Assassination File, 62-109060-217. Curry retracted his allegations later that day.

27. Gale's report of 12/10/1963 is available at *Investigation of the Assassination of President John F. Kennedy: Hearings before the Select Committee on Assassinations of the U.S. House of Representatives,* 95 Congress, 2d session (Washington, D.C.: U.S. Government Printing Office 1979); for further analysis of the Gale Report and the subsequent controversy concerning it, see McKnight, *Breach of Trust*, 247–81.

28. Warren Commission Exhibit 833; Hearings before Commission, vol. 17, 787.

29. At the time, FBI Assistant Director Alex Rosen of the General Investigative Division wrote to Belmont that the Bureau "did not have need" of the autopsy report or the medical evidence, including the X-rays and the medical photographs.

30. Nuclear activation analysis seeks to identify extremely small trace elements in a given substance by firing a beam of neutrons at it. The neutrons cause radioactive elements in the sample to decay and emit characteristic radiations that make it possible to construct a detailed chemical profile.

31. For example, the Warren Commission relied extensively on Howard Brennan's testimony that he saw Oswald at the southeast corner of the sixth floor of the Depository building at the time of the assassination. After the assassination, Brennan failed to identify Oswald at a line-up. The FBI knew that Brennan changed his story three times over the next two months, at times asserting that he saw Oswald at the window and other times withdrawing this claim.

32. One indication of the extent of Hoover's efforts in this regard is that he encouraged C.D. DeLoach to meet with Representative Gerald Ford and Deputy Attorney General Nicholas Katzenbach on a regular basis to gain insight into the activities and mind-set of the Commission members. See e.g., DeLoach to Mohr, 12/12/63, TNA, PRO, FBIHQ Liaison with Commission File, 62-109090-37. According to Assistant Director William Sullivan, Ford "was 'our man' on the Warren Commission and it was to him that we looked to protect our interests and keep us fully advised of any development that we would not like, that mitigated against us, and he did." Quoted in Bugliosi, *Reclaiming History*, 329.

Chapter 12

The Warren Commission and the Kennedy Assassination

Warren's dual responsibilities as Chief Justice and Chair of the Warren Commission made the first nine months of 1964 perhaps the most difficult period of his life. As he described it, "I would just come here to the Court for every conference, come here for every session of the Court, and then as soon as that was over I would run over there to that building (Warren Commission headquarters across the street) and work on that (Commission business) until maybe midnight . . . I think it took a good bit out of me . . . to be doing that, (but) I didn't want to give up my work on the Court . . . and I did carry on my work throughout that year."[1] In a later interview, Earl Warren Jr. stated that the experience of chairing the Commission "was obviously a terrible, terrible strain" on his father.[2] Warren's law clerks noted that the overall experience was "terribly exhausting and most unpleasant" for Warren and that he "didn't like to reminisce" about it.[3] The physical, intellectual, and psychological demands on Warren at this time show the depth of his commitment to the American people.

Warren's arduous new assignment exposed him to the horrible details of the assassination. He had been close to President Kennedy, and the investigation eventually became emotionally draining. Even as he worked himself to exhaustion, Warren approached his service on the Commission with the signature values that had long been his trademark. From his work on the school desegregation cases, Warren valued consensus, and his interactions with the Commissioners, as reflected in the Executive Session Transcripts, showed a masterful ability to run formal group meetings in a thoughtful, respectful, and productive way. He prepared carefully in advance, expressed his viewpoints cogently, and, if necessary, compromised in the interest of group unity. At times, the ideological diversity and conflicting political agendas of the Commissioners and other key actors in the investigation made this difficult, as Warren's interactions with fellow Commissioner Gerald Ford or with FBI Director J. Edgar Hoover repeatedly show. In what may have been the highpoint of Warren's tenure as Commission Chair, he successfully defended Professor Norman Redlich from Hoover's and Ford's accusation that Redlich's ties to leftist and communist organizations warranted his dismissal from the Warren Commission staff.

Warren's long years in public life and the controversy of his own father's murder led him to value the interest of family privacy. His work on the Commission reflects this point of view. Warren protected the Kennedy family by blocking the release of autopsy photographs and X-rays of the slain president. He shielded controversial witnesses such as Marina Oswald, Marguerite Oswald, and Jack Ruby from harsh cross-examination and treated them with respect as they testified before the Commission. As was his pattern throughout his professional life, Warren relied heavily on trusted insiders, conducted his affairs with personal integrity and good will, and assumed that others would respond in like terms. He handled federal law enforcement and national security organizations with a mixture of patriotism and naïve deference, in a spirit of good faith and mutual confidence that others did not always reciprocate.

THE FBI AND THE WARREN COMMISSION

The first meeting of the Warren Commission took place on December 5, 1963. Warren began the meeting by laying out his vision for what the mission and focus of the Commission should be. He asserted, "Now I think our job here is essentially one for the evaluation of evidence as distinguished from being one of gathering evidence, and I believe that at the outset at least, we can start with the premise that we can rely upon the reports of the various agencies that have been engaged in investigating the matter, the FBI, the Secret Service, and others that I may not know about at the present time."[4] For this reason, Warren initially opposed granting the Commission subpoena power or power to grant witnesses immunity from prosecution in exchange for their testimony. He also opposed the creation of a staff of investigators since this would replicate the work of the FBI and other federal investigatory agencies.

Representative Boggs and Senator Russell disagreed. They envisioned the need for a professional staff that could assist the Commission in analyzing the reports that various government agencies prepared on the assassination. John McCloy took this argument one step further, asserting: "I have the feeling that we have another obligation than the mere evaluation of the reports of agencies . . . . There is a potential culpability here on the part of the Secret Service and even the FBI, and these reports, after all, human nature being what it is, might have a self-serving aspect to them. And I think that if we didn't have the right to subpoena documents, the right to subpoena witnesses, . . . that this Commission's standing might be somewhat impaired."[5]

Boggs, Russell, and Ford agreed with McCloy's reasoning, and based on their arguments, the Commission formally voted in favor of seeking subpoena power. When McCloy extended his argument to embrace the idea that the Commission should seek a General Counsel, Chief Justice Warren readily agreed. Warren then suggested that his former deputy from the Alameda County District Attorney's Office, Warren Olney III, serve this function. During the 1950s, Olney had served as Assistant Attorney General in the Criminal Division of the U.S. Department of Justice, where he led an investigation into organized crime. The Commission decided to take Warren's proposal under advisement, and it determined that a subcommittee of Warren, Dulles, Ford, and Russell should try to resolve the matter within the next several days.

Later that afternoon, when word leaked out about Olney's contemplated nomination, Hoover resisted.[6] Not only had Olney crossed swords with the FBI during the organized crime hearings of the 1950s, when the FBI denied as illusory the very concept of organized crime in America, but, in Hoover's view, Olney was Earl Warren's sycophant. Hoover would have none of it. At his urging, Katzenbach and Ford initiated a "dump Olney" campaign, with Ford agreeing to keep FBI Assistant Director DeLoach "thoroughly advised as to the activities of the Commission."[7]

Warren had his reasons for preferring Olney. Over their long careers in California local and state government, the two had collaborated closely on highly sensitive matters including the *Point Lobos* murder cases and the Japanese internment. Warren trusted the independent-minded Olney. As one FBI agent remarked, "Olney was the only guy who had balls enough to stand up to Hoover."[8] Upon learning that Chief Justice Warren had proposed Olney as General Counsel, Hoover characteristically issued a one-word written reply on an internal memorandum, "Horrible."[9]

When the December 5 morning session ended, Warren, Dulles, Ford, and McCloy met in the early afternoon to resolve the matter. During this meeting, Ford reported, Warren fought hard for Olney, and he backed down only when Ford and Dulles threatened to resign from the Commission if Olney were appointed. A short time after this meeting, Ford disclosed its details to FBI Assistant Director DeLoach, who wrote the following report to his Headquarters:

> Ford said he was 'somewhat disturbed' by the way Warren was carrying on his Chairmanship and that his first mistake was an attempt to establish a 'one man commission' by appointing a chief counsel, Warren Olney, that was his

> own protégé. Ford stated that at the mention of Olney's name, Allen Dulles, former director of CIA, protested quite violently. At their second meeting, Ford and Hale Boggs joined with Dulles. Boggs told Warren flatly that Olney would not be acceptable and that he (Boggs)would not work on the commission with Olney. Warren put up a stiff argument. But a compromise was made when the name of Lee Rankin was mentioned. Warren stated he knew Rankin and could work with him.[10]

The Commission reassembled at 3 p.m. the next day. At that point, Warren asserted, "(T)he matter of Olney is closed." In the ensuing conversation, however, Warren also expressed his distaste for the idea of FBI involvement in the selection of General Counsel for the Commission. Warren stated, "I think it would be a great mistake for us to either feel ourselves, or to give the impression to the public, that we sought the assistance of the FBI or the Department of Justice in selecting our counsel."[11] The Commission later voted in favor of appointing J. Lee Rankin as General Counsel.

Rankin's background included service as Assistant Solicitor General and then Solicitor General during the Eisenhower Administration. He had presented one of the oral arguments in the *Brown* school desegregation case.[12] In contrast to Olney, Rankin had a more deferential relationship with Hoover and the FBI. Arguably, the outcome of the Warren Commission's investigation may have been different had Warren prevailed in his initial choice for general counsel. Certainly it is fair to conclude, as Professor Gerald McKnight does, that Warren assumed a passive stance in his management of the Commission's affairs in the wake of the Olney defeat. On the other hand, at the end of the day, Warren genuinely believed and later actively endorsed the Commission's conclusions. If he harbored serious reservations about Rankin's work, Warren would not have taken this course.

At its December 5, 1963 executive session, the Commissioners confronted what they perceived to be an active effort on the part of FBI Headquarters to provide the media with leaked information from its official report on the assassination, scheduled for release on a confidential basis to the White House on December 9. The Commissioners expressed their profound frustration over the leaking of the FBI report. Chief Justice Warren asserted that there was not "anything in the report that has not been leaked to the press," and Senator Russell responded in frustration, "How much of their findings does the FBI propose to release to the press before we present the findings of this Commission?"[13] Although the FBI's actions sent the clear message that Hoover and his staff had solved the crime and the Commission merely needed to rubber stamp their conclusions, a number of Commissioners, including John McCloy, viewed the report with skepticism. The FBI's characterization of Kennedy's wounds proved particularly troublesome. The Commission decided that the FBI report should not be made public and that the Commission would need its own investigative staff.

Following the meeting, Warren issued a public statement that "(T)he reports we are receiving are merely summary reports of what happened and in more or less skeleton form, and in order for us to evaluate them we will have to see some of the materials upon which those reports are based."[14] This prompted Hoover to write in the margin of a news clipping on the matter, "Certainly a statement not befitting a Chief Justice."[15]

By early January, J. Lee Rankin assembled the staff to assist him in conducting the investigation and constructing the final report. His staff consisted of several individuals who later would rise to prominence in American law and politics. They included John Hart Ely, Richard M. Mosk, Stuart Pollak, Burt W. Griffin, and Arlen Specter.[16] The staff set up its operations at the Veterans of Foreign Wars building on the corner of Second Street N.E. and Maryland Avenue in Washington, D.C., in close proximity to the Supreme Court. Chief Justice Warren stated that he expected the investigation to be completed by June 1.[17]

Rankin prepared a nine-page working outline of the assassination, which reflected the assumptions of the FBI report that Oswald had acted alone. With the completion of this outline on January 11, the Commission made arrangements to begin taking witness testimony in early February. Eleven days later, on January 22, a bombshell struck that shook the Commission to its core. That morning, Texas Attorney General Waggoner Carr called Rankin to report that "word had come out" that Oswald had been an undercover FBI agent under badge number 179 and had been paid $200 a month from September 1962 until the week of the assassination. Dallas County District Attorney Henry Wade reported, based on information from confidential sources, that Oswald had been an informant for the CIA under the assigned number 110669. The allegations prompted Warren to call an emergency meeting of the Commission that same day.

The transcript of the January 22 executive session, which was supposed to have been destroyed, reveals a Commission agonizing over the realization that there may have been a conspiracy behind the assassination, despite the FBI's assertions to the contrary.[18]

On January 24, Rankin and Warren met secretly in Washington with Dallas County District Attorney Henry Wade and Dean Robert G. Storey, past president of the American Bar Association and dean emeritus of Southern Methodist University Law School, to gain greater insight into the "Agent Oswald" allegations. What transpired at this meeting is not known, but apparently the sources of the allegations were *Houston Post* reporter Lonnie Hudkins and Allen Sweatt of the Dallas Sheriff's Office.

By the next meeting of the Commission on January 27, Rankin's demeanor completely changed. In reporting the results of the January 24 session, Rankin limited his remarks to the allegation that Oswald had been a paid informant of the FBI. Ignoring entirely (and not disclosing to the Commission) the charge that Oswald might have had ties to the CIA under badge number 110669, Rankin simply reported that Oswald could not have been assigned FBI number 179, since the FBI had no such numbering system for its informants. "We do have a dirty rumor that is very bad for the Commission . . . and it must be wiped out insofar as it is possible to do so by this Commission," he told the Commissioners.[19]

At the meeting, the Commissioners confronted a dilemma: they could not investigate the Agent Oswald allegations without incurring the wrath of J. Edgar Hoover. Yet if they chose to ignore the conspiracy allegations, they would be abdicating their responsibility to uncover the truth. Warren contended that the Commission should maintain its independence by simultaneously making inquiries of both the FBI Director and the journalists who were the apparent source of the Agent Oswald allegations. At a crucial juncture of the meeting, he entered into a debate with Rankin:

> *Warren:* "I wouldn't be in favor of going to any agency and saying, 'We would like to do this.' I think we ought to know what we are going to do, and do it, and take our chances one way or the other.
>
> "I don't believe we should apologize or make it look that we are in any way reticent about making any investigation that comes to the Commission."
>
> *Rankin:* "What I was fearful of was the mere process will cause him (Hoover) to think, in light of these people (the journalists) being here and all, and the meetings of the Commission, that we are really investigating him."
>
> *Warren:* "If you tell him we are going down there (to Texas) to do it, we are investigating him aren't we?"
>
> *Mr. Rankin:* "I think it is inherent."[20]

Warren persuaded the Commission to adopt his two-prong strategy. Rankin agreed to meet in person with Hoover to inquire whether Oswald had been a paid FBI informer. Meanwhile, the Commission staff conducted its own inquiry into the journalists' allegations.[21] Allen Dulles and several other Commissioners voiced skepticism about whether the FBI would ever admit to having ties with Oswald. Dulles, who had more expertise on covert affairs than any other member of the Commission, suspected that the FBI had paid Oswald in cash to try to penetrate the Fair Play for Cuba Committee, a left-wing organization that supported Fidel Castro.[22] The Commission finally decided to conduct "extensive and thorough hearings of as many witnesses as necessary, and where doubts were cast on any U.S. agency, independent experts (should) be hired and the investigation conducted in such a way as to avoid reliance on a questioned authority."[23] Ironically, Warren began his involvement with the Commission with the presupposition that there would be no need to call witnesses or conduct an investigation that was independent of the work of other federal agencies. Now, two months into the investigation, the Agent Oswald allegations led him to precisely the opposite conclusion.

Later that spring, when Rankin met with J. Edgar Hoover to pursue the issue of Oswald's possible ties to the FBI, Hoover used the occasion to give Rankin a long lecture about the unfairness of Chief Justice Warren's "carping criticism" of the FBI's report and Warren's allegation that the FBI's analysis was "skeletal."

Hoover eventually agreed to submit a sworn affidavit attesting that the FBI had never employed Oswald in any capacity. CIA Director John McCone did likewise. Hoover also offered to allow the Commission to undertake an independent review of the FBI files on Oswald, but Warren declined the offer. Warren contended that if the Commission or its staff undertook such a review, every American citizen should have the same right, and this, in turn, would jeopardize national security since the files contained confidential information and sources.[24] In view of the extensive records that the FBI, the CIA, and Office of Naval Intelligence actually had on Oswald's activities between his defection to the Soviet Union in 1959 and the date of the assassination, this decision proved unfortunate.[25]

In the wake of the Agent Oswald controversy and the stormy meeting with Hoover, Rankin prepared a formal list of thirty questions for the FBI. They involved three central themes: What did the FBI know about Oswald? When did it acquire this information? And what had the FBI done with the information it found?[26] The request left Hoover fuming, and, in the wake of Rankin's request, relations between the FBI and the Commission reached a new low.

The FBI's extensive answers to Rankin's questions reflected Hoover's animosity. After he received the FBI's reply, Rankin responded with a memo on behalf of the Warren Commission praising the Bureau's thoroughness and the quality of its experts' opinions. This prompted Hoover to write a note at the bottom of the memo, "I place no credence in any complimentary remarks made by Warren or the Commission. They were looking for FBI 'gaps' and having found none, yet they try to get 'syrupy.'"[27]

The Warren Commission began its hearings on February 3, 1964, and the hearings extended intermittently until the completion of the Commission report in September. Warren chaired many of the more important hearings, and commission staff or Rankin himself led the questioning of witnesses. During the hearings, the Commission heard from eyewitnesses whose testimony proved important to the Commission's conclusions. One of the eyewitnesses, Howard L. Brennan, stood across the street from the Texas School Book Depository as the motorcade passed by. He testified that he saw a figure fire a rifle out of an upper-story window of the building. Another witness, Mrs. Mary Bledsoe, who had been Lee Harvey Oswald's landlady, recognized him as he boarded a bus headed for the Oak Cliff neighborhood of Dallas shortly after the shooting took place. For the Commissioners, the testimony of these two witnesses helped to confirm the FBI hypothesis that Oswald had acted alone.

In addition to his role in chairing the hearings, Warren worked closely with Rankin in managing the staff investigation and overseeing the preparation of the Commission report. In early May, his supervisory responsibilities assumed greater importance when a controversy involving staff member Professor Norman Redlich threatened to erupt into a major firestorm. The controversy arose out of routine background investigations the FBI had performed on all proposed Commission staff in December 1963. FBI agents in New York determined that Redlich, a law professor at New York University, had ties to several leftist organizations. Since the mid-1950s, Redlich had given speeches at rallies sponsored by the Emergency Civil Liberties Committee, an organization that the FBI considered a communist front group. In his speeches, Redlich had called for the abolition of the House Committee on Un-American Activities and had criticized Supreme Court opinions involving the Fifth Amendment privilege against self-incrimination. In a report to Rankin dated December 31, 1963, FBI Headquarters implied that it would be inappropriate for Redlich to serve on the Commission staff.[28]

Several months later, Congressman Ralph F. Beerman (R-Nebraska) raised the issue on the House floor, criticizing Redlich's alleged pro-communist activities and calling his appointment "a tragic mistake." When Commission member Gerald Ford called for Redlich's dismissal, Warren placed the issue on the Commission's agenda for its May 19 meeting. At the meeting, Earl Warren sparred repeatedly with Ford. Warren defended Redlich against the charge that Redlich was a communist. Invoking the principles of due process and fair play that he had championed during the McCarthy era, Warren asserted, "Gentlemen, I just couldn't discharge this man without giving him a trial, either for misconduct or something. I just could not do that. When a man comes here and takes employment from us honorably, he is entitled to honorable treatment, and to discharge him without showing cause and without giving him an opportunity to defend himself against any charges it seems to me would be unseemly."[29] Warren convinced Russell, Boggs, Cooper, and McCloy to join with him, and the motion to dismiss Redlich failed.

Although Warren maintained a climate of fairness and respect during the hearings and conducted the personnel affairs of the Commission with integrity, in another sense the very work of his Commission threatened fundamental human rights. In the absence of a formal criminal trial for the accused assassin, the Commission played the conflicting roles of prosecutor, judge, and jury. No one assumed the formal responsibility of gathering exculpatory evidence or pointing out flaws in the staff attorneys' direct examination of the witnesses.

In late February, about three weeks after the hearings began and following Mauraurete Oswald's unsuccessful efforts to permit her attorney, Mark Lane, the opportunity of cross-examination during her testimony before the Commission, Warren asked the President of the American Bar Association, Walter E. Craig, to attend the hearings and advise the Commission if, in his judgment, the proceedings squared with the fundamental requirements of American justice. Following Warren's announcement of Craig's appointment, attorney Louis Nizer praised Warren's decision as "an exquisite blend of the reputation of thorough probing and preservation of the rights of the individual (including even the reputation of the accused slayer) in accordance with the great traditions of Anglo-American jurisprudence."[30] Yet nowhere in the 26 volumes of the Commission's Hearings and Exhibits or its 888 page report does Craig say or do anything of substance. His presence, apparently, was only symbolic. No one had the responsibility of serving as Oswald's advocate or presenting evidence on his behalf. At no point did this omission become more serious than in the Commission's review of the forensic evidence.

THE FORENSIC INVESTIGATION

From the outset, the investigation into the Kennedy assassination suffered from the failure of law enforcement agencies to control the crime scene and effectively gather evidence from it. As Professor Michael L. Kurtz (2008) has argued, over seven hundred people were present in Dealey Plaza as the motorcade passed by, yet for nearly forty-five minutes afterward, the bystanders came and went at will. No one in authority sealed off the crime scene, and the perpetrator or perpetrators apparently escaped without difficulty. Abraham Zapruder, whose film images represented crucial evidence in the case, also left the crime scene with his camera. No one combed the grassy area on either side of Elm Street on the afternoon of the assassination, and the next day an individual named Billy Harper found a piece of the president's skull on the southern edge of the Dealey Plaza grounds.[31] Even when the focus of the investigation concentrated on the Texas School Book Depository, police did not immediately search the entire sixth floor for criminal evidence. Only several weeks later did they discover Oswald's clipboard and blue jacket there. Finally, when medical workers and police located a bullet on one of the stretchers at Parkland Hospital on the afternoon of the shooting, no one photographed the bullet in place, nor did anyone make identifying initials on it to establish a chain of custody.

From a forensic point of view, the two most important pieces of evidence that police gathered from the crime scene were the Zapruder film and the World War II era Italian-made Mannlicher-Carcano rifle they found on the sixth floor of the School Book Depository.[32] When used in tandem, these objects helped investigators determine the sequence and timing of the shots that may have come from this weapon. The shutter speed of Zapruder's camera was 18.3 frames per second, and the rifle took a minimum of 2.3 seconds to recycle. These parameters helped investigators draw important conclusions about the assassination.

After he developed the film, Zapruder gave a copy to the Secret Service, which asked the CIA's National Photographic Intelligence Center to analyze it. The NPIC concluded that the first shot did not come from the sixth floor of the Texas School Book Depository and that there were at least two gunmen in Dealey Plaza. McKnight reports that these findings conflicted with the FBI's theory of the crime, and the FBI suppressed them.[33]

Warren and the Commissioners relied extensively on the Zapruder film as the best evidence of what had occurred in Dealey Plaza. They concluded that a bullet first struck Kennedy at approximately frame 210 of the film and that frame 238 showed Kennedy and Connally reacting to their wounds.[34] This difference of 28 frames translates into a time span of 1.6 seconds, an insufficient amount of time for the assassin to reload the purported murder weapon. Thus, the Zapruder film forced investigators into one of two possible conclusions: either two assassins were in Dealey Plaza or one shot hit both Kennedy and Connally, causing the Texas Governor to display a delayed reaction to his wounds. Staff members Arlen Specter and Norman Redlich opted for the latter explanation.[35]

During the period between early February and late August 1964, Rankin's staff worked intensively to study the FBI's investigation into Oswald and its analysis of forensic evidence from the crime scene. The staff then presented expert and lay witness testimony before the Commission. The Commission's findings of fact and overall conclusions are grounded in this evidence, as is the acrimonious debate concerning the accuracy of the Commission's work.[36] By way of summary, inquiry will focus on four important issues that came before the Commission: (1) Oswald's background; (2) the ballistic evidence; (3) Kennedy's autopsy; and (4) the development of the single bullet theory.

Lee Harvey Oswald

In the period immediately following the assassination, the FBI placed a high priority on gathering information concerning Oswald's background.

The Warren Commission extended the FBI's study by undertaking psychiatric analysis of Oswald's early and middle childhood years, as well as a more detailed examination of his activities in the military, his years as a defector in the Soviet Union, and his experience as a shadowy figure in the anti-Castro movement in New Orleans and Dallas.

Oswald's defection to the Soviet Union and his fledgling connection to communist organizations in the United States convinced both the FBI and the Warren Commission that he genuinely hatred western capitalism. As the Commission phrased it in its final report, "Oswald showed disdain for democracy, capitalism, and American society in general."[37] On the other hand, other investigators including New Orleans District Attorney Jim Garrison saw this as a ruse. Garrison used Oswald's involvement with the anti-Castro community in Louisiana as the basis for an unsuccessful prosecution of Clay Shaw in the plot to assassinate Kennedy.[38]

Two other incidents that took place in 1963 raise further suspicion that Oswald had ties to U.S. intelligence agencies as a low-level operative working with anti-Castro Cubans. In June 1963 Oswald applied for and then one day later received a passport to travel to Mexico in order to visit the Soviet and Cuban embassies in Mexico City. As a known defector to the Soviet Union, this application normally would have triggered more rigorous scrutiny. During the Commission's hearings on the subject, Earl Warren found it highly suspicious that a passport would be issued so promptly under such circumstances.[39]

The second incident occurred in late September 1963 immediately before Oswald went to Mexico City. Mrs. Sylvia Odio, an émigré active in the anti-Castro movement whose father was being held as a political prisoner in Cuba, contacted federal officials to report that three individuals had come to her home in Houston. One of them introduced himself as "Leon Oswald." The group sought money for the resistance against Castro. The next day, Odio received a phone call from an individual named "Leopoldo" who described Leon Oswald as a former Marine and a crack marksman who felt President Kennedy should have been shot after the unsuccessful Bay of Pigs invasion. Leopoldo also stated that Oswald was "loco" and the kind of person who could do anything, like kill Castro.[40] After the assassination, when Mrs. Odio saw images of Oswald on television, she identified him as the person who had appeared at her door.

On August 28, 1964, just weeks before it issued its final report on the assassination, the Warren Commission asked the FBI to investigate the Odio incident and identify the individuals who had visited her. The FBI determined that an individual by the name of William Seymour had impersonated Oswald in the encounter with Odio, and the Commission accepted this conclusion without further analysis.[41] Professor McKnight argues that the Commission's failure to come to terms with the import of the Odio incident represents one of its more important omissions. The Commission considered Odio's report to be credible enough to warrant FBI investigation, yet it ignored the implications of the report itself. Someone implicated Oswald in the assassination before it even took place, prima facie evidence of conspiracy.

Although the FBI and the Warren Commission provided answers to several key questions about Oswald's background, many more questions remain unresolved. These include how and why Oswald became fluent in the Russian language, why he found it so easy to defect and then return to the United States without prosecution, the ease with which he later acquired a passport to travel to Mexico City in September 1963, and the chain of events linking him to both pro- and anti-Castro political movements in the United States in the period leading up to the assassination. The failure of both the FBI and the Warren Commission to provide reasonable answers to these questions has fueled much of the continuing skepticism about the "lone assassination" hypothesis, and it became a central theme in the Schweiker-Hart Report of the Church Committee, which criticized the failure of intelligence agencies to cooperate with the Warren Commission.[42]

The Ballistic Evidence

A second key theme in the Commission investigation involved ballistic evidence from the crime scene. On the afternoon of the shooting, Dallas police discovered a rifle on the sixth floor of the Texas School Book Depository. Initially, they issued public statements that the weapon was a 7.65 mm German Mauser bolt action rifle. Later they identified the weapon as a 6.5 mm Mannlicher-Carcano. They found the weapon carefully hidden among stacks of book boxes. They also discovered one live round in the rifle, as well as three spent shell casings near a "sniper's nest" at the southeast window. Sebastian Latona, an FBI ballistics expert who testified before the Commission, described the rifle as a "cheap old weapon" manufactured in Italy during World War II.[43] Dial Ryder of the Irving (Texas) Sports Shop testified that the rifle was "real cheap, common, real flimsy looking (and) . . . very easily knocked out of adjustment."[44] When fully loaded, the rifle held seven bullets, but the evidence showed that it only contained four bullets that afternoon.

On March 31, 1964, Army expert Ronald Simmons testified before the Commission that he had examined the weapon and found it to be defective in several key respects.[45] "(C)onsiderable experience with this weapon (would be necessary) because of the amount of effort required to work the bolt," he said. "The pressure to open the bolt was so great that we tended to move the rife off the target, whereas with greater proficiency this might not have occurred." Another deficiency of the weapon involved the action of the two-stage trigger. The dangerously worn firing pin of the weapon heightened concern among FBI marksmen who attempted to use weapon during testing.[46] Experts at the Aberdeen Proving Ground notified Rankin that the telescopic lens on the weapon included two shims, each .015 inches thick, that elevated the scope in relation to the gun and that another shim .020 inches thick pointed the scope leftward in relation to the gun. They reported that the shims were installed "as if for a left-handed man."[47] Oswald was right handed.

The same day, FBI technician Robert A. Frazier testified concerning a simulation of the assassination he conducted with the help of three master-level marksmen who used the alleged murder weapon to fire at stationary targets from a distance of one hundred yards. The marksmen, whose skill with weaponry was superior to that of Oswald,[48] had the advantage of being able to aim the rifle before the timed shots began. They each fired three rounds within the allotted 8.3 seconds. Even so, they hit the target only one-third of the time. Frazier testified that the shots grouped high and to the right of the aiming point, which he attributed to maladjustment in the elevation of the telescopic sight. He speculated that the sight may have become unstable when Dallas police removed the sight to test the weapon for fingerprints. Frazier also testified that the shims on the telescope may have helped Oswald lead the vehicles as they moved at cruising speed along Elm Street.

Laboratory technicians also conducted spectrographic analysis of the composition of bullets and bullet fragments recovered from Parkland Hospital, lead scrapings from the bodies of Kennedy and Connally, and bullet fragments found on the windshield and floor of the limousine. FBI technician John F. Gallagher, with eighteen years of experience in the spectrographic laboratory, was the FBI's senior expert on these matters.

Yet staff counsel Arlen Specter chose not to call Gallagher as a witness. Instead, he selected Robert A. Frazier, who by his own admission had no expertise on spectrographic testing. Frazier testified that the lead fragments in question (the bullet found on the stretcher at Parkland Memorial Hospital and three bullet fragments found on the floor of the limousine) were "similar in composition."[49] Professor McKnight argues that there are literally hundreds of different trace elements in commercially manufactured bullets, and the mere fact that the fragments were "similar" is not tantamount to a finding that the bullets were "identical," the level of proof necessary in a criminal trial.[50]

Gallagher oversaw the highly sophisticated tests that technicians at Oak Ridge, Tennessee conducted on the ballistic evidence, using a revolutionary methodology known as neutron activation analysis to probe for commonalities in metallic composition. The nuclear activation tests could identify trace elements of gunpowder residue at the level of parts per billion and even parts per trillion, and this analysis could have gone a long way toward either proving or disproving the government's case against Oswald. The only portion of the Oak Ridge tests in which the Commission staff appeared to be interested, however, involved the paraffin tests that Dallas Police had conducted on Oswald's hands and right cheek to determine if Oswald had fired a weapon on the day of the assassination. Dallas officials had reported that the paraffin tests showed that Oswald did not have trace elements of gunpowder on his right cheek. The much more sophisticated Oak Ridge tests confirmed this result. By refraining from calling Gallagher to the stand, Specter deliberately chose not to bring this important piece of exculpatory evidence to the attention of the Commission.[51]

In late September, just before the final draft of the Commission's report went to the printing office, Specter suddenly reversed course and did call Gallagher as a witness. Specter simply wanted to know if Gallagher thought paraffin testing was reliable, and Gallagher responded in the negative. Apparently, Specter wanted this statement on the record to negate any inference arising out of the Dallas paraffin tests that Oswald might not have fired a weapon on the day of the murder.

In its final report, the Commission used the ballistic evidence to reach several other conclusions: Oswald had fired three shots from the Mannlicher-Carcano rifle; the cartridges, stretcher bullet, and bullet fragments found in the limousine were of "similar composition" and had been fired from the Mannlicher-Carcano rifle; and the paraffin test on Oswald's cheek could not reliably indicate whether he shot a weapon on the day of the assassination. The report did not disclose that the Oak Ridge National Laboratory had conducted nuclear activation analysis on other key pieces of evidence, including the bullet found on the stretcher at Parkland Hospital, bullet fragments found in Kennedy's brain, and bullet fragments from the floor of the limousine. Results from that analysis remain unknown.[52]

The Autopsy

Perhaps the most baffling of the various dimensions of the Kennedy investigation involves the autopsy evidence. In the chaotic aftermath of the assassination, three sets of medical professionals issued inconsistent reports concerning the nature of Kennedy's injuries. Ninety minutes after the shooting, the Parkland Hospital emergency room physicians (Drs. Malcolm Perry and Robert McClelland) gave a press conference and described "a wound of entrance" in the president's anterior neck and a gaping exit wound at the back of his skull.[53] Shortly thereafter, the president's personal physician, Admiral George G. Burkley, prepared the official death certificate for the State of Texas. In it, he noted another entrance wound in Kennedy's back "at the third thoracic vertebra," a wound he described as "nonfatal." All of these descriptions conflicted directly with the findings of the Bethesda autopsy report. According to that report, the autopsy doctors found no gaping wound at the back of Kennedy's head; instead, they described a small wound of entrance in the posterior skull, indicating that the head shot came from the rear. Additionally, the autopsy report described a second wound of entrance in the base of Kennedy's neck, three inches above the third thoracic vertebra. The evidence raised questions about the direction of the bullets, the pathway they took through Kennedy's body, and whether Kennedy and Connally could have been struck by the same bullet.[54]

The official position of the Commission staff, as developed by Norman Redlich and Arlen Specter, stated that Oswald fired three shots at the motorcade from the Texas School Book Depository. One shot entered Kennedy's neck and probably hit Governor Connally; one shot hit Kennedy in the head, killing him; and a third shot missed the motorcade entirely. The Commission could not determine which of the three shots missed its intended target.[55]

Although all three shots have been the subject of controversy, perhaps the greatest debate concerns the so-called "neck wound" and the "magic bullet" that allegedly caused it. As noted, Admiral Burkley originally described this wound as being at the third thoracic vertebra, approximately three inches below the anterior neck wound that Doctor Humes described in the Bethesda autopsy report. The Commission report consistently describes this wound as a "neck" wound, and for many years, critical readers wondered about the discrepancy.[56] Only after the Assassination Records Review Board released additional information about the Warren Commission in the 1990s did the origins of this alteration became clear. Commissioner Gerald Ford changed the description of Kennedy's back wound in a draft of the Commission report. Ford's language read, "A bullet had entered the base of the back of (Kennedy's) neck slightly to the right of the spine."[57] In 1997, Ford explained that he made the change in the interest of "clarity." As a proximate result of Ford's misrepresentation, a wound that occurred approximately one-quarter of the way down Kennedy's back became a "neck wound."

Staff member Arlen Specter then extended the "neck wound" allegation into a grand hypothesis that has since become known as the "single bullet" theory. Under Specter's reading of the evidence, the bullet that caused Kennedy's "neck wound" exited just below Kennedy's Adam's apple and continued into Governor Connally, hitting him in the right back, exiting through his chest near his right nipple, shattered his right wrist, and ended up in his left thigh. Specter contended that the bullet in question later fell out of Connally's thigh onto the stretcher at Parkland Hospital.

Testimony elicited at the Warren Commission hearings did not square with Specter's hypothesis. In late March 1964, Parkland Hospital physicians Malcolm Perry and Robert McClelland testified before the Commission.

Perry stated that while he performed a tracheotomy on the President in the emergency room, he noticed a small, circular wound approximately 5 millimeters in diameter below the Adam's apple. He described the wound as "roughly spherical to oval in shape, not a punched-out wound, actually, nor was it particularly ragged. It was rather clean cut."[58] When asked whether this appeared to be a wound of exit or entrance, Perry responded, "There is no way to determine from my examination as to exactly how accurately I could depict an entrance wound from an exit wound, without ascertaining the entire trajectory. . . . I had no way of ascertaining, as I said, the true trajectory."[59]

Dr. Perry's testimony does not provide affirmative support for the proposition that the neck wound was a wound of exit. In fact, his description of the edges of the wound as "clean" supported just the opposite inference.

Dr. McClelland testified that while he assisted with the tracheotomy, he had an opportunity to observe Kennedy's head wounds. He stated that the posterior skull had been damaged "so that you could actually look down into the skull cavity itself and see that probably a third or so at least, of the brain tissue, posterior cerebral tissue, and some of the cerebellar tissue had been blasted out."[60]

Dr. McClelland's statement that he saw cerebellar fluid flowing from the head wound is inconsistent with the assertion that the principal damage to the president's brain occurred in the upper left and right hemispheres of the cerebrum. His remarks go to the crucial question of whether at least one of the head shots came from the grassy knoll to the president's right and, if so, whether it "blasted out" the lower portions of the president's brain through the rear of his skull.[61]

The most controversial aspect of the president's autopsy concerns the draft autopsy report, which Dr. James J. Humes prepared over the weekend immediately following the assassination. On Sunday morning November 24, as Dr. Humes wrote the draft report, Jack Ruby shot Lee Harvey Oswald. At approximately that time, Dr. Humes burned the initial draft of his autopsy report together with his personal notes from the examination. It is unclear whether he did this on his own initiative or whether one of his superiors, perhaps Captain John H. Stover or Admiral Burkley, ordered him to do it. The second draft of the autopsy report differed significantly from the previous assertions of the Parkland emergency team and the death certificate in its discussion of the nature of the president's wounds. In the second draft, Humes concluded that Kennedy experienced four bullet wounds. The first, "presumably of entrance," occurred in his upper back. The second, "presumably of exit" occurred in the front of his neck, just below his Adam's apple. The third, "of entrance," occurred "slightly above" the occipital protuberance at the base of the skull, and the fourth, "of exit" occurred at the right side of the head partially in the parietal bone and "somewhat" in the temporal and occipital bones.[62]

Dr. Cyril Wecht, a leading critic of the Warren Commission, notes the unusual presence of the word "presumably" to describe matters that professional autopsy reports normally describe with greater scientific precision.[63] In his written criticism of the Commission's work, Wecht points out that that the autopsy team failed to trace the path of the bullet that struck Kennedy in the back, so that they might have determined whether the bullet made its way out of Kennedy's body through the Adam's apple, or whether there were two, unconnected wounds. The problems Dr. Wecht identifies indicate the inexperienced nature of the autopsy team and the lack of professionalism they displayed in the postmortem investigation.

Although the autopsy physicians made photographs and X-rays of the president's body during their examination, these materials did not become part of the official record of the Warren Commission. Chairman Earl Warren decided that they should not become part of the public record. In his *Memoirs*, Warren confided that when he saw the autopsy photographs from Bethesda, he found them so troubling that he could not sleep. He determined that the photographs would not be a part of the Commission record and that the Department of Justice would be given control over their disposition. Interested persons would only be able to examine them with the consent of the Kennedy family.[64] Although Warren made this decision with the best of intentions, he deprived both the Commission staff and subsequent researchers of indispensable technical evidence that may have quieted the growing controversy about the assassination.[65]

The Single Bullet Hypothesis

At the time of the assassination, bystander James Tague stood just ahead of the motorcade and to Kennedy's left. He immediately notified officials that one of the shots hit the curb of Elm Street and a fragment from the concrete had wounded him. Analysis of the curb where Tague had been standing showed evidence of a fresh bullet mark. The Warren Commission concluded that the mark in the curb could not be conclusively linked with any of the shots fired, but the Commission speculated that the mark was either a fragment from the shot that hit the president's head or a fragment from the missed shot.

Tague's testimony before the Commission precipitated a delay in the preparation of the final Commission report, originally scheduled for release in June, 1964. Of greater importance, his testimony triggered a crisis in the Commission's then-current explanation for how the assassination occurred. Given the time parameters set by the Zapruder film, the staff found it difficult to account for the curb shot while still maintaining that Oswald was the sole triggerman.

Furious at the delay, Warren pressured the staff to release their report before the presidential campaign heated up. Bugliosi notes that when Norman Redlich and Howard Willens informed Warren that the report could not be finished by the June 1 deadline, he became so angry and flushed that they feared he might have a heart attack.[66]

Staff member Norman Redlich proposed a way out of the crisis: Perhaps a single bullet caused some of Kennedy's and all of Connally's wounds. Given that the Commission had rejected the FBI's three-shots-three-hits scenario because one of the shots had backfired, Redlich reasoned that there simply was not enough time for three other shots to have taken place. Therefore, one of the remaining two shots must have hit both victims. Redlich noticed that frame 222 of the Zapruder film showed Kennedy and Connally to be aligned such that a single shot from the sixth floor of the Book Depository could have passed through Kennedy's neck and entered Connally's right back at a downward angle of 17 degrees.[67] At that point, Connally was holding his hat with his right hand. Building upon Redlich's theory, Arlen Specter argued the bullet continued into Connally's right wrist, shattered the radial bone, and then plunged three inches into Connally's left thigh.

On the other hand, if an independent shot hit Connally, causing at least some of his many wounds, then of necessity there had to be a second assassin. This is because the Mannlicher-Carcano weapon could not be recycled quickly enough to get a fourth shot in the allotted 8.3 seconds that the Zapruder film conclusively established as the timeframe within which all of the shots took place. Unfortunately, the Zapruder film does not provide definitive proof concerning the precise moment when Kennedy and Connally got hit. The presidential limousine passed behind a freeway sign, and the sign obscured the occupants of the vehicle for several seconds. The film does show a delay in the time the two leaders received their back wounds. Like many other aspects of the assassination, the nature of this delay has been the subject of intense debate.[68]

Specter's theory concerning the second shot rested on the assumption that the bullet in question was the one found in nearly perfect condition on the stretcher at Parkland Hospital. This precipitated yet another controversy: how could a bullet go through two people, produce seven different wounds, shatter one of the densest bones in the body, and penetrate deeply into the thigh, only to become dislodged and land nearly intact on a stretcher?

In their testimony before the Commission, several expert witnesses voiced their skepticism about Spector's theory. Three of the physicians who performed the autopsy at Bethesda—Doctors Humes, Boswell, and Finck—viewed the Zapruder film and then answered questions about the theory.

Doctor Humes testified that, in his view, Connally had been struck by two shots. The first went through Kennedy's neck, through Connally's chest, and dropped onto Connally's clothing. It was this bullet that Humes thought ended up on the stretcher at Parkland. A second bullet broke Connally's wrist and became lodged in Connally's thigh. It would account for the relatively large mass of bullet fragments that doctors found in Connally's wrist. Doctors Boswell, and Finck concurred with this analysis.[69]

Another expert, Dr. Joseph R. Dolce of the U.S. Army, met with the commission staff to review the Zapruder film and address the issue of Connally's wounds. Dolce served as a surgeon in World War II and had extensive experience as Chairman of the Wounds Ballistic Board. He told the staff that the pristine bullet found at Parkland could not have caused Connally's wrist wound and that in his opinion two different bullets had caused Connally's wounds. Following their meeting with Dolce, the Commission staff arranged for an experiment involving the firing of bullets from a Manlicher-Carcano rifle into the wrists of ten cadavers. When the bullets emerged substantially more deformed than the pristine bullet, the staff simply elected not to call Dolce as a witness. They substituted instead a team of veterinarians and physiologists who testified that the Parkland bullet in fact had caused all seven of Kennedy and Connally's "nonfatal wounds."[70]

THE COMMISSION'S FINAL REPORT

In early September, the staff issued a draft report for the Warren Commission's review. The draft accepted the single bullet theory and concluded that Oswald had acted alone in firing three shots at the motorcade from the School Book Depository. Upon review, Commission members Senator Richard Russell and Senator John Cooper disputed the single bullet hypothesis. On September 18, Senator Russell called the Commission into executive session to express his dissenting views. He alleged that the FBI and the CIA had failed to share all they knew about the assassination. He agreed that Oswald had shot the president, but he also believed that an independent bullet had struck Connally. In effect, this meant he thought there had been a conspiracy to assassinate Kennedy. Senator Cooper and Representative Boggs echoed at least some of these views.[71]

The Commission appeared to be in deadlock. Warren, Dulles, Ford, and McCloy agreed with the single bullet hypothesis, whereas Russell, Cooper, and Boggs rejected it. Chairman Warren pressed for unanimity. With the help of John McCloy, Warren sought compromise language that would allay the two Senators' concerns yet maintain a posture of unanimity on the Commission's central findings. The key to compromise lay in the words the

Commission used to describe the degree of confidence they had in the single bullet theory. Representative Ford thought there was "compelling" evidence that the hypothesis was true, while Senator Russell believed that the evidence was merely "credible." McCloy finally suggested the term "persuasive," and the Commissioners settled on it. The final language from the Report stated, "Although it is not necessary to any essential findings of the Commission to determine just which shot hit Governor Connally, there is very persuasive evidence from the experts to indicate that the same bullet which pierced the President's throat also caused Governor Connally's wounds. However, Governor Connally's testimony and certain other factors have given rise to some difference of opinion as to this probability but there is no question in the mind of any member of the Commission that all the shots which caused the President's and Governor Connally's wounds were fired from the sixth floor window of the Texas School Book Depository."[72]

The Warren Commission released its formal report on September 24, 1964. The report consisted of 888 pages as well as twenty-six bound volumes of transcripts and exhibits. The Commission staff had conducted 395 depositions, and 94 witnesses testified before the Commission. The budget for the Commission's work totaled approximately $1.2 million (in 1964 dollars). Like the initial FBI analysis of the assassination, the Warren Commission's report focused more on Oswald than on the assassination itself. Content analysis of the Commission's hearings, for example, shows that over 40% of the subject matter of the final report concerned the life of Lee Harvey Oswald.

The Commission concluded that President Kennedy suffered two bullet strikes: the first, which inflicted a nonfatal wound, entered at the back of his neck and exited through the lower front portion of his neck; the second, which caused a "massive" fatal wound, struck the right rear portion of Kennedy's head. The Commission found "no credible evidence" that any of the shots were fired from a location other than the Texas School Book Depository. It likewise found "no evidence" that anyone had assisted Oswald in the assassination or that any foreign government encouraged Oswald to commit it.

The Commission failed to resolve a number of critical questions. These include Oswald's possible relationship with U.S. intelligence agencies, the number and paths of the bullets, and the pristine condition of the bullet found on the stretcher at Parkland Hospital. In some cases, the Commission simply remained silent about crucial areas of inquiry, such as how Oswald became fluent in Russian, how he managed to travel with ease to and from the Soviet Union and Mexico City, or why someone was impersonating him at the Cuban and Soviet Embassies in Mexico. In other cases, it studiously avoided obtaining the best evidence or the best expert testimony concerning important forensic evidence, seeking instead evidence that supported its own *a priori* hypotheses.

The Warren Commission naively accepted the word of FBI Director J. Edgar Hoover and CIA Director John McCone when they testified under oath that Oswald had no formal or informal involvement with their agencies as an agent or informant. Subsequent events would show that federal domestic and international intelligence agencies did not forthrightly share classified information with the Commission.[73] In classic bureaucratic fashion, these agencies protected their institutional power base even at the cost of the truth. For his part, Warren refused to consider seriously the possibility that federal agencies concealed their activities from the Commission. His trust, in combination with the lack of substantive knowledge among the staff and nearly all of the Commissioners concerning the covert activities of U.S. intelligence agencies during the Cold War, led the Commission to accept the thesis that Oswald was a "lone nut" who had acted without conspiratorial ties to anti-Castro Cubans, the Soviet Union, or rogue members of U.S. intelligence agencies.[74] On the other hand, the Commission did more than merely ratify the conclusions of other investigatory agencies. It rejected the FBI's "three shots, three hits" analysis of the assassination and thereby incurred the wrath of FBI Headquarters and its powerful director.

Indisputably, the Commission's failure to challenge the FBI's and the CIA's self-serving denials of Oswald's connections to the U.S. intelligence community constituted one of the central weaknesses of its investigation. This failure, as well as the Commission's reluctance to engage the significant evidence that Oswald did not act alone, eventually led the House Select Committee on Assassinations to conclude in 1979 that the assassination of Kennedy did involve a conspiracy. Thus, three different federal agencies conducted formal inquiries into the events of Dallas, and they reached three contradictory conclusions.[75]

The Commission's weaknesses led to skepticism among the American public regarding whether the Commission had uncovered the truth about the Kennedy assassination. Within two years of the release of the Warren Commission report, both *Life Magazine* and the *Saturday Evening Post* called for a new investigation since the Commission had failed to explain the motion of the president's head back and to the left following the fatal head shot or the testimony of witnesses who saw smoke along the wall of the grassy knoll.[76] In 1966, a Harris Poll indicated that 46% of the American public believed a "broader plot" existed in the Kennedy assassination; by 2004, this figure increased to 70%.[77]

Warren dismissed the arguments of the critics and stood by the Commission's conclusions. In his *Memoirs*, he stated that he thought the case against Oswald was compelling and that on the basis of his experience as a district attorney who had tried many first-degree murder cases, had a criminal trial taken place, Oswald would have been convicted. Warren wrote, "(H)ad it not been for the prominence of the victim, the case against Oswald could have been tried in two or three days with little likelihood of any but one result."[78]

After the release of the Commission report, Warren refrained from public comment concerning the assassination. He contended that the report represented the most detailed statement of his thoughts on the subject and that no subsequent evidence had come to light that discredited its conclusions.[79]

But after he read the Commission's final report, an enraged J. Edgar Hoover dissented from its central findings. Not only did the Commission reject the FBI's three-shots-three-hits theory of the assassination, but it devoted several pages of its report to criticism of the FBI. The Commission, in a section that Earl Warren apparently focused on, found that the FBI had taken an "unduly restrictive" approach to its preventive intelligence work in the period leading up to the assassination and that it had failed to inform the Secret Service that Oswald, a defector and alleged communist sympathizer, worked at a building along the motorcade route.

Acting at the request of Hoover, FBI Agent Alex Rosen contacted Rankin by phone in early October to express the Bureau's displeasure about the Commission report. Rosen charged that the Commission had done the Bureau "a great disservice" and that it had "out-McCarthied McCarthy." After a lengthy silence, Rankin responded that the members of the Commission were "very strongly set in their views" and that their findings concerning the FBI were unanimous.[80]

For the rest of his life, Warren remained silent about his battles with Hoover over the work of the Commission. Whatever pain or resentment he felt about Olney's rejection, the realization that members of his own Commission leaked information to the FBI, or the weak resolution of the "Agent Oswald" controversy, he kept to himself. Warren perhaps took solace in the views of former President Lyndon Johnson, who, at a private dinner with the Warrens in the early 1970s, reportedly said, "Chief, of all the things you have done for your country, the most important was your work with the Commission on the assassination of President Kennedy."

Johnson had his own reasons of political expediency for drawing this conclusion, but Earl Warren clearly disagreed with him.[81] In bringing the work of the Warren Commission to a timely conclusion, Warren dutifully did as the commander in chief had demanded of him. Yet as his own comment about convicting Oswald in three days makes clear, Warren's role on the Commission crossed the line from judicial independence into unseemly prosecutorial bravado. In heading the Commission, Warren at least partially compromised his stature as Chief Justice. Because Oswald was dead, the case against him moot, and no one in the official inquiry had the responsibility of protecting his interests, the work of the Commission became one-sided, incomplete, and substantively dubious. The utter absence of due process and a criminal trial only served to fuel the ongoing controversy.

In the years since the completion of the Warren Commission Report, the controversy surrounding its account of the assassination has intensified. In 1979, the House Select Committee on Assassinations concluded that there probably was a conspiracy to assassinate President Kennedy. The Committee based its conclusions on the relatively large number of eyewitnesses who told investigators that they saw or heard shots coming from the grassy knoll to the President's right or smelled gunpowder there. It also stressed findings from acoustical studies of radio transmissions from the Dallas Police Department, which purportedly contained evidence of four impulses, consistent with gunshots, in sequences that correlated with the timing of shots recorded in a critical 8.3 second segment of the Zapruder film. To the Committee, the presence of a fourth shot provided clear evidence of conspiracy. Although critics responded that the radio recording was contaminated by "cross-talk" from another channel and that the impulses may not have been gunshots,[82] new research has attempted to rebut this criticism.[83] At this writing, the debate remains unresolved. Another area of controversy concerns the Warren Commission's failure to explore the role of organized crime as well as pro- and anti-Castro Cubans, in possible partnership with Lee Harvey Oswald and Jack Ruby, in an assassination plot. Given the absence of hard evidence, the subsequent deaths of key witnesses, and the passage of many decades, conclusions concerning these matters might best be described as reasonable speculation. Nevertheless, assessments about the adequacy of Warren's work as Chair of the Commission would be incomplete without at least some discussion of this new literature.

In a recent book, David Kaiser[84] argues that the Warren Commission failed to examine two contextual factors that helped to explain the Kennedy assassination: the intensive campaign against organized crime in the United States in the period between 1957 and 1963, especially under the leadership of Attorney General Bobby Kennedy; and the uneasy partnership between the CIA and covert organizations, such as the DRE (Student Revolutionary Directorate), JURE (Revolutionary Junta in Exile), Alpha-66, and MIRR (Insurrectional Movement for Revolutionary Recovery), in an effort to destabilize and eliminate Fidel Castro during these same years. In the wake of Castro's rise to power, organized crime leaders such as Santo Trafficante of Tampa and Miami, Sam Giancana of Chicago, and Carlos Marcello of New Orleans, experienced severe economic losses from the curtailment and closure of their lucrative resort and gambling interests in Cuba. In the late 1950s and early 1960s, they cooperated with secret governmental and nongovernmental initiatives to assassinate Castro. The Kennedy administration's unwillingness to intervene militarily during the Bay of Pigs attack on Cuba in 1961, together with its legal battles against Marcello, Giancana, and Teamsters' President Jimmy Hoffa, allegedly convinced these Mafia leaders to cooperate in removing Kennedy from power, both as a means of curtailing legal threats against them and as a way to spur a retaliatory U.S. military attack against Castro. Although hard evidence is sketchy, Kaiser makes a plausible case that in the climate of illegality and covert action that agents of the U.S. government themselves sanctioned, some of groups the CIA recruited to assassinate Castro eventually turned the plot against Kennedy.

Kaiser documents several incidents during the weeks leading up to Kennedy's assassination in which Oswald, someone posing as Oswald, or someone mentioning Oswald's name threatened to kill the President. In addition to the Odio incident discussed previously, either Oswald himself or someone posing as Oswald made similar statements to Dallas car salesman Albert K. Bogard. Likewise, Lillian Spingler, a clerk at the Parrot Jungle in Miami, Florida, reported that in early November 1963, a Cuban came into her shop and used Oswald's name in reference to a possible shooting of Kennedy. In all three instances, the eyewitnesses gave credible testimony to FBI officials, yet FBI leaders and the Warren Commission discounted their allegations. In a similar vein, Kaiser argues that Oswald's trip to Mexico City, his prominent arguments there with officials at the Cuban and Soviet Embassies, and an Oswald imposter's meeting in Mexico City with KGB assassination agent Valery Kostikov, show an extensive effort to link Oswald to the communists. Following the assassination, such links provided a basis for pressuring the United States to go to war against Cuba, and forces both inside and outside the administration urged President Johnson to take this step. Equally troubling is the evidence Kaiser presents concerning Jack Ruby's extensive ties to organized crime, which arose out of his operation of the Carousel Club, a strip joint in Dallas; his difficulties with the American Guild of Variety Artists, a mob-dominated union of show girls; and his history of running guns to anti-Castro Cubans. Such ties weaken J. Edgar Hoover's contention that Jack Ruby, like Lee Harvey Oswald, was a "lone nut," uninvolved with any wider conspiracy.

Other recent studies of the Warren Commission's portrait of the assassination document J. Edgar Hoover's unwillingness to take seriously evidence that pointed to conspiracy. For example, R. Andrew Kiel's study of Hoover offers a thorough discussion of the plethora of evidence pointing to conspiracy that the FBI suppressed.[85] Hoover's contention that Oswald was a "lone-nut" motivated by an attraction to communism, framed just hours after the assassination, overshadowed serious efforts to examine all of the evidence. His persistent and self-serving unwillingness to acknowledge the reality of organized crime in the United States, among other factors, may have induced him to protect the Mafia from scrutiny. Another factor may have been

Hoover's political opposition to Kennedy as well as his desire to avoid forced retirement. Apart from his critique of Hoover, another strength of Kiel's book involves his summaries of details concerning the assassination, which may be of great value to future researchers. These include inconsistencies between the medical notes of the Parkland and Bethesda medical staffs concerning the size and placement of Kennedy's cranial wound, contradictions in purported photographic images of Kennedy's skull that did not comport with eyewitness recollections, and the role of military leaders such as White House physician Admiral George Burkley and Admiral Calvin Galloway in limiting the scope of the Bethesda autopsy, even though Oswald was alive at the time and a criminal trial against him in Dallas was foreseeable.

Recordings of a conversation between President Johnson and Senator Richard Russell on the evening of November 29, 1963, in which Johnson persuaded a reluctant Russell to serve on the Warren Commission, reveal further evidence of Johnson's duplicity regarding the mission and focus of the Commission. During the conversation, Johnson described his recent meeting with Warren about serving as chair of the Warren Commission. He said:

> Bobby (Kennedy) and them went up to see him (Warren) today and he turned them down cold and said no. Two hours later I called him and I ordered him down here and he didn't want to come. Now I insisted he come, and he came down here and he told me no twice. I just pulled out what Hoover told me about the little incident in Mexico City, and I said, now I don't want Mr. Khrushchev to be told tomorrow . . . and be testifying before a camera that he killed this fellow and that Castro killed him and all I want you to do is look at the facts and bring in any other facts that you want in here and determine who killed the President. And I think you put on a uniform in World War I, fat as you are, and would do anything you could to save one American life, and now I'm surprised that you, the Chief Justice of the United States, would turn me down. And he started crying and he said well I won't turn you down, and I'll do whatever you say.[86]

In agreeing to chair the Commission and in his subsequent passive style of managing its investigation, Earl Warren played a key role in the achievement of Johnson's larger strategy of avoiding war. Only during the fight over Redlich and in the framing of the Commission's conclusions regarding lapses in the FBI's and the Secret Service's conduct in the period leading up to the assassination did Warren appear to assert himself. A variety of factors may explain this reticent stance, including his advancing age, the challenge of serving concurrently as Chair of the Commission and Chief Justice, and, perhaps, genuine intellectual disinterest. Warren rarely engaged the complex and contradictory issues that lay at the heart of the Commission's work, and he repeatedly blocked access to files, medical photographs, and lines of investigation that may have shed new light on the case. His mind often seemed more attuned to issues of administration than to issues of forensics, criminal investigation, or the broader implications of the threat that national security organizations posed to American democracy.

The Warren Commission resembles the many "blue-ribbon commissions" that modern presidents have used to blunt political criticism in the wake of national crises. Scholars of presidential commissions have noted numerous similarities between the work of the Warren Commission and the Roberts Commission that President Franklin Roosevelt chartered in the wake of the Japanese attack on Pearl Harbor in 1941.[87] Both commissions arose as the result of political crisis, and both had their origins in executive orders designed to preempt Congress from initiating its own investigations. Leadership of both commissions lay in the hands of a sitting member of the U.S. Supreme Court, and in both instances, executive branch officials regularly influenced their work. In the case of the Roberts Commission, Secretary of Defense Henry Stimson helped to select Commission members, chose Justice Roberts as the Chair, and on seven occasions had *ex parte* communications with them.[88] In the case of the Warren Commission, Deputy Attorney General Nicholas Katzenbach influenced the selection of the General Counsel, and FBI Director J. Edgar Hoover supervised nearly all of the forensic investigation. Both commissions conducted hasty inquiries, avoided serious scrutiny of national security records, and issued findings that endorsed the viewpoints of the president. Both commissions then released reports widely covered in the media, and in both instances, the president derived substantial political benefit from the commissioners' findings. In the end, the Warren Commission, like the Roberts Commission before it, failed to discharge its responsibility to speak truth to power.

NOTES

1. Quoted in Bugliosi, *Reclaiming History*, 325 (see chap. 11, n. 4).
2. See also, White, *Earl Warren: A Public Life*, 212, 82n (see chap. 1, n. 33).
3. Benno Schmidt, Jr., oral history 57, Columbia University Oral History Research Office, Butler Library, Columbia University, quoted in G. Edward White, *Earl Warren: A Public Life*, 212 83n.
4. Warren Commission, December 5, 1963, Executive Session Transcript, available at www.aarclibrary.org/publib/contents/wc/contents_wcexec.htm, at p. 4 (all page numbers from the Executive Session Transcripts cited herein refer to the numbering sequence in the digital images of the documents rather than the original page numbers of the documents themselves).
5. Ibid., 40.
6. One source of the leaked information was Deputy Attorney General Katzenbach. *See* DeLoach to Mohr, 12/6/1963, The National Archives (TNA): Public Records Office (PRO), FBIHQ Liaison with Commission File, 62-109090-6.

7. See DeLoach to Mohr, 12/7/1963, TNA:PRO, FBIHQ JFK Assassination File, 62–109060-1625; and DeLoach to Mohr, 12/12/63, TNA:PRO, FBIHQ Liaison with Commission File, 62–109090-37.

8. Quoted in Cray, *Chief Justice: A Biography of Earl Warren*, 418.

9. Belmont to Tolson, 12/3/1963 and 12/4/1963, TNA:PRO, FBIHQ Liaison with Commission File, 62-109090-8, 2.

10. DeLoach to Mohr, 12/7/1963. TNA:PRO, FBIHQ Liaison with Commission File, 62–109090-36; see also Hoover to Tolson, Belmont, Rosen, and DeLoach, 6/22/1964, TNA:PRO, FBI Record 124-10103-10087.

11. Warren Commission Executive Session Transcripts, 12/6/63, 11.

12. In his brief to the Court in *Brown v. Board of Education*, Rankin introduced the phrase "all deliberate speed" into the proceedings of the case.

13. Warren Commission Executive Session Transcripts, 12/5/1963, 11.

14. Warren Commission Executive Session Transcripts, 12/16/63, 62.

15. For Hoover's written comment, see TNA:PRO, FBIHQ Liaison with Commission File, 62-109090-19.

16. John Hart Ely served as a professor of law at Yale University and later at Harvard, Stanford, and the University of Miami. Richard M. Mosk is associate justice for the California Court of Appeal, Second Division, in Los Angeles. Stuart R. Pollak served as a law clerk for Chief Justice Earl Warren in the 1962 term and is associate justice for the California Court of Appeal, Third Division in San Francisco. Burt W. Griffin served as judge for the Court of Common Pleas, Cuyahoga County, Ohio, until his recent retirement. The late Arlen Specter was U.S. Senator from Pennsylvania from 1965 until 2011.

17. At the January 21, 1964 Commission meeting, Earl Warren stated, "I think if (the investigation) should go along too far and get into the middle of a campaign year that it would be very bad for the country to have this thing discussed at that particular time." Warren Commission Executive Session Transcripts, 1/21/64, 13.

18. Unbeknown to the Commissioners, a tape of the executive session survived, and the official transcript includes the portion of the meeting that took place prior to the point when the Commissioners went off the record. It is available at http:wwwaarc.library.org/publib/jfk/wc/contents_wcexec.htm.

According to the transcript, Rankin stated,

> (W)hen the Chief Justice and I were just briefly reflecting on this we said if (the Agent Oswald story) was true and it ever came out and could be established, then you would have people think that there was a conspiracy to accomplish this assassination that nothing the Commission did or anybody could dissipate.

He continued:

> They (the FBI) would like to have us fold up and quit. . . . They found the man. There is nothing more to do. The Commission supports their conclusions, and we can go home and that is the end of it.

Alan Dulles responded:

> But that puts the man right on them. If he was not the killer and they employed him, they are already it, you see. So your argument is correct if they are sure that this is going to close the case, but if it doesn't close the case, they are worse off than ever by doing this.

Boggs: Yes, I would think so. And of course, we are all even gaining in the realm of speculation. I don't even like to see this being taken down.

Dulles: Yes, I think this record ought to be destroyed. Do you think we need a record of this[?] Warren Commission Executive Session Transcripts, 1/22/1964, 13–14.

19. Warren Commission Executive Session Transcripts, 1/27/1964, 15.

20. Ibid., 40.

21. Although the Commission staff met with Lonnie Hudkins, Joe Goulden, Harold Feldman (journalist from the periodical *The Nation*), and Deputy Sheriff Sweatt, none of them testified before the Commission.

22. Warren Commission Executive Session Transcripts, 1/22/1964, 8.

23. Gerald Ford and John R. Stiles, *Portrait of the Assassin* (New York: Ballantine Books, 1966), 25.

24. *Hearings before Commission*, vol. 5, 13.

25. For a thorough analysis of the files U.S. intelligence agencies kept on Oswald during these years, see Newman, *Oswald and the CIA*. Newman's work is based on records released to the National Archives by the JFK Assassination Records Review Board and well as on Freedom of Information Act requests by scholars of the Kennedy assassination in the period since 1963.

26. Rankin to Hoover, 3/26/1964, TNA:PRO FBIHQ Liaison with Commission File, 62–109090-NR.

27. Belmont to Rosen, 4/4/1964, TNA: PRO, FBIHQ Liaison with Commission File, 62–109090-124 (written comment by J. Edgar Hoover).

28. The background investigation on Redlich is summarized in a memo from M.A. Jones to DeLoach, 3/11/64, TNA, PRO, FBIHQ Liaison with Commission File 62–109090-120; see also 62–109090-149.

29. Warren Commission Executive Session Transcripts, 5/19/1964, 47.

30. Quoted in Leo Sauvage, "Oswald's Case Against the Warren Commission," *New Leader*, 20 (Dec. 1965): 5–10.

31. Michael L. Kurtz, *The JFK Assassination Debates: Lone Gunman versus Conspiracy* (Lawrence, KS: University Press of Kansas, 2006), 25.

32. One of the more important sources of debate concerning the FBI's management of the investigation concerns the nature of the weapon officers found on the sixth floor of the Texas Book Depository. Several experienced officers at the scene, including Deputy Constable Seymor Weitzman, Deputy Sheriff Eugene Boone, and Homicide Chief Will Fritz, identified the rifle as a 7.65 Mauser bolt action rifle with a 4/18 scope and a thick leather-brownish, black sling on it. Deputy Sheriff Roger Craig stated to a reporter on the day of the assassination that the officers were approximately 6–8 inches away from the rifle and that they noted the stamp "7.65 Mauser" clearly visible on the barrel. For further analysis of these issues, see Meagher, *Accessories After the Fact*, 95, 102.

33. McKnight, Breach of Trust, 6.

34. Although many different versions of the Zapruder film are available on the Internet, students of the assassination should be advised that nearly all of them have been altered from the original.

35. One aspect of the Zapruder film that has proved problematic over the years involves Kennedy's reaction to the fatal head shot in frame 313. There, Kennedy's

head moves violently backward against the rear seat and then to the left. Critics of the FBI and Warren Commission argue that Kennedy could not have been thrust backward and to the left if he had been hit from the rear. The law of conservation of momentum dictates that objects hit by a bullet will travel in the same direction of the projectile, meaning that the shot must have hit Kennedy in the right front of his head and thrust his body backward and to the left. This implies that a second shooter, located in the grassy knoll, fired this shot. Defenders of the Commission, such as Louis Alvarez, have argued that kinetic energy created by a rear shot led to a "jet effect" of neuromuscular reaction that would have propelled Kennedy's head backward. However, neurosurgeons have disputed this hypothesis.

36. Current estimates of the number of monographs on the Kennedy assassination exceed two thousand books. They include serious works of scholarship, superficial diatribes, and sensationalistic fantasies. It is beyond the scope of this study to examine all of this literature and all of the major issues in the Kennedy assassination. Instead, I have presented what I consider to be the major issues that confronted the Warren Commission, the Commission's substantive conclusions about each, and several of the more important criticisms. Among the works that have been influential in my understanding of the subject are Sylvia Meagher's *Accessories after the Fact*, Gerald Posner's *Case Closed*, Vincent Bugliosi's *Reclaiming History*, Michael L. Kurtz's *The JFK Assassination Debates*, Gerald McKnight's *Breach of Trust*, and David Kaiser's *The Road to Dallas*.

37. Warren Commission Report, 32.

38. Garrison and many other conspiracy theorists allege that Oswald was involved in CIA-funded training camps for anti-Castro guerillas in Bedico Creek, Louisiana, and they criticize the Warren Commission for failing to explore this relationship in greater depth. Although the Commission emphasized Oswald's pro-Marxist posture and public pronouncements, they ignored his ties to anti-Castro organizations in Louisiana and Texas.

39. See Warren Commission Executive Session Transcripts, 12/16/1963, 25.

40. *Hearings before Commission*, vol. 11, 377.

41. Hoover to Rankin, 9/6/1964, TNA, PRO, FBIHQ Files, 105–8255-4920.

42. See Book V of the Church Committee Reports, "The Investigation of the Assassination of President John Fitzgerald Kennedy: Performance of the Intelligence Agencies," available at http:www.aarclibrary.org/publiclib/contents/church/contents_church_reports_book5.htm. This report was part of the House Select Committee on Assassinations investigations from the late 1970s.

43. *Hearings before Commission*, vol. 4, 29.

44. *Hearings before Commission*, vol. 11, 203.

45. *Hearings before Commission*, vol. 3, 449.

46. Warren Commission Report at 193–4; Commission Exhibit 2974.

47. Commission Exhibit 2560.

48. When Oswald entered the Marine Corps in 1959, he took a rifle proficiency test, scoring 191 on a scale of 190–250. This qualified him as a marksman, the minimum rifle classification used in the Marine Corps at that time.

49. *Hearings before Commission*, vol. 5, 67–9.

50. See McKnight, *Breach of Trust*, 204.

51. Gallagher testified on the last day of the hearings, even as the Commission's final report was already at the Government Printing Office. Redlich took Gallagher's brief testimony. Gallaher indicated that experts had performed nuclear activation tests on selected pieces of evidence and that the results of this testing were in the FBI's records. The test results never appeared as Commission exhibits, nor were they ever made public.

52. None of the findings from the Oak Ridge analysis of this evidence made it into the questioning of Gallagher or in the report of the Warren Commission. As Gerald McKnight and other critics of the Warren Commission have noted, a more rigorous investigation might have featured additional testing at Oak Ridge, including the unfired bullet found in the Mannlicher-Carcano rifle and scrapings from the limousine windshield.

53. Nine doctors and one nurse who worked on Kennedy at Parkland Hospital testified before the Commission concerning their impressions of the anterior neck wound, and nearly all of them described it as a wound of entrance. Hearings before Commission, vol. 6, 5–143. For detailed analysis of their testimony, the news conference, and the physicians' descriptions of Kennedy's head wound, see Meagher, *Accessories After the Fact*, 150–65.

54. Articles in the *New York Times* in December 1963 reflect these inconsistencies. See e.g., *New York Times*, December 6, 1963, December 17, 1963, December 18, 1963, and December 19, 1963.

55. See Warren Commission Report, 107–12.

56. Dr. Cyril Wecht's criticism of Dr. Shaw's description of the neck wound appears in Wecht's essay, "A Critique of President Kennedy's Autopsy" in the Appendix of Josiah Thompson, *Six Seconds in Dallas: A Micro-study of the Kennedy Assassination* (New York: B. Geis Associates, 1967).

57. See Kurtz, *JFK Assassination Debates*, 85–6 and 8n as well as the references cited therein. See also McKnight, *Breach of Trust*, 193 and Bugliosi, *Reclaiming History*, 425.

58. *Hearings before Commission*, 6, 9.

59. Ibid., 15.

60. Ibid., 33.

61. In testimony before the House Select Committee on Assassinations, four other individuals who were present at the Bethesda autopsy agreed that the president's skull contained a massive exit wound toward the rear. They included Drs. Robert Karnei, John Ebersole, David Osborne, Calvin Galloway, and George Burkley. See Kurtz, *JFK Assassination Debates*, 39–40. Other witnesses believed that one of the head shots came from a more powerful weapon than the Mannlicher-Carcino and that this high-velocity weapon fired bullets of a larger caliber. Photos of the autopsy, which are now available for public inspection at the National Archives, show that the rear of Kennedy's head is intact, except for a small bullet hole near the "cowlick." This has precipitated debate about the authenticity of the photographs. For further discussion, see Ibid., Chapters 3 and 4.

62. For a copy of the revised autopsy report, see Appendix IX of the Warren Commission Report. Further analysis of the autopsy protocol may be found in McKnight, *Breach of Trust*, 153–80; and Kurtz, *The JFK Assassination Debates*, 23–80.

63. Wecht's critiques of the Warren Commission are summarized in two articles, "Pathologist's View of the JFK Autopsy," 40 *Modern Medicine* 40 (Nov. 1972): 28–32 and "JFK Assassination: A Prolonged and Willful Cover-Up," *Modern Medicine* 42 (Oct. 24, 1974):40CC-40DD.

64. See Warren, *Memoirs*, 371.

65. In the absence of the X-rays and a dissection of the neck muscles during the autopsy to determine if there was a pathway between the back wound and the posterior neck wound, the commission staff constructed its own hypothesized conclusions. As it was, Dr. Humes testified that the nonfatal shot hit Kennedy's neck at a downward angle of 45 degrees, hit no bone, and exited the president just below the Adam's apple. Other officials who were present at Bethesda disputed this analysis. They included two FBI agents, who, like Dr. Berkley, described the president's nonfatal posterior wound as "one bullet hole located just below shoulders to the right of the spinal column." As critics of the Commission consistently have argued, it is difficult to see how a bullet entering the body at a point below the shoulder in the third thoracic vertebrae at a downward angle of 45 degrees, and hitting no bone, could exit at a point in the president's posterior neck that is above the point of entry in the rear. See McKnight, *Breach of Trust*, 193, 223–24.

66. Bugliosi, *Reclaiming History*, 356.

67. Although this angle of descent was different than the 25 degree angle that the Commission earlier had accepted, at no point did the Commission address the discrepancy.

68. For further details on this aspect of the debate, including the delay in Connally's reaction to being shot, the nature of his back wound, and the trajectory of the bullet(s), see Kurtz, *JFK Assassination Debates*, 112–13.

69. *Hearings before Commission*, vol. 2, 374–75 (Humes), 377 (Boswell), and 382 (Finck).

70. For analysis of Dr. Dolce's testimony, which was not used by the Commission, see McKnight, *Breach of Trust*, 186–87.

71. Apparently, Representative Hale Boggs also shared some of the Senators' concerns.

72. Warren Commission Report, 38.

73. In 1979, the House Select Committee on Intelligence (HSCA) concluded that federal investigatory agencies including the FBI and the CIA had withheld evidence from the Warren Commission and that there was a high probability that President Kennedy was assassinated as a result of a conspiracy. http://www.archives.gov/research/jfk/select-committee-report.

74. The one individual among the Commissioners who had detailed knowledge of the covert activities of U.S. intelligence agencies during the Cold War was Alan Dulles, former Director of the Central Intelligence Agency. However, Dulles was tight-lipped about these activities throughout the Warren Commission's investigation.

75. The FBI concluded that Oswald acted alone and that he fired three shots, each of which struck an occupant in the presidential limousine. The Warren Commission agreed that Oswald acted alone, but it concluded that one of the three shots missed the limousine entirely. The House Select Committee on Assassinations concluded that

there was a conspiracy to assassinate President Kennedy and four shots were fired at the motorcade.

76. See e.g., *Life Magazine*, 11/25/66, which contained a cover story entitled, "Did Oswald Act Alone? A Question of Reasonable Doubt." The article focused on Governor John Connally's contention that he and President Kennedy were hit by separate bullets. It concluded with the recommendation that a "new investigating body should be set up, perhaps at the initiative of Congress."

77. Gary Langer, "Legacy of Suspicion: Decades After, Few Accept the Official Explanation for JFK Assassination," http:abcnews.go.com/sections/wnt/US/JFK_poll_031116.html.

78. Warren, *Memoirs*, 367.

79. See Ibid., 366.

80. Rosen to Belmont, 10/2/1964, TNA, PRO, FBIHQ Liaison with Commission File, 62-109090-355.

81. As noted, Warren believed that his contributions to the law of legislative apportionment were his most significant achievement.

82. National Research Council, "Report of the Committee on Ballistics Acoustics," available at http://www.jfk-online.com/nas04.html#7. See especially sections II, III, IV-3, and Appendix D. See also, R. Linekar, R.L. Garwin, H. Chernoff, P. Horowitz, and N.F. Ramsay, "Synchronization of the Acoustic Evidence in the Assassination of President Kennedy," *Science & Justice* 45, no. 4 (2005): 207–26.

83. D.B. Thomas, "Echo Correlation Analysis and the Acoustic Evidence in the Kennedy Assassination Revisited," *Science & Justice* 41, no. 1 (2001): 21–32. See also, David Kaiser, *The Road to Dallas: The Assassination of John F. Kennedy* (Cambridge, MA: Belknap Press of Harvard University Press, 2008), 384–86.

84. Kaiser, *Road to Dallas*.

85. R. Andrew Kiel, *J. Edgar Hoover: The Father of the Cold War—How His Obsession with Communism Led to the Warren Commission Coverup and Escalation of the Vietnam War* (Lanham, MD: University Press of America, 2000).

86. National Archives and Records Administration, John F. Kennedy Assassination Related Recordings and Transcripts, 11/22/1963–3/28/1967, LBJ Recording of Telephone Conversation, K Series, Richard Russell, 8:55 p.m., 11/29/1963, LBJ Recording, 187355. A recording of the conversation is available at http://www.history-matters.com/archive/jfk/lbjlib/phone_calls/Nov_1963/audio/LBJ-Russell_11-29-63_2nd.htm; and at https://www.youtube.com/watch?v=YE6i2vYbY3I.

87. See e.g., Kenneth Kitts, *Presidential Commissions and National Security: The Politics of Damage Control* (Boulder, CO: Lynne Rienner Publishers, 2006).

88. Ibid., 35.

Part V

CONCLUSION

Chapter 13

The End of the Warren Court

The Warren Court's jurisprudence brought badly needed changes to American law, especially in the areas of racial justice, political representation, and law enforcement. Yet the social context of its criminal justice reforms left the liberal majority politically vulnerable. Street crime in the United States rose precipitously during the 1950s and 60s, and the high crime rate led to frequent calls for increased law and order. Judicial decorum and neutrality meant that the justices could not engage the debate openly, and conservative politicians stepped into the vacuum. The transformation of the Supreme Court from the liberalism of the Warren years to the retrenchment of the Burger and Rehnquist eras represents a milestone in Supreme Court history. Political scientist Robert A. Dahl has noted that "the policy views dominant on the Court are never long out of line with the policy views dominant among the lawmaking majorities of the United States."[1] The shift from liberalism to conservatism on the Court during the late 1960s and early 1970s confirms the truth of this assertion.

Dahl's early work on Supreme Court decision making, conducted in the 1950s, led him to conclude that on average each president during the course of a four-year term of office appoints two justices to the Supreme Court. In the period since Dahl conducted his research, this number has gradually decreased. In the 44-year period between 1969 and the present, eight presidents have appointed 16 justices to the Court, which averages out to one appointee for every 2.75 years that a president remains in office.[2] President Nixon's extraordinary opportunity to make four appointments to the Supreme Court in five years may have been a function of chance, but vagaries in the life cycle of individual justices and defects in the process by which President Johnson selected his nominees for the Court also played a role. In 1968, when Nixon won the presidency, three justices exceeded 70 years of age

(Warren, Black, and Douglas), and one was approaching seventy (Harlan). This increased the likelihood that Nixon would make more than two appointments to the Court. Lyndon Johnson's impetuous method of making Supreme Court appointments also contributed to the instability of the Court, and it ultimately unsettled the liberal ruling majority.

In his five years in the White House, Johnson made two appointments to the Court, Abe Fortas and Thurgood Marshall. The underlying circumstances of Fortas's appointment and Johnson's unsuccessful attempt to elevate Fortas to the office of Chief Justice in the summer of 1968 displayed a pattern of rash decision making and cronyism. During the four years between the beginning of 1965 and the end of 1968, Johnson played a game of musical chairs with the Court, seemingly giving little thought, consultation, or vetting to the selection process. In 1965, Johnson enticed Arthur Goldberg to leave the Court and accept a position as U.S. Ambassador to the United Nations. Johnson nominated his own friend and close advisor Abe Fortas as Goldberg's replacement. In 1967, Johnson nominated Ramsey Clark as Attorney General and precipitated the resignation of Ramsey's father Tom Clark from the Court so that the elder Clark would avoid conflict of interest problems. Johnson then nominated Thurgood Marshall as Clark's replacement. In 1968, Johnson nominated Abe Fortas to replace Earl Warren as chief justice and Homer Thornberry to fill Fortas's vacant seat as associate justice. In choosing Earl Warren as Chair of the Warren Commission and continually seeking Justice Abe Fortas's advice in framing the administration's approach to the Vietnam War, Johnson made a mockery of the principle of separation of power. Instead, he treated the Court as if it were an extension of the executive branch.

Johnson's impact on the Court began in 1965 with a series of discussions that led to Arthur Goldberg's resignation from the Court. Appointed in 1963 by President Kennedy, Goldberg had a background of successful work in labor negotiations as an attorney for the United Steel Workers and as Secretary of the U.S. Department of Labor. In World War II, he had worked for the Office of Strategic Services as an undercover agent in Palestine, Spain, and France, organizing resistance to the Nazis. During his tenure on the Court, Goldberg's groundbreaking opinions in the *Escobedo v. Illinois* custodial interrogation case, the *Bell v. Maryland* sit-in case, and the *Griswold v. Connecticut* right to marital privacy case showed his leadership potential. He developed a close working relationship with Earl Warren, and the two justices often met on a daily basis. Warren thought Goldberg would make an excellent choice for Chief Justice following his own retirement, and during their conversations, he openly said so.

On July 14, 1965, Adlai Stevenson, U.S. Ambassador to the United Nations, unexpectedly died. Stevenson had played an important role for the Johnson Administration maintaining good relations with influential liberals during the escalation of United States involvement in the Vietnam War earlier that year. Johnson initially approached Harvard economist and former Ambassador to India John Kenneth Galbraith as a replacement for Stevenson. Galbraith declined the offer and suggested Goldberg instead. Johnson invited Goldberg to accompany the White House staff during Stevenson's funeral in Bloomington, Illinois, and on the flight back to Washington, the President sought to persuade Goldberg to accept the position. Goldberg deeply opposed the Vietnam War and believed that his negotiation skills, honed from many decades of experience resolving labor-management disputes, might be useful in reaching a peaceful resolution of the war. According to notes later published in her memoirs, Dorothy Kurgans Goldberg, Arthur Goldberg's wife, shared her thoughts about the conversation:

> On the plane, returning from the funeral, the President and Arthur had a long conversation. Arthur told him it would be a very grave step for him to leave the Court and that he would need assurance before giving a final word of acceptance not only that the UN ambassadorship would be elevated in general foreign policy-making but that he would be a principal advisor and participant in all decision-making leading to a negotiated peace in Vietnam.
>
> Arthur asked the President point-blank if he were committed to such a peace. The President said that he was and that one of his basic reasons for asking Art to assume the UN role was to get the benefit of what he termed "America's greatest negotiator" in reaching a peaceful solution, and soon.[3]

Before accepting President Johnson's offer, Goldberg decided to consult with Chief Justice Warren. In her book, Dorothy Goldberg revealed the substance of that conversation. "(T)he Chief's reaction was, of course, one of great dismay," she wrote. "But Warren said: 'You and I have both been soldiers when our country needed us, and while I personally and officially do not want to lose you as a friend and colleague, nevertheless our country is at war and I can understand that you cannot refuse to put on the uniform again.'"[4] Like Justice Robert Jackson and Chief Justice Earl Warren before him, Justice Goldberg acceded to the requests of the chief executive.

Goldberg biographer David L. Stebenne[5] argues that Goldberg left his position on the Court for several reasons. Although the deepening crisis in Southeast Asia did pose an imminent threat to world peace and Goldberg's skills as a negotiator would be helpful to his country in a time of need, Stebenne contends that accepting Johnson's offer enabled Goldberg to put to rest a peccadillo arising from a party Goldberg organized for then Vice President Lyndon Johnson in 1962. Acting on Goldberg's behalf, Assistant Secretary of Labor Jerry Holleman inappropriately had raised funds from three of LBJ's longtime financial supporters, including Texas developer Billy Sol Estes. Holleman later resigned over the incident, and Goldberg may have wanted to help Johnson in order to erase any taint of wrongdoing. Accepting Johnson's offer and doing heavy lifting for the administration over the crisis in Indochina also might persuade Johnson to nominate Goldberg for Chief Justice when Warren retired.

Although the truth about Goldberg's motivations remains unclear, on its face Stebenne's argument appears unpersuasive. Johnson already had secured the benefits of the 1962 fundraiser, and it is not clear how Goldberg's service at the UN would erase, in Johnson's mind, any possible taint arising out of that affair. The cost of working as an advocate for peace might well exceed the benefit of a cessation of hostilities, at least as seen through the lens of the often-truculent White House. On a personal level, as an Assistant Justice, Goldberg already had the security of a lifetime appointment, and in the absence of any evidence of deeper levels of impropriety, it appeared doubtful that the fundraiser could threaten his current position on the Court. In the event Johnson later might nominate Goldberg for Chief Justice, any threat arising out of the fundraiser would come from hostile Republicans in the Senate, who would not be placated by any favors Goldberg might do Johnson at the UN, not from Johnson himself. Likewise, resigning a current position on the Court in the uncertain hope of later regaining a position as Chief Justice appears rather reckless conduct, wholly out of character of Arthur Goldberg. Why not simply retain the position on the Court, devote oneself to excellence as a jurist, and hope for the best?

In a 1983 interview with Ted Gittinger, Goldberg discussed his reasons for accepting Johnson's offer. When asked what prompted him to leave the Supreme Court and go to the United Nations, Goldberg responded:

> I should like to make clear that it was not because President Johnson twisted my arm, as I have read in many publications. A president of the United States cannot twist the arm of a Supreme Court justice, even Lyndon Johnson . . . .
>
> I left for this reason. I had the feeling, on the basis of what was developing, that we were going to get enmeshed in Vietnam. I also had the egotistical feeling, based upon my long experience with government and private life as a person who could influence policy, that I could influence the President to not get overly involved. . . .
>
> I made the decision based upon Johnson's assurances that I would play a key role in determining what we ought to do about Vietnam, that I would reluctantly leave the Supreme Court. I was not bored with the Supreme Court . . . . I did it as a national duty.[6]

Unfortunately, Goldberg failed to persuade Johnson to adopt a less bellicose posture in Vietnam. U.N.-sponsored negotiations with the North Vietnamese failed, and in March 1968 Johnson decided not to seek reelection. In the bargain, the Supreme Court lost one of its best hopes for liberal leadership in the coming decades.[7]

In the wake of Goldberg's resignation, President Johnson made a precipitous decision to nominate his friend and counselor Abe Fortas for the vacant position on the Court. A successful Washington lawyer, Fortas had helped to build the law firm Arnold and Fortas (later Arnold, Fortas, and Porter) and had represented Clarence Earl Gideon before the Supreme Court in 1963. As one of the best paid lawyers in the nation's capital, Fortas attracted many large corporations as clients. His principal interest lay in client advocacy, and he had little intellectual or financial interest in a position on the Supreme Court. The $39,500 annual salary for an associate justice at the time fell far below what Fortas had been accustomed to earning in private practice.

On the other hand, as Lyndon Johnson's close personal friend, Fortas had a difficult time saying no. The ties between the two dated back to the 1940s, when Fortas had represented Johnson in a dispute over vote fraud in the primary election that led to Johnson's initial election to the U.S. Senate. When Arthur Goldberg tendered his resignation, Lyndon Johnson determined that Abe Fortas should replace him, but Fortas remained ambivalent.

Years later, an interviewer asked Fortas if he had turned down the Supreme Court position that President Johnson offered him. Fortas responded:

> Yes. And he (LBJ) has in his files a handwritten letter which I wrote him to tell him the reasons why I was turning it down and thanking him. . . .
>
> What made you change your mind?
>
> He did. . . .
>
> The story has been published. I got a call from him asking me to come over. He was about to have a press conference—a televised press conference. I went over and he said, he was signing an order sending men to Viet Nam and he was going to announce at a televised conference that he'd appointed me to the Supreme Court. By that time we were half way down the hall to the press conference. To the best of my knowledge, and belief I never said yes.[8]

In his characteristic manner, Johnson ignored and then overcame Fortas' resistance. Senate confirmation quickly ensued.

As Goldberg's replacement, Fortas occupied the "Jewish seat" on the Court. In a tradition dating back to 1916, Justices Louis Brandeis, Felix Frankfurter, and Arthur Goldberg had given distinguished service to the Court and the American people. In Fortas' case, however, an important issue arose concerning his suitability for a position on the Court. Throughout his legal career, Fortas had become accustomed to giving legal and political advice to powerful corporate and governmental leaders. He liked this aspect of his prior work and found it impossible to say no when former clients, including Lyndon Johnson himself, sought his advice.

In defiance of both the constitutional principle of separation of power and the rules of judicial ethics, Fortas functioned as both a Supreme Court Justice and a de facto advisor to the President. Fortas helped to write Johnson's State of the Union Address in 1966, counseled the President during the Detroit riots of 1967, and urged Johnson to adopt a bellicose stance in Vietnam. Throughout American history, other justices—including William Howard Taft, Felix Frankfurter, and Fred Vinson—had offered political advice to the chief executive without apparent problems. In Fortas' case, however, the frequency and transparency of his meetings with Johnson led to controversy and criticism.

Fortas' role diffusion as Supreme Court justice and counselor to the president masked a broader set of ethical lapses. Three weeks after his appointment to the Court, Fortas accepted an offer from Louis Wolfson, a former client of Fortas's firm who had been accused of violating federal securities laws. Acting as chair of the Wolfson Family Foundation, Wolfson offered Fortas an annual stipend of $20,000 in exchange for Fortas's assistance in studying racial and religious relations. The agreement stipulated that the Foundation would make payments for the remainder of Fortas's life, and if Fortas's wife Carol Agger survived him, she too would continue to receive the payments for her life. Apparently, Fortas ignored the conflict of interest and appearance of impropriety problems that this arrangement represented. In July 1966, Fortas resigned from the board of the Wolfson Family Foundation, and the following December he quietly returned its funds.

Fortas did not publicly disclose the details of his arrangement with the Wolfson Family Foundation, nor did he report the gift on his federal tax returns. Subsequently, federal prosecutors convicted Wolfson on securities fraud charges, and Wolfson appealed his conviction to the Supreme Court. The Court declined to accept jurisdiction in the case, and Fortas properly recused himself from the vote. Wolfson later served a prison sentence of nine months, and the ethics controversy surrounding Fortas continued to swirl.

In January 1968, the North Vietnamese launched a devastating Tet Offensive against American and South Vietnamese forces. The unexpected severity of the fighting and increased demands for sacrifice from the American public proved problematic for President Johnson in an election year. Liberals opposed the war, and conservatives wanted to deepen American involvement. From his position as Ambassador to the United Nations, Arthur Goldberg became skeptical about Johnson's rosy predictions about impending U.S. victory in South Vietnam. In March 1968, Goldberg wrote a frank memo to Johnson in which he advocated de-escalation and the initiation of peace negotiations with the North Vietnamese. He followed up with a personal meeting with the President. Johnson allowed Goldberg to voice his opinions but then became angry about Goldberg's intransigence. Throughout his administration, Johnson had relied upon the advice of his "Wise Men," who included former Secretary of State Dean Acheson, former Undersecretary of State George Ball, Associate Justice Abe Fortas, and former U.S. Ambassador to South Vietnam, Henry Cabot Lodge. Contrary to Goldberg, these advisors urged Johnson to adopt a hawkish position toward the war. Johnson's rift with Goldberg doomed the Warren-Goldberg plan for Goldberg to become Chief Justice.[9]

On March 21, Goldberg met with Warren over lunch to discuss Goldberg's return to the Supreme Court. At the meeting, Warren reportedly voiced his concerns about the prospect that Richard Nixon might name Warren's successor as Chief Justice. Warren indicated that if Goldberg were to succeed him as Chief Justice, he would be willing to resign that spring. Goldberg tearfully responded that Warren should not resign. When Warren persisted, Goldberg disclosed the details of his recent disagreement with Johnson over Vietnam and predicted that under the circumstances, Johnson would never nominate him as Chief Justice. Warren responded by criticizing himself for waiting so long to retire from the Court. Goldberg replied that had Warren done so, it would have made no difference, given Goldberg's long-standing opposition to the war. Goldberg defended his decision to send Johnson the memo criticizing the administration's Vietnam policy, stating, "It was the right thing to do."[10]

Warren's conversations with Goldberg during the period between 1965 and the spring of 1968 show that Warren had been pondering retirement for some time. Several events that spring made the issue more pressing. At age 78, Warren faced serious medical problems. Doctors had informed him that he had a heart condition, and they prescribed nitroglycerine tablets to counter angina pain. In the meantime, President Johnson appeared to be having difficulty on the campaign trail. In February, Minnesota Senator Eugene McCarthy nearly defeated Johnson in the New Hampshire Democratic Primary, and in March, Senator Bobby Kennedy decided to enter the presidential campaign. On March 31, President Johnson announced that he would not be a candidate for President that fall.

Johnson's decision not to run for reelection increased the likelihood that Warren's longtime nemesis, Richard Nixon, would win the presidential election in November. Warren apparently placed his hopes on the prospect that Kennedy would win the Democratic nomination and go on to win the election.

On April 23, 1968, Arthur Goldberg submitted a letter to the President offering to resign as U.S. Ambassador to the United Nations. In his letter Goldberg stated, "I don't want the impression to be created that I am hanging around for a Supreme Court appointment. This is not good for the Court, Mr. President, nor is it personally dignified for me."[11] Two days later, Johnson accepted Goldberg's resignation.

Bobby Kennedy's assassination on June 5, 1968 and the imminent end of the Supreme Court's 1968 term finally persuaded Warren to act. On June 13th, Warren scheduled an appointment with President Johnson to discuss

Warren's retirement. In the meeting, Warren recommended that Johnson nominate Arthur Goldberg as the new Chief Justice; Johnson responded that he would take the matter under advisement. Warren then tendered a curiously worded letter of resignation in which he offered to retire "effective at your pleasure." By using this phrase, Warren apparently wanted to maximize President Johnson's options in selecting a new Chief Justice. With help from his counselor Abe Fortas, Johnson issued a written response: "With your agreement, I will accept your decision to retire effective at such time as a successor is qualified."

Upon learning the news, the *Washington Post* editorialized that Warren should provide a more definitive letter of resignation. Warren responded by giving a rare press conference in which he gave two unpersuasive reasons for the conditional resignation: his advancing age and the need for continuity in the administrative work of the Chief Justice. Although Warren's age and his undisclosed heart condition represented compelling reasons for retirement, both factors cut in favor of unconditional rather than conditional resignation. If President Johnson rejected Warren's conditional offer, Warren would only get older while he remained in office, and the continuity justification did not represent a special circumstance. It would arise whenever a new chief justice took over. In the eyes of his critics, Warren inappropriately sought to influence the politics of his succession.

Johnson responded to Warren's move by calling his two key advisors, Abe Fortas and Clark Clifford, to the White House. Johnson informed them that he wanted to nominate Fortas as Chief Justice and Homer Thornberry, an old friend of Johnson's who had served as a congressman from Texas, to fill Fortas' current seat on the Court. Notably absent on LBJ's short list was Arthur Goldberg.

If Warren's letter of resignation had come six months earlier, Johnson may have succeeded in his Fortas-Thornberry plan. But many senators resented the bullying they had taken from LBJ during the previous five years, and they opposed what appeared to be Johnson's eleventh-hour effort to reward his cronies with positions on the Court. Conservatives opposed the Warren Court's recent criminal justice decisions and did not want to defer to Johnson over the Chief Justiceship. Fortas' close and inappropriate ties to the White House only fueled the fire. When Senator James Eastland of Mississippi invited Fortas to make an appearance before the Senate Judiciary Committee in July and Fortas accepted the invitation, the fireworks began.

In accepting the invitation, Fortas made a big mistake. Precedent and respect for the principle of separation of power suggested that he should have refused to submit to the Committee's questions. Previously, when sitting Justices Edward White and Harlan Fiske Stone received nominations for promotion to chief justice, they declined to appear before the Senate Judiciary

Committee out of concern that they may have been asked to comment about past or future Supreme Court cases. In 1954, Warren himself had followed a similar path. Fortas apparently thought he could appear, give measured responses, and simply refrain from answering inappropriate questions. His appearance before the Committee opened the door to questions about his relationship with the Johnson Administration during Fortas' tenure on the Supreme Court. Asked about the frequency of his meetings with Johnson concerning Vietnam, his role in writing the 1966 State of the Union Address, and his involvement in framing the administration's response to the 1967 Detroit riots, Fortas downplayed the frequency and level of his involvement. When pressed, he simply lied about the matter.[12]

Republicans in the Senate sensed that the political winds favored the election of Richard Nixon that fall. They opposed any consideration of replacements for Warren until after the election. Seventeen Republican Senators signed a petition that declared "the next chief justice of the Supreme Court should be designated by the next President of the United States." In taking this position, the Senators repeated a pattern that had arisen on multiple occasions in American history. When politically weakened presidents attempted to make appointments to the Supreme Court, the Senate often had rejected their nominees. For example, in 1930 a politically shaken Herbert Hoover nominated conservative John J. Parker to replace retiring Justice Sanford, and the Senate rejected Parker by a vote of 39–41. To be sure, one of the most important Chief Justices in the country's history, John Marshall, had been a lame duck appointment. In Fortas' case, however, the Senate had legitimate grounds for questioning Fortas' nomination.

Following the confirmation hearings, the Senate adjourned for its traditional August recess. A short time later, investigators discovered that Fortas had accepted a supplemental teaching position at American University College of Law in the summers for a stipend of $15,000, nearly a third of his annual compensation as a member of the Supreme Court. Fortas' partners at Arnold and Porter had raised the funds for the position from their well-heeled clients. Although Fortas legitimately claimed that he knew nothing about these arrangements, the controversy fueled the perception that he lacked the ethical integrity to be Chief Justice of the United States. When the Senate reconvened in the fall, Republicans filibustered Fortas' confirmation vote. On October 1, only 45 Senators voted to end debate, and the cloture vote failed. Fortas then withdrew his nomination, and a few days later, Homer Thornberry followed suit. LBJ's dominance over the U.S. Senate had come to an ignominious end.

After the failure of the Fortas nomination, President Johnson apparently considered naming Arthur Goldberg as a recess appointment for chief justice, a prospect that Earl Warren apparently welcomed. In his interview with Ted Gittinger, Goldberg discussed the matter:

> When Fortas resigned, as a result of the [Louis] Wolfson scandal, the President did have a talk and he said, "Would you accept a recess appointment as chief justice?" That was in 1968. Before then, there were no conditions. I would not do that. And I said yes, I would accept it. He said, "Congress is in vacation." I said, "I will take my chances. I've always been confirmed unanimously," which was true, for all my offices, even by reactionaries. Then he called me the next day and said his staff had looked it up and they found a speech of his against recess appointments. So I said, "Then forget about it. If you feel that your statement is more important than getting a chief justice that would reflect liberal values (sic)."[13]

The situation left Warren in a quandary. Warren's letter of resignation stated that he would retire at the pleasure of the President, but just days before the start of the Supreme Court's 1969 term and one month before the presidential election, Johnson had no one else to fill the position. On October 7, Johnson bowed to the inevitable. He issued a statement that under normal circumstances the proper course would be for the president to select a new nominee. "However, these are not ordinary times. Under the circumstances, the foundations of government would be better served by the present Chief Justice remaining until emotionalism subsides, reason and justice prevail."[14] The temporary resolution of the vacancy question left the matter in the hands of the voters, who would select the next President of the United States four weeks later.

The Republican candidate for president, Richard Nixon, predicted that the political and cultural upheavals of the 1960s would trigger a backlash on the part of white-working and middle-class voters. Such voters saw themselves as having worked hard to earn their place in the economic hierarchy, and they resented the rapid expansion of the welfare state at the cost of their own financial security. The constant focus on racial equality, opposition to the war in Vietnam, and civil unrest in Watts, Newark, Detroit, and many other cities left them feeling threatened and alienated.

Nixon built his political future on appeals to such voters. One of his major talking points involved school desegregation, and he drew a fine line on the subject. In principle, he supported the *Brown* decision, but he opposed court decisions that required busing as a means of achieving racially balanced schools. Working-class whites overwhelmingly supported his position. They perceived that integration was "taking place on their backs" and that more affluent whites who supported integrated schools avoided the burdens of busing by escaping to suburbs where school districts had no legal duty to desegregate.

Nixon's campaign also emphasized cultural values rather than the improvement of economic conditions for working Americans. His appeals to patriotism, morality, and religion helped to shape a conservative cultural identity, even as elites at the top of the economic hierarchy engineered a new global economy that would move manufacturing jobs abroad and assemble a domestic economy built on a newly redesigned financial industry and on low-paying service jobs. In typical Nixon fashion, the strategy created a wedge between the civil rights community and labor, two central parts of the old New Deal coalition. In their analysis of this issue, Jefferson Cowie[15] and Paul Frymer[16] argue that these tensions reflected a policy gap between the Wagner Labor Relations Act of 1935 and Title VII of the 1964 Civil Rights Act. The former stressed a path to union membership for white immigrants and largely excluded black and female agricultural and service workers from the union movement. The latter, passed into law during the height of the civil rights movement, prohibited employment discrimination on the basis of race, gender, religion, or national origin. Together these laws formed the core of employment law in postwar America, but they cut in different directions, involved different departments of the federal government, and prevented the formation of a unified and diverse labor movement. Economically, the push for equal employment opportunity in the 1960s and 70s occurred against a background of declines in manufacturing that contributed to a Republican divide and conquer strategy. In the opening phase of this cultural and economic war, Nixon won the presidential election of 1968 by one of the narrowest margins in American history, 0.6%.

Warren remained at the helm of the Court during the 1969 term. The term featured several important First Amendment decisions, including *Tinker v. Des Moines School District* (1969) and *Brandenburg v. Ohio* (1969). In *Tinker*, the Court upheld the right of a high school student to wear a black armband to school as a silent symbolic protest against the Vietnam War. In *Brandenburg*, the Court reversed the conviction of a Ku Klux Klan leader who had been prosecuted under an Ohio criminal syndicalism statute that made it a crime to advocate an act of violence. In a *per curiam* opinion, the Court held that mere advocacy of violence could not be subject to criminal penalties unless the speech incites people to imminent lawless action.

The *Brandenburg* decision overruled *Whitney v. California* (1927), in which the Supreme Court sustained the constitutionality of California's criminal syndicalism act. Justice Holmes and Brandeis filed a famous concurring opinion in *Whitney*, in which they argued that only when speech presented a "clear and present danger" did the state have the constitutional authority to censor expression. Although the Supreme Court in the 1920s had given lukewarm support for clear and present danger test, in a series of cases during the Cold War, it used justifications such as the "bad tendency' test to balance First Amendment rights against legislative determinations that certain types of speech endangered national security. *Brandenburg*'s new test for First

Amendment protection strengthened the rights of political dissidents and elevated the Holmes-Brandeis approach into a majority rule.

Chief Justice Warren long had supported the Holmes-Brandeis "clear and present danger" test. In 1966, he used the test to review the Georgia House of Representatives' decision not to seat civil rights activist Julian Bond, whom voters duly elected to office. The House refused to administer the oath of office to Bond because he had publicly criticized the war in Vietnam and federal selective service laws. Writing on behalf of a unanimous Court in *Bond v. Floyd* (1966), Warren held that Bond had a First Amendment right to criticize the war and that he did not incite others to imminent lawless action. Warren concluded that under the First Amendment, the state legislature could not punish Bond for expressing unpopular views. The unanimous opinions of the Warren Court in *Bond* and *Brandenburg* strengthened freedom of expression, an important dimension of its constitutional legacy.

The *Bond* decision also illustrates the Warren Court's willingness to enforce constitutional rights in matters involving the administrative affairs of a coordinate branch of government. Traditionally, the Supreme Court shied away from exercising jurisdiction over cases that involved political questions in order to maintain the constitutional principle of separation of powers. The landmark *Baker v. Carr* decision led to a new, less deferential approach to the political question doctrine. Under *Baker*, only if a legal issue is textually committed to a coordinate branch or is of a type that lacks judicially manageable standards for its resolution will the Court decline to review it under the political question doctrine. In *Bond*, the Court asserted its power to enforce constitutional rights against a state legislature. During the 1968 term, it addressed an analogous issue involving the U.S. House of Representatives.

The new case arose out of the legal and political problems of Adam Clayton Powell, Jr., a representative from New York City who had refused to pay a civil judgment and ended up being held in contempt of court. The House of Representatives initiated an investigation and determined that Powell had misappropriated congressional funds and improperly paid some of them to his wife. When the voters of Powell's district reelected him in the 1966 election, the House—by a two-thirds majority—passed a resolution that prevented him from taking his seat. The resolution also censured Powell for misconduct, fined him $25,000, took away his seniority, and declared his seat vacant. Powell filed an action in federal court seeking declaratory and injunctive relief that would bar enforcement of the House resolution. During the time it took to litigate the case in the lower courts, the 1968 election took place, and Powell again won. When the new Congress convened in January, Powell regained his seat in the House of Representatives; however, he did not receive back pay nor did the House leadership restore his seniority.

Powell encountered difficulty in the lower courts. The district court denied jurisdiction over the case, and the appellate court dismissed on mootness grounds since Powell already had been seated in the House of Representatives following the 1968 election. The Supreme Court accepted jurisdiction in *Powell v. McCormack* (1969), and Chief Justice Warren assigned the opinion to himself. As Warren saw it, the complex issues in the case boiled down to four overlapping questions: (1) Was Powell's case moot because he already had been seated as a member of Congress? In the alternative, did his case raise a nonjusticiable political question? (2) Did Powell meet the constitutional qualifications to serve in the House of Representatives? (3) Did the House of Representatives, acting under a two-thirds majority, lawfully exclude or expel Powell from office? (4) Did Article I, Section 6 of the Constitution (the Speech or Debate Clause) bar Powell from suing congressional administrative assistants on his claim?

Warren disposed of the mootness question in short order. He determined that Powell still had live claims for back pay and seniority that the House of Representatives had not resolved. The issues involving the political question doctrine proved more complex. Under the *Baker v. Carr* precedent, determining whether the Constitution commits a given matter to another branch of government itself poses a "delicate exercise in constitutional interpretation," which the Supreme Court must undertake. The underlying question in this aspect of the case concerned whether the requirements for service in the House of Representatives in Article I, Section 2 (age, duration of citizenship, and residence) are exclusive or whether the House, using its power under Article I, Section 5 to punish and expel its members, may supplement the requirements.

In addressing this question, Warren extensively analyzed the history of Parliament, the Constitutional Convention, and the House of Representatives. He focused on the issue of legislative power to determine qualifications of membership and whether the people should have the power to determine who represents them or whether governing elites should play the predominant role in this determination. Warren came down decisively on the side of the people. As he phrased it:

> A fundamental principle of our representative democracy is, in Hamilton's words, "that the people should choose whom they please to govern them." (citing 2 Elliot's Debates 257). As Madison pointed out at the Convention, this principle is undermined as much by limiting whom the people can select as by limiting the franchise itself. In apparent agreement with this basic philosophy, the Convention adopted his suggestion limiting the power to expel. To allow essentially that same power to be exercised under the guise of judging qualifications would be to ignore Madison's warning . . . against "vesting an improper & dangerous power in the Legislature." (citing 2 Farrand 249).[17]

Warren reasoned that the House of Representatives had a legal duty to seat Powell once it determined that he met the eligibility requirements of the Constitution. He interpreted the House Resolution as an exclusion proceeding, not an expulsion proceeding, and therefore ruled that the House had acted unconstitutionally. He then examined the Court's precedents, especially *Kilburn v. Thompson* (1881), to determine if Powell could sue members of Congress for the violation of his constitutional rights. In *Kilburn*, the Court had held that although members of Congress enjoy absolute immunity from suit under the Speech or Debate Clause, parties may sue administrative officers of the Congress, such as the Sergeant of Arms of the House, who execute the decisions of Congress.

Thus, Warren concluded that Powell could maintain his action against the administrators of the House of Representatives who had violated his constitutional rights. Seven of the eight sitting justices joined Warren's opinion in *Powell*, and the decision represented his last and in many ways most academically impressive opinion for the Court.

Although the *Tinker*, *Brandenburg*, and *Powell* decisions established important precedents for the rights of students, political dissidents, and public officials, the most important event of Warren's final year on the Court involved the continuing controversy over Associate Justice Abe Fortas. The Nixon Administration sought to end the liberalism of the Warren era, and the simplest means of accomplishing this objective involved placing new personnel on the Court. Warren had already announced his imminent retirement, and foreseeably several other members of the Court would be retiring in the near future. As the administration searched for a replacement for Warren, attention turned to Abe Fortas. The Nixon Justice Department continued its investigation of the Wolfson Foundation and uncovered evidence of the $20,000 annual stipend that the Foundation paid to Fortas in 1966. Behind the scenes, Attorney General John Mitchell and his staff assembled information on Fortas from the Securities and Exchange Commission and federal income tax records.

On May 7, 1969, Mitchell scheduled an appointment with Chief Justice Warren to present the evidence the Justice Department had uncovered. Details of the meeting are not available. However, it appears that when Mitchell disclosed the evidence, Warren declined comment and simply said that he would "take the matter under advisement." Warren had no direct role in supervising Fortas, nor did he have any reason to be privy to the investigation in the absence of formal charges being brought against Fortas. Most scholars contend that Mitchell shared the information with Warren in order to place additional pressure on Fortas to resign. The administration apparently reasoned that Warren wanted to maintain the Supreme Court's high ethical standards, and on the eve of his retirement, Warren's expectations might become a factor in inducing Fortas to resign.

Troubled by the appearance of impropriety in Fortas's ties with Wolfson, Warren disapproved of Fortas's close relations with the Johnson Administration. On the other hand, Fortas strenuously denied the allegation that he had interceded with the Administration on Wolfson's behalf, and the brethren had no reason to doubt his word. Several days after Warren's meeting with Attorney General Mitchell, the justices held a difficult meeting to discuss the matter. Later that day, Fortas resigned from the Court.

In the meantime, the Administration pondered the issue of Chief Justice Warren's replacement. Throughout his campaign for president, Nixon had developed close ties with Warren E. Burger, a judge on the U.S. District Court for the District of Columbia. An outspoken critic of the Warren Court's due process revolution, Burger claimed that the exclusionary rule and the *Miranda* decision had tied the hands of law enforcement officials in the fight against street crime. In several influential speeches, Burger praised the criminal justice systems of Sweden and Norway, where courts focused less on the procedural rights of the defendant and more on the rehabilitation of offenders prior to their release from prison. In the spring of 1969, President Nixon nominated Burger as Warren's replacement, and the Senate confirmed Burger by a vote of 65 to 33.

Following the conclusion of the Court's 1969 term, Warren formally retired from the Supreme Court. It was a bittersweet moment. Warren reveled in his job, and his close ties with his colleagues on the Court sustained him. Now his long-standing adversary, Richard Nixon, would be selecting a new Chief Justice, and the prospect of sweeping ideological change on the Court appeared imminent. Nixon's presence at the retirement ceremonies also proved awkward. Yet both the President and the retiring Chief Justice maintained a diplomatic tone during the ceremonies. Nixon read a prepared statement that said in part:

> Over the last 16 years there have been great debates in this country. There have been some disagreements even within this Court. But standing over those debates has been the symbol of the Court as represented by the Chief Justice of the U.S.: fairness, integrity, dignity.

He concluded:

> (T)his period will be described, not only his but that of his successor, not as the Warren Court, not as the Burger Court, not in personal terms, but in this hallowed moment in this great Chamber, the Supreme Court. It was always that way; may it always be that way.[18]

Warren responded by thanking Nixon for his "personal, kind words." He continued:

> We do not always agree . . . . It is not likely ever, with human nature as it is, for nine men to agree always on the most important and controversial things of life. If it ever comes to pass, I would say that the Court will have lost its strength and will no longer be a real force in the affairs of our country. But so long as it is manned by men like those who have preceded us and by others like those who sit today, I have no fear of that ever happening.[19]

Although he succeeded in replacing Warren with a more conventional chief justice, Nixon encountered difficulty filling Justice Fortas's seat. Initially, Nixon nominated Clement F. Haynsworth of the U.S. Court of Appeals for the Fourth Circuit. A conservative with roots in South Carolina, Haynsworth had written several opinions that sustained the constitutionality of segregation and opposed the interests of labor unions. Senate Democrats and moderate Republicans resisted his nomination, and they eventually rejected Haynsworth's confirmation by a vote of 45 to 55. Desiring to cement his appeal to Southern voters, Nixon then nominated George Harold Carswell of the U.S. Court of Appeals for the Fifth Circuit. A graduate of Duke Law School, Carswell served as U.S. Attorney for Northern District of Florida during the 1950s and had accepted a position on the federal bench there in 1958. In 1969, President Nixon had appointed Carswell to the Fifth Circuit Court of Appeals, where Carswell served for six months before being nominated for a position on the Supreme Court. Like Haynsworth, Carswell encountered opposition because of his past positions on the issue of racial segregation. In 1948, Carswell had given a speech before the American Foreign Legion in rural Georgia in which he espoused white supremacist beliefs. The Senate rejected him by a vote of 45–51.

Next, Nixon nominated Judge Harry Blackmun of Minnesota. More moderate than either Haynsworth or Carswell, Blackmun had studied under Professor Felix Frankfurter at Harvard Law School during the 1930s and later served on the Eighth Circuit Court of Appeals. Blackmun won Senate confirmation by a vote of 94–0.

With his retirement, Warren had free time to focus on writing and public speaking. In 1972 he issued his first book, *A Republic If You Can Keep It*. In it, Warren traced the evolution and meaning of the concept of citizenship in American history, advocating the reestablishment of a moral tone of decency, honesty, and fair dealing in public and private life. Writing as if he foresaw the problems of radical individualism, gridlock, and secession that would come to threaten American society in the early years of the twenty-first century, Warren decried the tendency of citizens to live in isolation, their failure to be considerate of the needs of others, and their unwillingness to adjust their thoughts and actions to the needs of the community. He wrote:

> If every citizen or group should be adamant in demanding results strictly in accord with personal desires, the nation would be broken up into so many conflicting factions that consensus on anything would become impossible. We must, therefore, if we are to continue to have a viable government, consider yielding to the reasoning of others when it points the way toward accommodating the divergent groups which make up our body politic.[20]

Another theme in the book concerned the consequences of citizen apathy. Warren perceived that when citizens abandon their responsibilities and give unbridled power to tyrants—as they did in Nazi Germany, Stalinist Russia, and Fascist Italy—the path leads to the erosion of rights and barbarism. The threat, he contended, tends to come from within, not from without. To reinforce his point, he quoted from Justice Louis Brandeis, who once noted, "Those who won our independence believed . . . that the greatest menace to freedom is an inert people, that public discussion is a political duty and that this should be a fundamental principle of the American Government. . . . They eschewed silence coerced by law. . . ."[21]

Following publication of his book, Warren pursued an expanded agenda of public speaking engagements and international travel. He remained popular on the speaking circuit, particularly at law schools and conferences, and he retained his interest in the World Peace Through Law Foundation.

In the early 1970s Chief Justice Burger supported a proposal to create a new federal court of appeals to ease the Supreme Court's workload. A committee of legal scholars and attorneys headed by Professor Paul A. Freund of Harvard Law School examined statistics on the Supreme Court's case load and proposed that a panel of federal circuit judges screen petitions for review, selecting significant cases for the Court's jurisdiction. In effect, the proposal would have deprived the Court of the discretion to determine its own docket.

Warren strenuously opposed the Freund Committee's recommendations. In remarks that received significant media attention, Warren denounced Freund's statistical analysis and disputed the contention that the Supreme Court had lost its ability to manage the cases on its docket. Warren suspected that the Freund proposal originated in Chief Justice Burger's effort to deprive the Court of its ability to accept controversial cases. Many of the Warren Court's major decisions arose because law clerks combed petitions for certiorari to find appropriate cases that the Court later used to initiate legal reforms. Adopting the Freund Committee's recommendations would have hampered this approach. Warren's public stance against the Freund Committee's recommendations became an important factor in Congress's later decision to reject the proposal.

Throughout the early 1970s, Warren continued to have health problems. He gained weight and fought angina pain. For a time in 1972 he exercised more and managed to lose 18 pounds. He had always enjoyed swimming and taking walks, and the increased physical activity helped him cope with his heart condition. He resumed giving occasional speeches and worked intermittently on his *Memoirs* in his office at the Supreme Court.

As the first chief justice in American history to write a personal memoir, Warren approached the work with discretion. The first half of the book offered an upbeat discussion of his years in California politics. He avoided extensive analysis of controversial matters such as the Japanese internment and focused instead on his record of successfully combating corruption in Oakland and improving public services during his years as Governor. The buoyant discussion made it apparent that Warren believed his happiest years and greatest accomplishments lay in his work in California.

The second half of the book, which remained unfinished, was less sanguine. Warren struck back at the critics who attacked the Court's school desegregation and criminal justice reforms. He blamed the American Bar Association for failing to support the Court in its extension of constitutional rights. The chapter on the Kennedy assassination assailed opponents of the Warren Commission who, Warren contended, failed to amass any credible evidence of conspiracy in Kennedy's death. In keeping with his views about the importance of maintaining secrecy concerning the internal deliberations of the Supreme Court, Warren did not reveal any details about decisions the Court issued during his tenure as Chief Justice.

Although the vituperative nature of Warren's remarks seems out of step with his usually sunny disposition and diplomatic rhetoric, his feelings of pent-up frustration are understandable. Had he been able to finish the book, some of the raw commentary may have been edited out. His unconstrained thoughts underscore the central truth that the criticisms of the Court stung him and left him indignant about his inability to issue a public rebuttal. Nixon's successful effort to orchestrate the anti-Warren criticism made Warren's resentment all the deeper. His silence in the face of public criticism during his time as Chief Justice resembles the solitary leadership of his favorite president, Abraham Lincoln.

By the fall of 1973, the Watergate scandal gripped the nation. Since the late 1940s, Warren had distrusted Richard Nixon, and the President's problems during the scandal may have confirmed Warren's instincts that Nixon's flawed character and vindictive machinations made him a threat to constitutional democracy. Warren carefully followed the details of the Watergate investigation. The following January Warren suffered congestive heart failure and excessive fluid build-up in the lungs, and he entered the hospital in Los Angeles. Although he recovered enough to resume his speaking schedule, he gave his last address in May at Morehouse College in Atlanta. Speaking openly about Watergate, Warren noted that "the scandal . . . has shaken the faith of people. . . . Many people are so shocked by the disclosures that they are distrustful of all persons in public life and, what is even worse, they are becoming doubtful about the institutions upon which we have relied for so long to bring about the freedom which was promulgated in the Declaration of Independence two centuries ago. . . . The great virtue of our Government," he concluded, "is that people can do something about it."[22]

Several days after his Morehouse address, Warren suffered a heart attack in Washington, D.C. He was hospitalized repeatedly over the next seven weeks in Georgetown University Hospital, suffering from coronary artery disease and severe angina pectoris. Apart from immediate family members, Warren received several valued friends, including Edgar "Pat" Patterson, Warren's African American chauffeur from his days as Governor in Sacramento. The two reminisced about their trips to the Sierra Nevada Mountains and their conversations about segregated schools in the South.

Not all of Warren's visitors brought forward such pleasant memories. Robert Kirsch, book review editor for the *Los Angeles Times*, reported that when *New York Times* obituary writer Alden Whitman interviewed Warren at the hospital, Warren broke down and said: "It's difficult to conceive of anyone living to be 83 and having no regrets. If I had ever known what was going to happen to this country—and this court—I never would have resigned. They would have had to carry me out of here on a plank."[23]

On July 9, 1974, Justices Brennan and Douglas also called upon the ailing Chief. The previous day Brennan and Douglas heard oral arguments in *U.S. v. Nixon* (1974), the Watergate tapes case. From his hospital bed, Warren shared his views about the arguments President Nixon's attorneys had made before the courts in the Watergate proceedings. Warren expressed his disdain for the president's contention that the doctrine of executive privilege justified the withholding of documents subpoenaed by a grand jury investigating the scandal. Brennan and Douglas left the hospital at 5:30 p.m., and Nina and "Honey Bear" visited early that evening. During their visit, Warren's condition suddenly deteriorated. As they remained by his side, Warren died of cardiac arrest at 8:10 p.m. He was 83.

Warren's body lay in state in the Great Hall of the United States Supreme Court amid the beautiful columns of white marble that craftsmen had painstakingly polished and assembled during the construction of the Supreme Court building in the depths of the Great Depression. Behind the casket appeared Chief Warren's chair, his black judicial robe draped over the side. Above the chair hung a wreath, a gift from the United Nations, in symbolic tribute to the meaning of Warren's leadership for the world community. An estimated 10,000 persons filed silently by, paying their last respects to the

Chief. Warren was the first chief justice in American history to be honored in death in this manner.

On July 12, 1974, Warren's funeral service took place at Washington National Cathedral. Rabbi Alvin Fine, Professor of Humanities at San Francisco State University, offered one of the eulogies at the service. In his prayer, Rabbi Fine said, "One of the giants of our generation has fallen and a part of everyman has fallen with him. . . . *Zecher Zaddik Livrachah*. The memory of the Great and Righteous shall live as an everlasting blessing. Amen."

President and Mrs. Nixon asked Nina Warren for permission to accompany her as she walked down the aisle during the service, and photographers captured the moment. Draped in a long black veil, Nina stoically accepted the Nixon's support. Past and present members of the Supreme Court served as pall bearers.

Over 1,000 persons followed the funeral procession as it crossed the Potomac River into Arlington National Cemetery. At the front gate, the pall bearers moved Warren's casket into a caisson drawn by six black horses, which carried Warren to a grave site one and one-half miles away. As a military band softly played "Nearer My God to Thee," soldiers laid Warren's body to rest on a sunny hillside.

Warren's law clerks assembled quotations from his many opinions, speeches, and articles, and Nina made final selections for the inscriptions on the gravestone. The final statement reads:

> Where there is injustice, we should correct it; where there is poverty, we should eliminate it; where there is corruption, we should stamp it out; where there is violence, we should punish it; where there is neglect, we should provide care; where there is war, we should restore peace; and wherever corrections are achieved we should add them permanently to our storehouse of treasures.

NOTES

1. Robert Dahl, "Decision-Making in a Democracy: The Supreme Court as a National Policy-Maker," *Journal of Public Law*, 6 (Fall 1957): 279–95.

2. President Nixon served five years and made four appointments to the Court. In contrast, President Ford served three years and made one appointment; President Carter served four years and made no appointments; President Reagan served eight years and made three appointments; President George H.W. Bush served four years and made two appointments; President Clinton served eight years and made two appointments; President George W. Bush served eight years and made two appointments; and President Obama (to date) has served six years and made two appointments.

3. Dorothy Kurgans Goldberg, *A Private View of a Public Life* (Charterhouse Publishing, New York, 1975), 194.

4. Ibid.

5. David L. Stebenne, *Arthur J. Goldberg: New Deal Liberal* (New York: Oxford University Press, 1996).

6. Transcript, Arthur J. Goldberg Oral History Interview I, 3/23/83, by Ted Gittinger, Internet Copy, LBJ Library, http://www.lbjlib.utexas.edu/johnson/archives.hom/oralhistory.hom/GoldbergA/Goldberg.PDF.

7. In her book, Dorothy Goldberg also shared the pain and self-doubt that her husband endured as a result of his decision to leave the Supreme Court. She wrote, "The three years on the Court were like three days. There still was so much Arthur could have given to the law. When I thought of all those years of his work that neither of us had ever dreamed would be rewarded by so exalted an appointment, provided opportunity to truly serve; when I thought of all those preliminary years of "bicker and bargain and bustle"; when I thought of all the corporation lawyers' astonishment that anyone could arrive at the most revered position in the law doing everything the wrong way, the hardest way, then I had no heart for the usual public-face smiles of the devoted wife at the thought of his moving off the bench." Goldberg, *Private View*, 195.

8. Transcript, Abe Fortas Oral History Interview, 8/14/69, by Joe B. Frantz, Internet Copy, LBJ Library, http://www.lbjlib.utexas.edu/johnson/archives.hom/oralhistory.hom/fortasa/fortas01.pdf.

9. For further details on these events, see Stebenne, *Arthur J. Goldberg: New Deal Liberal*.

10. See Dorothy Kurgan Goldberg Diary, Library of Congress, Manuscript Division, Arthur Goldberg Papers (Dorothy Kurgans Goldberg Papers File), Part I, Boxes I:13-I: 22; see also, Sebenne, *Arthur J. Goldberg: New Deal Liberal*, 371–72.

11. Letter from Arthur J. Goldberg to Lyndon Baines Johnson, April 23, 1968, quoted in Dorothy Kurgans Goldberg Diary, Part I, Boxes I:13–I:22, Arthur Goldberg Papers, Manuscript Division, Library of Congress, Washington, D.C. See also, Stebenne, *Arthur J. Goldberg: New Deal Liberal*, 370–71.

12. For detailed analysis of Fortas' confirmation testimony, see Laura Kalman, *Abe Fortas: A Biography* (New Haven: Yale University Press, 1990), 335–58.

13. Transcript, Arthur J. Goldberg Oral History Interview I, 3/23/83, by Ted Gittinger, Internet Copy, LBJ Library, http://www.lbjlib.utexas.edu/johnson/archives.hom/oralhistory.hom/GoldbergA/Goldberg.PDF.

14. Newton, *Justice for All*, 496, 20n.

15. Jefferson Cowie, *Stayin' Alive: The 1970s and the Last Days of the Working Class* (New York: The New Press, 2010).

16. Paul Frymer, *Black and Blue: African Americans, the Labor Movement, and the Decline of the Democratic Party* (Princeton, NJ: Princeton University Press, 2008).

17. *Powell v. McCormack*, 395 U.S. 486, 547–48 (1969).

18. Richard Nixon, "Remarks at the Swearing In of Warren E. Burger as Chief Justice of the United States," June 23, 1969, courtesy Gerald Peters and John T. Woolley, The American Presidency Project, Santa Barbara, CA, available at http://www.presidency.ucsb.edu/ws/?pid=2107.

19. Quoted in Baker, *Miranda: Crime, Law, and Politics*, 286.

20. Warren, *A Republic, If You Can Keep It*, 168.
21. *Whitney v. California*, 274 U.S. 357, 375–76 (Brandeis, J., concurring).
22. Newton, *Justice for All: Earl Warren and the Nation He Made*, 511 74n.
23. Robert Kirsch, "Earl Warren's Day in Court," *Los Angeles Times*, May 7, 1979.

Chapter 14

The Legacy of Earl Warren

> "He will free the poor man who calls to him and those who need help. He will have pity on the poor and feeble and save the lives of those in need. He will redeem their lives from exploitation and outrage. Their lives will be precious in his sight."
>
> Psalm 72:12-14, read at the funeral of Earl Warren, July 12, 1974.

Earl Warren served as a public official for nearly fifty years, and his influence extends over many of the key events of his time. His complex career involved positions in both the executive and judicial branches of government and in every layer of American federalism from county administration to state and national offices. The breadth of his experience and the integrity he brought to his life's work made Warren one of the most important public figures of his generation. From humble origins, he rose to positions of great political power. Yet his commitment to conscience, fairness, and humanism rarely left him. He understood the problems of ordinary Americans and insisted that socially excluded groups be given a seat at the table. The very embodiment of the American dream in his own personal journey, he did much to further the aspirations and opportunities of others.

Warren's view of the world reflected the ideals of the Declaration of Independence, the U.S. Constitution, and the golden rule. As a journalist from *Time* magazine phrased it at the time of Warren's passing, "Warren was not an ideologue or a radical. Rather he was a pragmatist who came to the bench with no preconceived vision or grand design, nor strongly held or elaborately developed theory of society or even the law itself. He did right as he learned to see the right; the key word was learned."[1]

During Warren's funeral service, Archbishop Philip M. Hannan delivered one of the eulogies. A priest at St. Patrick's Church in Washington, D.C. during the 1950s and 60s, Hannan recalled the many times Earl and Nina attended the annual Pan-American mass for Latin Americans and joined the congregation for a celebration afterward. Hannan's tribute to Warren offers insight into the legacy of the Chief. His remarks, summarized here, show that he understood the values and historical impact of his departed friend:

> Our beloved former Chief Justice Earl Warren believed that the life of everyman was as precious in the sight of the government and of the law, as it was in the sight of God. . . .
>
> He subjected government policy and law to the test of conscience. . . . He related principles to persons, not to legal abstractions. And because he believed that law floats in a sea of ethical principles, he judged the Constitution also by his conscience, his set of ethical principles. This controlling viewpoint shaped his character, and made him the attractive, unpretentious, gracious personality that helped our country pass through one of the most tumultuous periods in its history.
>
> . . . Fortunately, for our country, at the age of seventeen he worked as a railroad brakeman. This experience, of which he was very proud, taught him the need for the protection of the rights of the struggling wage earner. . . .
>
> It seemed to me that it was always like a good Pastor. It is not sufficient to be right, you need also to lead people.
>
> His hopes and aspirations were expressed I think by a student in this prayer: "I hope that I will always be for each man what he needs me to be." That prayer epitomized the life of Chief Justice Earl Warren. And God grant that it epitomize the life of a country he so deeply loved and served so well.[2]

The central elements of Archbishop Hannan's eulogy—Warren's humble origins, his faith in individual dignity, and his development of a jurisprudence of conscience—capture well the meaning of Earl Warren's life. Warren's youthful experiences as a railroad worker raised his awareness of the problems of laborers, a concern that he later extended to the rights of racial and ethnic minorities. Behind Warren's progressive philosophy and belief in fundamental fairness lay a strong moral conscience that shaped his approach to the law. He analyzed abstract legal principles in terms of their concrete effects on everyday people, which made him both an effective litigator and a good communicator. Although critics derided the simplicity of Warren's jurisprudence, Warren's focus on the moral meaning of the Constitution transformed the equal protection and due process clauses into new sources of individual rights. Like Gandhi, who synthesized the principles of Christian activism and Hindu passivism in framing a new approach to civil disobedience, Warren combined conscience and the text of the Constitution to meet the social crisis of his time. He became what his country needed him to be.

Warren's career consisted of two distinct periods, his years as elected politician and his service on the federal bench. Assessments of his legacy must recognize both the values he championed throughout his career—progressivism, ethics in public administration, the ideals of fairness and equality—and the differences in public policy that sometimes separated Warren the politician from Warren the jurist. In elected office, Warren often seemed to act as a delegate of the people, firmly carrying out their political will notwithstanding his own contrary personal views, as illustrated by his involvement in the administration of the death penalty. Conversely, as Chief Justice, he appeared more willing to exercise his own independent judgment concerning the vexing and unresolved social problems of his day.

In the period before 1946, Warren often assumed the role of a law and order conservative. During Frank F. Merriam's campaign for governor of California in 1934, Warren spoke out against the alleged communist overtones of Upton Sinclair's End Poverty in California plan, and Warren's successful prosecution of the *Point Lobos* murder cases in the late 1930s underscored his opposition to labor union militancy. His endorsement of proposals to remove Japanese Americans from the Pacific coast during World War II linked his name and reputation to one of the most flagrant violations of civil liberties in American history. Indeed, Warren's unwillingness to offer an unconditional public apology for his role in the internment may represent his greatest human failure.

On the other hand, traces of Warren the reformer can be found in his years in elected office. During the 1930s, he joined Berkeley Police Chief August Vollmer in opposing coercive interrogations of criminal suspects; instead, he encouraged police officers to utilize scientific methods in the gathering of physical evidence from crime scenes. Politically, he ran bipartisan campaigns and maintained political independence from special interests and downstate business leaders, as illustrated by his unsuccessful effort in the late 1940s to build a system of public health insurance in California.

In his many years in public office, Warren adopted a utilitarian approach to public policy that constrained the development of a comprehensive political philosophy. In the period before 1954, he opposed much of Franklin Roosevelt's New Deal, especially those aspects of Roosevelt's policies that removed autonomy and discretion from state and local officials. In a speech in the spring of 1945, Warren asserted: "I am one who deplores the loss of state responsibility to the federal government during the last quarter of a century. . . . The more responsibility that can be lodged in local government, the greater participation in government by the average citizen will be achieved. The closer the government can be kept to the people, the greater will be our chances for preserving the spirit as well as the letter of our republican form of government."[3]

Warren the politician resented federal intrusion into the affairs of state and local government. Warren the jurist had no qualms about requiring the states to follow the federal Bill of Rights and selective incorporation. The tension embedded in these two positions represents one central incongruity in Warren's political thought. Part of its reconciliation lies in the shifting roles that Warren occupied during the course of his career. In elected political office, he reflexively defended the interests of the State of California. As Chief Justice, he freely pursued his own view of the world. Warren's former law clerk and Warren Commission staff member John Hart Ely expressed this point well: "The difference between District Attorney Warren and Chief Justice Warren may have been less that the man changed as he grew older than that during his Court years he became increasingly true to himself."

In an interview with *New York Times* reporter Alden Whitman, conducted shortly before Warren's death,[4] the Chief reflected on his evolution from a law and order district attorney to liberal leader of the Warren Court. Warren admitted that his position on the Court led him to view the world differently. As he phrased it, "No man can sit on the Court over 16 years and remain parochial, for he must look out over all the United States." Warren continued, "On the Court, I saw (things) in a different light."

As Chief Justice, Warren's principal accomplishments lay in his administrative and leadership skills and in his substantive contributions to American constitutional law. In measuring the administrative and leadership skills of a chief justice, political scientists[5] have emphasized three factors: length of time in office; performance as a leader of the judicial branch generally; and skill in the managerial work of the Supreme Court itself.

In some respects, the length of time one serves in office may appear an arbitrary and irrelevant measure of individual effectiveness in the position of chief justice. Throughout the country's history, most chief justices have begun their tenure at a relatively advanced age, and accordingly, their time in office often turns on longevity and other circumstances beyond their personal control. Nevertheless, the amount of time a given chief has to implement new policies and reforms may determine his or her ultimate success, since those who serve ephemerally have little time to impact the administration of the law. At this writing, seventeen persons have served as chief justices, only five of them for periods longer than Earl Warren. Warren held office for 5,740 days. In contrast, John Marshall served 12,570 days, Roger B. Taney 10,425 days, Melville Fuller 7,938 days, William Rehnquist 6,917 days, and Warren E. Burger 6,304 days.

One of the managerial reforms of Warren's tenure involved his work on the Judicial Conference of the United States. Created by Congress in 1922, the Judicial Conference oversees the administration of federal trial and appellate courts throughout the country. In 1958, Warren appointed his former aide,

Warren Olney III, as Director of the Administrative Office of the U.S. Courts. Olney formed a committee to study the workloads and administrative needs of the lower federal courts, whose caseloads had been increasing sharply since the end of World War II. The study committee recommended a series of research projects and education programs for federal judges, but limited resources and the absence of a permanent staff made it difficult to implement the recommendations. In 1966, Warren asked former Justice Stanley Reed to chair a new study group to examine the needs of federal judges, and Reed's group recommended the formation of a new center on the federal judiciary to improve the training of federal judges and help them manage complicated cases. At Warren's behest, President Johnson endorsed the recommendations of the Reed Committee, and in 1967 Congress appropriated funds for the Federal Judicial Center.

Warren served as Chair of the Board for the new Center, and he advocated the appointment of his former colleague, Justice Tom C. Clark, as the Center's first director. Warren believed that continuing education for federal judges and the appointment of magistrate judges would help to reduce the backlog of cases and improve the quality of justice in the federal courts. Warren's ideas served as the impetus for reform of the federal judiciary in the 1960s and, indirectly, the 1970s. Although Warren himself did not undertake the difficult task of automating the lower federal courts, the administrative structure that he created made such reforms possible under his successor, Warren E. Burger. Under Burger's guidance, the staff of the Federal Judicial Center and the Administrative Office of the U.S. Courts rationalized court office functions, improved docket management, and streamlined the administration of bankruptcy cases throughout the country.

As noted, the chief justice also assumes principal responsibility for managing the administrative affairs of the Supreme Court, including chairing the Court's weekly conferences, in which the justices make decisions about case selection and present their views concerning the merits of cases that have been briefed. During these meetings, which often last seven or eight hours, the justices cast votes and determine who will write the opinion of the Court. The chief justice exercises considerable discretion over the management of conference meetings, and if the chief votes with the majority of the Court, s/he assigns writing responsibilities to an individual justice, an important power.

Leadership of the Court involves both a social and a task dimension. Social leadership includes building cohesion, defusing tension, and finding common ground, whereas task leadership focuses on the development of legal doctrine and the resolution of cases. Warren excelled at both.

In the forty years preceding Warren's appointment to the Court, five persons served as chief justice, Edward White (1910–1921), William Howard Taft (1921–1930), Charles Evans Hughes (1930–1941), Harlan Fisk Stone

(1941–1946), and Fred Vinson (1946–1953). Two served with distinction, and three had difficulty discharging the responsibilities of the office. Those who succeeded, Taft and Hughes, paid attention to the "personal equation," developing an atmosphere of cordiality and respect among the justices. To build doctrinal unity, they developed close relationships with "lieutenants" on the Court. Those who failed, White, Stone, and Vinson, usually had trouble managing the Court's conferences. White found it difficult to present case summaries in a concise and clear manner, and he allowed the justices to wander off point in their discussions.[6] Stone exhibited similar problems and complicated the difficulty by interrupting his colleagues to argue with them. Vinson lacked the intellectual skills needed for the position, and, in the words of Justice Robert Jackson, was "just plain lazy."[7] In contrast, Warren excelled at social cohesion and mediation, worked tirelessly to prepare for the Court's weekly conferences, and consulted closely with his chief lieutenant, Justice William Brennan, on issues of strategy and legal doctrine.

Throughout Warren's tenure the Supreme Court experienced eleven "natural courts," a term that denotes time periods in which no personnel change among the justices occurs. Scholars differ in their definition of the term "natural court." Some emphasize only "strong natural courts," that is those periods in which the Supreme Court is fully staffed, while others include "weak natural courts," periods following resignations or deaths in which the Court has vacancies and must continue with its work until a new justice is appointed. Including both strong and weak natural courts, Warren served on eleven natural courts. This relatively high number reflects not only the age of his colleagues but also other factors such as lack of suitability for the work and the desire for early resignation (e.g., Justice Whittaker), pressure from the President to perform other assignments (e.g., Justice Goldberg), and resignations to avoid conflict of interest problems (e.g., Justices Clark and Fortas). Warren welcomed eight new justices to the Supreme Court: Associate Justices John Marshall Harlan II, William Brennan, Charles Whittaker, Potter Stewart, Byron White, Arthur Goldberg, Abe Fortas, and Thurgood Marshall. Warren devoted significant attention to helping newly appointed justices adapt to the demands of the job, and the personal dynamics of the Court often flourished as a result.

Another measure of Warren's effectiveness involves the number of dissents and narrow 5–4 rulings the Court issued during his tenure. Prior to World War II, the Court experienced a relatively low number of dissents, averaging 9% of the total case load during the Taft years, and 15% during the Hughes years. In the 1940s, as the number of civil liberties cases on the Court's docket increased, the dissent rate reached 50% in the Stone Court and 57% in the Vinson Court. In fairness, some of this increase may have been due to other factors besides weak leadership, including changes in the nature of the Court's docket, ideological and personal tensions among the justices, and changes in the social environment of the country itself. During the Warren Court, the cumulative rate of dissents rose to 60%.

Rulings of 5–4 imply instability in the law. They send a message that changes in the composition of the court could affect legal outcomes. Historically, from 1801 until 1943, the proportion of cases decided by a one-vote margin never exceeded 10.0% annually.[8] During the Warren years, the percentage ranged from a low of 1.6% in 1967 to a high of 21.7% in 1959, averaging 11.3% across the entire 16-year period. The highest percentages occurred in the periods 1957–1960 in the wake of the Red Monday controversy and in 1966, the year the Court decided *Miranda v. Arizona*.[9]

Chief Justice Warren achieved a remarkable record of judicial reform in a relatively short time. In its "late period" between 1961 and 1968, the Warren Court incorporated eleven provisions of the Bill of Rights, and it overturned 32 precedents, many in the field of criminal procedure. As a result, the public defender system, the exclusionary rule, and *Miranda* warnings became part and parcel of the American legal landscape. The Court expanded First Amendment freedoms by strengthening the clear and present danger test and adopting stronger standards for separation of church and state in school prayer cases. It protected unenumerated rights involving reproductive freedom and the liberty interest in choosing marital partners, rights never previously recognized. Its legislative apportionment and voting rights decisions elevated voting to the status of a fundamental right.

Warren's approach to tactical leadership began with the *Brown I* opinion, which shaped him into the justice he would later become. He viewed the issues in the case from the point of view of children, protecting the interest in equal educational opportunity, and he wrote simply, from the heart, avoiding extended discussion of legal technicalities. The ninth paragraph of his opinion encapsulates all of these themes:

> Today, education is perhaps the most important function of state and local governments. Compulsory school attendance laws and the great expenditures for education both demonstrate our recognition of the importance of education to our democratic society. It is required in the performance of our most basic public responsibilities, even service in the armed forces. It is the very foundation of good citizenship. Today it is a principal instrument in awakening the child to cultural values, in preparing him for later professional training, and in helping him to adjust normally to his environment. In these days, it is doubtful that any child may reasonably be expected to succeed in life if he is denied the opportunity of an education. Such an opportunity, where the state has undertaken to provide it, is a right which must be made available to all on equal terms.[10] .

At the risk of posing a counterfactual question, one wonders what the school desegregation decisions or the later struggle over civil rights would have looked like if President Eisenhower had selected John Foster Dulles,

Thomas E. Dewey, or John W. Davis for the position of chief justice in Warren's place.

Warren's opinion in *Brown* contains all the elements of what later would be considered signature aspects of his jurisprudence: constitutional interpretation based on moral insight; a philosophy of legal realism that stressed the role of courts in resolving conflicts between social forces in the broader community;[11] and a plainly worded opinion shorn of legalese, consciously designed to communicate with ordinary Americans. Every major decision Warren issued, from the school desegregation cases to his reapportionment, criminal justice, and right to marry cases, shared these attributes. Warren's writing style did not always make him popular with legal scholars. As former professor and judge Louis H. Pollak later remarked:

> A lot of the criticism [of the *Brown* decision] is based on the notion that the opinion should have been written to satisfy lawyers and professors. But it wasn't written for that. If it was 50 pages long, like many opinions today, it would never have gotten unanimous support. The purpose was to write short, tight and bring the opinion as soon as possible. It was to be readable by the American people.[12]

In his interview with Alden Whitman, Warren acknowledged that his innovative style of opinion writing reflected a philosophy of improving lines of communication between the Supreme Court and the American people. "Expressing the concepts of the Constitution in common language was part of my idea of the Court as a people's court," he noted. Conventional wisdom in the legal community holds that the Court's audience should consist of the parties to litigation, the bar, legal scholars, and, in appropriate cases, political leaders. Instead, Warren wrote primarily to the audience of everyday Americans in an effort to raise awareness about public responsibility and constitutional rights.

Warren's efforts to precipitate dialogue between federal courts and the nation on issues of racial equality accelerated the pace of social change. The *Brown* decision convinced many persons sympathetic to the cause of civil rights to undertake greater levels of activism, as shown in the popularity of the Montgomery Bus Boycott in 1955–1956. In addition, as Professor Michael J. Klarman argues, the *Brown* decision radicalized Southern politics and put the struggle against Jim Crow into the national and international spotlight. The brutal and savage attacks against civil rights protestors that took place during the period of massive resistance in the South persuaded many Americans to support the goals of the movement.

The various forms of direct action undertaken in the South often led to litigation as the protestors or their opponents turned to the courts to advance their respective causes. In what might be considered a symbiotic relationship with the civil rights activists, the Warren Court repeatedly weighed in on the side of the extension of civil rights, issuing a total of 45 decisions that overruled precedents in this field. Its decisions desegregating schools, parks, swimming pools, golf courses, bus stations, and restaurants helped African Americans gain full legal rights as citizens. Likewise, its rulings in civil rights cases brought reforms in other areas of the law, including dignitary torts and the freedom to criticize public officials, new interpretations of the state action requirement, and determinations of the scope of congressional power to undertake civil rights reforms under the Commerce Clause and the Enforcement Clauses of the Reconstruction Amendments. In each of these ways, the Warren Court advanced the scope of civil rights in the United States.

The dynamics of the relationship between the Court and civil rights reformers has given rise to controversy in interpretations of the history of the civil rights movement. In the 1950s and 1960s, heated discussions took place within the movement about the relative merits of using courts or direct action as a means of social change. Although much of the debate involved conflicts over ego and organizational power—illustrated by fights between NAACP leaders, such as Roy Wilkins and Thurgood Marshall, and Dr. King over the need to direct limited funds into the fight to desegregate schools rather than support boycotts, sit-ins, and legal representation of protestors—other elements of the disagreement concerned the respective role of legal elites and mass movements in the struggle for civil rights. In 1960, Marshall tempered his indifference toward public protests and undertook major legal appeals on behalf of the protestors. The litigation included void for vagueness challenges against disturbing the peace statutes that had been used against civil rights protestors and challenges against states that attempted to force civil rights organizations to disclose their membership lists. Today, in histories of the movement, the controversy lingers in discourse concerning the interplay between "gradualist" legal reform strategies and mass-based direct action tactics. Did the strategies operate independently or did they function in tandem with one another? Is elite-based social change fundamentally incompatible with and inferior to a mass-based social movement?

Recently, three scholars, coming from different ideological perspectives, have raised the issue. First, of course, Professor Gerald Rosenberg emphasizes the distinction between direct action and litigation in his arguments concerning the weaknesses of courts in the fight for social change. Second, Professor Michael J. Klarman raises the issue in a slightly different context in descriptions of the tactics of the movement. He writes, "Sit-ins, Freedom Rides, and street demonstrations fostered black agency much better than did litigation, which encouraged blacks to place their faith in elite black lawyers and white judges rather than in themselves."[13] Third, Professor Michelle Alexander makes a similar point when she says, "In recent years, . . . a bit of mythology has sprung up regarding the centrality of litigation to racial justice struggles" . . . creating "a widespread perception that civil rights lawyers are the most important players in racial justice advocacy."[14] Three admonitions concerning these contentions must be kept in mind.

First, as Klarman acknowledges, in the 1940s and early 1950s, the decision to become a plaintiff in a case challenging racial segregation was itself a political act, fraught with heightened risk of retaliation.[15] The failure of the black community in Wilmington, Ohio to support Ted Lewis' challenge against the Wilmington School Board and the hesitation of black residents of Clarendon County South Carolina to join the NAACP action in the opening stages of *Briggs v. Elliot* illustrate this phenomenon. The alienating experiences of black veterans in World War II and the growing perception that segregated schools could not prepare black children for success in a competitive world eventually convinced would-be plaintiffs that the benefits of involvement in NAACP-sponsored litigation outweighed the risks. But in the context of their day, the plaintiffs' decisions to challenge Jim Crow laws in court unequivocally was a form of protest.

The second point is that in the overall context of the civil rights movement, the perception of strict dichotomies between direct action and litigation is illusory. On countless occasions, direct action protestors ended up in the courts. Some of the most critical incidents in the history of the movement were resolved, in whole or in part, through high-stakes litigation, from the early sit-in cases and the "Heed Their Rising Voices" controversy to the march from Selma to Montgomery. In fundamental ways, the struggle for civil rights concerned the intersection between direct action and litigation, not either strategy standing alone.

Finally, when the litigation phase of these direct action cases ended up in the U.S. Supreme Court, or when challenges against key civil rights legislation came there, the Warren Court nearly always ruled on the side of the movement. What would have happened if some or all of these decisions had gone the other way? The Roberts Court's recent decisions in the *Shelby County v. Holder* (2013)[16] case (striking down the preclearance provisions of the 1965 Voting Rights Act) and in several challenges against voter identification laws show that adverse legal decisions can have a devastating impact on the exercise of civil rights. Much of the discourse about the superiority of direct action over legal gradualism seems to assume that federal courts will support the legal rights of protestors, and in the Warren era this premise certainly was true. One should not overlook the role that the Warren Court played in the process of reform during the Second Reconstruction, for without its supportive decisions, the task of reform would have been even more arduous, an observation that may be relevant for future of such movements in the United States.

Although the Warren Court functioned as an important ally of the civil rights movement, its rulings in social justice cases also contained shortcomings. Warren and his colleagues stumbled in their efforts to devise remedies for the constitutional violation they found in *Brown*. They waited too long to reject the Briggs Dictum and other obstructionist strategies for undermining the intent of the school desegregation decisions. By 1964, ten years after the *Brown* decision, 98% of black students in the South still attended segregated schools. The Court lost valuable time in this waiting game, and by the late 1960s, the opponents of school integration launched a political, legal, and economic counterattack that over the next four decades has isolated inner-city neighborhoods and blocked avenues of upward mobility for inner-city youth. A key aspect of the counterattack involved the unpopularity of the Court's criminal justice reforms among ordinary Americans. Badly needed as they were, the Court's criminal justice reforms occurred against the backdrop of a dramatic rise in street crime throughout the mid-to-late 1960s, and, they helped to trigger a political backlash.

Some of the most stinging criticism of the Warren Court came from one of its own members, Justice John Marshall Harlan. Dissenting in *Reynolds v. Sims* (1964), a reapportionment case, Harlan wrote:

> These decisions give support to the current mistaken view of the Constitution and the constitutional function of this Court. This view, in a nutshell, is that every major social ill in this country can find its cure in some constitutional 'principle,' and that this Court should "take the lead" in promoting reform when other branches of Government fail to act. The Constitution is not a panacea for every blot upon the public welfare, nor should this Court, ordained as a judicial body, be thought of as a general haven for reform movements.[17]

In their assessments of the Warren era, many scholars have echoed Harlan's concern. Professor G. Edward White has observed that the Warren Court gave "disproportionate attention" to matters of policy rather than law."[18] Professor Mark Tushnet described the Warren Court's incorporation and major constitutional decisions as "willful—in reaching out for the correct result even when doctrinal tools . . . were not readily at hand."[19] Others have attacked the Warren Court for engaging in a pattern of counter-majoritarianism and for utilizing unwarranted levels of "creativity" in the invention of constitutional rights. In this view, the justices of the Warren Court functioned as platonic guardians, who contended that they knew what was best for American society even though the public did not necessarily approve of where the Court was taking them.[20]

In the popular mind, the principal critic of Earl Warren was Richard Nixon himself. Nixon's attacks on the Warren Court for favoring lawless elements over the forces of law and order and for excessive social engineering on behalf of racial minorities appealed to many Americans, especially white ethnic voters of diverse economic backgrounds, suburbanites, and conservative Southerners. Nixon saw the roots of crime not in social conditions but in the permissive attitudes of parents and judges. He opposed the "welfare class," attacked the alleged moral depravity of the counterculture, and denounced the critics of the Vietnam War. His cultural appeals to the working class yielded substantial electoral support and provided a model for Republican candidates over the next two decades, even as the Republican Party's support for deindustrialization, free trade, and globalization eroded the financial stability of middle- and lower-class Americans.

For all their public discord, Warren and Nixon shared many common roots. Both came of age in relatively poor families facing a plethora of challenges in small California towns. Both rose to prominence in the California Republican Party by attacking alleged communists, and both encountered controversy in the early stages of their national careers, Warren as a result of the Japanese internment and Nixon due to the HUAC investigation of Alger Hiss. Both drew the ire of President Dwight Eisenhower, Warren because of the school desegregation decisions and Nixon because of his Checkers speech in the 1952 campaign. The similarities between Warren and Nixon also extended to their reverence for the national security state. During the Japanese internment crisis and in his management of the Warren Commission, Warren deferred to military and national security officials. He resisted proposals to resettle Japanese Americans into the eastern United States as an alternative to internment and, as Chair of the Warren Commission, declined to scrutinize the history of Oswald's relationships with the federal officials. Likewise, President Nixon maintained a posture of secrecy in the prosecution of the Indochina War and the repression of his domestic critics. Both leaders failed to stop the concentration of power in the hands of the national security state and in this sense both contributed to growing levels of cynicism and distrust in government in the 1960s and 1970s.

The differences between Warren and Nixon appear most clearly in their respective conceptions of citizenship. From its origins, the United States featured limited citizenship rights, as women, slaves, Native Americans, and, in some states, those not owning real estate did not receive the right to vote and could not sit on juries, hold public office, or perform combat duties in the military. In theory, by 1920, many restrictions on the franchise had been lifted, but in many parts of the South, literacy tests, poll taxes, and white primaries of Jim Crow system effectively prevented blacks from voting. Warren's conception of the rights, privileges, and obligations of citizenship was grounded in the federal constitution. There he found a set of broad principles that guaranteed the right to equality under the law and the right to be free from the constraints of government-endorsed caste systems. They included the right to participate in the political process on an equal basis with others, the right to a comprehensive set of due process protections including freedom from oppressive law enforcement practices, and the right to equal opportunity in the pursuit of education and other avenues for self-actualization. His concept of citizenship also embraced the obligation to maintain transparent, good, and efficient government, constraints on excessive partisanship, and the promotion of public welfare above private interest, ideas he absorbed from William Carey Jones, one of his professors at the University of California.

In contrast, Nixon's vision of citizenship promoted the interest of national security over the legal rights of individuals. In his mind, the duly elected chief executive functioned as the managerial leader of the body politic, overshadowing the competing policy preferences of the other branches of government in the separation of power system. In the interest of defeating the perceived enemies of the United States, Nixon advocated a series of covert activities in both foreign and domestic affairs in order to preserve American affluence, its culture of competitive individualism, and (indirectly) the economic interests of the white middle and upper class. In practice, this meant secrecy in the conduct of war; extensive domestic surveillance and repression of critics; discontinuance of liberal policies involving the War on Poverty and school integration; easing of constitutional restrictions on law enforcement; and the creation of a set of political norms based on nationalism, lack of transparency, and public indifference to the details of government activities in exchange for the preservation of power and wealth in the hands of selected portions of the community. Philosophically, while Warren perceived federal courts as a constitutional counterweight to the majoritarian thrust of the political branches of government, Nixon stressed the need for federal judges to defer to the political will of the majority.

Warren's views of citizenship gained expression in the jurisprudence of the Warren Court, and, in a narrow sense, none of the major decisions of the Warren era has been overturned. Yet in the years since Warren's retirement from the Court, many of the underlying principles of Warren Court case law have been scaled back, reinterpreted, or ignored. To a large extent, Nixon's transformation of the Supreme Court through the appointment power, in conjunction with the changes wrought by President Reagan, George H.W. Bush, and George W. Bush, ended the Court's protection of racial minorities and reinforced the majoritarian preferences of the political branches.

The newly constituted Burger Court abandoned many of the initiatives of the Warren era, particularly in school desegregation and criminal justice cases. In *Keyes v. School District* (1973), *Milliken v. Bradley* (1974), and *Washington v. Davis* (1976), the Court stressed the requirement of intentional discrimination in equal protection analysis, and it prohibited federal courts from using interdistrict school desegregation remedies in the absence of proof of interdistrict violations of constitutional rights. In *Rodriguez v. San Antonio* (1973), the Court refused to recognize education as a fundamental right and accepted the legality of substantial differences in school funding across local districts. In these ways, the Burger Court sanctioned the phenomenon of white flight in urban America.

Although the Burger Court allowed major Warren Court criminal justice precedents to remain law, it emaciated them through the creation of numerous exceptions and limiting interpretations. In so doing, it complicated the field of criminal procedure and made it easier for prosecutors to secure criminal convictions. In *U.S. v. Leon* (1984), for example, the Burger Court created a good faith exception to the exclusionary rule. In *Illinois v. Gates* (1983), it adopted a totality of the circumstances approach to the issuing of search warrants based on informant tips, and in *New York v. Quarles* (1984), it recognized a public safety exception to *Miranda*. Its decision in *Wainwright v. Sykes* (1976) narrowly construed the broad approach to habeas corpus jurisdiction the Warren court had endorsed in *Fay v. Noia* (1963). *Wainwright* opened the door to a raft of state procedural default rules that prevented criminal defendants from presenting their cases for federal habeas corpus review.

On the other hand, in the areas of women's rights, privacy, and reproductive freedom, the Burger Court in some ways extended the rulings of the Warren Court. Several of the new appointees, including Henry Blackmun, Louis Powell, and John Paul Stevens, adopted moderate stances on controversial social issues, including those involving capital punishment, abortion, and affirmative action. Their positions reflected the division within the American public on these issues. Thus, while the Republican-dominated Burger Court blocked the expansion of the Warren Court's due process and equal protection decisions, in other ways it consolidated a number of Warren-era reforms.

The contrasting values of the Warren Court and those of its successors, the Burger, Rehnquist, and Roberts Courts, appear most starkly in racial justice cases. The Roberts Court's most recent pronouncement on the resegregation of public schools shows that it has all but abandoned the effort to maintain racial balance and equality of opportunity under the auspices of the federal Constitution. In 2007, the Court issued its decision in the companion cases *Parents Involved in Community Schools v. Seattle* and *Meredith v. Jefferson County*.[21] Both involved challenges against school boards that used race as a "tie-breaker" in assigning students to particular schools. Chief Justice Roberts, joined by Justices Scalia, Thomas, Alito, and Kennedy (concurring), struck down the policies, finding that the use of race in making student assignments did not constitute a narrowly tailored solution to the problem. Roberts and three other justices also held that all racial classifications trigger strict scrutiny. They read *Brown* to mean that public school boards must assign students to schools on a nonracial basis.

The dissenting justices (Stevens, Breyer, Ginsburg, and Souter) took special aim at Chief Justice Roberts' interpretation of *Brown*. Justice Stevens accused the Chief Justice of mistakenly recasting the school desegregation decisions into a defense of an individual's rights to live under a color-blind constitution. "The Chief Justice fails to note that it was only black school children who were told where they could or could not attend school," he wrote. In Stevens' view, *Brown* stood for the need to remedy the history of inequality for blacks as a class, and the case did not create an ironclad right to individual equality. "No member of the Court that I joined in 1975 would have agreed with today's decision," he concluded. In a separate dissent, Justice Breyer criticized the plurality for issuing legal rules that hindered state and local governments that sought to remedy the growing problems of school resegregation.

The Court's recent school segregation cases show that the ideology of individualism looms large in conservative approaches to the Equal Protection Clause. In the name of meritocracy and the construction of a color-blind constitution, the Court has ignored the legacy of white privilege that arises from slavery and the Jim Crow era. Its criminal justice rulings, part of an overarching policy of mass incarceration, have had devastating consequences for poor persons of color. Taken together, the school segregation and criminal justice decisions have had the effect of reinforcing the social and economic distance between white and black America and thus perpetuate the color line. According to recent analysis by the Pew Research Center, based on the Federal Reserve's Survey of Consumer Finances, the median wealth of white households in the United States in 2013 was 13 times the median wealth of black households and 10 times the wealth of Hispanic households.[22] Much of this difference comes from the value of real estate, a factor that reflects both historical discrimination and patterns of family inheritance, as well as continued high levels of racial segregation in suburban neighborhoods.

Warren's rulings in the fields of school desegregation, legislative malapportionment, and criminal justice overturned discriminatory and unfair practices and forced elected officials in the legislative and executive branches to protect the interests of minority groups and political outsiders. Today, as shown in the Court's partisan gerrymandering, campaign finance, and corporate personhood decisions, the Court merely reinforces the power of political interests that already predominate in the legislative and executive branches.

Public attitudes about Chief Justice Warren closely follow views concerning the role of courts in American democracy. Professor Yale Kamisar once noted that "Whether Earl Warren was a great Chief Justice is hopelessly intertwined with one's concept of the role of the Court in our society—with the extent to which one believes the Court sits to do good when no other agency of government will do it and good is desperately needed, with whether one believes the Office of the Chief Justice calls primarily for statesmanship, a sense of history, an understanding of people or creative thinking and analytical brilliance."[23] Former federal appellate judge Michael William McConnell echoed these words when he recently described the Warren Court as "a bit of a Rorschach test, because for some it's an almost imaginary romantic past when there was this noble Supreme Court that was doing justice with little regard to expediency and thus . . . bringing about social change and reform. . . . (F)or others, it's an almost imaginary or at least highly exaggerated vision of a court that was doing politics instead of law and thus distorting what a court is really all supposed to be about."[24]

Earl Warren and the Warren Court exercised power with integrity and compassion. Warren's insistence that the law follow a moral compass moved constitutional jurisprudence beyond the sphere of self-indulgent individualism into a broader quest for inclusion and justice for the socially dispossessed. His decisions opened up avenues of political participation for minority groups and voters residing in malapportioned electoral districts; in certain parts of the county, his decisions removed barriers that denied or diluted the voting rights of numerical majorities. Yet whether Warren's ideals will have lasting resonance turns on the value preferences of the American public. As Richard Nixon's successful presidential campaigns in 1968 and 1972 demonstrate, dominant groups rarely surrender power without a struggle. Chief Justice Warren often noted this phenomenon, which he summarized in a maxim that often appeared in his speeches: "The same human nature that craves justice and freedom under law is too often willing to deny them to others." On the other hand, as long as conflict arises between the powerful and the powerless, Warren's life teachings and constitutional legacy may have continued relevance and appeal.

In his book *A Republic, If You Can Keep It,* Warren wrote eloquently about American citizenship and the problems of a multiracial society. Warren contrasted the experience of twenty million immigrants who entered America at Ellis Island in New York harbor with the experience of African American slaves. He quoted from Emma Lazarus' famous inscription on the Statue of Liberty: "Give me your tired, your poor, Your huddled masses yearning to be free. The wretched refuse of your teeming shore. Send these, the homeless, tempest-tossed to me. I lift my lamp beside the golden door." Noting the upward mobility that many European and Asian immigrants have enjoyed at many points in American history, Warren reflected upon the experience of African Americans. "What a breach of trust it it—as well as a betrayal of a commitment to our own ideals—whenever any of these people, because of their race, or color, or creed, find hostility here instead of hospitality, or are awarded not light and warmth from the 'lamp beside the golden door' but a badge of inferiority for conditions they are powerless to change," he observed.[25]

In his many legal opinions, Warren strove to expand the conscience of American citizens concerning the social and economic plight of the underprivileged. As a progressive reformer, he refused to cede all political authority to a special-interest dominated political process. He carved out a role for professional public administrators and courts to play in the making of public policy, and he promoted the interests of rationality and morality as counterweights to the market-driven values of capitalist democracy. His social vision and moral consciousness asked much of American citizens, perhaps too much for the "silent majority" of his day. Yet just as his major decisions have been set aside rather than overturned, his vision of social justice remains an integral part of the American mind. May the members of a new generation rekindle and extend the ideals for which Earl Warren stood.

NOTES

1. "Earl Warren's Way: Is It Fair?" *Time*, July 22, 1974, 66.

2. Archbishop Philip M. Hannan, Eulogy for Chief Justice Earl Warren, Washington National Cathedral, July 12, 1974, available at https://www.youtube.com/watch?v=-yJUZfR8BU4. Archbishop Hannan had a long record of distinguished service for the church. During World War II, he volunteered as a paratroop chaplain in the European theater and earned the nickname "Jumping Padre" because he joined troops for airborne assaults in France. As priest of St. Patrick's Church in Washington, D.C., Hannan conducted the annual Red Mass for government officials involved in the administration of law. A friend and religious advisor to John F. Kennedy, he gave the eulogies for both President Kennedy and Senator Robert Kennedy. In 1964, he conducted reburial services so the two infant sons of President and Mrs. Kennedy could be interred at Arlington National Cemetery near their father. Later in life, Hannan served at St. Louis Cathedral in the French Quarter in New Orleans where he worked extensively with the poor.

3. Container 437, "Research and Reference: Governor: Public Addresses," p. 14, Irving Stone Papers, The Bancroft Library, University of California, Berkeley.

4. Alden Whitman, "Earl Warren, 83, Who Led High Court in Time of Vast Social Change, is Dead," *New York Times*, July 10, 1974.

5. David J. Danielski, "The Influence of the Chief Justice in the Decisional Process," in *American Court Systems: Readings in Judicial Process and Behavior*, 2d ed., ed. Sheldon Goldman and Austin Sarat (New York: Longman, 1989), 486.

6. According to Charles Evans Hughes, who served initially under Chief Justice White from 1910 until Hughes' resignation in 1916, White "completely lacked executive ability" and was "very unsatisfactory at Conferences, as he would talk for an hour, yet not be well prepared, and not take a position on most of the cases." Del

Dickson, *The Supreme Court in Conference (1940–1985)* (New York: Oxford University Press, 2001), 70. See also, Merlo Pusey, *Charles Evans Hughes* (New York: Macmillan, 1951), 286–87.

7. See Melvin I. Urofsky, *Division and Discord: The Supreme Court under Stone and Vinson* 1941–1953 (Columbia, SC: University of South Carolina Press, 1997), 149. See also, Dickson, *The Supreme Court in Conference*, 100.

8. See Lee Epstein, Jeffrey A. Segal, Harold J. Spaeth, and Thomas G. Walker, *The Supreme Court Compendium* (Los Angeles: Sage Press, 2012), 262–67.

9. For further information on the annual rate of 5–4 decisions in the Warren Court, see Ibid.

10. *Brown v. Board of Education*, 347 U.S. 483, 493 (1954).

11. Legal realism was an influential school of thought that arose in the late nineteenth and early twentieth centuries as a critique of the role of reason and judicial formality in American law. It emphasized the social context of law and the process by which policy makers and judges choose between competing conceptions of rights. By way of illustration, in the interwar period plaintiffs in tort actions relied upon the theory of legal realism to persuade legislators and judges to endorse strict products liability and no-fault approaches to personal injury law. Likewise, plaintiffs in contract cases used it as a means of overturning traditional theories of "offer and acceptance" on the supposition that the parties often lacked equality of bargaining power. In both situations, legal realists contended that decision makers should look outside the parameters of existing legal rules to the broader cultural and socioeconomic reality in order to resolve legal disputes.

In Earl Warren's America, the forces of reform and reaction competed in the streets, courtrooms, and legislative chambers of the country over the meaning of the Declaration of Independence, the Bill of Rights, and the Fourteenth Amendment as these legal documents applied to the dynamics of Jim Crow society.

12. Quoted in Richard Brust, "The Court Comes Together: A New Chief Led a Fractious Supreme Court to Unanimity in Overturning Segregation," *ABA Journal*, April 1, 2004, available at www.abajournal.com/magazine/article/the_court_comes_together.

13. Klarman, *From Jim Crow to Civil Rights*, 467.

14. Alexander, *New Jim Crow*, 225.

15. Ibid.

16. 133 S. Ct. 2612 (2013).

17. *Reynolds v. Sims*, 377 U.S. 533, 624–25 (Harlan, J., dissenting).

18. White, *Earl Warren: A Public Life*, 269.

19. Mark Tushnet, "The Warren Court as History: An Introduction," in *The Warren Court in Historical and Political Perspective*, ed. Mark Tushnet (Charlottesville, VA: University Press of Virginia, 1993), 10.

20. See e.g., Berger, *Government by Judiciary*. See also, Horowitz, *The Courts and Social Policy*; and Glazer, "Toward an Imperial Judiciary," 104–23. Since the late 1960s, many of these points of view have been reflected in Republican presidential platforms. Republican candidates have denounced judicial activism and legislating from the bench, favoring instead the jurisprudence of strict construction. In contrast, in their approach to constitutional interpretation, Democrats have endorsed the

principle of a living and breathing constitution. One observation about the tension between these two ideological positions comes from Professor Justin Driver, who noted that "(t)he jurisprudential divide on the Supreme Court regarding high-profile legal issues now appears to map almost perfectly onto the political divide that exists in the larger nation." "In a Reversal, Rulings Could Goad Democratic Voters," *New York Times*, April 5, 2012, at A14.

21. 551 U.S. 701 (2007).

22. See Rakeh Kochhar and Richard Fry, "Wealth Inequality Has Widened Along Racial, Ethnic Lines Since End of Great Recession," at http://www.pewresearch.org/fact-tank/2014/12/12/racial-wealth-gaps-great-recession/.

23. Yale Kamisar, *Los Angeles Times*, Sunday June 15, 1969.

24. Nina Totenberg, "Earl Warren's Legacy" All Things Considered June 30, 2008, http://www.npr.org/templates/story/story.php?, quoting The Hon. Michael McConnell.

25. Warren, *A Republic, If You Can Keep It*, 52.

Bibliography

MANUSCRIPTS, TRANSCRIPTS, AND SPECIAL COLLECTIONS

Attorney General Office Papers, Earl Warren, California State Archives, Sacramento.

Burton, Harold H. Papers. Manuscript Division, Library of Congress, Washington, D.C.

Douglas, William O. Papers. Manuscript Division, Library of Congress, Washington, D.C.

FBI Records (including JFK Assassination File, FBI Headquarters File, and FBI Headquarters Liaison with Warren Commission File), Public Records Office, National Archives and Records Administration, Washington, D.C.

Fry, Amelia R. and Miriam Feingold Stein, "Earl Warren: The Governor's Family, Oral History Transcript and Related Material, 1970–1980," typescript of an oral history conducted 1970–1978, Regional Oral History Office, The Bancroft Library, University of California, Berkeley, 1980, p. 265, http://bancroft.berkeley.edu/ROHO/projects/ewge.

Goldberg, Arthur J. Papers. Manuscript Division, Library of Congress, Washington, D.C.

Jackson, Robert Hughwout. Papers. Manuscript Division, Library of Congress, Washington, D.C.

Levenson, Rosemary, Amelia Fry, and Miriam Feingold Stein, "The Japanese-American Relocation Reviewed," typescript of an oral history conducted 1974, Vol. II: The Internment, Regional Oral History Office, The Bancroft Library, University of California, Berkeley, 1974, p. 267, http://bancroft.berkeley.edu/ROHO/projects/ewge.

NAACP Records. Manuscript Division, Library of Congress, Washington, D.C.

Nixon, Richard, radio address, October 21, 1972, courtesy Gerhard Peters and John T. Woolley, The American Presidency Project, Santa Barbara, CA, available at http://www.presidency.ucsb.edu/ws/?pid=3637.

Nixon, Richard, "The Need for Leadership: An Address in Greensboro, North Carolina," August 17, 1960, courtesy Gerhard Peters and John T. Woolley, The American Presidency Project, Santa Barbara, CA, available at http://www.presidency.ucsb.edu/ws/?pid=25385.

Olney, Warren, III, "Law Enforcement and Judicial Administration in the Earl Warren Era," typescript of an oral history conducted 1970–1977 by Miriam Stein and Amelia R. Fry, Regional Oral History Office, The Bancroft Library, University of California, Berkeley, 1981, p. 533, http://bancroft.berkeley.edu/ROHO/projects/ewge.

Powers, Robert B., "Law Enforcement, Race Relations: 1930–1960," typescript of an oral history conducted 1969 by Amelia R. Fry, Regional Oral History Office, The Bancroft Library, University of California, Berkeley, 1971, p. 180, http://bancroft.berkeley.edu/ROHO/projects/ewge.

Schmidt Jr., Benno, "Reminiscences of Benno C. Schmidt Jr.: Oral History, 1975," Columbia University Oral History Research Office, Butler Library, Columbia University, New York, 1984, p. 386.

State of California, Office of the Attorney General, Collection on the Pre-Evacuation Location of Japanese Americans, The Bancroft Library, University of California, Berkeley.

Sweigert, William,"Administration and Ethics in the Governor's Office and the Courts, California, 1937–1975," transcript of an oral history conducted 1972–1975 by Amelia Fry, Regional Oral History Office, The Bancroft Library, University of California, Berkeley, 1987, p. 266, http://bancroft.berkeley.edu/ROHO/projects/ewge.

Transcript of Record, *People of California v. King*, 30 Cal. App. 2d 185 (Cal. Ct. App. 1938) (Crim. No. 1947) (1938 Cal. App. LEXIS 467).

Warren, Earl. Papers. Manuscript Division, Library of Congress, Washington, D.C.

Whitaker, Clem and Leone Baxter, "California Election News," (footage of film shorts covering California's 1934 gubernatorial campaign), available at http://www.youtube.com/watch?v=M9vfWjmON0.

BOOKS AND ARTICLES

Adler, Jeffrey S. *First in Violence, Deepest in Dirt: Homicide in Chicago, 1875–1929*. Cambridge, MA: Harvard University Press, 2006.

Alexander, Michelle. *The New Jim Crow: Mass Incarceration in the Age of Colorblindness*. New York: The New Press, 2012.

Ambrose, Stephen E. *Eisenhower. Vol. 2, The President*. New York: Simon & Schuster, 1984.

———. *Nixon: The Triumph of a Politician, 1962–1972*. Los Angeles: Premier Digital Publishing, 1989.

"American Schools Still Heavily Segregated by Race, Income: Civil Rights Project Report." Huffington Post, September 20, 2012, http://www.huffingtonpost.com/2012/09/20/american-schools-still-he_n_1901583.html.

Atkins, Raymond A. and Paul H. Rubin. "Effects of Criminal Procedure on Crime Rates: Mapping Out the Consequences of the Exclusionary Rule." *Journal of Law and Economics* 46, no. 1 (2003): 157–79.

Baker, Liva. *Miranda: Crime, Law, and Politics*. New York: Atheneum Books, 1983.

Barnum, David G. "The Supreme Court and Public Opinion: Judicial Decision Making in the Post-New Deal Period." *The Journal of Politics* 47, no. 2 (1985): 652–66.

Basler, Ray, ed. *The Collected Works of Abraham Lincoln*. Washington, D.C.: Abraham Lincoln Association, 1959.

Baum, Lawrence. *American Courts: Process and Policy*. Boston: Houghton Mifflin, 1990.

———. *The Supreme Court*. Washington, D.C.: CQ Press, 2010.

Belknap, Michal R. *The Supreme Court under Earl Warren, 1953–1969*. Columbia, SC: University of South Carolina Press, 2005.

Bell, Derrick A. "Racial Realism." *24 Conn. LO. Rev*. 363 (1991).

———. "Brown v. Board of Education: Forty-five Years after the Fact." *Ohio N.U.L.Rev*. 171 (2000).

Berger, Raoul. *Government by Judiciary: The Transformation of the Fourteenth Amendment*. Indianapolis: Liberty Fund, 1997.

Bernstein, Barton J. "Plessy v. Ferguson: Conservative Sociological Jurisprudence." *Journal of Negro History* 48 (1963): 196–196-205.

Black, Charles. "The Lawfulness of the Segregation Decisions." 69 *Yale Law Journal* 421 (1960).

Branch, Taylor. *At Canaan's Edge: America in the King Years, 1965–68*. New York: Simon & Schuster, 2006.

———. *Parting the Waters: America in the King Years,1954–63*. New York: Simon & Schuster, 1989.

———. *Pillar of Fire: America in the King Years, 1963–65*. New York: Simon & Schuster, 1999.

Brust, Richard. "The Court Comes Together." *ABA Journal*, 90 (2004): 40–44.

Buenker, John D., John C. Burnham, and Robert M. Crunden. "What Was Progressivism?" *America* 51 (1969): 175–93.

Bugliosi, Vincent. *Reclaiming History: The Assassination of President John F. Kennedy*. New York: W.W. Norton & Co., 2007.

Burns, Stewart, ed. *Daybreak of Freedom: The Montgomery Bus Boycott*. Chapel Hill: University of North Carolina Press, 1997.

———. *Social Movements of the 1960s: Searching for Democracy*. Boston: Twayne Publishers, 1990.

Carson, Clayborne. *In Struggle: SNCC and the Black Awakening of the 1960s*. Cambridge, MA: Harvard University Press, 1981.

Carte, Gene E. and Elaine H. Carte. *Police Reform in the United States: The Era of August Vollmer,* 1905–1932. Berkeley: University of California Press, 1975.

Choper, Jesse H. "Earl Warren—A Law Clerk's Memory of the Man and the Court." In *Earl Warren and the Warren Court: The Legacy in American and Foreign Law*. Edited by Harry N. Scheiber. New York: Lexington Books, 2007.

Christman, Henry M., ed. *The Public Papers of Chief Justice Earl Warren*. Westport, CT: Greenwood Press, 1974.

Collingwood, R.G. *The Idea of History*. Oxford: Clarendon Press, 1993.

Compston, Christine. *Earl Warren: Justice for All*. New York: Oxford University Press, 2001.

Comptroller General of the United States. *Impact of the Exclusionary Rule on Federal Criminal Prosecutions*. Washington, D.C.: Government Printing Office, 1979.

Cowie, Jefferson. *Stayin' Alive: The 1970s and the Last Days of the Working Class*. New York: The New Press, 2010.

Cox, Archibald. *The Warren Court: Constitutional Decision as an Instrument of Reform*. Cambridge, MA: Harvard University Press, 1968.

Cray, Ed. *Chief Justice: A Biography of Earl Warren*. New York: Simon & Schuster, 1997.

Cushman, Clare and Melvin I. Urofsky, eds. *Black, White, and Brown: The Landmark School Desegregation Case in Retrospect*. Washington, D.C.: Supreme Court Historical Society, 2004.

Dahl, Robert. "Decision-Making in a Democracy: The Supreme Court as a National Policy-Maker." *Journal of Public Law* 6 (Fall 1957): 279–95.

Dallek, Robert. *Lyndon Johnson and His Times*. Vol. 2, *Flawed Giant*, 1961–1973. New York: Oxford University Press, 1998.

Dickson, Del, ed. *The Supreme Court in Conference: The Private Decisions Behind Nearly 300 Supreme Court Decisions*. New York: Oxford University Press, 2001.

"Disenfranchised Felons." *New York Times*, July 15, 2012.

Douglas, William O. *The Court Years*, 1939–1975*: The Autobiography of William O. Douglas*. New York: Random House, 1980.

———. *Go East, Young Man: The Early Years—The Autobiography of William O. Douglas*. New York: Vintage Books, 1983.

DuBois, W.E.B. "Does the Negro Need Separate Schools?" *Journal of Negro Education* (1935): 328–35.

Duster, Troy. "Pattern, Purpose, and Race in the Drug War: The Crisis of Credibility in Criminal Justice." In *Crack in America: Demon Drugs and Social Justice*. Edited by Craig Reinarman and Harry G. Levine. Berkeley: University of California Press, 1997.

Dyson, Michael Eric. *I May Not Get There With You: The True Martin Luther King Jr*. New York: Free Press, 2000.

Elliott, Ward Y.E. *The Rise of Guardian Democracy: The Supreme Court's Role in Voting Rights Disputes*, 1845–1969. Cambridge, MA: Harvard University Press, 1974.

Epstein, Lee and Jeffrey A. Segal. *The Supreme Court Compendium: Data, Decisions, and Developments*. Thousand Oaks, CA: CQ Press, 2012.

Epstein, Sandra P. *Law at Berkeley: The History of Boalt Hall*. Berkeley: Institute of Government Studies Press, University of California, Berkeley, 1997.

Ewald, William B., Jr. *Eisenhower the President: Crucial Days*, 1951–1960. Englewood Cliffs, NJ: Prentice Hall, 1981.

Feingold, Miriam. "The King-Ramsey-Connor Case: Labor, Radicalism, and Law in California, 1936–1941." *Dissertation Abstracts* 37, no. 6 (1976): 3850–4689.

Filene, Peter G. "An Obituary for 'The Progressive Movement.'" *American Quarterly* 22, no. 1 (Spring, 1970): 20–34.

Ford, Gerald and John R. Stiles. *Portrait of the Assassin*. New York: Ballantine Books, 1966.

Frank, Jerome. *Law and the Modern Mind*. New York: Coward-McCann, 1930.

Frantz, Joe B. "Interview with Former Chief Justice Earl Warren, 1971." Lyndon Baines Johnson Library, Austin, Texas, http://glifos.lbjf.org/gsm/index.php/Warren_Earl_OHInt1_092171.

Frymer, Paul. *Black and Blue: African Americans, the Labor Movement, and the Decline of the Democratic Party*. Princeton, NJ: Princeton University Press, 2008.

Gara, Lenna Mae. "Separate and Unequal: The Closing of Midland School." *Timeline Magazine,* June/July 1991: 41–54.

Garrow, David J., ed. *Birmingham, Alabama,* 1956–1963*: The Black Struggle for Civil Rights*. Brooklyn, NY: Carlson, 1989.

Gentry, Curt. *J. Edgar Hoover: The Man and the Secrets*. New York: W.W. Norton & Company, 1991.

Ghurye, G.S. *Caste and Race in India*. London: Routledge and Degan Paul, 1932.

Glazer, Nathan, "Towards an Imperial Judiciary." *Public Interest* 40 (Fall 1975): 104–23.

Goldberg, Arthur J. "Earl Warren: The Flame Burned Bright." *Virgin Island Daily News*, September 30, 1974, p. 19. News.google.com/newspapers?nid=757&dat=19740930.

Goldberg, Dorothy Kurgans. *A Private View of a Public Life*. New York: Charterhouse Publishing, 1975.

Goldman, Sheldon and Thomas P. Jahnige. *The Federal Courts as a Political System*. New York: Harper and Row, 1976.

Goodman, James. *Stories of Scottsboro*. New York: Vintage Books, 1995.

Goodwin, Doris Kearns. *Lyndon Johnson and the American Dream*. New York: St. Martin's Griffin, 1993.

Greenberg, Jack. *Crusaders in the Courts: How a Dedicated Band of Lawyers Fought for the Civil Rights Revolution*. New York: BasicBooks, 1994.

Gregor, A. James. "The Law, Social Science, and School Segregation: An Assessment." 14 *Western Reserve Law Review* 626 (1963).

Grodzins, Morton. *Americans Betrayed: Politics and the Japanese Evacuation*. Chicago, University of Chicago Press, 1949.

Haag, Ernest Van den. "Social Science Testimony in the Desegregation Cases." 6 *Villanova Law Review* 69 (1960).

Hamilton, Alexander. "Federalist No. 78." In *The Federalist Papers*. Edited by Clinton Rossiter. New York: Signet Classics, 2003.

Hart, Henry M., Jr. "Hart Says Confirmation First." *Harvard Crimson*, October 5, 1953.

Hess, Diana E. "Brown as a Classroom Icon." In *Black, White, and Brown: The Landmark School Desegregation Case in Retrospect*. Edited by Clare Cushman and Melvin I. Urofsky. Washington, D.C.: Congressional Quarterly Press, 2004.

Hofstadter, Richard. *The Age of Reform from Bryan to F.D.R.* New York: Knopf, 1955.

Horwitz, Bernard J. *The Warren Court and the Pursuit of Justice*. New York: Hill and Wang, 1998.

Horwitz, Morton J. *The Warren Court and the Pursuit of Justice*. New York: Hill and Wang, 1998.

Hill, Gladwin. "Nixon Denounces Press as Biased." *New York Times*, November 8, 1962, A-1.

Hockett, Jeffrey D. *New Deal Justice: The Constitutional Jurisprudence of Hugo L. Black, Felix Frankfurter, and Robert H. Jackson*. Lanham, MD: Rowman & Littlefield Publishers, 1996.

Horowitz, Donald. *The Courts and Social Policy*. Washington, D.C.: Brookings Institution, 1977.

House Select Committee on Assassinations (Church Committee Report). "The Investigation of the Assassination of President John Fitzgerald Kennedy: Performance of the Intelligence Agencies." http:www.aarclibrary.org/publiclib/contents/church/contents_church_reports_book5.htm.

Hutchinson, Dennis J. "Hail to the Chief: Earl Warren and the Supreme Court." 81 *Michigan Law Review* 922 (1983).

"In a Reversal, Rulings Could Goad Democratic Voters." *New York Times*, April 5, 2012.

Irons, Peter H. *The Courage of Their Convictions: Sixteen Americans Who Fought Their Way to the Supreme Court*. New York: Penguin, 1990.

———. *Jim Crow's Children: The Broken Promise of the Brown Decision*. New York: Penguin Group, 2002.

———. *Justice at War*. New York: Oxford University Press, 1983.

———. *A People's History of the Supreme Court*. New York: Viking, 1999.

Jones, William Carey. *Elements of Civil Government*. Sacramento: State of California Printing Office, 1891.

———. "Present Day Problems of Democracy." *Collected Writings of William Carey Jones*. Bound in Faculty Library, Boalt Hall, University of California, Berkeley.

"Jurist's Joyful Junket." *Life*. September 17, 1956. http://books.google.com/books.

Kagen, Robert A., Lawrence M. Friedman, and Stanton Wheeler. "The Business of State Supreme Courts, 1870–1970." 30 *Stanford Law Review* 121 (1977).

Kaiser, David. *The Road to Dallas: The Assassination of John F. Kennedy*. Cambridge, MA: Belknap Press of Harvard University Press, 2008.

Kalman, Laura. *Abe Fortas: A Biography*. New Haven: Yale University Press, 1990.

Kamisar, Yale. "Earl Warren: Law Enforcement Leads to Defendants' Rights." *Law Quad Notes* 47, no. 3, (2005): 87–8.

———. "How Earl Warren's Twenty-Two Years in Law Enforcement Affected His Work as Chief Justice." *Ohio State Journal of Criminal Law* 3, no.1 (2005): 11–32.

———. "On the Fortieth Anniversary of the Miranda Case: Why We Needed It, How We Got It—And What Happened To It." *Ohio State Journal of Criminal Law* 5 (2007): 163.

Katcher, Leo. *Earl Warren: A Political Biography*. New York: McGraw-Hill, 1967.

Keller, William W. *The Liberals and J. Edgar Hoover: The Rise and Fall of a Domestic Intelligence State*. Princeton, NJ: Princeton University Press, 2014.

Keyssar, Alexander. *The Right to Vote: The Contested History of Democracy in the United States*. New York: Basic Books, 2000.

Kiel, R. Andrew. *J. Edgar Hoover: The Father of the Cold War—How His Obsession with Communism Led to the Warren Commission Coverup and Escalation of the Vietnam War*. Lanham, MD: University Press of America, 2000.

King, Martin Luther, Jr. *Stride toward Freedom: The Montgomery Story*. New York: Harper & Row, 1958.

———. *Where Do We Go From Here: Chaos or Community?* Boston: Beacon Press, 1968.

———. *Why We Can't Wait.* New York: Penguin, 1964.

Kirsch, Robert. "Earl Warren's Day in Court," *Los Angeles Times*, May 7, 1979.

Kitts, Kenneth. *Presidential Commissions and National Security: The Politics of Damage Control.* Boulder, CO: Lynne Rienner Publishers, 2006.

Klarman, Michael J. *From Jim Crow to Civil Rights: The Supreme Court and the Struggle for Racial Equality.* New York: Oxford University Press, 2004.

Kluger, Richard. *Simple Justice: The History of Brown v. Board of Education and Black America's Struggle for Equality.* New York: Knopf, 1976.

Kochhar, Raken and Richard Fry. "Wealth Inequality has Widened Along Racial, Ethnic Lines Since End of Great Recession." At http://www.pewresearch.org/fact-tank/2014/12/12/racial-wealth-gaps-great-recession/.

Kousser, J. Morgan. *Colorblind Injustice: Minority Voting Rights and the Undoing of the Second Reconstruction.* Chapel Hill, NC: The University of North Carolina Press, 1999.

———. *Dead End: The Development of 19th-Century Litigation on Racial Discrimination in Schools.* New York: Oxford University Press, 1986.

Kozol, Jonathan. *The Shame of the Nation: The Restoration of Apartheid Schooling in America.* New York: Three Rivers Press, 2005.

Kurland, Philip B. *Politics, the Constitution, and the Warren Court.* Chicago: University of Chicago Press, 1970.

Kurtz, Michael L. *The JFK Assassination Debates: Lone Gunman versus Conspiracy.* Lawrence, KS: University Press of Kansas, 2006.

Lain, Corinna Barrett. "Countermajoritarian Hero or Zero?" 152 *University of Pennsylvania Law Review* 1361 (2004).

Lane, Mark. *Plausible Denial: Was the CIA Involved in the Assassination of JFK?* New York: Thunder's Mouth Press, 1991.

Langer, Gary. "Legacy of Suspicion: Decades After, Few Accept the Official Explanation for JFK Assassination." http:abcnews.go.com/sections/wnt?US?JFK_poll_031116.html.

Levy, David W. "Before Brown: The Racial Integration of American Higher Education." In *Black, White, and Brown: the Landmark School Desegregation Case in Retrospect.* Edited by Clare Cushman and Melvin I. Urofsky. Washington, D.C.: Supreme Court Historical Society, 2004.

Lewis, Anthony. "A Talk with Warren on Crime, the Court, and the Country." *New York Times Magazine*, October 19, 1969.

Liptak, Adam. "Inmate Court in U.S. Dwarfs Other Nations." *New York Times*, April 23, 2008.

McKnight, Gerald D. *Breach of Trust: How the Warren Commission Failed the Nation and Why.* Lawrence, KS: University Press of Kansas, 2005.

Meagher, Sylvia. *Accessories after the Fact: The Warren Commission, the Authorities, and the Report.* New York: Vintage Books, 1967.

Mitchell, Greg. *The Campaign of the Century Upton Sinclair's Race for Governor of California and the Birth of Media Politics.* New York: Random House, 1992.

Mowry, George E. *The California Progressives.* Chicago: Quadrangle Books, 1963.
Murphy, Paul L. *The Constitution in Crisis Times,* 1918–1969. New York: Harper & Row, 1972.
Myer, Dillon S. *Uprooted Americans: The Japanese Americans and the War Relocation Authority during World War II.* Tucson, AZ: University of Arizona Press, 1971.
National Commission on Law Observance and Law Enforcement. *Report on Lawlessness in Law Enforcement.* Washington, D.C.: Government Printing Office, 1931.
Neier, Aryeh. *Only Judgment: The Limites of Litigation in Social Change.* Middletown, CT: Wesleyan University Press, 1982.
Newman, John. *Oswald and the CIA: The Documented Truth about the Unknown Relationship Between the U.S. Government and the Alleged Killer of JFK.* New York: Skyhorse Publishing, 2008.
Newman, Roger K. *Hugo Black: A Biography.* New York: Pantheon Books, 1994.
Newton, Jim. *Justice for All: Earl Warren and the Nation He Made.* New York: Riverhead Books, 2006.
Orfield, Gary and Erica Frankenberg. "Reviving Brown v. Board of Education: How Courts and Enforcement Agencies Can Produce More Integrated Schools." In *Brown at 50: The Unfinished Legacy: A Collection of Essays.* Edited by Deborah L. Rhode and Charles J. Ogletree, Jr. Chicago: American Bar Association, 2004).
Orfield, Gary and Hohn T. Yun. "Resegregation in American Schools." Civil Rights Project, Harvard University, 1999.
Orth, John V. *Due Process of Law: A Brief History.* Lawrence, KS: University Press of Kansas, 2003.
Oshinsky, David M.*"Worse Than Slavery": Parchman Farm and the Ordeal of Jim Crow Justice.* New York: Free Press, 1996.
Patterson, James T. *Brown v. Board of Education: A Civil Rights Milestone and Its Troubled Legacy.* New York: Oxford University Press, 2001.
Perlstein, Rick. *Nixonland: The Rise of a President and the Fracturing of America.* New York: Schriber, 2008.
________, ed. *Richard Nixon: Speeches, Writings, Documents.* Princeton, NJ: Princeton University Press, 2008.
Perry, Michael. *The Constitution, the Courts, and Human Rights: An Inquiry into the Legitimacy of Constitutional Policymaking by the Judiciary.* New Haven, CT: Yale University Press, 1982.
Pollack, Jack Harrison. *Earl Warren: The Judge Who Changed America.* Englewood Cliffs, NJ: Prentice Hall, 1979.
Posner, Gerald. *Case Closed: Lee Harvey Oswald and the Assassination of JFK.* New York: Doubleday, 1993.
Posner, Richard A. "Objectivity and Hagiography in Judicial Biography." 70 New York *University Law Review*, 502 (1995).
Powe, Lucas A. *The Warren Court and American Politics.* Cambridge, MA: Belknap Press of Harvard University Press, 2000.
Prettyman, E. Barrett. "Thoughts on Justice Jackson's Unpublished Opinion." October 8, 2003. http://www.roberthjackson.org/the_man/speeches-articles/speeches/speeches-related-to-robert-h-jackson/thoughts-on-jacksons-unpublished -opinion/.

Przybyszewski, Linda. *The Republic According to John Marshall Harlan*. Chapel Hill, NC: University of North Carolina Press, 1999.

Purdum, Todd S. "Presidents, Picking Justices, Can Have Backfires." *New York Times*, July 5, 2005.

Radke, Marian J. and Helen G. Trager. "Children's Perceptions of the Social Roles of Negroes and Whites." *Journal of Psychology* 29, no. 1 (1950): 3–33.

Ramadas, Sandhya. "How Earl Warren Previewed Today's Civil Liberties Debate—And Got It Right In the End. 16 *Asian American Law Journal* 73 (2009).

Ray, Julie. "Reflections on the 'Trouble in Little Rock.'" Part II. Gallup.com.

Rehnquist, William H. "Chief Justice Warren's Role in Brown v. Board of Education." In *Brown at 50: The Unfinished Legacy*. Edited by Deborah L. Rhode and Charles J. Ogletree, Jr. Chicago: American Bar Association, 2004.

———. "Who Writes Decisions of the U.S. Supreme Court?" *U.S. News & World Report*, December 13, 1957.

Reisner, Marc. *Cadillac Desert: The American West and Its Disappearing Water*. New York: Viking Press, 1986.

Rhode, Deborah L. and Charles J. Ogletree, Jr. *Brown at 50: The Unfinished Legacy*. Chicago: American Bar Association, 2004.

Rodgers, Daniel T. "In Search of Progressivism." *Reviews in American History* 10, no. 4 (Dec., 1982): 113–32.

Rosenberg, Gerald N. *The Hollow Hope: Can Courts Bring About Social Change?* Chicago: University of Chicago Press, 1991.

Saphire, Richard B. "The Search for Legitimacy in Constitutional Theory: What Price Purity?" 42 *Ohio State Law Journal* 335 (1981).

Saphire, Richard B. and Paul Moke. "Litigating Bush v. Gore in the States: Dual Voting Systems and the Fourteenth Amendment." 51 *Villanova Law Review* 229 (2006).

Sauvage, Leo. "Oswald's Case Against the Warren Commission." *New Leader*, December 20, 1965: 5–10.

Scheiber, Harry N., ed. *Earl Warren and the Warren Court:The Legacy in American and Foreign Law*. Lanham, MD: Lexington Books/Rowman & Littlefield Publishers; Berkeley, IGS Press for the Institute for Legal Research at the University of California, 2007.

Schell, Jonathan. *The Time of Illusion: An Historical and Reflective Account of the Nixon Era*. New York: Vintage Books, 1976.

Schmidhauser, John R. *The Supreme Court: Its Politics, Personalities, and Procedures*. New York: Holt, Rinehart, and Wilson, 1960.

Schwartz, Bernard. *Super Chief: Earl Warren and His Supreme Court, A Judicial Biography*. New York: New York University Press, 1983.

Simon, James F. *In His Own Image: The Supreme Court in Richard Nixon's America*. New York: David McKay Co., 1973.

Sinclair, Upton. *I, Candidate for Governor: And How I Got Licked*. Pasadena, CA: The Author, 1935.

Smith, A. Wade. "Tolerance of School Desegregation." *Social Forces* 59, no. 4 (1981): 1256–74.

"Southern Poverty Law Center Provides List of Unresolved Civil Rights Era Deaths to FBI." http://www.splcenter.org/civil-rights-memorial/history.

Starr, Kevin. *Endangered Dreams: The Great Depression in California*. New York: Oxford University Press, 1996.

Stebenne, David L. *Arthur J. Goldberg: New Deal Liberal*. New York: Oxford University Press, 1996.

Stone, Irving. *Earl Warren: A Great American Story*. New York: Prentice Hall, 1948.

Stuntz, William J. *The Collapse of American Criminal Justice*. Cambridge, MA: Belknap Press of Harvard University Press, 2011.

Totenberg, Nina. "The Supreme Court and Brown v. Board of Education." Available at http://www.npr.org/templates/story/story.php?storyId=1537409.

Tushnet, Mark V. *Making Constitutional Law: Thurgood Marshall and the Supreme Court,* 1936–1961. New York: Oxford University Press, 1994).

———. *Making Constitutional Law: Thurgood Marshall and the Supreme Court,* 1961–1991. New York: Oxford University Press, 1997.

———. *The NAACP's Legal Strategy against Segregated Education,* 1925–1950. Chapel Hill: University of North Carolina Press, 1987.

———. "The Warren Court as History." In Mark V. Tushnet, ed., *The Warren Court in Historical and Political Perspective*. Charlottesville, VA: University Press of Virginia, 1993.

Uchida, Craig D. and Timothy S. Bynum. "Search Warrants, Motions to Suppress, and 'Lost Cases:' The Effects of the Exclusionary Rule in Seven Jurisdictions," *Journal of Criminal Law and Criminology* 81, no. 4 (Winter, 1991): 1034–1066.

Ulmer, S. Sidney. "Bricolage and Assorted Thoughts on Working in the Papers of Supreme Court Justices." *The Journal of Politics*, 35, no. 2 (May, 1973): 286–310.

———. "Earl Warren and the Brown Decision." *The Journal of Politics*, 33, no. 3 (Aug., 1971): 609–702.

U.S. Department of Justice, Office of Justice Programs, Bureau of Justice Statistics. "Correctional Population in the United States, 2010." www.bjs.gov/content/pub/pdf/cpus10.pdf.

United States. Warren Commission. *Report of the President's Commission on the Assassination of President John F. Kennedy*. Washington, D.C.: U.S.G.P.O., 1964.

———. Warren Commission Executive Session Transcripts, www.aarclibrary.org/publib/contents/wc/contents_wcexec.htm.

Wald, Michael, Richard Ayres, David W. Hess, Mark Schantz, and Charles H. Whitebread. "Interrogations in New Haven: The Impact of Miranda." 76 *Yale Law Journal* 1519 (1967).

Walton, Hanes, Jr., Sherman C. Puckett, and Donald R. Deskins, Jr. *The African American Electorate: A Statistical History, Vol. 1*. Thousand Oaks, CA: CQ Press, 2012).

Warren, Earl. "The Law and the Future." In *The Public Papers of Chief Justice Earl Warren*. Edited by Henry M. Christman. Westport, CT: Greenwood Press, 1974.

———. *The Memoirs of Chief Justice Earl Warren*. New York: Madison Books, 1977.

———. *A Republic If You Can Keep It*. New York: Quadrangle Books, 1972.

Washington, James Melvin, ed. *Testament of Hope: The Essential Writings and Speeches of Martin Luther King, Jr.* San Francisco: HarperSanFrancisco, 1991.

Weaver, John D. *Warren: The Man, the Court, the Era*. London: Victor Gollancz Ltd., 1968.
Wechsler, Herbert. "Toward Neutral Principles of Constitutional Law." 73 *Harvard Law Review* 1 (1959).
Wecht, Cyril. "A Critique of President Kennedy's Autopsy." In Josiah Thompson, *Six Seconds in Dallas: A Micro-study of the Kennedy Assassination*. New York: B. Geis Associates, 1968.
———. "Pathologist's View of the JFK Autopsy." 40 *Modern Medicine* 28, November 27, 1972.
———. "JFK Assassination: A Prolonged and Willful Cover-Up." 42 *Modern Medicine* 40, September–December 1974.
White, G. Edward. *The American Judicial Tradition: Profiles of Leading American Judges*. New York: Oxford University Press, 2007.
———. *Earl Warren: A Public Life*. New York: Oxford University Press, 1982.
———. *Patterns of American Legal Thought*. New Orleans: Quid Pro Books, 2010.
Whitman, Alden. "Earl Warren, 83, Who Led High Court in Time of Vast Social Change, is Dead," *New York Times*, July 10, 1974.
Wicker, Tom. *One of Us: Richard Nixon and the American Dream*. New York: Random House, 1991.
Wiebe, Robert H. *The Search for Order, 1877 to 1920*. New York: Hill and Wang, 1967.
Woodward, C. Vann. *Reunion and Reaction: The Compromise of 1877 and the End of Reconstruction*. Boston: Little, Brown, 1966.
———. *The Strange Career of Jim Crow*. New York: Oxford University Press, 1974.

CASES

Adamson v. California, 332 U.S. 46, 68 (1947) (Black, J., dissenting).
Aguilar v. Texas, 378 U.S. 108 (1964).
Ashcroft v. Tennessee, 322 U.S. 143 (1944).
Baker v. Carr, 369 U.S. 186 (1962).
Barr v. City of Columbia, 378 U.S. 146 (1964).
Bell v. Maryland, 378 U.S. 226 (1964).
Belton v. Gebhart, 33 Del. Ch. 144, 87 A.2d 862 (Del. Ch. 1952), *aff'd,* 91 A.2d 137 (Del. 1952).
Belton v. Maryland, 395 U.S. 784 (1969).
Betts v. Brady, 316 U.S. 455 (1942).
Bouie v. City of Columbia, 378 U.S. 374 (1964).
Bram v. U.S, 168 U.S. 532 (1897).
Brandenburg v. Ohio, 395 U.S. 444 (1969).
Briggs v. Elliott, 98 F. Supp. 529 (E.D. South Carolina 1951), *rev'd,* 347 U.S. 483 (1954).
Brown v. Board of Education, 98 F. Supp. 797 (D. Kansas 1951), *rev'd,* 347 U.S. 483 (1954).
Brown v. Mississippi, 297 U.S. 278 (1936).

Burton v. Wilmington Parking Authority, 365 U.S. 715 (1961).
Chambers v. Florida, 309 U.S. 227 (1940).
Colegrove v. Green, 328 U.S. 549 (1946).
Cory v. Carter, 48 Ind. 327 (1874).
Cox v. Louisiana, 379 U.S. 536 (1965).
Crawford v. Washington, 541 U.S. 36 (2004).
Davis v. County School Board of Prince Edward County, 149 F. Supp. 431 (E.D. Va. 1952), *rev'd*, 249 F.2d 462 (4th Cir. 1957).
Dawson v. Mayor and City Council of Baltimore, 350 U.S. 877 (1955)(per curiam).
Dennis v. U.S., 341 U.S. 494 (1951).
District of Columbia v. Heller, 554 U.S. 570 (2008).
Dred Scott v. Sandford, 60 U.S. (19 How.) 393 (1857).
Duncan v. Louisiana, 391 U.S. 145 (1968).
Edwards v. California, 314 U.S. 160 (1941).
Engel v Vitale, 370 U.S. 421 (1962).
Escobedo v. Illinois, 378 U.S. 478 (1964).
Ex parte Endo, 323 U.S. 283 (1944).
Galven v. Press, 347 U.S. 522 (1954).
Garner v. Louisiana, 368 U.S. 157 (1961).
Gideon v. Wainwright, 372 U.S. 335 (1963).
Gomillion v. Lightfoot, 364 U.S. 339 (1960).
Griffin v. Maryland, 378 U.S.130 (1964).
Griffin v. School Board, 377 U.S. 218 (1964).
Griswold v. Connecticut, 381 U.S. 479 (1965).
Guinn v. U.S., 238 U.S. 347 (1915).
Hammer v. Dagenhart, 247 U.S. 251 (1918).
Harper v. Virginia State Board of Elections, 383 U.S. 663 (1966).
Harrison v. Day, 200 Va. 439, 106 S.E.2d 636 (Va. 1959).
Heart of Atlanta Motel v. U.S., 379 U.S. 241 (1964).
Henderson v. U.S., 339 U.S. 816 (1950).
Hirabayashi v. U.S., 320 U.S. 81 (1943).
Holmes v. Atlanta, 350 U.S. 879 (1955)(per curiam).
Irvine v. California, 347 U.S. 128 (1954).
Jones v. Alfred H. Mayer, 392 U.S. 409 (1968).
Katz v. U.S., 389 U.S. 347 (1967).
Katzenbach v. McClung, 379 U.S. 294.
Katzenbach v. Morgan, 384 U.S. 641 (1966).
Ker v. California, 374 U.S. 23 (1963).
Klopfer v. North Carolina, 386 U.S. 213 (1967).
Korematsu v. United States, 323 U.S. 214 (1944).
Lochner v. New York, 198 U.S. 45 (1905).
Loving v. Virginia, 388 U.S. 1 (1967).
Malloy v. Hogan, 378 U.S. 1 (1964).
Mapp v. Ohio, 367 U.S. 643 (1961).
Massiah v. United States, 377 U.S. 201 (1964).

McDonald v. City of Chicago, 561 U.S. 742 (2010).
Meyer v. Nebraska, 262 U.S. 390 (1923).
Miranda v. Arizona, 384 U.S. 436 (1966).
Moore v. Dempsey, 261 U.S. 86 (1923).
*Morgan v. Virginia,*328 U.S. 373 (1946).
Muller v. Oregon, 208 U.S. 412 (1908).
NAACP v. Alabama, 357 U.S. 449 (1958).
New York Times v. Sullivan, 376 U.S. 254 (1964).
Norris v. Alabama, 294 U.S. 587 (1935).
Palko v. Connecticut, 302 U.S. 319 (1937).
Pennsylvania v. Nelson, 350 U.S. 497 (1956).
Pierce v. Society of Sisters, 268 U.S. 510 (1925).
Plessy v. Ferguson, 163 U.S. 537 (1896).
Pockman v. Leonard, 249 P.2d 267 (1952).
Pointer v. Texas, 380 U.S. 400 (1965).
Powell v. Alabama, 287 U.S. 45 (1932).
Powell v. McCormack, 395 U.S. 486 (1969).
People v. Cahan, 282 P.2d 905 (1955).
People v. Gonzales, 24 Cal. 2d 870 (1942).
People v. Taylor, 187 Cal. 378, 203 P. 85 (1921).
Reynolds v. Sims, 377 U.S. 533 (1964).
Robinson v. California, 370 U.S. 660 (1962).
*Robinson v. Florida,*378 U.S. 153 (1964).
Rochin v. California, 342 U.S. 165 (1952).
Roe v. Wade, 410 U.S. 113 (1973).
Schnell v. Davis, 336 U.S. 933 (1949).
Shapiro v. Thompson, 394 U.S. 618 (1969).
Shelley v. Kraemer, 334 U.S. 1 (1948).
Skinner v. Oklahoma, 316 U.S. 535 (1942).
Slaughterhouse Cases, 83 U.S. 36 (1873).
Smith v. Allwright, 321 U.S. 649 (1944).
South Carolina v. Katzenbach, 383 U.S. 301 (1966).
Spano v. New York, 369 U.S. 315 (1959).
Standard Oil Co. of New Jersey v. U.S., 221 U.S. 1 (1911).
State, ex rel. Gaines v. McCann, 21 Ohio St. 198 (1872).
Terminello v. Chicago, 337 U.S. 1 (1949).
Terry v. Ohio, 392 U.S. 1 (1968).
Tinker v. Des Moines School Board, 393 U.S. 503 (1969).
Tolman v. Underhill, 39 Cal. 2d 708 (1952).
Townsend v. Sain, 372 U.S. 293 (1963).
Twining v. New Jersey, 211 U.S. 78 (1908).
U.S. v. Caroline Products Co., 304 U.S. 144 (1938).
U.S. v. Guest, 383 U.S. 745 (1966).
U.S. v. Jefferson County Board of Education, 372 F.2d 836 (1966).
U.S. v. Leon, 468 U.S. 897 (1984).

Walker v. City of Birmingham, 388 U.S. 307 (1967).
Washington v. Texas, 388 U.S. 14 (1967).
Watkins v. U.S., 354 U.S. 178 (1957).
Westbury v. Sanders, 376 U.S. 1 (1964).
Westminster School District v. Mendez, 64 F. Supp. 544 (S.D. Cal. 1946), *aff'd en banc*, 161 F.2d 774 (9th Cir. 1947).
Whitney v. California, 274 U.S. 357 (1927).
Williams v. State of Texas, 88 Tex. Cr. Rep. 87, 225 S.W. 177 (1920).
Wolf v. Colorado, 338 U.S. 25 (1949).
Yasui v U.S., 320 U.S. 115 (1943).
Yates v. U.S., 354 U.S. 298 (1957).

Index

About the Author

Paul Moke is professor of political science at Wilmington College in Wilmington, Ohio and adjunct professor of law at the University of Dayton School of Law. A graduate of Ohio State University College of Law and the University of Cincinnati, he is an active civil liberties lawyer and author of several articles on voting rights, judicial selection, and correctional policy.